JEFFERSON

MAGNIFICENT POPULIST

Other Books by the Same Author

Milton and Servetus
The Theory of Logical Expression
The Modernity of Milton
The Plaster Saint
The Religion of the Occident
Wanton Sinner
Church Wealth and Business Income
The Essene Heritage
The Great Tax Fraud
The Churches: Their Riches, Revenues, and Immunities
Praise the Lord for Tax Exemption
When Parochial Schools Close
Tax Revolt: U.S.A!
The Federal Reserve and Our Manipulated Dollar
The Religious Empire
The Story of Christian Origins
How to Defend Yourself against the Internal Revenue Service
The Essence of Jefferson
How to Establish a Trust and Reduce Taxation
The Essene-Christian Faith
How You Can Save Money on Your Taxes This Year
The Continuing Tax Rebellion
The IRS vs. The Middle Class

The painting on the cover, *Thomas Jefferson* by Gilbert Stuart, is the promised gift of Thomas Jefferson Coolidge IV in memory of his great-grandfather, Thomas Jefferson Coolidge, his grandfather, Thomas Jefferson Coolidge II, and his father, Thomas Jefferson Coolidge III, 1979. It is reprinted by permission of the National Gallery of Art, Washington, D.C.

JEFFERSON
Magnificent Populist

Martin A. Larson

The Inscription on Jefferson's Seal
"Rebellion to Tyrants is Obedience to God"

Devin-Adair, Publishers
Greenwich, Connecticut

Devin-Adair, Publishers Greenwich, Connecticut

DEVIN-ADAIR, PUBLISHERS, is America's foremost publisher of quality conservative books. Founded in 1911, the company had championed the cause of the Thinking Right and historically had published the work of major conservative writers. In recent years Devin-Adair has increased its emphasis in this area and today is considered the leading publishing firm of the right.

The company also has a long-standing reputation for works in the fields of ecology, Irish literature, health and nutrition. It publishes superbly illustrated nature and travel books on the Eastern seaboard through its Chatham Press subsidiary.

Devin-Adair's newest emphasis is in the area of books, programs and software relating to the personal computer.

Devin-Adair operates the Veritas Book Club for conservative readers, the Ecological Book Club for nature and health audiences, and the Irish-American Book Society.

Manufactured in the United States of America.

Library of Congress Cataloging in Publication Data

Jefferson, Thomas, 1743-1826.
Jefferson, magnificent populist.

Reprint. Originally published: Washington:
R.B. Luce, c1981.
Includes index.
1. United States—Politics and government—
Revolution, 1775-1783—Addresses, essays, lectures.
2. United States—Politics and government—1783-1809—
Addresses, essays, lectures. I. Larson, Martin
Alfred, 1897- . II. Title.
[E302.J442 1984b] 973.4'6'0924 84-21352
ISBN 0-8159-5902-8 (pbk.)

Devin-Adair, Publishers
6 North Water Street
Greenwich, Connecticut 06830
EXCELLENCE, SINCE 1911

Contents

Farewell Address to Thomas Jefferson, President of the United States — Feb. 7, 1809

(Similar addresses were prepared and presented to Jefferson by various other legislative bodies. No other president has ever received such accolades.)

ME XVII 398-401

Sir, — The General Assembly of your native State cannot close their session, without acknowledging your services in the office which you are just about to lay down, and bidding you a respectful and affectionate farewell.

We have to thank you for the model of an administration conducted on the purest principles of republicanism; for pomp and state laid aside; patronage discarded; internal taxes abolished; a host of superfluous officers disbanded; the monarchic maxim "that a national debt is a national blessing," renounced, and more than thirty-three millions of our debt discharged; the native right to nearly one hundred millions of acres of our national domain extinguished; and, without the guilt or calamities of conquest, a vast and fertile region added to our country, far more extensive than her original possessions, bringing along with it the Mississippi and the port of Orleans, the trade of the west to the Pacific ocean, and in the intrinsic value of the land itself, a source of permanent and almost inexhaustible revenue. These are points in your administration which the historian will not fail to seize, to expand, and teach posterity to dwell upon with delight. Nor will he forget our peace with the civilized world, preserved through a season of uncommon difficulty and trial; the good will cultivated with the unfortunate aborigines of our country, and the civilization humanely extended among them; the lesson taught the inhabitants of the coast of Barbary, that we have the means of chastising their piratical encroachments, and awing them into justice; and that theme, on which, above all others, the historic genius will hang with rapture, the liberty of speech and of the press preserved inviolate, without which genius and science are given to man in vain.

In the principles on which you have administered the government, we see only the continuation and maturity of the same virtues and abilities, which drew upon you in your youth the resentment of Dunmore. From the first brilliant and happy moment of your resistance to foreign tyranny, until the present day, we mark with pleasure and with gratitude the same uniform, consistent character, the same warm and devoted attachment to liberty and the republic, the same Roman love of your country, her rights, her peace, her honor, her prosperity.

How blessed will be the retirement into which you are about to go! How deservedly blessed will it be! For you carry with you the richest of all rewards, the recollection of a life well spent in the service of your country, and proofs the most decisive, of the love, the gratitude, the veneration of your countrymen.

That your retirement may be as happy as your life has been virtuous and useful; that our youth may see in the blissful close of your day, an additional inducement to form themselves on your model, is the devout and earnest prayer of your fellow citizens who compose the General Assembly of Virginia.

Lincoln's Tribute to Jefferson

ME X xv-xvii

But soberly, it is now no child's play to save the principles of Jefferson from total overthrow in this nation. One would state with great confidence that he could convince any sane child that the simpler propositions of Euclid are true; but nevertheless, he would fail, utterly, with one who would deny the definitions and axioms.

The principles of Jefferson are the definitions and axioms of free society and yet they are denied and evaded, with no small show of success. One dashingly calls them "glittering generalities." Another bluntly calls them "self-evident lies;" and others insidiously argue that they apply to "superior races." These expressions, differing in form, are identical in object and effect — the supplanting the principles of free government, and restoring those of classification, caste, and legitimacy. They could delight a convocation of crowned heads plotting against the people. They are the vanguard, the miners and sappers of returning despotism. We must repulse them, or they will subjugate us. This is a world of compensation; and he who would be no slave must consent to have no slave. Those who deny freedom to others deserve it not for themselves, and, under a just God, cannot long retain it.

All honor to Jefferson — to the man, who in the concrete presence of a struggle for national independence by a single people, had the coolness, forecaste, and sagacity to introduce into a merely revolutionary document an abstract truth, applicable to all men and all times, and so embalm it there that to-day and in all coming days it shall be a rebuke and a stumbling block to the very harbingers of reappearing tyranny and oppression.

Citation Sources

ME — *Writings of Thomas Jefferson,* edited by Baugh and Lipscomb, and Published by the Thomas Jefferson Memorial Association, Washington, D.C., 1903-05, 20 Volumes.

BW — *Basic Writings of Thomas Jefferson,* edited by Philip S. Foner, Published by the Wiley Book Company, New York, 1944, 1 Volume.

CE — *Writings of Thomas Jefferson,* the Congressional Edition, Edited by H. A. Washington, and Published by Taylor and Maury, 1853-54, 9 Volumes.

FORD — *Writings of Thomas Jefferson,* edited by Paul Leiscester Ford, Published by G. P. Putnams Sons, 1892-99, 10 Volumes.

WC — *Jefferson's Letters,* Arranged by Willson Whitman, Published by E. M. Hale and Company.

CB — *Jefferson in Power,* by Claude G. Bowers, Published by Houghton, Mifflin Company, 1936, 1 Volume.

The letters which appear at the head of each citation indicate the source from which it is taken; thus, for example,

BW 156-59 Notes on Virginia, 1781

means that the quoted material is from the *Notes on Virginia,* found in the volume called *Basic Writings,* pages 156-59, and published in 1781.

The following heading

ME XIII 394-403 John Adams 10-28-13

means that following material is from a letter written by Jefferson to John Adams on October 28, 1813, and is found in Volume XIII of the Memorial Edition of the *Writings of Thomas Jefferson,* pages 394-403.

Introduction

We call Thomas Jefferson the magnificent populist because he was the American leader who sought to establish on this continent the world's first great nation dedicated to the interests of its productive citizens. At that time, this was a revolutionary concept so startling, so far-reaching, as to be almost incomprehensible. Against him and his colleagues were arrayed every species of privilege, tyranny, oppression, and extortion; but without those whose interests he represented, victory over British imperialism would have been impossible. Their triumph was not merely over this entrenched and global enemy, but even more over a social structure which had existed for many generations and was so firmly established that its elimination in this nation required efforts, fortitude, courage, and statesmanship unparalleled in the annals of history.

The reader will discover that each of the twenty-three chapters into which this volume is divided constitutes a separate treatise and, therefore, may be read with equal profit in any sequence; he can turn at once to whatever subject seems to him or her most interesting or attractive. It is important that the date of any letter or other composition be noted in order to place it in the proper framework of Jefferson's life and activity. As a guide to this, it may be helpful to indicate the principal divisions of his life, which were as follows:

1773	Worked with the Committee of Correspondence
1774	Wrote the *Summary View of the Rights of British America*
1775	Elected a delegate to the Continental Congress
1776	Drafted the first Constitution for Virginia
	Wrote the Declaration of Independence
	Introduced the Bill to Abolish Entails in Virginia
1779	Elected Governor of Virginia
	Introduced the Bill to Establish Religious Freedom
	Prepared the Revisal of the Virginia Code of Laws
1780	Re-elected Governor of Virginia
1781	Resigned as Governor of Virginia

1783	Elected delegate to the Continental Congress
1784-89	Minister in residence in France
1789-93	Secretary of State in Washington
1794-95	At home in Monticello
1796-00	Vice President under John Adams
1801-09	President of the United States
1809-26	At Monticello
1817	Education Bill passed in Virginia
1818-25	Engaged primarily in Establishing the University of Virginia
1809-26	Wrote hundreds of important letters

We should never forget that although Jefferson's fame rests primarily on his contributions as a statesman and political leader, his interests were almost universal; his mind was encyclopaedic and all embracing; he stated that he found far greater delight in scientific and philosophic pursuits than in the public labors and duties which were constantly forced upon him. Of the several thousand letters published in various compendia, at least half deal with non-political themes; and they show that among his various intellectual occupations, he was versed, often deeply, in theology, architecture, orthography, exploration, grammar, prosody, animal husbandry and breeding, medicine, surgery, arts, belles lettres, manufactures, philosophy (especially in ethics and morals), history, educational theory and practice, economics, monetary science, anatomy, zoology, botany, in flora and fauna, inventions, patents, mathematics, pendulums, geology, anthropology, antiquarian society, sculpture, painting, naval warfare, military science, printing presses, languages, aeronautics, physics, meteorology, astronomy, paleontology, natural history, civil engineering, agriculture, rural development, and human advancement in every field. A mere roster of his principal interests, exclusive of those which placed him in the public domain, constitutes an impressive catalog.

However, we should note also that whether he was in or out of office, his interest in every facet pertaining to the public interest continued to engage his most intense scrutiny and continued attention. When he was in France, he wrote a stream of letters to friends commenting on American issues and developments; and in all of these, he spoke with the voice, not only of wisdom, but that of authority. When he retired from the Presidency in 1809 to spend the remainder of his life at Monticello, there emerged from his pen — and from his heart and his mind — a constant stream of epistles to friends and public figures, almost every one of which is a disquisition on religion, money, finance, monetary science, economics, foreign policy, and a host of other subjects, all of which constitute a literary treasure without equal in American history. Although he declared repeatedly that he was in delightful retirement, it is obvious that his interest in national affairs remained as keen and wide-ranging as ever; and he wrote as if conscious of being the National Oracle and supreme Fountain of Wisdom. He not only issued these declarations with the greatest care and circumspection as if they were official papers from the White House: he also preserved all this correspondence with the greatest care so that it would be available to posterity. Of the more than 18,000 letters he kept on file, several thousand have been published, all of which are of especial interest to students of history and constitute a source of superb and undying wisdom.

Jefferson did not write what may be called formal "books." The nearest to such a composition is probably his *Notes on Virginia,* 1781, and the *Anas,* 1821. His *Answers to de Meusnier,* 1786, is an important work, written in Francc; as is the *Autobiography,* 1821, which, unfortunately, ends in 1790 shortly after his return from Europe.

When we began this labor of love, the mass of material accumulated rapidly, until it reached more than one thousand pages, all of which we would have liked to reproduce; however, since it was obvious that all this would make the volume too large, we lopped off nearly half of it, by excluding material covered, fully or partially, in other citations. Then, finding the remainder still too extensive, we went through every quotation with a sharp pruning knife, which eliminated another eighty or a hundred pages. Wherever possible, we left out a paragraph, a sentence, a line, or even a phrase not essential to convey the intended meaning; wherever such omissions occur, we have indicated the fact by a series of periods.

Since Jefferson sometimes wrote single paragraphs that run into pages, we have taken the liberty, without noting it, of breaking up material into shorter paragraphs when there is a change in the sequence of thought. This, we believe, will facilitate the perusal.

We consider Jefferson not only as incomparably the leader among our Founding Fathers, but also the greatest statesman in American history. And yet, a strange phenomenon has occurred; even though two of the greatest monuments in Washington (the Library of Congress and the magnificent Pantheon in which his heroic statue is enshrined) are dedicated to him, and although almost universal lip service is offered to his memory, his ideals and political philosophy have been shamefully ignored, especially since 1913 and more particularly since 1933. Strange indeed it is that many who will quote a sentence or a part of it, refuse to read, or listen to, other statements of his dealing with the same subject. He advocated a social and political structure which has been almost completely betrayed during the last fifty years in the United States.

Still, his fame is imperishable and indestructible. His greatness cannot be questioned or challenged as long as this nation or freedom survives.

Gems From Jefferson

Personal Philosophy

A right to property is founded in natural wants... . (42)

There is a natural aristocracy among men. The grounds for this are virtue and talents... . There is also an artificial aristocracy, founded on wealth and birth, without either virtue or talents; for *with* these, it would belong in the first class. The natural aristocracy I consider as the most precious gift of nature, for the instruction, the trusts, and the government of society. (8)

...to make an opening for the aristocracy of virtue and talent, which nature has wisely provided for the direction of the interests of society, and scattered with equal hand through all its conditions, was deemed essential to a well-ordered republic. To effect this, no violence was necessary, no deprivation of natural right, but rather an enlargement of it by the repeal of the law [of primogeniture]. (8)

I know also, that laws and institutions must go hand in hand with the progress of the human mind. (89)

... to offer drudgery and subsistence only to those entrusted with the administration, — [is] a wise and necessary precaution against the degeneracy of the public servants. (94)

Agriculture, manufacture, commerce, and navigation, the four pillars of our prosperity, are the most thriving when left free to individual enterprise. (94)

You will perhaps have been alarmed, as some have been, at the proposition to abolish the whole of the internal taxes. But it is perfectly safe... . By suppressing at once the whole internal taxes, we abolish three-fourths of the offices now existing, and spread over the land... . (96)

The God who gave us life, gave us liberty at the same time; the hand of force may destroy it, but cannot disjoin them. (148)

If we can prevent the government from wasting the labors of the people under the pretense of taking care of them, they must become happy. (19)

If a nation expects to be ignorant and free, in a state of civilization, it expects what never was and never will be. (251)

When public opinion changes, it is with the rapidity of thought. (241)

Truth and reason are eternal. They have prevailed. And they will eternally prevail. (257)

But we must await, with patience, the workings of an overriding Providence, and hope that that is preparing the deliverance of these, our suffering brethren [the slaves]. When the measure of their tears shall be full, when their groans shall have involved heaven itself in darkness, doubtless, a God of justice will awaken to their distress, and by diffusing light and liberality among their oppressors, or, at length, by his exterminating thunder, manifest His attention to the things of this world and that they are not left to the guidance of blind fatality. (306)

...truth is great and will prevail if left to herself, ... she is the proper and sufficient antagonist to error, and has nothing to fear from the conflict, unless by human interposition disarmed of her natural weapons, free argument and debate... (319)

It is error alone which needs the support of government. Truth can stand by itself. (321)

An honest man can feel no pleasure in the exercise of power over his fellow-citizens. (360)

The People The Depository of Power

Educate and inform the whole mass of the people. Enable them to see that it is to their interest to preserve peace and order, and they will preserve them. And it requires no high degree of education to convince them of this. They are the only sure reliance for the preservation of liberty. (83)

...governments are republican only in proportion as they embody the will of their people, and execute it. (84)

I would say that the people, being the only safe depository of power, should exercise in person, every function which their qualifications enable them to exercise... . (96)

We believed... that man was a rational animal, endowed by nature with rights, and with an innate sense of justice; and that he could be restrained from wrong and protected in right, by moderate powers, confided to persons of his own choice, and held to their duties by dependence on his own will. (122)

Independence can be trusted nowhere but with the people in mass. They are inherently independent of all but moral law... . (138)

I know of no safe depository of the ultimate powers of the society, but the people themselves. (138)

Jefferson Magnificent Populist

I am not among those who fear the people. They, and not the rich, are our dependence for continued freedom. (210)

Do not be frightened... by the alarms of the timid, or the croakings of wealth against the ascendancy of the people. (84)

Preach... a crusade against ignorance; establish and improve the law for educating the common people. Let our countrymen know that the people alone can protect us against these evils [of tyrannical government]. (250)

The people of every country are the only safe guardians of their own rights, and are the only instruments which can be used for their destruction. (250)

...the most effectual means of preventing [tyranny]... would be to illuminate, as far as practicable, the minds of the people at large... that those persons, whom nature hath endowed with genius and virtue, should be rendered by liberal education worthy to receive, and able to guard, the sacred deposit of rights and liberties of their fellow-citizens; and that they should be called to that charge without regard to wealth, birth, or other accidental condition or circumstance... . (249)

The Excellence of the American Government

And the system of government which shall keep us afloat amidst the wreck of the world, will be immortalized in history. (45)

In general, our affairs are proceeding in a train of unparalleled prosperity. This arises from the real improvements of our government, from the unbounded confidence reposed in it by the people, their zeal to support it, and their conviction that a solid Union is the best rock of their safety... ; so that I believe I may say with truth, that there is not a nation under the sun enjoying more present prosperity, nor with more in prospect. (48)

Peace, then, has been our principle, peace is our interest, and peace has saved the world this only plant of free and rational government existing upon it. (50)

Were we to break [the Union] to pieces, it would damp the hopes and efforts of the good, and give triumph to those of the bad, through the whole enslaved world... it is our sacred duty... not to blast the confidence we have inspired of proof that a government of reason is better than one of force. (96)

Our Argosy... has stood the waves into which she was steered with a view of sinking her. We will now show by the beauty of her motions, the skill of her builders... . A just and solid republican government maintained here, will be a standing monument and example for the aims and imitation of the people in other countries... and will ameliorate the condition of man over a great portion of the globe. (92).

[We pursue] with temper and perseverance the great experiment which shall prove that man is capable of living in society, governing itself, by laws self-imposed, and securing to its members the enjoyment of life, liberty, property, and peace... . (110)

[Our purpose] will be chiefly to reform the waste of public money, and thus drive away the vultures who prey upon it... . (207)

In the hour of death, we shall have the consolation to see established in the land of our fathers the most wonderful work of wisdom and disinterested patriotism that has ever appeared on the globe. (366)

All eyes are opened, or opening, to the rights of man... that the mass of mankind has not been born with saddles on their backs, nor a favored few booted and spurred, ready to ride them legitimately, by the grace of God. (374)

Government: Division or Despotism

...in government, as well as in every other business of life, it is by division and subdivision of duties alone, that all matters, great and small, can be managed to perfection. (16)

...whensoever the General Government assumes undelegated powers, its acts are unauthoritative, void, and of no force... . (58-59)

...confidence is everywhere the parent of despotism — free government is founded in jealousy, and not in confidence... . (61)

The further the departure from direct and constant control by the citizens, the less has the government of the ingredient of republicanism... . (98)

Were we directed from Washington, when to sow, when to reap, we should soon want bread. (98)

What has destroyed the rights of man in every government under the sun? The generalizing and concentrating all cares and powers in one body... . (99)

My idea is that we should be one nation in every case concerning foreign affairs, and separate ones in what is merely domestic... . (103)

They [the States] would, indeed, consider such a rupture [of the Union] as among the great calamities which could befall them; but not the greatest. There is yet one greater, submission to a government of unlimited powers. It is only when the hope of avoiding this shall become absolutely desperate, that further forebearance could not be indulged... . (110)

It is a singular phenomenon, that while our State governments are the very best in the world, without exception or comparison, our General Government has, in the rapid course of nine or ten years, become more arbitrary, and has swallowed more of the public liberty than even that of England. (112)

If this vast country is brought under a single government, it will be one of the most extensive corruption... . (140)

...when all government... shall be drawn to Washington as the centre of power, it will render powerless the checks provided of one government on another, and will become as venal and oppressive as the government from which we separated... . (141)

The natural progress of things is for liberty to yield, and government to gain ground. (85)

...experience hath shown, that even under the best forms, those entrusted with power have, in time, and by slow operations, perverted it into tyranny... . (249)

Juries and the Judiciary

I consider that [the trial by jury] as the only anchor ever yet imagined by man, by which a government can be held to the principles of its constitution. (134)

The juries [are] our judges of fact, and of the law when they choose... . (134)

That there should be public functionaries independent of the nation, whatever may be their demerit, is a solecism in a republic, of the first order of absurdity and inconsistency. (140)

The judiciary of the United States is the subtle corps of sappers and miners constantly working underground to undermine the foundations of our confederated fabric. They are construing our Constitution from a co-ordination of general and special government into a general and supreme one alone. (141)

The Dangers of Public Debt

I... place economy among the first and most important of republican virtues, and public debt as the greatest of the dangers to be feared. (96)

I wish it were possible to obtain a single amendment to our Constitution. I would be willing to depend on that alone for the reduction of the administration of our government to the genuine principles of the Constitution: I mean an additional article taking from the federal government the power of borrowing. (207)

I consider the fortunes of our republic as depending, in an eminent degree, on the extinguishment of the public debt before we engage in any war; because, that done, we shall have revenue enough to improve our country in peace and defend it in war, without recurring either to new taxes or loans. But should the debt once more be swelled to a formidable size, its entire discharge will be despaired of, and we shall be committed to the English career of debt, corruption, and rottenness, closing with revolution. The discharge of the debt, therefore, is vital to the destinies of our government. (210)

We must make our election between *economy and liberty* or *profusion and servitude.* If we run into such debts, as that we must be taxed in our meat and in our drink, in our necessaries and our comforts, in our labors and our amusements, for our callings and our creeds, as the people of England are, our people, like them, must come to labor sixteen hours in the twenty-four, give the earnings of fifteen of these to the government for their debts and daily expenses; and... have no time to think, no means of calling the mismanagers to account; but be glad to obtain subsistence by hiring ourselves out to rivet our chains on the necks of our fellow-sufferers. (210)

Banks, Specie, and Paper (Fiat) Money

I deem no government safe which is under the vassalage of any self-constituted authorities, or any other authority than that of the nation, or its regular functionaries. What an obstruction could not this Bank of the United States, with all its branch banks, be in time of war!... it is the greatest debt we owe to the safety of our Constitution, to bring this powerful enemy to a perfect subordination... . (224)

I sincerely believe... that [private] banking institutions are more dangerous than standing armies; and that the principle of spending money to be paid by posterity, under the name of funding, is but swindling futurity on a large scale. (227)

The bank mania... is raising up a moneyed aristocracy in our country which has already set the government at defiance, and... their principles are unyielded and unyielding. (227)

I now deny their power of making paper money... a legal tender. (228)

The sum of what has been said is, that... specie is the most perfect medium, because it will preserve its own level; because, having intrinsic and universal value, it can never die in our hands; and it is the surest resource of reliance in time of war... that it [a paper currency] is liable to be abused, has been, is, and forever will be abused, in every country where it is permitted... . (230)

I should say, put down all banks [of issue], admit none but a metallic circulation that will take its proper level with the like circulation of other countries... . (230)

The unlimited emission of bank paper [carried France to bankruptcy]... as it did us, and will us again, and every country permitting paper to be circulated, other than that by public authority, rigorously limited to the just measure of circulation. (233)

Bank paper must be suppressed, and the circulating medium must be restored to the nation to whom it belongs. (234)

...the medium of gold and silver [should] be universally restored. (242)

Interdict forever to both the State and national governments, the power of establishing any paper bank; for without this interdiction, we shall have the same ebbs and flows of medium, the same revolutions of property to go through every twenty or thirty years. (246)

No one has a natural right to the trade of money-lender, but he who has the money to lend. (233)

Religion

...to compel a man to furnish contributions of money for the propagation of opinions which he disbelieves and abhors, is sinful and tyrannical. (319)

What has been the effect of [religious] coercion? To make one half of the world fools, the other half hypocrites. (322)

I never will, by word or act, bow to the shrine of intolerance, or admit a right of enquiry into the religious opinions of others. On the contrary, we are bound... to make common cause, even with error itself, to maintain the common right of freedom of conscience. (323)

It is an insult to our citizens... and blasphemy against religion to suppose that it cannot stand the test of truth and reason. (324)

I am a sect by myself, so far as I know. (330)

I have sworn upon the altar of God, eternal hostility against every form of tyranny over the mind of man. (328)

I must ever believe that religion substantially good which produces an honest life; and we have been authorized by One whom you and I equally respect, to judge the tree by the fruit. (334)

I do not believe it is for the interest of religion to invite the civil magistrate to direct its exercises, its discipline, or its doctrines; nor of the religious societies, that the General Government should be invested with the power of effecting any uniformity of time or matter among them. (341)

Believing with you that religion is a matter which lies solely between man and his God, that he owes account to none other for his faith or his worship, that the legislative powers of government reach actions only, and not opinions, I contemplate with sovereign reverence that act of the whole American people which declared that their legislature should "make no law respecting an establishment of religion, or prohibiting the free exercise thereof," thus building a wall of separation between Church and State. (341)

JEFFERSON

MAGNIFICENT POPULIST

1. Philosophy: Personal and Political

Commentary

At the outset, we consider some of the basic elements in Jefferson's personal philosophy which were the beacon lights of his lifelong activity. Although he rejected the dogmas of the contemporary churches, he was deeply religious in his own way; and, what is more important, his was a stern morality which never could, even for a moment, countenance the smallest degree of fraud, deceit, or unethical concealment.

Again and again he declared that we must never tell an untruth; for this, once done, leads to another; deceit then becomes habitual; and will become so obvious to others that the liar loses all credibility even when he tells the truth. The same criterion applies to all transactions: without honesty, we cannot hope to enjoy the esteem of our countrymen, or to receive any measure of honor from them.

Although Jefferson sometimes expressed the hope and belief that felicity awaited him in an afterlife, we do not believe that this was the basis for his stern morality; on the contrary, it stemmed from his conviction that it is the duty of all men to treat others at least as well as they would be treated in return. It was based also on his profound desire to be loved and honored by all who knew him. Is there any stronger basis for a stern moral code?

Any one who is under the impression that Jefferson considered all men equal has certainly not read his many statements dealing with this subject. He even referred to the ignorant and unpropertied as the swinish multitude and the canaille *of the European cities. He declared that there exists in every society an aristocracy of virtue and talent, natural* aristoi, *scattered abroad among all classes regardless of birth, wealth, parentage, or social position. One can never predict where these superior individuals will be found; but they will be distinguished by their congenital drive, their innate desire to excel and succeed, their determination to learn, to achieve, to serve humanity. They become discernible even while children, as they distinguish themselves in classroom and in competition; and these are the individuals who should be encouraged and given every opportunity to reach their highest potential.*

Contrasted to these are the idle, worthless progency of the rich, the landed aristocrats, who consider themselves superior simply because they were born in wealthy or privileged families or of royal lineage. They are the parasites, who riot on the production of the useful citizens, the hogs of society, who must be put down and who, under a truly republican government, will be replaced by a natural aristocracy of virtue and talent.

It is obvious that Jefferson had the highest regard for those hardworking individuals (whom we now call the Middle Class) who labor in productive enterprise which requires not only their labor, but also capital investment. Such were the independent farmers, whose brightest and most ambitious children were destined to become the future aristoi.

Jefferson was well aware of the evil propensities that lurk in the human soul. Although he evinces no understanding of the three-fold nature of the human psyche, as analyzed by Emanuel Swedenborg, Warren Felt Evans, and finally by Sigmund Freud, he had concluded that it is the nature of those who seek high office or special privileges to be dishonest seekers for power, pelf, profit, and dominance. They should, therefore, never be trusted; and only by developing a large number of minor and major aristoi, *would it ever be possible to prevent such individuals from seizing the government and transforming it into a despotism.*

However, Jefferson also declared that no matter how great the necessity for even-handed generosity may be in daily intercourse, the necessity of self-preservation is the first law of life. And rather than lose our own lives or permit the destruction of our nation, it becomes our right, and our duty, in extremity, to commit acts which are beyond the purlieus of strictly statutory law.

We reproduce in this chapter two of Jefferson's most explicit declarations of political principle: he stood for a thrifty and limited federal government which would trim away all waste and extravagance, all unnecessary offices and expenditures; he was determined that parasites should not live on the labors of producers. He was fervently devoted to the political rights of the people: freedom of conscience and religion, free individual enterprise, and freedom of speech and the press; he would permit the Federalists the right to preach near-treason without restriction, so long as reason was free to combat it. He was bitterly opposed to the alien and sedition laws; he advocated trials in all cases — civil as well as criminal — by juries impartially selected; and he insisted on the right of habeas corpus.

He was for extinguishing the public debt as rapidly as possible and for paying the entire obligation sacredly with hard money; he was opposed to standing armies, always used as instruments of oppression; he relied on an armed citizenry organized into militias for the public defence. He wanted no entangling alliances, and only a small diplomatic corps; he was always urging neutrality, friendship, and free commerce with all nations.

Most of all, perhaps, he made it a principal lifetime objective to prevent the federal government from aggrandizing to itself the power and activities mandated by the Constitution to the States. All government, he declared, should be wise and frugal, charged only with the duty of protecting its citizens in their rights and preventing them from injuring each other. He declared that it is by division and subdivision and not by consolidation in the political structure, that all things may be managed to perfection.

After Jefferson had been President six or seven years, it became apparent to him that, with continued peace and prosperity, the public debt would soon be liquidated. Since about eighty per cent of the federal budget had gone to pay the interest on this and to reduce the principal, and since the annual per capita cost of operating the General Government was less than fifty cents, he proposed that an amendment be added to the Constitution permitting the Treasury to disburse otherwise idle sums to the respective states, to be employed by them for the construction of roads and canals, for promoting the arts, the sciences, and education, and for building and subsidizing colleges and universities.

What would Jefferson have said, could he have foreseen what our federal government has been doing, especially since 1933!

Throughout his life, he was consistent: whenever he changed an outlook, it was because profound changes had occurred, as in his beliefs concerning the relationship between agriculture and manufacture. But, as he said in one place, "I may err in my measures, but shall never deflect from the intention of fortifying the public liberty by every possible means, and to put it out of the power of the few to riot on the labors of the many."

We must prevent the government from wasting the labors of the people on the pretext of caring for them; if they do not control the politicians, they will use their position to perpetuate themselves in power and wealth and pervert the government into an instrument of oppression. The people are the only safe depository of power, because they, and they alone, are honest. Even in 1823, the government had become overloaded with parasites living on the labor of the industrious.

The works of Jefferson are studded with such gems of purest ray serene — and where else, in all the range of literature, will we find anything comparable? And where shall we find a more total patriotism or devotion to his own country than actuated the philosophy and life-long activity of Thomas Jefferson?

Ethical Principles

ME VII 43-44 Peter Carr 5-28-88

Health, learning, and virtue will insure your happiness; they will give you a quiet conscience, private esteem, and public honor. Beyond these, we want nothing but physical necessaries, and they are easily obtained.

Ford IV 372, 387 Martha Jefferson 1787

Nothing can contribute more to your future happiness (moral rectitude always excepted), than the contracting a habit of industry and activity. Of all the cankers of human happiness, none corrodes with so silent, yet so baneful an influence, as indolence. Body and mind both unemployed, our being becomes a burden, and every object about us loathsome, even the dearest. Idleness begets *ennui, ennui* the hypochondriac, and that a diseased body.

Determine never to be idle. No person will have an occasion to complain of the want of time who never loses any. It is wonderful how much may be done if we are always doing.

ME VI 256-62 Peter Carr 8-10-87

Moral Philosophy: I think it lost time to attend lectures on this branch. He who made us would have been a pitiful bungler, if He had made the rules of our moral conduct a matter of science... . He has endowed [man] with a sense of right and wrong... . This sense is as much a part of his nature, as the sense of hearing, seeing, feeling; it is the true foundation of morality... . The moral sense, or conscience, is as much a part of man as his leg or arm. It is given to all human beings in a stronger or weaker degree... . It may be strengthened by exercise, as may any particular limb of the body. This sense is submitted, indeed, in some degree, to the guidance of reason; but... even less than what we call common sense. State a moral case to a ploughman and a professor. The former will decide it as well, and often better, than the latter, because he has not been led astray by artificial rules.

ME XII 314-316 James Fishback 9-27-09

Reading, reflection, and time have convinced me that the interests of society require the observation of those moral precepts only in which all religions agree (for all forbid us to steal, murder, plunder, bear false witness); and that we should not intermeddle with the particular dogmas in which all religions differ, and which are totally unconnected with morality. In all of them, we see good men, and as many in one as in another. The varieties in the structure and action of the human mind, as in those of the body, are the work of the Creator, against which it cannot be a religious duty to erect a standard of uniformity. The practice of morality being necessary for the well-being of society, He has taken care to impress its precepts so indelibly on our hearts that they shall not be effaced by the subtleties of the brain.

ME XVI 110-11 Thomas Jefferson Smith 2-21-25

Adore God. Reverence and cherish your parents. Love your neighbor as yourself. Be just. Be true. Murmur not at the ways of Providence. So shall the life into which you have entered, be the portal to one of eternal and ineffable bliss... .

A Decalogue of Canons for Observation in Practical Life.

1. Never put off till to-morrow what you can do to-day.
2. Never trouble another for what you can do yourself.
3. Never spend your money before you have it.
4. Never buy what you do not want, because it is cheap; it will be dear to you.
5. Pride costs us more than hunger, thirst, and cold.
6. We never repent of having eaten too little.
7. Nothing is troublesome that we do willingly.
8. How much pain have cost us the evils that have never happened.
9. Take things always by their smooth handle.
10. When angry, count ten, before you speak; if very angry, an hundred.

ME V 82-87 Peter Carr 8-19-85

When your mind shall be well improved with science, nothing will be necessary to place you in the highest point of view, but to pursue the interests of your country, the interests of your friends, and your own interests also, with the purest integrity, the most chaste honor. The defect of these virtues can never be made up by all the other acquirements of body and mind. Make these, then, your first object.

Give up money, give up fame, give up science, give up the earth itself and all it contains, rather than do an immoral act. And never suppose, that in any possible situation, or under any circumstances, it is best for you to do a dishonorable thing, however slightly so it may appear to you. Whenever you are to do a thing, though it can never be known but to yourself, ask yourself how you would act were all the world looking at you, and act accordingly.

Encourage all your virtuous dispositions, and exercise them whenever an opportunity arises; being assured that they will gain strength by exercise, as a limb of the body does, and that exercise will make them habitual. From the practice of the purest virtue, you may be assured you will derive the most sublime comforts in every moment of life, and in the moment of death. If ever you find yourself environed with difficulties and perplexing circumstances, out of which you are at a loss how to extricate yourself, do what is right, and be assured that that will extricate you the best out of the worst situations. Though you cannot see, when you take one step, what will be the next, yet follow truth, justice, and plain dealing, and never fear their leading you out of the labyrinth, in the easiest manner possible. The knot which you thought a Gordian one, will untie itself before you. Nothing is so mistaken as the supposition, that a person is to extricate himself from a difficulty by intrigue, by chicanery, by dissimulation, by trimming, by an untruth, by an injustice. This increases the difficulties tenfold; and those who pursue these methods, get themselves so involved at length, that they can turn no way but their infamy becomes more exposed.

It is of great importance to set a resolution, not to be shaken, never to tell an untruth. There is no vice so mean, so pitiful, so contemptible; and he who permits himself to tell a lie once, finds it much easier to do it a second and third time, till at length it becomes habitual; he tells lies without attending to it, and truths without the world's believing him. This falsehood of the tongue leads to that of the heart, and in time depraves all its good dispositions.

An honest heart being the first blessing, a knowing head is the second.

ME XIV 487-93 Dupont de Nemours 4-24-16

Liberty, truth, probity, honor, are declared to be the four cardinal principles of your society. I believe with you that morality, compassion, generosity, are innate elements of the human constitution; that there exists a right independent of force; that a right to property is founded in our natural wants, in the means with which we are endowed to satisfy these wants, and the right to what we acquire by those means without violating the similar rights of other sensible beings; that no one has a right to obstruct another, exercising his faculties innocently for the relief of sensibilities made a part of his nature; that justice is the fundamental law of society; that the majority, oppressing an individual, is guilty of a crime, abuses its strength, and by acting on the law of the strongest, breaks up the foundations of society; that action by the citizens in person, in affairs within their reach and competence, and in all others by representatives, chosen immediately, and removable by themselves, constitutes the essence of a republic; that all governments are more or less republican in proportion as this principle enters more or less into their composition; and that a government by representation is capable of extension over a greater surface of country than one of any other form.

ME XII 196-201 Thomas Jefferson Randolph 1-24-08

But thrown on a wide world, among entire strangers, without a friend or guardian to advise, so young too, and with so little experience of mankind, your dangers are great, and still your safety must rest with yourself. A determination never to do what is wrong, prudence and good humor, will go far towards securing to you the estimation of the world.

When I recollect that at fourteen years of age, the whole care and direction of myself was thrown on myself entirely, without a relation or friend qualified to advise or guide me, and recollect the various sorts of bad company with which I associated from time to time, I am astonished I did not turn off with some of them, and become as worthless to society as they were. I had the good fortune to become acquainted very early with some characters of very high standing, and to feel the incessant wish that I could ever become what they were. Under temptations and difficulties, I would ask myself what would Dr. Small, Mr. Wythe, or Peyton Randolph do in this situation? What course in it will insure me their approbation?

I am certain that this mode of deciding on my conduct, tended more to correctness than any reasoning power I possessed. Knowing the even and dignified line they pursued, I could never doubt for a moment which of two courses would be in character with them. Whereas, seeking the same object through a process of moral reasoning, and with the jaundiced eye of youth, I should often have erred. From the circumstances of my position, I was often thrown into the society of horse racers, card players, fox hunters, scientific and professional men, and of dignified men; and many a time have I asked myself, in the enthusiastic moment of the death of a fox, the victory of a favorite horse, the issue of a question eloquently argued at the bar, or in the great council of the nation, well, which of these kinds of reputation should I prefer? That or a horse jockey? a fox hunter? an orator? or the honest advocate of my country's rights? Be assured, my dear Jefferson, that these little returns into ourselves, this self-catechising habit, is not trifling nor useless, but leads to the prudent selection and steady pursuit of what is right... .

ME XVII 103 Miscellaneous Papers

What a stupendous, what an incomprehensible machine is man! who can endure toil, famine, stripes, imprisonment, and death itself, in vindication of his own liberty, and, the next moment, be deaf to all those motives whose power supported him through his trial, and inflict on his fellow men a bondage, one hour of which is fraught with more misery, than ages of that which he rose in rebellion to oppose.

ME IX 357-60 James Madison 1-1-97

What is called civilization seems to have no other effect on him [man] than to teach him to pursue the principle of *bellum omnium in omnia* on a larger scale, and in place of the little contests of tribe against tribe, to engage all the quarters of the earth in the same work of destruction. When we add to this that as to the other species of animals, the lions and tigers are mere lambs compared with man as a destroyer, we must conclude that it is in man alone that nature has been able to find a sufficient barrier against the too great multiplication of other animals and of man himself, an equilibrating power against the fecundity of generation.

Aristocracy — Real and Perverted

ME VIII 394-408 President of the United States 9-9-92

I hold it to be one of the distinguishing excellencies of elective over hereditary successions, that the talents which nature has provided in sufficient proportion, should be selected by the society for the government of their affairs, rather than that this should be transmitted through the loins of knaves and fools, passing from the debauches of the table to those of the bed.

ME XIII 395-403 John Adams 10-28-13

I agree with you that there is a natural aristocracy among men. The grounds for this are virtue and talents... . There is also an artificial aristocracy, founded on wealth and birth, without either virtue or talents; for *with* these, it would belong to the first class. The natural aristocracy I consider as the most precious gift of nature, for the instruction, the trusts, and the government of society. And indeed, it would have been inconsistent in creation to have formed man for the social state, and not to have provided virtue and wisdom enough to manage the concerns of society. May we not even say that that form of government is the best, which provides the most effectually for a pure selection of these natural aristoi into the offices of government? The artificial aristocracy is a mischievous ingredient in government, and provision should be made to prevent its ascendancy.

BW 430 Autobiography 1821

In the earlier times of the colony, when lands were to be obtained for little or nothing, some provident individuals procured large grants; and, desirous of founding great families for themselves, settled them on their descendants in fee tail. The transmission of this property from generation to generation, in the same name, raised up a distinct set of families, who, being privileged by law in the perpetuation of their wealth, were thus formed into a Patrician order, distinguished by the splendor and luxury of their establishments. From this order, too, the king habitually selected his counsellors of State; the hope of which distinction devoted the whole corps to the interests and will of the crown. To annul this privilege, and, instead of an aristocracy of wealth, of more harm and danger, than benefit, to society, to make an opening for the aristocracy of virtue and talent, which nature has wisely provided for the direction of the interests of society, and scattered with equal hand through all its conditions, was deemed essential to a well-ordered republic. To effect this, no violence was necessary, no deprivation of natural right, but rather an enlargement of it by the repeal of the law.

ME XIII 395-403 John Adams 10-28-11

At the first session of our legislature [in Virginia] after the Declaration of Independence, we passed a law abolishing entails. And this was followed by one abolishing the privilege of primogeniture, and dividing the lands of intestates equally among all their children, or other representatives. These laws, drawn by myself, laid the axe to the root of pseudo-aristocracy. And had another which I prepared been then adopted by the legislature, our work would have been complete. It was a bill... to provide for the annual selection of the best subjects from these schools, who might receive, at the public expense, a higher degree of education at a distant school; and from these district schools to select a certain number of the most promising subjects, to be completed at an university, where all the useful sciences should be taught. Worth and genius would thus have been sought out from every condition of life, and completely prepared by education for defeating the competition of wealth and birth for public trusts.

CE IX 281 M. de Meusnier 1786

An industrious farmer occupies a more dignified place in the scale of being, whether moral or political, than a lazy lounger, valuing himself on his family, too proud to work, and drawing out a miserable existence by eating on that surplus of other men's labor, which is the sacred fund of the helpless poor.

Ford X 11-16 George Logan November 1816

I hope we shall crush... in its birth the aristocracy of our moneyed corporations, which dare already to challenge our government to a trial of strength and bid defiance to the laws of our country.

ME XIII 395-403 John Adams 10-28-13

I think that to give them [the artificial aristoi] power in order to prevent them from doing mischief, is arming them for it, and increasing instead of remedying the evil.... Nor do I believe them necessary to protect the wealthy; because enough of these will find their way into every branch of the legislation, to protect themselves. From fifteen to twenty legislatures of our own, in action for thirty years past, have proved that no fears of an equalization of property are to be apprehended from them. I think the best remedy is exactly that provided by all our [State] constitutions, to leave to the citizens the free election and separation of the aristoi from the pseudo-aristoi, of the wheat from the chaff. In general, they will elect the really good and wise. In some instances, wealth may corrupt, and birth blind them; but not in sufficient degree to endanger the society.

Kings: Ultimate Corruption of False Aristocracy

ME XII 373-379 John Langdon 3-5-10

The practice of Kings marrying only in the families of Kings, has been that of Europe for some centuries. Now, take any race of animals, confine them in idleness and inaction, whether in a stye, a stable, or a state-room, pamper them with high diet, gratify all their sexual appetities, immerse them in sensualities, nourish their passions, let everything bend before them, and banish whatever might lead them to think, and in a few generations they become all body and no mind; and this, too, by a law of nature, by that very law by which we are in the constant practice of changing the characters and propensities of animals we raise for our own purposes. Such is the regimen in raising Kings, and in this way they have gone on for centuries... . Louis the XVI was a fool, of my own knowledge... . The King of Spain was a fool, and of Naples the same. They passed their lives in hunting and despatched two couriers a week, one thousand miles, to let each other know what game they had killed the preceding days. The King of Sardinia was a fool. All these were Bourbons. The Queen of Portugal, a Braganza, was an idiot by nature. And so was the King of Denmark. Their sons, as regents, exercised the powers of government. The King of Prussia, successor to the great Frederick, was a mere hog in body as well as in mind. Gustavus of Sweden, and Joseph of Austria, were really crazy, and George of England, you know, was in a straight waistcoat. There remained, then, none but old Catherine, who had been too lately picked up to have lost her common sense. In this state Bonaparte found Europe, and it was this state of its rulers which lost it with scarce a struggle. These animals had become without mind and powerless and so will every hereditary monarch be after a few generations... . And so endeth the book of Kings, from all of whom may the Lord deliver us... .

ME VI 231-2 Benjamin Hawkins 8-4-87

I am astonished at some people's considering a kingly government as a refuge. Advise such to... [come to] Europe, to see something of the trappings of monarchy, and I will undertake that every man shall go back thoroughly cured. If all the evils which can arise among us, from the republican form of government, from this day to the day of judgment, could be put into a scale against what this country [France] suffers from its monarchical form in a week, or England in a month, the latter would preponderate... . No race of kings has ever presented above one man of common sense in twenty generations. The best they can do is to leave things to their ministers... . If the king can meddle, it is but to do harm.

ME VI 278-80 Colonel Humphreys 8-14-87

So much for the blessings of having Kings, and magistrates who would be Kings. From these events our young Republic may learn useful lessons, never to call on foreign powers to settle their differences, to guard against hereditary magistrates, to prevent their citizens from becoming so established in wealth and power, as to be thought worthy of alliance by marrying with the nieces, sisters, etc., of Kings... . Let us besiege the throne of heaven with eternal prayers, to extirpate from creation this class of human lions, tigers, and mammoths called Kings: from whom, let him perish who does not say, "good Lord, deliver us!"

The Law of Self-preservation

ME XII 418-22 J. B. Colvin 9-20-10

A strict observance of the written laws is doubtless *one* of the high duties of a good citizen, but it is not the *highest.* The laws of necessity, of self-preservation, of saving our country when in danger, are of higher obligation. To lose our country by a scrupulous adherence to written law, would be to lose the law itself, with life, liberty, property, and all those who are enjoying them with us; thus absurdly sacrificing the end to the means... .

A ship at sea in distress for provisions, meets another having abundance, yet refusing a supply; the law of self-preservation authorizes the distressed to take a supply by force... . Further to exemplify the principle, I will state an hypothetical case. Suppose it had been made known to the Executive of the Union in the autumn of 1805, that we might have the Floridas for a reasonable sum, that the sum had not indeed been appropriated by law, but that Congress were to meet within three weeks and might appropriate it on the first or second day of their session. Ought he, for so great an advantage to his country, to have risked himself by transcending the law and making the purchase? The public advantage offered, in this supposed case, was indeed immense; but a reverence for law, and the probability that the advantage might still be *legally* accomplished by a delay of only three weeks, were powerful reasons against hazarding the act. But suppose it foreseen that a John Randolph would find means to protract the proceeding on it by Congress, until the ensuing spring, by which time new circumstances would change the mind of the other party. Ought the Executive, in that case, and with that foreknowledge, to have secured the good of the country, and to have trusted to their justice for the transgression of the law? I think he ought, and that the act would have been approved.[a]

ME XII 182-85 Doctor James Brown 10-27-08

.... under the maxim of the law itself, that *inter arma silent leges,* that in an encampment expecting daily attack from a powerful enemy, self-preservation is paramount to all law, I expected that instead of invoking the forms of the law to cover traitors, all good citizens would have concurred in securing them. Sould we have ever gained our Revolution, if we had bound our hands by manacles of the law, not only in the beginning, but in any part of the revolutionary conflict? There are extreme cases where the laws become inadequate even to their own preservation, and where the universal resource is a dictator, or martial law.

The Theory of Government Structure

ME X 75-86 Elbridge Gerry 1-26-99

I do then, with sincere zeal, wish an inviolable preservation of our present federal Constitution, according to the true sense in which it was adopted by the States, that in which it was advocated by its friends, and not that which its enemies apprehended, who therefore became its enemies; and I am opposed to the monarchising its features by the forms of its administration, with a view to conciliate a first transition to a President and Senate for life, and from that to an hereditary tenure of these offices, and thus to worm out the elective principle.

I am for preserving to the States the powers not yielded by them to the Union, and to the legislature of the Union its constitutional share in the division of powers; and I am not for transferring all the powers of the States to the General Government, and all those of that government to the executive branch.

I am for a government rigorously frugal and simple, applying all the possible savings of the public revenue to the discharge of the national debt; and not for a multiplication of officers and salaries merely to make partisans, and for increasing, by every device, the public debt, on the principle of its being a public blessing. I am for relying, for internal defence, on our militia solely, till actual invasion, and for such a naval

a. It is very interesting indeed to note that Jefferson is here describing precisely the conditions under which he made the Louisiana Purchase, a transaction not strictly constitutional and performed without congressional consent or approval. He even paid down $2 million from the Treasury without permission. However, his wisdom has been proclaimed in this regard and his action has ever since been hailed as perhaps his greatest achievement—even more splendid than his authorship of the Declaration of Independence.

force only as may protect our coasts and harbors from such depredations as we have experienced; and not for a standing army in time of peace, which may overawe the public sentiment; nor for a navy, which, by its own expenses and eternal wars in which it will implicate us, will grind us with public burthens, and sink us under them.

I am for free commerce with all nations; political connection with none; and little or no diplomatic establishment. And I am not for linking ourselves by new treaties with the quarrels of Europe; entering that field of slaughter to preserve their balance, or joining in the confederacy of kings at war against the principles of liberty.

I am for freedom of religion, and against all manoeuvress to bring about a legal ascendancy of one sect over another; for freedom of the press, and against all violations of the Constitution to silence by force and not by reason the complaints or criticisms, just or unjust, of our citizens against the conduct of their agents. And I am for encouraging the progress of science in all its branches; and not for raising a hue and cry against the sacred name of philosophy; for awing the human mind by stories of raw-head and bloody bones to a distrust of its own vision, and repose implicitly on that of others; to go backwards instead of forwards to look for improvement; to believe that government, religion, morality, and every other science were in the highest perfection in ages of the darkest ignorance, and that nothing can ever be devised more perfect than what was established by our forefathers.

To these I will add, that I am a sincere well-wisher to the success of the French revolution, and still wish it may end in the establishment of a free and well-ordered republic; but I have not been insensible under the atrocious depredations they have committed on our commerce.

The first object of my heart is my own country. In that is embarked my family, my fortune, and my own existence. I have not one farthing of interest, nor one fibre of attachment out of it, nor a single motive of preference of any one nation to another, but in proportion as they are more or less friendly to us. But though deeply feeling the injuries of France, I did not think war the surest means of redressing them. I did believe, that a mission sincerely disposed to preserve peace, would obtain for us a peaceable and honorable settlement and retribution; and I appeal to you to say, whether this might not have been obtained, if either of your colleagues had been of the same sentiment with yourself.

These, my friend, are my principles, they are unquestionably the principles of the great body of our fellow-citizens, and I know there is not one of them which is not yours also.

BW 332-335 First Inaugural Address 3-4-01

Let us, then, fellow-citizens, unite with one heart and one mind. Let us restore to social intercourse that harmony and affection without which liberty and even life itself are but dreary things. And let us reflect that having banished from our land that religious intolerance under which mankind so long bled and suffered, we have yet gained little if we countenance a political intolerance as despotic, as wicked, and as capable of as bitter and bloody persecutions.

During the throes and convulsions of the ancient world, during the agonizing spasms of infuriated man, seeking through blood and slaughter his long-lost liberty, it was not wonderful that the agitation of the billows should reach even this distant and peaceful shore... . But every difference of opinion is not a difference of principle. We are all republicans — we are federalists. If there be any among us who would wish to dissolve this Union or to change its republican form, let them stand undisturbed as monuments of the safety with which error of opinion may be tolerated where reason is left free to combat it.

I know, indeed, that some honest men fear that a republican government cannot be strong; that this government is not strong enough. But would the honest patriot, in the full tide of successful experiment, abandon a government which has so far kept us free and firm, on the theoretic and visionary fear that this government, the world's best hope, may by possibility want energy to preserve itself? I trust not. I believe this, on the contrary, the strongest government on earth. I believe it is the only one where every man, at the call of the laws, would fly to the standard of the law, and would meet invasions of the public order as his own personal concern. Sometimes it is said that man cannot be trusted with the government of himself. Can he, then, be trusted with the government of others? Or have we found angels in the forms of kings to govern him? Let history answer this question.

Let us, then, with courage and confidence pursue our own federal and republican principles, our attachment to our union and representative government. Kindly separated by nature and a wide ocean from the exterminating havoc of one quarter of the globe; too high-minded to endure the degradations of the others; possessing a chosen country, with room enough for our descendants to the hundreth and thousandth generation; entertaining a due sense of our equal right to the use of our own faculties, to the acquisitions of our industry, to honor and confidence from our fellow-citizens, resulting not from birth but from our actions and their sense of them; enlightened by a benign religion, professed, indeed, and practiced in various forms, yet all of them including honesty, truth, temperance, gratitude, and the love of man; acknowledging and adoring an overruling Providence, which by all its dispensations proves that it delights in the happiness of man here and greater happiness hereafter; with all these blessings, what more is necessary to make us a happy and prosperous people?

Still one thing more, fellow citizens — a wise and frugal government, which shall restrain men from injuring one another, which shall leave them otherwise free to regulate their own pursuits of industry and improvements, and shall not take from the mouth of labor the bread it has earned. This is the sum of good government, and this is necessary to close the circle of our felicities.

About to enter, fellow citizens, on the exercise of duties which comprehend everything dear and valuable to you, it is proper that you should understand what I deem the essential principles of our government, and consequently those which ought to shape its administration. I will compress them within the narrowest compass they will bear, stating the general principle, but not all its limitations.

Equal and exact justice to all men, of whatever state or persuasion, religious or political; peace, commerce, and honest friendship with all nations — entangling alliances with none; the support of the State governments in all their rights, as the most competent administrations for our domestic concerns and the surest bulwarks against anti-republican tendencies; the preservation of the general government in its whole constitutional vigor, as the sheet anchor of our peace at home and safety abroad; a jealous care of the right of election by the people — a mild and safe corrective of abuses which are lopped by the sword of revolution where peaceable remedies are unprovided; absolute acquiescence in the decisions of the majority — the vital principle of republics, from which there is no appeal but to force, the vital principle and immediate parent of despotism; a well-disciplined militia — our best reliance in peace and for the first moments of war, till regulars may relieve them; the supremacy of the civil over the military authority; economy in the public expense, that labor may be lightly burdened; the honest payment of our debts and sacred preservation of the public faith; encouragement of agriculture, and of commerce as its handmaid; the diffusion of information and the arraignment of all abuses at the bar of public reason; freedom of religion; freedom of the press; freedom of the person under the protection of *habeas corpus;* and trial by juries impartially selected — these principles form the bright constellation which has gone before us, and guided our steps through an age of revolution and reformation. The wisdom of our sages and the blood of our heroes have been devoted to their attainment. They should be the creed of our political faith — the text of our civil government and instruction — the touchstone by which to try the services of those we trust; and should we wander from them in moments of error or alarm, let us hasten to retrace our steps and to regain the road which alone leads to peace, liberty, and safety.

ME XV 32-44 Samuel Kercheval 7-12-16

We should thus marshall our government into, 1, the general, federal republic, for all concerns foreign and federal; 2, that of the State, for what relates to our citizens exclusively; 3, the county republics, for the duties and concerns of the county; and 4, the ward republics, for the small, and yet numerous and interesting concerns of this neighborhood; and in government, as well as in every other business of life, it is by division and subdivision of duties alone, that all matters, great and small, can be managed to perfection. And the whole is cemented by giving to every citizen, personally, a part in the administration of the public affairs.

The sum of these amendments, 1. General Suffrage. 2. Equal representation in the legislature. 3. An executive chosen by the people. 4. Judges elective or amovable. 5. Justices, jurors, and sheriffs elective. 6. Ward divisions. And 7, Periodical amendments to the Constitution.

How Should Thrifty Government Use its Surplus?

BW 369-75 Sixth Annual Message 12-2-06

The question, therefore, now comes forward — to what other objects shall these surpluses be appropriated, and the whole surplus of impost, after the entire discharge of the public debt, and during those intervals when the purposes of war shall not call for them?

Shall we suppress the impost and give that advantage to foreign over domestic manufactures? On a few articles of more general and necessary use, the suppression in due season will doubtless be right, but the great mass of the articles on which impost is paid is foreign luxuries, purchased by those only who are rich enough to afford themselves the use of them. Their patriotism would certainly prefer its continuance and application to the great purposes of the public education, roads, rivers, canals, and such other objects of public improvement as it may be thought proper to add to the constitutional enumeration of federal powers.

By these operations, new channels of communication will be opened between the States; the lines of separation will disappear, their interests will be identified, and their union cemented by new and indissoluble ties. Education is here placed among the articles of public care, not that it would be proposed to take its ordinary branches out of the hands of private enterprise, which manages so much better all the concerns to which it is equal; but a public institution can alone supply those sciences which, though rarely called for, are yet necessary to complete the circle, all the parts of which contribute to the improvement of the country, and some of them to its preservation.

The subject is now proposed for the consideration of Congress, because, if approved by the time the State legislatures shall have deliberated on this extension of the federal trusts, and the laws shall be passed, and other arrangements made for their execution, the necessary funds will be on hand without employment. I suppose an amendment to the Constitution, by consent of the States, necessary, because the objects now recommended, are not among those enumerated in the Constitution, and to which it permits public moneys to be applied.

Love of Peace and Neutrality

ME IX 284-86 Tench Coxe 5-1-94

I love peace, and am anxious that we should give the world another useful lesson, by showing them other modes of punishing injuries than by war, which is as much a punishment to the punisher as to the sufferer. I love, therefore, Mr. Clarke's proposition of cutting off all communication with the nation which has conducted itself so atrociously. This, you will say, may bring war. If it does, we will meet it like men; but it may not bring war; and then the experiment will have been a happy one.

ME X 55-59 Samuel Smith 8-22-98

I know my own principles to be pure, and therefore am not ashamed of them. On the contrary, I wish them known, and therefore willingly express them to every one. They are the same I have acted on from the year 1775 to this day, and are the same, I am sure, with those of the great body of American people. I only wish the real principles of those who censure mine were also known. But warring against those of the people, the delusion of the people is necessary to the dominant party [the Federalist]. I see the extent to which that delusion [the XYZ] has already been carried, and I see there is no length to which it may not be pushed by a party in possession of the revenues and the legal authorities of the United States... long enough to admit much particular mischief. There is no event, therefore, however atrocious, which may not be expected [from the Federalists.]

I am for peace with both countries [England and France]. I know that both of them have given... sufficient cause for war; that in defiance of the laws of nations, they are every day trampling on the rights of the neutral powers, whenever they can thereby do any injury, either to the other.

BW 349-54 Third Annual Message 10-17-03

We should be most unwise, indeed, were we to cast away the singular blessings of the position in which nature has placed us, the opportunity she has endowed us with of pursuing, at a distance from foreign contentions the paths of industry, peace, and happiness; of cultivating general friendship, and of bringing collisions of interest to the umpirage of reason rather than of force.

How desirable then must it be, in a government like ours, to see its citizens adopt individually the views, the interests, and the conduct which their country should pursue, divesting themselves of those passions and partialities which tend to lessen useful friendships, and to embarrass and embroil us in the calamitous scenes of Europe!

Confident, fellow citizens, that you will duly estimate the importance of neutral dispositions toward the observance of neutral conduct, that you will be sensible how much it is our duty to look on the bloody arena spread before us with commiseration indeed, but with no other wish than to see it closed, I am persuaded you will cordially cherish these dispositions in all discussions among yourselves, and in all communications with your constituents; and I anticipate with satisfaction the measures of wisdom which the great interests now committed to *you* will give you an opportunity of providing, and *myself* that of approving and carrying into execution with the fidelity I owe to my country.

ME XIII 92-94 John W. Eppes 9-29-11

I believe it will place us high in the scale of wisdom, to have preserved our country tranquil and prosperous during a contest which prostrated the honor, power, independence, laws, and property of every country on the other side of the Atlantic. Which of them have better preserved their honor? Has Spain, has Portugal, Italy, Switzerland, Holland, Prussia, Austria, the other German powers, Sweden, Denmark, or even Russia? And would we accept of the infamy of France or England in exchange for our honest reputation, or of the result of their enormities, despotism to the one, and bankruptcy and prostration to the other, in exchange for the prosperity, the freedom, and independence which we have preserved safely through the wreck?

Defense: A People's Militia vs. a Standing Army

Ford II 27 The Proposed Virginia Constitution 1776

There will be no standing army but in time of actual war.

ME VI 29-32 William Carmichael 12-26-86

I am satisfied the good sense of the people is the strongest army our government can ever have, and that it will not fail them.

ME X 365-66 To 2-23-03

I take the liberty of urging on you the importance and indispensable necessity of vigorous exertions, on the part of the State governments, to carry into effect the militia system adopted by the national legislature, agreeable to the powers reserved to the States respectively, by the Constitution of the United States, and in a manner the best calculated to ensure such a degree of military discipline, and knowledge of tactics, as will, under the auspices of a benign providence, render the militia a sure and permanent bulwark of national defence.

Blessings of Independence & Limited Government

ME VIII 193-98 James Monroe 5-28-92

It were contrary to feeling, and indeed, ridiculous to suppose, that a man had less rights in himself than one of his neighbors, or, indeed, than all of them put together. This would be slavery, and not that liberty which the bill of rights has made inviolable, and for the preservation of which our government has been charged. Nothing could so completely divest us of that liberty as the establishment of the opinion, that the State has a perpetual right to the services of all its members. This to men of [our way] . . . of thinking, would be to annihilate the blessings of existence, and to contradict the Giver of Life, who gave it for happiness, and not for wrtechedness. And certainly, to such it were better that they had never been born.

ME III 60 Official Papers 7-15-90

Every man, every body of men on earth, possesses the right of self-government. They receive it with their being from the hand of nature. Individuals exercise it by a single will; collections of men by that of their majority; for the law of the *majority* is the natural law of every society of men. When a certain description of men are to transact together a particular business, the times and places of their meeting and separating, depend on their own will; they make a part of the natural right of self-government. This, like all other rights, may be abridged or modified in its exercise by their own consent, or by the law of those who depute them, if they meet in the rights of others; but as far as it is not abridged or modified, they retain it as a natural right, and may exercise it in what form they please, either exclusively by themselves, or in association with others, or by others altogether.

ME X 341-43 Thomas Cooper 1-29-02

If we can prevent the government from wasting the labors of the people, under the pretense of taking care of them, they must become happy.

ME XI 32-35 Judge John Tyler 6-28-04

I may err in my measures, but shall never deflect from the intention of fortifying the public liberty by every possible means, and to put it out of the power of the few to riot on the labors of the many.

Jefferson Magnificent Populist

ME XIII 135-37 F.A. Van der Kemp 3-22-12

Unless the mass retains sufficient control over those intrusted with the powers of their government, these will be perverted to their own oppression, and to the perpetuation of wealth and power in the individuals and their families selected for the trust.

CE VII 36 Samuel Kercheval 1823

No other depositories of power [but the people themselves] have ever yet been found, which did not end in converting to their own profit the earnings of those committed to their charge.

ME XV 480-90 Monsieur A. Coray 10-31-23

.... the people, especially when moderately instructed, are the only safe, because the only honest, depositories of public rights, and should, therefore, be introduced into the administration of them in every function to which they are sufficient; they will err sometimes and accidentally, but never designedly, or with a systematic and persevering purpose for overthrowing the free principles of the government.

ME XVI 74-76 William Ludlow 9-6-24

I think myself we have more machinery of government than is necessary, too many parasites living on the labor of the industrious. I think it might be much simplified, to the relief of those who maintain it.

2. Opinions and Declarations

Commentary

Since Jefferson's overwhelming and lifelong passion was to establish a republican form of government in which the self-employed and self-reliant citizens would constitute a ruling majority, it is no accident that his pride on preparing four legislative measures for the Virginia Assembly perhaps exceeded every other emotion: these were (1) the law terminating the importation of slaves; (2) that abolishing entails (which required all real estate to remain in the same family); (3) that abolishing primogeniture (which fixed the inheritance on the eldest son); and (4) the law establishing religious freedom, which abolished the union of the state with the Anglican or any other denomination.

These laws, he declared, laid the axe to the root of an aristocracy based on wealth or inheritance, and made it possible for another to develop — one founded on virtue, talent, and personal effort.

Since the eradication of caste and privilege was Jefferson's principal objective, he viewed with alarm the establishment of the Order of Cincinnati — at first an innocent organization of revolutionary soldiers, which, however, when taken over by the Federalist-Monocrats, threatened to become a privileged order, somewhat similar to the European nobility and to be incorporated into the government. Jefferson fought against this, and after he became President in 1801, its extinction followed in course.

Since Jefferson's interests were as broad and deep as life itself, we need not wonder that he had definite opinions concerning the medical profession. In his University, no theory *in this field would be taught; only clinical practice, based on specific knowledge and observation.*

He hailed every proven victory over disease, as in the case of vaccination over smallpox; he also hoped and believed that the science would make great strides in the future, probably resulting from accidental discoveries. Interestingly enough, he wrote extensively and approvingly of a doctor who used placebos *for the cure of illness, which were really psychosomatic curatives; in this, he was a forerunner of such men as Phineas Parkhurst*

Quimby and others who declared that the mind can overcome a host of physical illnesses.

It seems that a full treatment of Jefferson would focus heavily on his multitude of diversified scientific interests; for it was largely by accident and because of his supreme abilities, that he was drawn or forced into a career of politics and statecraft — which have made his fame forever immortal. We have found that at least half of his correspondence and other writings deal, in one way or another, with some scientific subject; and he stated emphatically that if he could, he would have devoted his life entirely to scientific pursuits.

We include a small sampling of statements concerning science which ranged from making a sun dial to a plan for a drydock; from raising blooded sheep to a disquisition on the Anglo-Saxon language; from an interest in gunboats and steam engines, to the digging of the Panama Canal, Indian vocabularies, and the bones of mammoths. How could he find time to write 18,000 letters with his sore wrist and preserve them for posterity?

Although it was Jefferson's fervent desire to preserve and extend the Union, he wished to do so on the basis of self-rule; we need, therefore, not be surprised to find him declaring that we should never be twenty years without a rebellion; and he added that rulers should be warned from time to time that the tree of liberty must be refreshed with the blood of patriots and tyrants — for this is the natural fertilizer of freedom.

One of the principal events of Jefferson's life was the act of giving his great collection of books to the Congress of the United States. When the original library was destroyed by the British raid on Washington in 1814, the stage was set for this far-reaching conveyance. It was the beginning of the present Library of Congress, now totalling more than 45,000,000 titles, which certainly ranks with the British Museum as one of the largest and most complete collections of literary treasure to be found anywhere in the world.

We understand that he received $23,500 for his collection of books, an average of somewhat more than $2.00; he used this to pay a portion of the debt he had incurred during his twelve consecutive years of tenure as vice-president and president of the United States.

Laws of Entail and Primogeniture

ME 1 64 Autobiography 1821

As the law of Descents and the criminal law fell of course within my portion, I wished the committee to settle the leading principles of these, as a guide for me in framing them; and, with respect to the first, I proposed to abolish the law of primogeniture, and to make real estate descendible in parcenary to the next of kin, as personal property is, by the statute of distribution. Mr. Pendleton wished to preserve the right of primogeniture, but seeing at once that that would not prevail, he proposed that we should adopt the Hebrew principle, and give a double portion to the elder son. I observed that if the eldest son could eat twice as much, and do double work, it might be natural evidence of his right to a double portion; but being on a par in his powers and wants, with his brothers and sisters, he should be on a par also in the distribution of the patrimony; and such was the decision of the other members [of the Assembly].

ME XVII 461 Miscellaneous Papers

[The law prohibiting the importation of slaves] was followed by the abolition of entails, which broke up the hereditary and high-handed aristocracy, which, by accumulating immense masses of property in single lines of families, had divided our country into two distinct orders, of nobles and plebians.

But further to complete the equality among our citizens so essential to the maintenance of republican government, it was necessary to abolish the principle of primogeniture. I drew the law of descents, giving equal inheritance to sons and daughters, which made a part of the revised code.

BW 440 Autobiography 1821

I considered four of these bills [including the abolition of slave importation and the disestablishment of the Anglican Church], passed or reported, as forming a system of which every fibre would be eradicated of ancient or future aristocracy. The repeal of the laws of entail would prevent the accumulation and perpetuation of wealth, in select families, and preserve the soil of the country from being daily more and more absorbed in mortmain. The abolition of primogeniture, and equal partition of inheritances, removed the feudal and unnatural distinction which made one member of every family rich, and all the rest poor, substituting equal partition, the best of all Agrarian laws.

The Order of the Cincinnati

ME I 215-220 General Washington 4-16-84

When the army was about to be disbanded, and the officers to take final leave, perhaps never again to meet, it was natural for men who had accompanied each other through so many scenes of hardship, of difficulty, and danger... to seize with fondness any proposition which promised to bring them together again, at certain and regular periods. And this, I take for granted, was the origin and object of this institution [the Cincinnati]; and I have no suspicion that they foresaw, much less intended, those mischiefs which exist... .

Jefferson Magnificent Populist

ME I 267 The Anas

The next effort was [a movement for]... the establishment of a hereditary order under the name of the Cincinnati, ready prepared by that distinction to be ingrafted into the future form of government, and placing General Washington still at their head... .

ME IV 215-20 General Washington 4-16-84

The objections of those who are opposed to the institution [of the Cincinnati] shall be briefly sketched... . They urge that it is against the Confederation — against... the natural equality of man, the denial of every pre-eminence attached to birth; that a... time may come, when a change of dispositions would render these flattering, when a well-directed distribution of them might draw into the order all the men of talents, of office and wealth, and in this case, would probably procure an ingraftment into the government; that in this, they will be supported by their foreign members, and the wishes and influence of foreign courts; that experience has shown that the hereditary branches of modern governments are the patrons of privilege and prerogative, and not of the natural rights of the people, whose oppressors they generally are; that, besides these evils, which are remote, others may take place more immediately; that a distinction is kept up between the civil and military, which it is for the happiness of both to obliterate; that when the members assemble, they will be proposing to do something, and what that something may be, will depend on actual circumstances; that, being an organized body, under habits of subordination, the first obstruction to enterprise will be already surmounted; that the moderation and virtue of a single character [Washington] have probably prevented this Revolution from being closed, as most others have been, by a subversion of that liberty it was intended to establish; that he is not immortal, and his successor, or some of his successors, may be led by false calculation into a less certain road to glory.

ME XVII 80-91 Miscellaneous Papers 1786

General Washington... was sometimes present, when his officers were fashioning, in their conversations, their newly proposed society [of the Cincinnati]. He saw the innocence of its origin... . Far from thinking it a moment to multiply the causes of irritation, by thwarting a proposition which had absolutely no other basis but that of benevolence and friendship, he was rather satisfied to find himself aided in his difficulties by this new incident, which occupied, and, at the same time, soothed, the minds of the officers [because of their lack of pay]... .

As to the question, then, whether evil can proceed from the institution as it stands at present, I am of opinion there may. 1. From the meetings. These will keep the officers formed into a body; will continue a distinction between the civil and military, which it would be for the good of the whole to obliterate, as soon as possible; and the military assemblies will not only keep alive the jealousies and fears of the civil government, but give ground for these fears and jealousies... . 2. The charitable part of the institution is still more likely to do mischief, as it perpetuates the dangers apprehended in the preceding clause. For here is a fund provided of permanent existence. To whom will it belong? To the descendants of American officers of a certain description. These descendants, then, will form a body, having sufficient interest to keep up an attention to their description, to continue meetings, and perhaps, in some moment, when the political eye shall be slumbering, or the firmness of their fellow-citizens relaxed, to replace the insignia of the order and revive all its pretensions... .

How are these evils to be prevented? 1. At their first general meeting, let them distribute the funds on hand to the existing objects of their destination, and discontinue all further contributions. 2. Let them declare, at the same time, that their meetings, general and particular, shall thenceforth cease. 3. Let them melt up their eagles and add the mass to the distributable fund, that their descendants may have no temptation to hang them in their buttonholes.

ME XVI 52-69 Martin van Buren 6-29-24

When the first meeting was called for the establishment [of the Society of the Cincinnati], I was a member of the Congress then sitting at Annapolis. General Washington wrote to me, asking my opinion of that proposition, and the course, if any, which I thought Congress would observe respecting it. I wrote him frankly my own disapprobation of it; that I found the members of Congress generally in the same sentiment: that I thought they would take no notice of it, but that in all appointments of trust, honor, or profit, they would silently pass by all the candidates of that order, and give an uniform preference to others.

On his way to the first meeting in Philadelphia, which I think was in the spring of 1784, he called on me at Annapolis... . While he was feelingly indulgent to the motives which might induce the officers to promote it, he concurred with me entirely in condemning it; and when I expressed an idea that if the hereditary quality were suppressed, the institution might perhaps be indulged during the lives of the officers now living, and who had actually served: "No," he said, "not a fibre of it ought to be left, to be an eyesore to the public, a ground for dissatisfaction, and a line of separation between them and their country;" and he left with a determination to use all his influence for its entire suppression.

On his return from the meeting, he called on me again, and related to me the course the thing had taken. He said that from the beginning he had used every endeavor to prevail on the officers to renounce the project altogether, urging the many considerations which would render it odious to their fellow citizens, and disreputable and injurious to themselves; that he had at length prevailed on most of the old officers to reject it, although with great and warm opposition from others, and especially the younger ones... . But that in this state of things... . Major L'Enfant arrived from France, with a bundle of eagles, for which he had been sent there, with letters from the French officers who had served in America, praying for admission into the order, and a solemn act of their King permitting them to wear its ensign. This, he said, changed the face of matters at once, produced an entire revolution of sentiment, and turned the torrent so strongly in an opposite direction that it could no longer be withstood; all he could then obtain was a suppression of the hereditary quality.

ME IX 293-97 James Madison 12-28-94

The denunciation of the democratic societies [established by Jefferson] is one of the extraordinary acts of boldness of which we have seen so many from the faction of the monocrats. It is wonderful indeed, that the President should have permitted himself to be the organ of such an attack on the freedom of discussion, the freedom of writing, printing, and publishing.

It must be a matter of rare curiosity to get at the modifications of those rights proposed by them, and to see what line their ingenuity would draw between democratical societies, whose avowed object is the nourishment of the republican principles of our Constitution, and the society of the Cincinnati, a *self-created one,* carving out for itself hereditary distinctions, lowering over our Constitution eternally, meeting together in all parts of the Union, periodically, with closed doors, accumulating a capital in their separate treasury, corresponding secretly and regularly, and of which society the very persons denouncing the democrats are themselves the fathers, founders, and high officers. Their sight must be perfectly dazzled by the glittering of crowns and coronets, not to see the extravagance of the proposition to suppress the friends of general freedom, while those who wish to confine that freedom to the few, are permitted to go on in their principles and practices. [These democratic societies were republican organizations which printed and published analyses and criticisms of Federalist policies and practices. Unfortunately, Hamilton was able to persuade George Washington to join in their condemnation].

Doctors, Medicine, and Medical Theory

ME XI 242-48 Doctor Casper Wister 6-21-07

We know, from what we see and feel, that the animal body is in its organs and functions, subject to derangement, inducing pain, and tending to its destruction. In this disordered state, we observe nature providing for the re-establishment of order, by exciting some salutary evacuation of the morbific matter, or by some other operation which escapes our imperfect senses and researches. She brings on a crisis, by stools, vomiting, sweat, urine, expectoration, bleeding, etc., which, for the most part, ends in the restoration of healthy action. Experience has taught us, also, that there are certain substances, by which, applied to the living body, internally or externally, we can at will produce these same evacuations, and thus do, in a short time, what nature would do but slowly, and do effectually, what perhaps she would not have strength to accomplish... .

So far, I bow to the utility of medicine. It goes to the well-defined forms of disease, and happily, to those the most frequent. But the disorders of the animal body, and the symptoms indicating them, are as various as the elements of which the body is composed. The combinations, too, of these symptoms are so infinitely diversified, that many associations of them appear too rarely to establish a definite disease; and to an unknown disease, there cannot be a known remedy.

Here, then, the judicious, the moral, the humane physician should stop. Having been so often a witness to the salutary efforts which nature makes to re-establish the disordered functions, he should rather trust to their action, than hazard the interruption of that, and a greater derangement of the system, by conjectural experiments on a machine so complicated and so unknown as human life. Or, if the appearance of doing something be necessary to keep alive the hope and spirits of the patient, it should be of the most innocent character.

One of the most successful physicians I have ever known, has assured me that he has used more bread pills, drops of colored water, and powders of hickory ashes, than of all other medicines put together. It was certainly a pious fraud.

But the adventurous physician goes on, and substitutes presumption for knowledge. From the scanty field of what is known, he launches into the boundless region of what is unknown. He establishes for his guide some fanciful theory... which lets him into all of nature's secrets at short hand. On the principle which he thus assumes, he... arrays his diseases into families, and extends his curative treatment, by analogy, to all the cases he has thus arbitrarily marshalled together... .

I believe we may safely affirm, that the inexperienced and presumptuous band of medical tyros let loose upon the world, destroys more of human life in one year, than all the Robin Hoods, Cartouches, and MacHeaths do in a century. It is in this part of medicine that I wish to see a reform, an abandonment of hypothesis for sober facts, the first degree of value set on clinical observation, and the lowest on visionary theories. I would wish the young practitioner, especially, to have deeply impressed on his mind, the real limits of his art, and that when the state of his patient gets beyond these, his office is to be a watchful, but quiet spectator of the operations of nature, giving them fair play by a well-regulated regimen, and by all the aid they can derive from the excitement of good spirits and hope in the patient.

I have no doubt, that some diseases not yet understood may in time be transferred to the table of those known. But, were I a physician, I would rather leave the transfer to the slow hand of accident, than hasten it by guilty experiments on those who put their lives into my hands.

The only sure foundations of medicine are an intimate knowledge of the human body, and observation on the effects of medicinal substances on that. The anatomical and clinical schools, therefore, are those in which the young physician should be formed. If he enters with innocence that of the theory of medicine, it is scarcely possible he should come out untainted with error. His mind must be strong indeed, if, rising above juvenile credulity, it can maintain a wise infidelity against the authority of his instructors, and the bewitching delusions of their theories.

You see that I estimate justly that portion of instruction which our medical students derive from your labors; and, associating with it one of the chairs which my old and able friend, Doctor Rush, so honorably fills, I consider them as the two fundamental pillars of the edifice. Indeed, I have such an opinion of the talents of the professors of the other branches which constitute the school of medicine with you, as to hope and believe, that it is from this side of the Atlantic, that Europe, which taught us so many other things, will at length be led into sound principles in this branch of science, the most important of all others, being that to which we commit the care of our health and life.

ME XIV 199-202 Thomas Cooper 2-7-14

.... the theory (not the practice) of medicine... is the charlatanerie of the body... .

ME XV 207-11 John Brazier 8-24-19

The physician [finds in the Latin language]... as good a code of his art as has been given us to this day. Theories and systems of medicine, indeed, have been in perpetual change from the days of the good Hippocrates, to the days of the good Rush, but which of them is the true one? the present, to be sure, as long as it is the present, but to yield its place in turn to the next novelty, which is then to become the true system, and is to mark the vast advance of medicine since the days of Hippocrates. Our situation is certainly benefitted by the discovery of some new and very valuable medicines; and substituting those for some of his with the treasure of facts, and of sound observations recorded by him (mixed, to be sure, with the anilities of the day), and we shall have nearly the sum of the healing art.

ME XIII 226-26 Dr. Benjamin Rush 3-6-13

That there are certain diseases of the human body, so distinctly pronounced by well-articulated symptoms, and recurring so often, as not to be mistaken, wherein experience has proved that certain substances applied, will restore order, I cannot doubt. Such are Kindina in Intermittants, Mercury in Syphilis, Castor Oil in Dysentery, etc. And so far, I go with the physicians.

But there are also a great mass of indistinct diseases, presenting themselves under no form clearly characterized, nor exactly recognized as having occurred before, and to which of course the application of no particular substance can be known to have been made, nor its effect on the case experienced. These may be called unknown cases, and they may in time be lessened by the progress of observation and experiment.

Observing that there are in the construction of the animal system some means provided unknown to us, which have tendency to restore order, when disturbed by accident... , I think it safer to trust to this power in the unknown cases, than to uncertain conjectures built on the ever-changing hypothetical systems of medicine.

Now, in the Veterinary department, all are unknown cases. Man can tell his physician the seat of his pain, its nature, history, and sometimes its cause, and can follow his directions for the curative process — but the poor dumb horse cannot signify where his pain is, what it is, or when or whence it came, and resists all process for its cure. If in the case of a man, then, the benefit of medical interference in such cases admits of question, what must it be in that of the horse? And to what narrow limits is the real importance of the Veterinary art reduced? When a boy, I knew a Doctor Seymour, neighbor to our famous botanist Clayton, who imagined he could cure the diseases of his tobacco plants; he bled some, administered lotions to others, sprinkled powders on a third class, and so on — they only withered and perished the faster.

Examples of Artistic and Scientific Interest

ME V 134-37 James Madison 9-20-85

You see, I am an enthusiast on the subject of the arts. But it is an enthusiasm of which I am not ashamed, as its object is to improve the taste of my countrymen, to increase their reputation, to reconcile to them the respect of the world, and procure their praise.

ME VI 11-15 Charles Thompson 12-17-86

Since writing... I have had a conversation on the subject of steam mills, with the famous Boulton... . He compares the effort of steam with that of horses, in the following manner: Six horses, aided with the most advantageous combination of the mechanical powers hitherto tried, will grind six bushels of flour in an hour... . They can work thus, six hours in the twenty-four, grinding thirty-six bushels of flour, which is six to each horse, for the twenty-four hours. His steam mill in London consumes one hundred and twenty-four bushels of coal in twenty-four hours, turns ten pairs of stones, which grind eight bushels of flour an hour each, which is nineteen hundred and twenty bushels in the twenty-four hours. This makes a peck and a half of coal perform exactly as much as a horse, in one day, can perform.

ME VII 26-30 William Carmichael 5-27-88

With respect to the Isthmus of Panama, I am assured by Burgoyne... that a survey was made, that a canal appeared practicable, and that the idea was suppressed for political reasons altogether.

ME VII 241-44 Thomas Paine 12-23-88

I will begin with the subject of your bridge, in which I feel myself interested; and it is with great pleasure that I learn... that the execution of the arch of experiment exceeds your expectations. In your former letter, you mention, that instead of arranging your tubes and bolts as ordinates to the cord of the arch, you had reverted to your first idea, of arranging them in the direction of the radii.

ME XI 362-63 Thomas Paine 9-6-07

I received last night your... model of a contrivance for making a gunboat do nearly double execution. It has all the ingenuity and simplicity which generally mark your inventions... . I send it this day to the Secretary of the Navy, within which department it lies to try and judge it. Believing myself, that gunboats are the only *water* defense that can be useful to us, and protect us from the ruinous folly of a navy, I am pleased with everything which promises to improve them.

ME XI 118-21 James Bowdoin 7-10-06

I believe that when you left America, the invention of the polygraph had not yet reached Boston. It is for copying with one pen while you write with the other, and without the least additional embarrassment or exertion to the writer. I think it the finest invention of the present age, one so much superior to the copying machine, that the latter will never be continued a day by anyone who tries the polygraph.

ME XIII 191-93 Robert Patterson 12-27-12

I am very thankful for the description of Redhefer's machine. I had never before been able to form an idea of what his principle of deception was. He is the first of the inventors of perpetual motion within my knowledge, who has had the cunning to put his visitors on a false pursuit, by amusing them with a sham machinery whose loose and vibratory motion might impose on them the belief that it is the real source of the motion they see. To this device, he is indebted for a more extensive delusion than I have before witnessed on this point. We are full of it as far as this State, and I know not how much farther. In Richmond they have done me the honor to quote me as having said that it was a possible thing. A poor Frenchman who called on me the other day, with another invention of perpetual motion, assured me that Dr. Franklin, many years ago, expressed his opinion that it was not impossible... .

Redhefer seems to be reaping a rich harvest from the public deception. The office of science is to instruct the ignorant. Would it be unworthy of some one of its votaries who witness this deception, to give a popular demonstration of the insufficiency of the ostensible machinery, and of course of the necessary existence of some hidden mover? And who could do it with more effect on the public mind than yourself?

ME X 176-80 Robert B. Livingston 12-14-00

I have heard of the discovery of some large bones, supposed to be of the mammoth, at about thirty or forty miles distant from you; and among the bones found, are said to be some of which we have never been able to procure. The first interesting question is, whether they *are* the bones of the mammoth? The second, what are the particular bones, and could I possibly procure them? The bones I am most anxious to obtain, are those of the head and feet, which are said to be among those found in your State, as also *casa innominata,* and *scapula.* Others would also be interesting, though similar ones may be possessed, because they would show by their similarity that the set belong to the mammoth. Could I so far venture to trouble you on this subject, as to engage some of your friends near the place, to procure for me the bones above mentioned?

ME XII 380-81 Robert Fulton 3-17-10

I have duly received your favor of February 24th covering one of your pamphlets on the Torpedo. I have read it with pleasure. This was not necessary to give them favor in my eye. I am not afraid of new inventions or improvements, nor bigoted to the practices of our forefathers... . I am much pleased that Congress is taking up the business. Where a new invention is supported by well-known principles, and promises to be useful, it ought to be tried. Your torpedoes will be to cities what vaccination has been to mankind. It extinguishes their greatest danger. But there will still be navies. Not for the destruction of cities, but for the plunder of commerce on the high seas. That the tories should be against you is in character, because it will curtail the power of their idol, England.

ME XII 389-91 James Madison 5-13-10

Give all the full-blooded males [rams] we can raise to the different counties of our State, one to each, as fast as we can furnish them. And as there must be some rule of priority for the distribution, let us begin with our own counties, which are contiguous and nearly central to the State, and proceed, circle after circle, till we have given a ram to every county. This will take about seven years, if we add to the full descendants those which will have passed to the fourth generation from common ewes. To make the benefit of a single male as general as practicable to the county, we may ask some known character in each county to have a small society formed which shall receive the animal and prescribe rules for his care and government. We should retain ourselves all the full-blooded ewes, that they may enable us the sooner to furnish a male to every county. When all shall have been provided with rams, we may, in a year or two more, be in a condition to give an ewe also to every county, if it be thought necessary.

ME XIII 80-81 Charles Clay 8-23-11

I have amused myself with calculating the hour lines of an horizontal [sun] dial for the latitude of this place, which I find to be $37°22'25_0$. The calculations are for every five minutes of time, and are always exact within less than half of a second of a degree.

ME XIII 108-10 Robert Patterson 11-10-11

I have a curiosity to try the length of the pendulum vibrating seconds here, and would wish Mr. Voigt to prepare one which would be substituted for that of a clock occasionally... .

ME XIII 347-49 John Wilson 8-17-13

(A letter dealing with orthography, English spellings, etc.)

ME XVIII 365-411 Essay on Anglo-Saxon

(A 47-page disquisition on the Anglo-Saxon language, grammar, spelling, and sentence-structure.)

ME XV 153-57 J. Correa de Serra 11-25-17

I have taken measures to obtain the crested turkey, and will endeavor to perpetuate that beautiful and singular characteristic, and shall be not less earnest in endeavors to raise the Moronnier.

ME XVI 135-38 Lewis M. Wiss 11-27-25

(This, written only a few months before Jefferson's death, contains an elaborate plan for a drydock in which to build and repair ships.)

Jefferson: The Recipient of Honors

ME V 311-12 William Drayton 5-6-86

I am very sensible of the honor done me by the South Carolina Society for Promoting and improving Agriculture and other rural concerns, when they were pleased to elect me to be of their body; and I beg leave, Sir, to convey to them my grateful thanks for this favor.

ME VI 25-26 Mr. Stiles 12-24-86

I feel myself very much honored by the degree which has been conferred on me by the Senatus Academicus of Yale College, and I beg leave, through you, Sir, to express to them how sensible I am of this honor and that it is to their and your indulgence, and not to any merit of my own, that I am indebted for it.

ME VI 165-69 T.M. Randolph of the Society for the Encouragement of Natural History 7-6-87

Will you be so good, Sir, as to return my most respectful thanks for the diploma with which I am honored by the Society for the Encouragement of Natural History?

ME VII 325-29 Doctor Willard 3-24-89

I have been lately honored with your letter of September the 24th, 1788, accompanied by a diploma for a Doctorate of Laws, which the University of Harvard has been pleased to confer on me. Conscious how little I merit it, I am the more sensible of their goodness and indulgence to a stranger, who has had no means of serving or making himself known to them.

ME VIII 11 Doctor Joseph Willard 4-1-90

I have duly received the letter wherein you are so good as to notify to me the honor done me by the American Academy of Arts and Sciences, in electing me one of their members, together with the diploma therein enclosed; and I beg leave through you, Sir, to return to the Academy the homage of my thanks for this favor, and to express to them the gratified sense I have of it.

ME XI 212-13 M. Sylvester, Secretaire de La Societe D'Agriculture de Paris 5-29-07

Sir, — I have received, through the care of General Armstrong, the medal of gold by which the Society of Agriculture at Paris have been pleased to make their approbation of the form of a mould-board which I prepared [for a plough very similar to modern ones]... .

ME XI 382-83 Doctor W. S. Barton 10-18-07

I received last night a diploma from the Linnaean Society of Philadelphia, doing me the honor of associating with their body.

ME XI 419-20 To the Philosophical Society 1-9-08

I duly received your favor of the 1st instant, informing me that at an election of officers of the American Philosophical Society, held at their hall on that day, they were pleased unanimously to elect me as their President for the ensuing year. I repeat, with great sensibility, my thanks to the Society for these continued proofs of their good will.

ME XII 230 Thomas C. James, Secretary of the American Philosophical Society 1-14-09

I have received your favor... informing me that the American Philosophical Society has been pleased, at their late election, to re-elect me President of the Society... I shall obey it with dutifulness and be ever anxious to avail myself of every occasion of being useful to them...

ME XII 381-82 To the Royal Institute of Sciences, of Literature, and of Fine Arts, at Amsterdam 5-2-10

Your letter of the 10th of May of the last year but lately came into my hands. I am duly sensible of the honor done me by the first class of the Royal Institute of Sciences, of Literature, and of Fine Arts, in associating me to their class, and by the approbation which his Majesty, the King of Holland, has condescended to give to their choice... I shall be happy at all times in fulfulling any particular views which the Society may extend to this region of the globe...

ME XIII 119-20 Thomas Sully 1-8-12

I have duly received your favor of December 22d, informing me that the Society of Artists of the United States has made me an honorary member of their Society. I am very justly sensible of the honor they have done me, and I pray you to return them my thanks for this mark of their distinction.

On The Theory of Insurrection

ME I 196 Appendix to Autobiography 1774

There are extraordinary situations which require extraordinary interposition. An exasperated people, who feel they possess power, are not easily restrained within limits strictly regular. A number of them assembled in the town of Boston, threw the tea into the ocean, and dispersed without doing any other act of violence.

ME VI 155-56 B. Hollis 7-2-87

You will have seen that one of our republics [Massachusetts] has experienced those commotions [Shay's Rebellion] which the newspapers have been always ascribing to all of them. I am not satisfied what has been the cause of this, but the most probable account is, that these individuals were of those who have so imprudently involved themselves in debt; and that a vigorous exertion in their government to enforce the payment of private debts, and raise money for the public ones, occasioned the insurrection. One insurrection in thirteen States in the course of eleven years that they have existed, amounts to one in any individual State in one hundred and forty-three years, say a century and a half. This will not weigh against the inconveniences of a government of force, such as monarchies and aristocracies. You see I am not discouraged by this little difficulty; nor have I any doubt that the result of our experiment will be, that men are capable of governing themselves without a master.

ME VI 371-73 Colonel Smith 11-13-87

God forbid we should ever be twenty years without such a rebellion. The people cannot be all, and always, well informed. The part which is wrong will be discontented, in proportion to the importance of the facts they misconceive. If they remain quiet under such misconceptions, it is lethargy, the forerunner of death to the public liberty. We have had thirteen States independent for eleven years. There has been one rebellion. That comes to one rebellion in a century and a half, for each State. What country before, ever existed a century and a half without a rebellion? And what country can preserve its liberties, if its rulers are not warned from time to time, that the people preserve the spirit of resistance? Let them take arms. The remedy is to set them right as to facts, pardon and pacify them. What signify a few lives lost in a century or two? The tree of liberty must be refreshed from time to time, with the blood of patriots and tyrants. It is its natural manure. Our convention has been too much impressed by the insurrection in Massachusetts, and on the spur of the moment, they are setting up a kite to keep the hen yard in order. I hope in God, this article will be rectified before the Constitution is accepted.

ME IX 293-97 James Madison 12-28-94

And with respect to the transactions against the excise law, it appears to me that you are all swept away in the torrent of governmental opinions, or that we do not know what these transactions have been. We know of none which, according to the definitions of the law, have been anything more than riotous. There was indeed a meeting to consult about a separation. But to consult on a question does not amount to a determination of that question in the affirmative, still less to the acting on such a determination; but we shall see, I suppose, what the court lawyers, and courtly judges, and would-be ambassadors will make of it.

The excise law is an infernal one. The first error was to admit it by the Constitution; the second, to act on that admission; the third and last will be, to make it the instrument for dismembering the Union, and setting us all afloat to choose that part of it we will adhere to.

The information of our militia, returned from the westward [Pennsylvania], is uniform, that though the people there let them pass quietly, they were the objects of their laughter, not of their fear; that one thousand men could have cut off their whole force in a thousand places of the Allegheny; that their detestation of the excise law is universal, and has now associated to it a detestation of the government... .

I expected to have seen some justification of arming one part of the society against another; of declaring a civil war the moment before the meeting of that body which has the sole right of declaring war; of being so patient of the kicks and scoffs of our enemies, and rising at a feather against our friends, of adding a million to the public debt... .

Jefferson Gives His Library to Congress

ME XIII 176-78 Thomas Cooper 7-10-12

I am making a fair copy of the catalogue of my library, which I mean to have printed merely for the use of the library. It will require correct orthography in so many languages, that I hardly know where I can get it done.

ME XIV 190-194 Samuel H. Smith, Esq. 9-21-14

I learn from the newspapers that the vandalism of our enemy has triumphed at Washington over science as well as the arts, by the destruction of the public library with the noble edifice in which it was deposited... .

You know my collection [of books], its condition and extent. I have been fifty years making it, and have spared no pains, opportunity, or expense, to make it what it is. While residing in Paris, I devoted every afternoon I was disengaged, for a summer or two, in examining all the principal bookstores, turning over every book with my own hand, and putting by everything which related to America, and indeed whatever was rare and valuable in every science.

Besides this, I had standing orders during the whole time I was in Europe, on its principal book marts, particularly Amsterdam, Frankfort, Madrid, and London, for such works relating to America as could not be found in Paris. So that in that department particularly, such a collection was made as probably can never again be effected, because it is hardly probable that the same opportunities, the same time, industry, perseverance, and expense, with some knowledge of the bibliography of the subject, would again happen to be in concurrence.

During the same period, and after my return to America, I was led to procure, also, whatever related to the duties of those in the high concerns of the nation. So that the collection, which I suppose is of between nine and ten thousand volumes, while it includes what is chiefly valuable in science and literature generally, extends more particularly to whatever belongs to the American statesman. In the diplomatic and parliamentary branches, it is particularly full.

It is long since I have been sensible it ought not to continue private property, and had provided that at my death, Congress should have the refusal of it at their own price. But the loss they have now incurred, makes the present the proper moment for their accommodation without regard to the small remnant of time and the barren use of my enjoying it. I ask of your friendship, therefore, to make for me the tender of it to the Library Committee of Congress, not knowing myself of whom the Committee consists. I enclose you the catalogue, which will enable them to judge of the contents. Nearly the whole are well bound, abundance of them elegantly, and of the choicest editions existing. They may be valued by persons named by themselves; and the payment made convenient to the public... . They may enter... into immediate use of it, as eighteen or twenty wagons would place it in Washington in a single trip of a fortnight... The return of the catalogue will of course be needed, whether the tender be accepted or not. I do not know that it contains any branch of science which Congress would wish to exclude from their collection; there is, in fact, no subject to which a member of Congress may not have occasion to refer. But such a wish would not correspond with my views of preventing its dismemberment. My desire is either to place it in their hands entire, or to preserve it so here. I am engaged in making an alphabetical index of the author's names, to be annexed to the catalogue, which I will forward to you as soon as completed; any agreement you shall be so good as to take the trouble of entering into with the Committee, I hereby affirm.

ME XIV 290-94 James Madison, President of the United States 3-23-15

Mr. Smith wrote to me on the transportation of the library, and, particularly, that it is submitted to your direction... . I am now employing as many hours every day as my strength will permit, in arranging the books, and putting every one in its place on the shelves, corresponding with its order in the catalogue, and shall have them numbered correspondently. This operation will employ me a considerable time yet.

Then I should wish a competent agent to attend, and, with the catalogue in his hand, see that every book is on the shelves, and have their lids nailed on, one by one, as he proceeds... . I enclose you a letter from Mr. Milligan, offering his service, which would not cost more than eight or ten days' reasonable compensation. This is necessary for my safety and your satisfaction, as a just caution for the public... . If you approve of it, therefore, as soon as I am through the review, I will give notice to Mr. Milligan, or any other person you will name, to come on immediately.

ME XIV 294-96 L. H. Girardin 3-27-15

It is with real regret I inform you that the delivery of the library is close at hand. A letter by last mail informs me that Mr. Milligan is ordered to come on the instant I am ready to deliver. I shall complete the arrangement of the books on Saturday. There will then remain only to paste on them their numbers, which will be begun on Sunday. Of this, Mr. Milligan has notice, and may be expected every hour after Monday next. He will examine the books by the catalogue, and nail up the presses, one by one, as he gets through them. But it is indispensable for me to have all the books in their places when we begin to number them... .

[This extraordinary collection of books became the nucleus of the great Congressional Library, which now has some fifty million titles and documents and occupies three magnificent buildings. The original of these has now been named the Jefferson Library; what was, for many years, called the Jefferson Annex is now the John Adams Annex; and across the street stands the new and opulent Madison Addition. And so these three close friends, after many years, are immortalized together in these fitting and splendid monuments to their memory and their fame.]

3. The American vs. the European Man

Commentary

We should note that when Jefferson uses the term manufactures, *he means the proletarians — propertyless wage-earners — employed in European factories or sweatshops. In these, he had no confidence, and, for a long time, did not wish to see such industry established in the United States for the simple and all-important reason that such employees cannot be relied upon to support a republican form of government. Above all else, he wished to encourage producers who perform labor in occupations which require their ownership of the means of production. In short, he wanted an American population which would consist overwhelmingly of what we today call the middle class of proprietors who, in one way or another, are in business for themselves.*

Such individuals, especially independent farmers, he called the chosen people of God, the most virtuous and the most independent of all citizens. They are the self-reliant, economic-political units who will think for themselves; every such person, he declared in a letter to John Adams, "by his property, or by his satisfactory situation, is interested in the support of law and order. And such men may safely and advantageously reserve to themselves a wholesome control over the public affairs, and a degree of freedom which, in the hands of the canaille *of the cities of Europe, would be instantly perverted to the demolition and destruction of everything, public and private."*

Thus, a nation consisting largely of middle-class citizens will not only be prosperous and self-reliant, but will prove also that a minimum of government is sufficient as well as salutary. In such a state, the rich, the over-privileged, and the paupers will be few in numbers. It will maintain an orderly and powerful organization; it will have no standing or central army, but a people's militia prepared at all times for defence.

When the Federalists attempted to establish a privileged order of Cincinnati, who would live in idleness on government pensions, Jefferson told these would-be noblesse that they, like others, should earn their livings by honest labor on the land.

However, as the years brought new situations and especially as English goods were interdicted by the embargo, the non-intercourse laws, the continuing piracies, and the war, Jefferson's opinions concerning manufacture underwent a considerable alteration: but not as drastic as might have been thought. What he wanted to see and what actually happened to a considerable degree, was the transformation of most farms from mere cultivators of the soil into combination agrarian-manufacturing entities. And this was in no sense contrary to Jefferson's ideal: such producers of clothing, nails, lumber, and many other products, were still using their own materials and equipment to fabricate a multitude of articles for their own use. And this gave the country something else in addition, worth fully as much as the virtues of farming: namely, independence from foreign sources of goods.

No doubt Jefferson foresaw the development of larger plants in the cities, which would employ many manufactures — as he called them — and produce ploughs, wagons, guns, rifles, ships, etc., beyond the scope of family activity. However, he consoled himself with the thought that such workers would command decent incomes, for they could, at any time, acquire land and soon achieve comfort and independence thereon.

All facets of Jefferson's social, political, and economic philosophy meld into a single structure: the creation of a republican government, which would serve the interests of property-owning producers. It was no accident, therefore, that when he became president one of his first acts was to abolish the Internal Revenue Service, which, under the Federalists, had created "unnecessary offices, useless establishments, and expenses," which, "covering our land with officers, and opening our doors to their intrusions, had already begun that process of domiciliary vexation, which, once entered, is scarcely to be restrained from reaching successively every article of produce and property." The Federalists, like our modern government, had continued to invent manifold methods of taxing every article of produce and property and increasing the size and complexity of the central government. Jefferson terminated all of these, as well as the positions of the bureaucrats who administered them: by instituting economies in the federal structure, he reduced the taxes dramatically; and yet, at the same time, instead of increasing the national debt, as the Federalists had been doing, he paid off nearly one-half of it in eight years; and he did so without taking so much as a penny from the productive middle class.

Jefferson never tired of expatiating on the vast gulf which separated the producers of Europe from those of the United States. Many of those in England — as he explained elsewhere — were so poor that, starving, they demanded bread or the gallows. Perhaps nothing gave him greater pleasure than seeing the indigent of Europe, no matter how downtrodden, become respectable and self-reliant citizens when offered the opportunity of work for decent remuneration here; and how they found honest labor more pleasant and profitable than a life of vice and violence on the other side of the ocean.

Thus, under the leadership of Jefferson and the Republicans, the oppressed of Europe came to the United States, where their labor and fidelity contributed to the creation of the wealthiest, most prosperous, and most powerful nation that has ever existed on this earth.

Early Desirability of Agricultural Expansion

BW 161-2 Notes on Virginia 1781

The political economists of Europe have established it as a principle, that every State should endeavor to manufacture for itself; and that principle, like many others, we transfer to America, without calculating the difference of circumstance which should often produce a difference of result. In Europe, the lands are either cultivated, or locked up against the cultivator. Manufacture must therefore be resorted to of necessity, not of choice, to support the surplus of their people. But we have an immensity of land courting the industry of the husbandman. Is it best, then, that all our citizens should be employed in its improvement, or that one half should be called off from that to exercise manufactures and handicraft arts for the other?

Those who labor in the earth are the chosen people of God, if ever He had a chosen people, whose breasts He has made His peculiar deposit for substantial and genuine virtue. It is the focus in which He keeps alive that sacred fire, which otherwise might escape from the face of the earth. Corruption of morals in the mass of cultivators is a phenomenon of which no age or nation has furnished an example. It is the mark set on those, who, not looking up to heaven, or to their own soil and industry, as does the husbandman, for their subsistence, depend for it on casualties and caprice of customers.

Dependence begets subservience and venality, suffocates the germ of virtue, and prepares fit tools for the designs of ambition. This, the natural progress and consequence of the arts, has sometimes perhaps been retarded by accidental circumstances; but, generally speaking, the proportion which the aggregate of the other classes of citizens bears in any State to that of its husbandmen, is the proportion of its unsound to its healthy parts, and is a good enough barometer whereby to measure its degree of corruption.

While we have land to labor [on] then, let us never wish to see our citizens occupied at the work-bench, or twirling a distaff... for the general operations of manufacture, let our workshops remain in Europe. It is better to carry provisions and materials to workmen there, than to bring them [here]... and with them their manners and principles. The loss by the transportation of commodities across the Atlantic, will be made up in happiness and permanence of government.

The mobs of the great cities add just so much to the support of pure government, as sores do to the strength of the human body. It is the manners and spirit of a people which preserve a republic in vigor. A degeneracy in these is a canker which soon eats to the heart of its laws and constitutions... .

I repeat it again, that the cultivators of the earth are the most virtuous and independent citizens. It might be time to seek employment for them at sea, when the land no longer offers it.

ME V 93-96 John Jay 8-23-85

Cultivators of the earth are the most valuable citizens. They are the most vigorous, the most independent, the most virtuous, and they are tied to their country and wedded to its liberty and interests, by the most lasting bonds. As long, therefore, as they find employment in this line, I would not convert them into mariners, artisans, or anything else... . I consider the class of artificers as the panders of vice, and the instruments by which the liberties of a country are generally overturned.

ME VI 385-93 James Madison 12-20-87

I think we shall be so [virtuous] as long as agriculture is our principal object, which will be the case, while there remain vacant lands in any part of America. When we get piled upon one another in large cities, as in Europe, we shall become corrupt as in Europe, and go to eating one another, as they do there.

ME XV 27-31 William Crawford 6-20-16

The agricultural capacities of our country constitute its distinguishing feature; and the adapting our policy and pursuits to that, is more likely to make us a numerous and happy people, than the mimicry of an Amsterdam, a Hamburg, or a city of London... . We have the most abundant resources of happiness within ourselves, which we may enjoy in peace and safety... .

CE VI Dupont de Nemours 1816

A right to property is founded in our natural wants, and the means with which we are endowed to satisfy those wants, and the right to what we acquire by those means without violating the similar rights of other similar sensible beings.

ME XI 1-3 Jean Baptiste Say 2-1-04

...Malthus' work on population [is one]... of sound logic... . [However, in Europe] Supernumerary births... add only to your mortality. Here the immense extent of uncultivated and fertile lands enables every one who will labor, to marry young, and to raise a family of any size. Our food, then, will increase geometrically with our laborers and our births... . Again, there the best distribution of labor is supposed to be that which places the manufacturing hands alongside the agricultural; so that one part shall feed both, and the other part furnish both with clothes and other comforts. Would that be best here?... . Or would it be better that all our laborers should be engaged in agriculture? In this case, a double or treble portion of fertile lands would be brought into culture, a double or treble creation of food be produced, and its surplus go to nourish the now perishing births of Europe, who, in return, would manufacture and send us in exchange our clothes and other comforts... . In solving this question, too, we should allow its just weight to the moral and physical preferences of the agricultural over the manufacturing man.

ME XI 55-56 Mr. Lithson 1-4-05

As yet our manufacturers are as much at their ease, as independent and moral as our agricultural inhabitants, and they will continue so as long as there shall be vacant lands for them to resort to; because whenever it shall be attempted by the other classes to reduce them to the minimum of subsistence, they will quit their trades and go to laboring the earth... .

[Is it] desirable for us to receive at present the dissolute and demoralized handicraftsmen of the old cities of Europe? A second and more difficult one is, when even good handicraftsmen arrive here, is it better for them to set up their trade, or go to the culture of the earth? Whether their labor in their trade is worth more than their labor on the soil, increased by the creative energies of the earth? Had I time to revise that chapter [in the *Notes on Virginia*], this question should be discussed, and other views of the subject taken, which are presented by the wonderful changes which have taken place here since 1781... .

Equality: The New American Man

BW 231-32 Answers to de Meusnier 1786

It should be further considered, that in America no other distinction between man and man had ever been known, but that of persons in office, excercising powers by authority of the laws, and private individuals. Among these last, the poorest laborer stood on equal ground with the wealthiest millionaire, and generally on a more favored one, whenever their rights seemed to jar. It has been seen that a shoemaker or other artisan, removed by the voice of his country from his workbench into a chair of office, has instantly commanded all the respect and obedience which the laws ascribe to his office.

But of distinction by birth and badge, they had no more idea than they had of the mode of existence in the moon... . A due horror of the evils which flow from these distinctions, could be excited in Europe only, where the dignity of man is lost in arbitrary distinctions, where the human species is classed into several stages of degradation, where the many are crushed under the weight of the few, and where the order established, can present to the contemplation of the thinking being, no other picture than that of God Almighty and his angels, trampling under foot the host of the damned. No wonder, then, that the institution of the Cincinnati should be innocently conceived by one order of American citizens, should raise in the other orders only a slow, temperate, and rational opposition, and should be viewed in Europe as detestable parricide.

ME VI 55-59 Colonel Edward Carrington 1-16-87

European governments... under pretense of governing... have divided their nations into two classes, wolves and sheep. I do not exaggerate. This is a true picture of Europe. Cherish, therefore, the spirit of our people, and keep alive their attention... for experience declares that man is the only animal which devours his own kind; [for] I can apply no milder term to the governments of Europe, and to the general prey of the rich on the poor.

BW 232-33 Answers to de Meusnier 1786

What good can the officers [of the Cincinnati] propose, which may weigh against these possible evils? The securing their descendants against want? Why afraid to trust them to the same fertile soil and the same genial climate, which will secure from want the descendants of their other fellow citizens?... . They will be rendered thereby both more honest and happy. An industrious farmer occupies a more dignified place in the scale of beings, whether moral or political, than a lazy lounger, valuing himself on his family, too proud to work, and drawing out a miserable existence, by eating on that surplus of other men's labor, which is the sacred fund of the helpless poor.

ME XIII 394-403 John Adams 10-28-13

With respect to aristocracy, we should further consider, that before the establishment of the American States, nothing was known to history but the man of the old world, crowded within limits either small or overcharged, and steeped in the vices which that situation generates. A government adapted to such men would be one thing; but a very different one, that for the man of these States. Here every one may have land to labor for himself, if he chooses; or, preferring the exercise of any other industry, may exact for it such compensation as not only to afford a comfortable subsistence, but wherewith to provide for a cessation from labor in old age. Every one, by his property, or by his satisfactory situation, is interested in the support of law and order. And such men may safely and advantageously reserve to themselves a wholesome control over their public affairs, and a degree of freedom which, in the hands of the *canaille* of the cities of Europe, would be instantly perverted to the demolition and destruction of everything public and private. The history of the last... forty years in America, nay of its last two hundred years, proves the truth of both parts of this observation.

ME X 355-57 Mr. Pictet 2-5-03

Our citizens almost all follow some industrious occupation, and, therefore, have little time to devote to abstract science. In the arts, and especially in the mechanical arts, many ingenious improvements are made in consequence of the patent right giving exclusive use of them for fourteen years. But the great mass of our people are agricultural; and the commercial cities, though, by the command of the newspapers, they make a great deal of noise, have little effect in the direction of the government. They are as different in sentiment and character from the country people as any two distinct nations, and are clamorous against the order of things established by the agricultural interest. Under this order, our citizens generally are enjoying a very great degree of liberty and security in the most temperate manner. Every man being at his ease, feels an interest in the preservation of order, and comes forth to preserve it at the first call of the magistrate. We are endeavoring, too, to reduce the government to the practice of a rigorous economy, to avoid burdening the people and arming the magistrate with a patronage of money, which might be used to corrupt and undermine the principles of our government.

American Society Contrasted with European

ME XII 170-73 Doctor Walter Jones 3-5-10

Our difficulties are indeed great, if we consider ourselves alone. But when viewed in comparison to those of Europe, they are as the joys of Paradise. In the eternal revolutions of ages, the destinies have placed our portion of existence amidst such scenes of tumult and outrage, as no other period, within our knowledge, has presented. Every government but one on the continent of Europe, demolished, a conqueror roaming over the earth with havoc and destruction, a pirate spreading misery and ruin over the face of the ocean. Indeed, my friend, ours is a bed of roses. And the system of government which shall keep us afloat amidst the wreck of the world, will be immortalized in history.

ME XIV 20-25 Baron Alexander von Humboldt 12-6-13

The European nations constitute a separate division of the globe; their localities make them part of a distinct system; they have a set of interests of their own, in which it is our business never to engage ourselves. America has a hemisphere to itself. It must have its separate system of interests, which must not be subordinated to those of Europe. The insulated state in which nature has placed the American continent, should so far avail it that no spark of war kindled in other quarters of the globe should be wafted across wide oceans which separate us from them. And it will be so. In fifty years more, the United States alone will contain fifty millions of inhabitants, and fifty years are soon gone over.

ME XIV 179-90 Thomas Cooper 9-10-14

The population of England is composed of three descriptions of persons (for those of minor note are too inconsiderate to affect a general estimate). These are, 1. The aristocracy, comprehending the nobility, the wealthy commoners, the high grades of priesthood, and the officers of government. 2. The laboring class. 3. The eleemosynary class, or paupers, who are about one-fifth of the whole.

The aristocracy, which have the laws and government in their hands, have so managed them as to reduce the third description below the means of supporting life, even by labor; and to force the second, whether employed in agriculture or the arts, to the maximum of labor which the construction of the human body can endure, and to the minimum of food, and of the meanest kind, which will preserve it in life, and in strength sufficient to perform its functions. To obtain food enough, and clothing, not only their whole strength must be unremittingly exerted, but the utmost dexterity also which they can acquire; and those of great dexterity only can keep their ground, while those of less must sink into the class of paupers.

Nor is it manual dexterity alone, but the acutest resources of the mind also which are impressed into this struggle for life; and such as have means a little above the rest, as the master-workmen, for instance, must strengthen themselves by acquiring as much of the philosophy of their trade as will enable them to compete with their rivals, and keep themselves above ground. Hence the industry and manual dexterity of their journeymen and day-laborers, and the science of their master-workmen, keep them in the foremost ranks of competition with those of other nations; and the less dexterous individuals, falling into the eleemosynary ranks, furnish materials for armies and navies to defend their country, exercise piracy on the ocean, and carry conflagration, plunder and devastation on the shores of all those who endeavor to withstand their aggressions.

A society thus constituted possesses certainly the means of defence. But what does it defend? The pauperism of the lowest class, the abject oppression of the laboring, and the luxury, the riot, the domination and the vicious happiness of the aristocracy. In their hands, the paupers are used as tools to maintain their own wretchedness, and to keep down the laboring portion by shooting them whenever the desperation produced by the cravings of their stomachs drives them into riots. Such is the happiness of scientific England; now let us see the American side of the medal.

And, first, we have no paupers, the old and crippled among us, who possess nothing and have no families to take care of them, being too few to merit notice as a separate section of society, or to affect a general estimate. The great mass of our population is of laborers; our rich, who can live without labor, either manual or professional, being few, and of moderate wealth. Most of the laboring class possess property, cultivate their own lands, have families, and from the demand for their labor are enabled to exact from the rich and the competent such prices as enable them to be fed abundantly, clothed above mere decency, to labor moderately and raise their families. They are not driven to the ultimate resources of dexterity and skill, because their wares will sell, although not quite so nice as those of England.

The wealthy, on the other hand, and those at their ease, know nothing of what the Europeans call luxury. They have only somewhat more of the comforts and decencies of life than those who furnish them. Can any condition of society be more desirable than this?... .

Now let us compute by numbers the sum of happiness of the two countries. In England, happiness is the lot of the aristocracy only; and the proportion they bear to the laborers and paupers, you know better than I do. Were I to guess them to be four in every hundred, then the happiness of the nation would be to its misery as one in twenty-five. In the United States, it is as eight millions to zero, or as all to none... .

The Greeks and Romans had no standing armies, yet they defended themselves. The Greeks by their laws, and the Romans by the spirit of their people, took care to put into the hands of their rulers no such engine of oppression as a standing army. Their system was to make every man a soldier, and oblige him to repair to the standard of his country, whenever that was reared. This made them invincible; and the same remedy will make us so.

ME XV 257-64 William Short 8-4-20

The excess of population in Europe and want of room, render war, in their opinion, necessary to keep down that excess of numbers. Here, room is abundant, population scanty, and peace the necessary means for producing men, to whom the redundant soil is offering the means of life and happiness. The principles of society there and here, then, are radically different; and I hope no American patriot will ever lose sight of the essential policy of interdicting in the seas and territories of both Americas, the ferocious and sanguinary contests of Europe.

How America Transforms Its Immigrants

BW 219-20 Answers to de Meusnier 1786

Indented servants... were poor Europeans who went to America to settle themselves. If they could pay their passage, it was well. If not, they must find means of paying it. They were at liberty, therefore, to make an agreement with any person they chose, to serve him such a length of time as they agreed on, upon condition that they would repay to the master of the vessel the expenses of their passage... . This contract was by deed indented, which occasioned them to be called indented servants. Sometimes, they were called redemptioners, because by their agreement with the master of the vessel, they could *redeem* themselves from his power by paying their passage, which they frequently effected by hiring themselves on their arrival, as is before mentioned... .

So mild was this kind of servitude that it was very frequent for foreigners, who carried to America money enough not only to pay their passage, but to buy themselves a farm, to indent themselves to a master for three years for a certain sum of money, with a view to learn the husbandry of the country.

I will here make a general observation. So desirous are the poor of Europe to get to America, where they may better their condition, that being unable to pay their passage, they will agree to serve two or three years on their arrival here, rather than not go. During the time of that service, they are better fed, better clothed, and have lighter labor, than while in Europe. Continuing to work for hire a few years longer, they buy a farm, marry and enjoy all the sweets of their own domestic society.

ME VIII 196-98 Mr. Dumas 5-13-91

In general, our affairs are proceeding in a train of unparalleled prosperity. This arises from the real improvements of our government, from the unbounded confidence reposed in it by the people, their zeal to support it, and their conviction that a solid Union is the best rock of their safety, from the favorable seasons which for some years past have co-operated with a fertile soil and genial climate to increase the productions of agriculture, and from the growth of industry, economy, and domestic manufactures; so that I believe I may say with truth, that there is not a nation under the sun enjoying more present prosperity, nor with more in prospect.

ME XIII 180-82 Colonel William Duane 8-4-12

Experience will soon teach the newcomers how much more plentiful and pleasant is the subsistence gained by wholesome labor and fair dealing, than a precarious and hazardous dependence on the enterprises of vice and violence.

CE VI 507-10 Dupont de Nemours 12-31-15

For twenty years to come we should consider peace as the *summun bonum* of our country... . At the end of that period we shall be twenty millions in number, and forty in energy, when encountering the starved and rickety paupers and dwarfs of English workshops.

ME XVI 74-6 William Ludlow 9-6-24

I have observed the march of civilization advancing from the seacoast passing over us like a cloud of light, increasing our knowledge and improving our condition, insomuch as that we are at this time more advanced in civilization here than the seaports were when I was a boy. And where this progress will stop, no one can say. Barbarism has, in the meantime, been receding before the steady step of amelioration; and will in time, I trust, disappear from the earth.

How the Wealthy Pay the Taxes

ME VII 109-11 Count de Moustier 12-3-90

The powers of the government for the collection of taxes, are found to be perfect, so far as they have been tried. This has been as yet only by duties on consumption. As these fall principally on the rich, it is a general desire to make them contribute the whole money we want, if possible. And we have a hope that they will furnish enough for the expenses of government and the interest of our whole public debt, foreign and domestic.

If they do this for the present, their increase, from the increases of population and consumption, (which is at the rate of five per centum per annum,) will sink the capital [i.e., will pay off the public debt] in thirteen or fourteen years, as it will operate in the way of compound interest... . We are now going on with the census of our inhabitants. It will not be completed till next summer; but such progress is already made as to show our numbers will very considerably exceed our former estimates.

BW 359-63 Second Inaugural Address 3-4-05

The suppression of unnecessary offices, of useless establishments and expenses, enabled us to discontinue our internal taxes. These, covering our land with officers, and opening our doors to their intrusions, had already begun that process of domiciliary vexation which, once entered, is scarcely to be restrained from reaching successively every article of produce and property... .

The remaining revenue on the consumption of foreign articles, is paid cheerfully by those who can afford to add foreign luxuries to domestic comforts, being collected on our seaboards and frontiers only; and, incorporated with the transactions of our mercantile citizens, it may be the pleasure and pride of an American to ask, what farmer, what mechanic, what laborer, ever sees a tax-gatherer of the United States?

ME XIII 40-43 General Thaddeus Kosciusko 4-13-11

But when we see two antagonists... so eager for mutual destruction... prudent bystanders, whom some of them may wound, instead of thinking it cause to join in the maniac contest, get out of the way as well as they can, and leave the cannibals to mutual ravin. It would have been perfect Quixotism in us to have encountered these Bedlamites... .

We have, therefore, remained in peace, suffering frequent injuries, but, on the whole, multiplying, improving, prospering beyond all example... . When these gladiators shall have worried each other into ruin or reason, instead of lying among the dead, we shall have acquired a growth and strength which will place us *hors d'insulte.*

Peace, then, has been our principle, peace is our interest, and peace has saved the world this only plant of free and rational government existing upon it. If it can still be preserved, we shall soon see the final extinction of our national debt, and liberation of our revenues for the defence and improvement of our country. These revenues will be levied entirely on the rich, the business of household manufacture being now so established that the farmer and laborer clothe themselves entirely. The rich alone use imported articles, and on these alone the whole taxes of the General Government are levied. The poor man who uses nothing but what is made in his own farm or family, or within his own country, pays not a farthing of tax to the General Government.

Our revenues liberated by the discharge of the public debt, and its surplus applied to canals, roads, schools, etc., the farmer will see his government supported, his children educated, and the face of the country made a paradise by the contributions of the rich alone, without his being called on to spend a cent from his earnings... .

And this, I believe, is the only legitimate object of government, and the first duty of governors, and not the slaughter of men and devastation of the countries placed under their care... .

America Turns to Domestic Manufacture

ME XII 293-98 Monsier Dupont de Nemours 6-28-09

The interruption of our commerce with England, produced by our embargo and non-intercourse law, and the general indignation excited by her barefaced attempts to make us accessories and tributaries to her usurpation of the high seas, have generated in this country an universal spirit for manufacturing for ourselves, and of reducing to a minimum the number of articles for which we are dependent on her. The advantages, too, of lessening the occasions of risking our peace on the ocean, and of planting the consumer in our own soil by the side of the grower of produce, are so palpable, that no temporary suspension of injuries on her part, or agreements founded on that, will now prevent our continuing in what we have begun.

The spirit of manufacture has taken deep root among us, and its foundations are laid in too great expense to be abandoned... the principal articles wanted in every family are now fabricated within itself. This mass of *household* manufacture, unseen by the public eye, and so much greater than what is seen, is such at present that, let our intercourse with England be opened when it may, not one half the amount of what we have heretofore taken from her will ever again be demanded... .

Among the arts which have made great progress among us is that of printing. Heretofore, we imported our books, and with them much political principle from England. We now print a great deal, and shall soon supply ourselves with most of the books of considerable demand.

ME XII 236-38 Thomas Leiper 1-21-09

I have lately inculcated the encouragement of manufactures to the extent of our own consumption, at least, in all articles of which we raise the raw material. On this, the federal papers... have sounded the alarm... that is to say, the iron which we make must not be wrought here into ploughs, axes, hoes, etc., in order that the ship-owners may have the profit of carrying it to Europe, and bringing it back in a manufactured form, as if, after manufacturing our own raw materials for our own use, there would not be a surplus of produce sufficient to employ a due proportion of navigation in carrying it to market and exchanging it for those articles of which we have not the raw material... .

But I trust the good sense of our country will see that its greatest prosperity depends on a balance between agriculture, manufactures, and commerce, and not in this protuberant navigation which has kept us in hot water from the commencement of our government, and is now engaging us in war.

FORD X 73 William Sampson 1817

I was once a doubter whether the labor of the cultivator, aided by the creative powers of the earth itself, would not produce more value than that of the manufacturer, alone and unassisted by the dead subject on which he acted. In other words, whether the more we could bring into action the energies of our boundless territory, in addition to the labor of our citizens, the more would not be our gain? But the inventions of later times, by labor-saving machines, do as much now for the manufacturers as the earth for the cultivator. Experience, too, has proved that mine was but half of the question. The other half is whether dollars and cents are to be weighed in the scale against real independence.

ME XIV 387-93 Benjamin Austin 1-9-15

We must now place the manufacturer by the side of the agriculturist; the former question is suppressed, or rather assumes a new form. Should we make our own comforts, or go without them, at the will of a foreign nation? He, therefore, who is now against domestic manufacture, must be for reducing us either to dependence on that foreign nation, or to be clothed in skins, and to live like beasts in dens and caverns. I am not one of these; experience has taught me that manufactures are now as necessary to our independence as to our comfort; and if those who quote me as of a different opinion, will keep pace with me in purchasing nothing foreign where an equivalent of domestic fabric can be obtained, without regard to difference in price, it will not be our fault if we do not soon have a supply at home equal to our demand, and wrest that weapon of distress from the hand that wielded it.

ME XIV 306-11 Thomas Leiper 6-12-15

It is our business to manufacture for ourselves whatever we can, to keep our markets open for what we can spare or want; and the less we have to do with the amities or enmities of Europe, the better. Not in our day, but at no distant one, we may shake a rod over the head of all, which may make the stoutest of them tremble. But I hope our wisdom will grow with our power, and teach us, that the less we use our power, the greater it will be.

ME XIII 206-13 John Melish 1-13-13

I had no conception that manufactures had made such progress there, [in the Western States] and particularly of the number of carding and spinning machines dispersed through the whole country. We are but beginning here to have them in our private families. Small spinning jennies of from half a dozen to twenty spindles, will soon, however, make their way into the humblest cottages, as well as the richest houses... .

The continuance of the war will fix the habit generally, and out of the evils of impressment and of the orders of council, a great blessing for us will grow. I have not formerly been an advocate for great manufactories. I doubted whether our labor, employed in agriculture, and aided by spontaneous energies of the earth, would not procure us more than we could make ourselves of other necessaries. But other considerations entering into the question, have settled my doubts.

ME XIII 122-25 John Adams 1-21-12 [Thanks him for homespuns.]

Every family in the country is a manufactory within itself, and is very generally able to make within itself all the stouter and middling stuffs for its own clothing and household use... . The economy and thriftiness resulting from our household manufactures are such that they will never again be laid aside; and nothing more salutary for us has ever happened than the British obstructions to our demands for their manufactures. Restore free intercourse when they will, their commerce with us will have totally changed its form, and the articles we shall in future want from them will not exceed their own consumption of our produce.

ME XIII 168-72 General Thaddeus Kosciusko 6-28-12

Our manufacturers are now very nearly on a footing with those of England. She has not a single improvement which we do not possess, and many of them better adapted by ourselves to our ordinary use. We have reduced the large and expensive machinery for most things to the compass of a private scale for their household purposes [and]... nothing is more certain than that, come peace when it will, we shall never again go to England for a shilling where we have gone for a dollar's worth. Instead of applying to her manufacturers there [for work], they must starve or come here to be employed.

4. The Alien and Sedition Laws

Commentary

The Alien and Sedition Laws were so closely intertwined with the XYZ delusion that it is difficult to separate them. The forgeries which produced it arrived in the United States on October 22, 1797; the Alien and Sedition Laws were passed July 14, 1798.

At the end of 1793, Jefferson, then Secretary of State, had found himself so isolated, frustrated, and browbeaten in President Washington's cabinet and government, that he resigned, vowing never again to leave Monticello. However, he accepted the vice-presidency in 1796, a position in which he again found himself isolated and deserted by despairing fellow republicans, who returned to their states, where they hoped to promote their principles. Only Jefferson, Gallatin, Livingston, Nicholas, and a few others of stature and influence remained. Had they not done so, the Federalists might have emerged completely victorious, and this nation would have embarked on an entirely different course.

If the Greek dictum is true that those whom the gods would destroy, they first make mad, this assuredly applies to the Federalists between 1796 and 1799. They went mad with power, and rode roughshod over the people. They came within an eyelash of forcing a declaration of war against France, which wanted only peace and accommodation. And then they took one step after another which, within two years, caused them to be hurled from the seats of power.

As Jefferson said over and over, a free press is the safest instrument for the preservation of responsible government; no despotism, therefore, can permit it and survive, in a nation where the people can read and write and think for themselves.

In order to understand the situation of 1796-97, we must go back to 1793-94, when Jefferson resigned from the government; in order to combat its consolidationist tendencies, he helped to organize the Whig and Jeffersonian presses — papers which sprang up in various parts of the Union, proclaimed the republican principles of the Founding Fathers, and sought to curb the expansionist policies in vogue in the general government. Since the Federalists were well aware that, in order to achieve their objectives, these publications would have to be silenced, they passed the Alien and Sedition Laws — the former so that they could rid the nation of republican voices such as those of Gallatin, Volney, and others. We should note that in those days, 14 years of residence were required for citizenship.

Hamilton and the Federalists had fought bitterly against the addition of the Bill of Rights to the Constitution, saying that nothing not permitted therein would be forbidden to it in its powers or activities. In 1798, however, their true purposes were revealed; without the first ten amendments, it would have been comparatively simple and easy for them to modify or interpret the Constitution according to their wishes; and now it eventuated that, in spite of the most specific prohibitions, *they sought to establish a tyranny which made even the English newspapers blush with shame. The federal marshalls invaded the homes of republican-Jeffersonian printers and publishers in the middle of the night, dragged them from their beds, and threw them into prison; and then, after illegal trials, subjected them to heavy fines and prison terms. In the meantime, their presses and printing establishments were destroyed.*

Jefferson, as Vice-President, could not take an open part in fomenting the Rebellion of the States; however, without divulging its authorship, he wrote The Kentucky Resolutions, *which certainly rank with the* Declaration of Independence, *the* Summary View of the Rights of British America, *and the* Bill to Establish Religious Freedom in Virginia, *as one of the most significant documents in the political history of this nation. Every reader should study it with care — and even memorize its most salient passages. We reproduce almost the entire text of this in the present chapter.*

In Virginia, James Madison, in collaboration with Jefferson, introduced a bill somewhat similar to the Kentucky Resolutions *into the Assembly, where it was approved.*

Probably no other man in American history has been so maligned and calumniated by political enemies, as was Jefferson. One of the worst, and most contemptible, was the English emigrant, James Callendar, whose spite and venom — impartially directed at almost everyone — were beyond belief. He, among many others, was imprisoned under the Sedition Act during the administration of John Adams, who had also been the object of the man's hatred. He it was who had first published the tale of Jefferson's alleged liaison with Sally Hemmings, and declared that he was the father of her children. The Federalist presses were filled with lurid and obscene material and a multitude of lascivious ballads and satires depicting Jefferson engaging in miscegenist orgies.

When Mrs. Adams accused Jefferson of pardoning a wretch who had defamed her husband, he replied simply that he had done so because the law under which he was convicted was unconstitutional and therefore null and void. And it should be noted that the filth this degenerate directed toward

Jefferson Magnificent Populist

Mr. Adams was like unto the attar of roses compared to the stench he spewed out about Mr. Jefferson, who nevertheless pardoned this monster, because, as he said, justice should be applied equally to everyone. He also pardoned others who had maligned him in the press or in public statements.

And just where else shall we find anything comparable?

Conspirators At Work

ME X 31-33 James Madison 4-26-98

One of the war party, in a fit of unguarded passion, declared sometime ago, they would pass a citizen bill, an alien bill, and a sedition bill; accordingly, some days ago, Coit laid a motion on the table of the House of Representatives for modifying the citizen law. Their threats pointed at Gallatin, and it is believed they will endeavor to reach him by this bill. Yesterday, Mr. Hillhouse laid on the table of the Senate a motion for giving power to send away suspected aliens. This is understood for Volney and Collot.

But it will not stop there when it gets into a course of execution. There is now only wanting, to accomplish the whole declaration before mentioned, a sedition bill, which we shall certainly see soon proposed. The object of that, is the suppression of the Whig presses [If this happens]... republicanism will be entirely browbeaten... .

The Committee on Ways and Means have voted a land tax. An additional tax on salt will certainly be proposed in the House, and probably prevail to some degree. The stoppage of interest on the public debt will also perhaps be proposed, but not with effect. In the meantime, the paper [i.e., government bonds], cannot be sold.

The popular movement in the Eastern States is checked, as we expected, and war addresses are showering in from New Jersey and the great trading towns. However, we still trust that a nearer view of war and a land tax will oblige the great mass of the people to attend. At present, the war hawks talk of septembrizing [massacres like those in Paris of September, 1792], a deportation, and the examples for quelling sedition set by the French executive. All the firmness of the human mind is now in a state of requisition.

ME X 38-40 James Monroe 5-21-98

The tax on lands, houses, and negroes, will be a dollar a head on the population of each State [to raise an army]. There are alien bills, sedition bills, etc., also before both houses. The severity of their aspect determines a great number of French to go off.

ME X 40-41 James Madison 5-31-98

The alien bill will be ready to-day... a most detestable thing... . This bill will unquestionably pass the House... the majority there being very decisive, consolidated, and bold enough to do anything. I have no doubt from the hints dropped, they will pass a bill to declare the French treaty void. I question whether they will think a declaration of war prudent... . It is suspected that they mean to borrow money of individuals in London, on the credit of the land tax, and perhaps the guarantee of Great Britain... .

Volney and a shipload of others will sail on Sunday night.

ME X 49-53 James Madison 6-21-98

They have brought into the lower house a sedition bill, which, among other enormities, undertakes to make printing certain matter criminal, though one of the amendments to the Constitution has so expressly taken religion, printing presses, etc., out of their coercion. Indeed, this bill, and the alien bill, are both so palpably in the teeth of the Constitution as to show they mean to pay no respect to it.

ME X 63-66 John Taylor 11-26-98

It is a singular phenomenon, that while our State governments are *the very best in the world*, without exception or comparison, our General Government has, in the rapid course of nine or ten years, become more arbitrary, and has swallowed more of the public liberty than even that of England. I enclose you a column, cut out of a London paper, to show you that the English, though charmed with our making their enemies, our enemies, yet blush and weep over our sedition law.

The Constitution Subverted

ME XVIII xiii-xiv Section 2 of the Sedition Law of 7-14-98

"And be it further enacted that if they shall write, print, utter, or publish, or shall cause or procure to be written, printed, uttered, or published, or shall knowingly and willingly assist or aid in writing, printing, uttering, or publishing any false, scandalous, and malicious writing or writings against the government of the United States, or either House of the Congress of the United States with an intent to defame the said government or either House of the said Congress, or the President, or to bring them or either of them into contempt or disrepute, or to excite against them or either of them the hatred of the good people of the United States, etc., then such persons, being thereof convicted before any court of the United States having jurisdiction thereof, shall be punished by a fine not exceeding two thousand dollars, and by imprisonment not exceeding two years."

ME XV 350-52 Mr. Nicholas 12-11-21

At the time when the republicans of our country were so much alarmed at the proceedings of the federal ascendency in Congress, in the executive and the judiciary departments, it became a matter of serious consideration how head could be made against their enterprises on the Constitution. The leading republicans in Congress found themselves of no use there, browbeaten, as they were, by a bold and overwhelming majority. They concluded to retire from that field, take a stand in the State legislatures, and endeavor there to arrest their progress.

The alien and sedition laws furnished the particular occasion. The sympathy between Virginia and Kentucky was more cordial, and more intimately confidential, than between any other two States of republican policy. Mr. Madison came into the Virginia legislature. I was then in the Vice-presidency, and could not leave my station. But your father, Colonel W. C. Nicholas, and myself happening to be together, the engaging the co-operation of Kentucky in an energetic protestation against the constitutionality of those laws, became a subject of consultation. Those gentlemen pressed me strongly to sketch resolutions for that purpose, your father undertaking to introduce them to that legislature, with a solemn assurance, which I strictly required, that it should not be known from what quarter they came. I drew and delivered them to him, and in keeping their origin secret, he fulfilled his pledge of honor.

Some years after this, Colonel Nicholas asked me if I would have any objection to its being known that I had drawn them. I pointedly enjoined that it should not. Whether he had unguardedly intimated it before to any one, I know not; but I afterwards observed in the papers repeated imputations of them to me; on which, as has been my practice on all occasions of imputation, I have observed entire silence.

In Defence of the Constitution

ME XVIII 379-91 The Kentucky Resolutions Relative to the Alien and Sedition Laws 1798-99

1. *Resolved,* That the several States composing the United States of America, are not united on the principle of unlimited submission to their General Government; but that, by a compact under the style and title of a Constitution for the United States, and of amendments thereto, they constituted a General Government for special purposes, — delegated to that government certain definite powers, reserving, each State to itself, the residuary mass of right to their own government; and that whensoever the

General Government assumes undelegated powers, its acts are unauthoritative, void and of no force: that to this compact each State acceded as a State, and is an integral party, its co-States forming, each as to itself, the other party: that the government created by this compact was not made the exclusive or final judge of the extent of the powers delegated to itself; since that would have made its discretion, and not the Constitution, the measure of its powers; but that, as in all other cases of compact among powers having no common judge, each party has an equal right to judge for itself, as well of infractions as of the mode and measure of redress.

2. *Resolved,* That the Constitution of the United States, having delegated to Congress a power to punish treason, counterfeiting the securities and current coin of the United States, piracies, and felonies committed on the high seas, and offences against the law of nations, and no other crimes whatsoever; and it being... one of the amendments to the Constitution... that "the powers not delegated to the United States by the Constitution, nor prohibited by it to the States, are reserved to the States respectively, or to the people," therefore the act of Congress, passed on the 14th day of July, 1798, and intituled "An... Act for the punishment of certain crimes against the United States is... altogether void, and of no force; and that the power to create, define, and punish such other crimes is reserved, and, of right, appertains solely and exclusively to the respective States, each within its own territory.

3. *Resolved,* That it is... also expressly declared by one of the amendments to the Constitution, that... no power over the freedom of religion, freedom of speech, or freedom of the press being delegated to the United States by the Constitution, nor prohibited by it to the States, all lawful powers respecting the same did of right remain, and were reserved to the States or the people... insomuch, that whatever violated either, throws down the sanctuary which covers the others, and that libels, falsehood, and defamation, equally with heresy and false religion, are withheld from the cognizance of federal tribunals. That, therefore, the act of Congress of the United States, passed on the 14th day of July, 1798, intitled "An... Act for the punishment of certain crimes against the United States," which does abridge the freedom of the press, is not law, but is altogether void, and of no force.

4. *Resolved,* That alien friends are under the jurisdiction and protection of the laws of the State wherein they are: that no power over them has been delegated to the United States, nor prohibited to the individual States... [therefore] the act of the Congress of the United States, passes on the ______ day of July, 1798, intituled "An Act concerning aliens," which assumes powers over alien friends, not delegated by the Constitution, is not law, but is altogether void, and of no force... .

6. *Resolved,* That the imprisonment of a person under the protection of the laws of this commonwealth, on his failure to obey the simple

order of the President to depart out of the United States, as is undertaken by said act intituled "An Act concerning aliens," is contrary to the Constitution... is therefore not law, but utterly void, and of no force... .

7. *Resolved,* That the construction applied by the General Government (as is evidenced by sundry of their proceedings) to those parts of the Constitution of the United States which delegate to Congress a power "to lay and collect taxes, duties, imports, and excises, to pay the debts, and provide for the common defense and general welfare of the United States,"... goes to the destruction of all limits prescribed to their power by the Constitution: that words meant by the instrument to be subsidiary only to the execution of limited powers, ought not to be so construed as to give themselves unlimited powers, nor a part to be so taken as to destroy the whole residue of that instrument... .

8. *Resolved,* That a committee of conference and correspondence be appointed, who shall have in charge to communicate the preceding resolutions to the legislatures of the several States; to assure them that this commonwealth continues in the same esteem of their friendship and union which it has manifested from that moment at which a common danger first suggested a common union: that it considers union, for specified national purposes, and particularly to those specified in their late federal compact to be friendly to the peace, happiness, and prosperity of all the States: that faithful to that compact, according to the plain intent and meaning in which it was understood and acceded to by the several parties, it is sincerely anxious for its preservation.

That it does also believe, that to take from the States all the powers of self-government and transfer them to a general and consolidated government, without regard to the special delegations and reservations solemnly agreed to in that compact, is not for the peace, happiness, or prosperity of these States; and that therefore this commonwealth is determined, as it doubts not its co-States are, not to submit to undelegated, and consequently unlimited powers in any man, or body of men on earth: that in cases of an abuse of the delegated powers, the members of the General Government, being chosen by the people, a change by the people would be the constitutional remedy; but, where powers are assumed which have not been delegated, a nullification of the act is the rightful remedy.

That every State has a natural right in cases not within the compact, (*casus non foederis,*) to nullify of their own authority all assumptions of power by others within their limits: that without this right, they would be under the dominion, absolute and unlimited, of whosoever might exercise this right of judgment for them: that nevertheless, this commonwealth, from motives of regard and respect for its co-States, has wished to communicate with them on the subject: that with them alone it is proper to communicate, they alone being parties to the compact, and solely authorized to judge in the last resort of the powers exercised under it.

[That] Congress being not a party, but merely the creature of the compact, and subject as to its assumptions of power to the final judgment of those by whom, and for whose use itself and its powers were all created and modified: that if the acts before specified should stand, these conclusions would flow from them: that the General Government may place any act they think proper on the list of crimes, and punish it themselves whether enumerated or not enumerated by the Constitution as cognizable by them: that they may transfer its cognizance to the President, or any other person, who may himself be the accuser, counsel, judge and jury, whose *suspicions* may be the evidence, his *order* the sentence, his *officer* the executioner, and his breast the sole record of the transaction: that a very numerous and valuable description of the inhabitants of these States being by this precedent, reduced, as outlaws, to the absolute dominion of one man, and the barrier of the Constitution thus swept away from us all, no rampart now remains against the passions and the powers of a majority in Congress to protect from a like exportation, or other more grievous punishment, the minority of the same body, the legislatures, judges, governors, and counsellors of the States, nor their other peaceable inhabitants, who may venture to reclaim the constitutional rights and liberties of the States and people, or who, for other causes, good or bad, may be obnoxious to the views, or marked by the suspicions of the President, or be thought dangerous to his or their election, or other interest, public or personal.

That the friendless alien has indeed been selected as the safest subject of a first experiment; but the citizen will soon follow, or, rather, has already followed, for already has a sedition act marked him as its prey: that these and successive acts of the same character, unless arrested at the threshold, necessarily drive these States into revolution and blood, and will furnish new calumnies against republican government, and new pretexts for those who wish it to be believed that man cannot be governed but by a rod of iron.

That it would be a dangerous delusion were a confidence in the men of our choice to silence our fears for the safety of our rights: that confidence is everywhere the parent of despotism — free government is founded in jealousy, and not in confidence; it is jealousy and not confidence which prescribes limited constitutions, to bind down those whom we are obliged to trust with power: that our Constitution has accordingly fixed the limits to which, and no further, our confidence may go; and let the honest advocate of confidence read the Alien and Sedition acts, and say if the Constitution has not been wise in fixing limits to the government it created, and whether we should be wise in destroying those limits.

Let him say what the government is, if it be not a tyranny, which the men of our choice have conferred on our President, and the President of our choice has assented to, and accepted over the friendly strangers to whom the mild spirit of our country and its laws have pledged hospitality and protection: that the men of our choice have more respected the bare *suspicions* of the President, than the solid right of innocence, the claims of justification, the sacred force of truth, and the forms and substance of law and justice.

In questions of power, then, let no more be heard of confidence in man, but bind him down from mischief by the chains of the Constitution. That this commonwealth does therefore call on its co-States for an expression of their sentiments on the acts concerning aliens, and for the punishment of certain crimes herein before specified, plainly declaring whether these acts are or are not authorized by the federal compact. And it doubts not that their sense will be so announced as to prove their attachment unaltered to limited government, whether general or particular. And that the rights and liberties of their co-States will be exposed to no dangers by remaining embarked in a common bottom with their own.

That they will concur with this commonwealth in considering the said acts as so palpably against the Constitution as to amount to an undisguised declaration that that compact is not meant to be the measure of the powers of the General Government, but that it will proceed in the exercise over these States, of all powers whatsoever: that they will view this as seizing the rights of the States, and consolidating them in the hands of the General Government, with a power assumed to bind the States, (not merely as the cases made federal, *casus foederis,*) but in all cases whatsoever, by laws made, not with their consent, but by others against their consent: that this would be to surrender the form of government we have chosen, and live under one deriving its powers from its own will, and not from our authority; and that the co-States, recurring to their natural right in cases not made federal, will concur in declaring these acts void, and of no force and will each take measures of its own for providing that neither these acts nor any others of the General Government not plainly and intentionally authorized by the Constitution, shall be exercised within their respective territories.

9th. *Resolved,* That the said committee be authorized to communicate... with any person or persons who may be appointed by any one or more co-States... and that they lay their proceedings before the next session of Assembly.

ME X 61-62 S. T. Mason 10-11-98

I consider these laws as merely an experiment on the American mind, to see how far it will bear an avowed violation of the Constitution.

ME X 63-67 John Taylor 11-17-98

For the present, I should be for resolving the alien and sedition laws to be against the Constitution and merely void, and for addressing the other States to obtain similar declarations, and I would not do anything at this moment which should commit us further... .

ME X 104-110 Edmund Pendleton 2-14-99

In this State [Pennsylvania], we fear that the ill-designing may produce insurrection. Nothing could be so fatal. Anything like force would check the progress of the public opinion, and rally them around the government... keep away all the show of force, and they will bear down the evil propensities of the government.

Pardoning Those Convicted of Sedition

ME XI 42-45 Mrs. John Adams 7-22-04

My charities to Callendar are considered as rewards for his calumnies. As early, I think, as 1796, I was told in Philadelphia that Callendar, the author of the Political Progress of Britain, was in that city, a fugitive from persecution for having written that book, and in distress. I had read and approved the book; I considered him as a man of genius, unjustly persecuted. I knew nothing of his private character, and immediately expressed my readiness to contribute to his relief... . Himself I did not see till long after, nor ever more than two or three times... .

But another fact is, that I "liberated a wretch who was suffering for a libel against Mr. Adams." I do not know who was the particular wretch alluded to; but I discharged every person under punishment or prosecution under the sedition law, because I considered, and now consider, that law to be a nullity, as absolute and as palpable as if Congress had ordered us to fall down and worship a golden image; and that it was as much my duty to arrest its execution in every stage, as it would have been to have rescued from the fiery furnace those who should have been cast into it for refusing to workship the image. It was accordingly done in every instance, without asking what the offenders had done, or against whom they had offended, but whether the pains they were suffering were inflicted under the pretended sedition law. It was certainly possible that my motives for contributing to the relief of Callendar, and liberating sufferers under the sedition law, might have been to protect, encourage, and reward slander; but they may also have been those which inspire ordinary charities to objects of distress, meritorious or not, or the obligation of an oath to protect the Constitution, violated by an unauthorized act of Congress. Which of these were my motives, must be decided by a regard to the general tenor of my life. On this I am not afraid to appeal to the nation at large, to posterity, and still less to that Being who sees himself our motives, who will judge us from his own knowledge of them and not on the testimony of Porcupine or Fenno [professional Federalist libellers.]

5. XYZ Delusion: On the Brink of War

Commentary

The Federalists, riding high and totally contemptuous of the people, plunged the nation into the worst crisis it had ever known shortly after their unwitting tool, John Adams, took the oath of office in March, 1797. They lost no time in putting their conspiracies into effect; and had it not been for Jefferson and a few other staunch republicans who remained in Washington, it is very doubtful that our constitutional republic could have survived.

Their object was to involve the nation in a devastating war against France, to effect a solid union with England, create enormous debts, levy the most onerous system of taxation conceivable, reduce the states into political non-entities, expand the general government into an all-powerful and omnipresent colossus, wipe out all the rights and protections established by the Bill of Rights, and develop, as rapidly as possible, a tyrannical form of government that could exceed the most hideous despotisms in the Old World. They were utterly without ethics, mercy, or respect for the people or the principles on which the republic was founded. They regarded the productive citizens as precisely on a level with beasts of burden.

At the head of this Party, stood Alexander Hamilton, a man of genius, but of obscure origin, whose danger and power stemmed precisely from his personal and incorruptible honesty. He and Jefferson were the supreme antagonists in a battle which would determine the destiny of the western world.

The Federalists wished to raise armies to invade, conquer, colonize, and dominate South America; but their greatest ploy was to send three Federalists — Dana, Marshall, and Pinckney — to France for the purpose of persuading our people to declare war upon her. They therefore prepared a set of forgeries, known as the XYZ Papers, devised by themselves, but purportedly delivered to them by the French government, which included outrageous demands upon the American people, such as tribute and large loans and threatening the capture of American ships on the high seas.

And just as meetings were being held in many states condemning the obvious plans of the government, these forgeries arrived, were reprinted by the hundreds of thousands, and distributed everywhere, with the result that even many staunch republicans, unable to comprehend the infamy of their enemies, were ready to declare war.

In this crisis, Jefferson urged caution and delay; and he was instrumental in sending Elbridge Gerry to Paris, where it soon became evident that the XYZ Papers were blatant forgeries intended to mislead the American people into slavery and possible destruction.

While the Federalists withheld Gerry's communications from Congress and the people, laws were passed levying a whole galaxy of new taxes, increasing the federal income, expanding the army and navy far beyond current needs, and, in general, using the crisis to transfer all power from the states to the general government.

However, as the Federalist lies and conspiracies gradually became known, the people recovered from their awful delusion. The Federalists had gone too far; they had mistaken the temper and intelligence of the American people; by cooperating with them as their servant, John Adams committed political suicide; and the episode contributed substantially to Federalist repudiation by the electorate. It would not be long before Hamilton would fall victim to a bullet fired by Aaron Burr, his former friend and collaborator.

As the mania subsided, Jefferson became exultant; the outcome proved to him more certainly than ever, that the people can be trusted with self-government; that they can make correct decisions when informed of facts; and that it is not necessary for good government that it rule its subjects with a rod of iron.

Forged Dispatches from France: Public Delirium

ME X 74-86 Elbridge Gerry 1-26-99

When Pinckney, Marshall, and Dana were nominated to settle our differences with France, it was suspected by many, from what was understood of their dispositions, that their mission would not result in a settlement of differences, but would produce circumstances tending to widen the breach, and to provoke our citizens to consent to a war with that nation, and union with England. Dana's resignation and your appointment gave the first gleam of hope of a peaceable issue to the mission. For it was believed that you were sincerely disposed to accommodation; and it was not long after your arrival there, before symptoms were observed of that difference of views which had been suspected to exist.

In the meantime, however, the aspect of our government towards the French republic had become so ardent, that the people of America generally took the alarm. To the southward, their apprehensions were early excited. In the Eastern States also, they at length began to break out. Meetings were held in many of your towns, and addresses to the government agreed in opposition to war. The example was spreading like wildfire. Other meetings were called in other places, and a general concurrence of sentiment against the apparent inclinations of the government was imminent; when, most critically for the government, the despatches of October 22, [1797), prepared by your colleague Marshall, with a view to their being made public, dropped into their laps. It was truly a God-send to them, and they made the most of it. Many thousands of copies were printed and dispersed gratis, at the public expense; and the zealots for war co-operated so liberally, that there were instances of single individuals who printed and dispersed ten or twelve thousand copies at their own expense.

The odiousness of the corruption supposed in those papers excited a general and high indigation among the people. Unexperienced in such manoeuvres, they did not permit themselves even to suspect that the turpitude of private swindlers might mingle itself unobserved, and give its own hue to the communications of the French government, of whose participation there was neither proof nor probability.

It served, however, for a time, the purpose intended. The people, in places, gave a loose to the expressions of their warm indignation, and of their honest preferences to war over dishonor. The fever was long and successfully kept up, and in the meantime, war measures as ardently crowded. Still, however, as it was known that your colleagues were coming away, and yourself to stay, though disclaiming a separate power to conclude a treaty, it was hoped by the lovers of peace, that a project of treaty would have been prepared *ad referendum,* on principles which would have satisfied our citizens, and overawed any bias of the government towards a different policy. But... the suggestions of the person charged with your despatches, and his probable misrepresentations of the real wishes of the American people, prevented these hopes. They had then only to look forward to your return for such information, either through the executive, or from yourself as might present to our view the other side of the medal.

The despatches of October 22, 1797 [the XYZ forgeries], had presented one face. That information, to a certain degree, is now received, and the public will see from your correspondence with Talleyrand, that France, as you testify, "was sincere and anxious to obtain a reconciliation, not wishing us to break the British treaty, but only to give her equivalent stipulations; and in general was disposed to a liberal treaty." And they will judge whether Mr. Pickering's report shows an inflexible determination to believe no declarations the French government can make, nor any opinion which you, judging on the spot and from actual view, can give of their sincerity, and to meet their designs of peace with operations of war.

The alien and sedition acts have already operated in the south as powerful sedatives to the X.Y.Z. inflammation. In your quarter, where violations of principle are either less regarded or more concealed, the direct tax is likely to have the same effect, and to excite inquiries into the object of the enormous expenses and taxes we are bringing on. And your information supervening, that we might have a liberal accommodation, if we would, there can be little doubt of the reproduction of that general movement which had been changed, for a moment, by the despatches of October 22... .

The unquestionable republicanism of the American mind will break through the mist under which it has been clouded, and will oblige its agents to reform the principles and practices of their administration.

ME X 63-67 John Taylor 11-26-98

But there is a most respectable part of our State [Virginia] who have been enveloped in the XYZ delusion, and who destroy our unanimity for the present moment. This disease of the imagination will pass over, because the patients are essentially republicans. Indeed, the Doctor is now on his way to cure it, in the guise of the tax-gatherer. But give time for the medicine to work, and for the repetition of stronger doses, which must be administered. The principle of the present majority, is *excessive expense,* money enough to fill all their maws, or it will not be worth the risk of their supporting. They cannot borrow a dollar in Europe, or above two or three millions in America. This is not the fourth of the expenses of this year, unprovided for. Paper money would be perilous even to the paper men. Nothing then but excessive taxation can get us along; and this will carry reason and reflection to every man's door, and particularly in the hour of election.

The Federalists Conceal the Truth

ME X 67-68 James Madison 1-3-99

Gerry's correspondence with Talleyrand, promised by the President at the beginning of the session, is still kept back. It is known to show France in a very conciliatory attitude, and to contradict some executive assertions. Therefore, it is supposed they will get their war measures well taken before they will produce this damper.

Taxes, War, and Insurrection

ME X 89-92 Colonel Nicholas Lewis 1-30-99

You will see by Mr. Pickering's report that we are determined to believe no declarations they [the French government] can make, but to meet their peaceable professions with acts of war... .

Yesterday, the House of Representatives voted six ships of 74 guns and six of 18, making 552 guns. These would cost in England $5,000 a gun. They would cost here $10,000, so the whole will cost five and a half millions of dollars... . And this is only a part of what is proposed; the whole contemplated being twelve 74's, 12 frigates, and about 25 smaller vessels. The state of our income and expense is (in round numbers) nearly as follows.

Imports, seven and a half millions of dollars; excise, auctions, licenses, carriages, half a million; postage, patents, and bank stock, one-eighth of a million, making eight and on-eighth millions. To these the direct tax and stamp tax will add two millions clear of expenses, making in the whole ten and one-eighth millions. The expenses on the civil list, three-fourths of a million, foreign intercourse, half a million, interest on the public debt, four millions, the present navy two and a half millions, the present army one and a half millions, making nine and one-quarter... .

The additional army will be two and a half millions, the additional navy three millions, and interest on the new loan near one-half a million, in all, fifteen and one-quarter millions; so, in about a year or two, there will be five millions annually to be raised by taxes in addition to the ten millions we now pay. Suppose our population is now five millions, this would be three dollars a head. This is exclusive of the outfit of the navy, for which a loan is opened to borrow five millions at eight per cent... .

In the meantime, the sentiments of the people in the Middle States are visibly turning back to their former direction, the X.Y.Z. delusion being abated, and their minds become sensible to the circumstances surrounding them, to wit: the alien and sedition acts, the vexations of the stamp act, the direct tax, the follies of the additional army and navy, money borrowed for these at the usurious interest of eight per cent., and Mr. Gerry's communications showing that peace is ours unless we throw it away. But if the joining the revolted subjects (negroes) of France, and surrounding *their* islands with our armed vessels, instead of their merely cruising on our own coasts to protect our own commerce, should provoke France to a declaration of war, these measures will become irremediable.

ME X 104-106 Edmund Pendleton 2-14-99

The fate of this country, whether it shall be irretrievably plunged into a form of government rejected by the makers of the Constitution, or shall get back to the true principles of that instrument, depends, on the turn which things take within a short period of time ensuing the present moment. The violations of the Constitution, propensities to war, to expense, and to a particular foreign connection, which we have lately seen, are becoming evidence to the people, and are dispelling that mist which X.Y.Z. had spread before their eyes... .

The People Recover From X.Y.Z.

ME X 86-89 Edmund Pendleton1-29-99

You know what a wicked use has been made of the French negotiation; and particularly the X.Y.Z dish cooked up by ***** where the swindlers are made to appear as the French government. Art and industry combined, have certainly wrought out of this business a wonderful effect on the people.

Yet they have been astonished more than they have understood it, and now that Gerry's correspondence comes out, clearing the French government of that turpitude, and showing them "sincere in their dispositions for peace, not wishing us to break the British treaty, and willing to arrange a liberal one with us," the people will be disposed to suspect that they have been duped.

But these communications are too voluminous for them, and beyond their reach. A recapitulation is now wanting of the whole story, stating everything according to what we may now suppose to have been the truth, short, simple and levelled to every capacity. Nobody in America can do it so well as yourself... and so concise as, omitting nothing material, may yet be printed in hand bills, of which we could print and disperse ten or twelve thousand copies under letter covers, through all the United States by the members of Congress when they return home.

If the understanding of the people could be rallied to the truth on this subject, by exposing the dupery practised on them, there are so many other things about to bear on them favorably for the resurrection of their republican spirit, that a reduction of the administration to constitutional principles cannot fail to be the effect. These are the alien and sedition laws, the vexations of the stamp act, the disgusting particularities of the direct tax, the additional army without an enemy, and recruiting officers lounging at every court-house to decoy the laborer from the plough, a navy of fifty ships, five millions to be raised to build it, on the usurious interest of eight per cent, the perseverance in war on our part, when the French government shows such an anxious desire to keep at peace with us, taxes of ten millions now paid by four millions of people, and yet a necessity, in a year or two, of raising five millions more for annual expenses. These things will immediately be bearing on the public mind, and if it remain not still blinded by the supposed necessity, for the purposes of maintaining our independence and defending our country, they will set things to rights.

ME X 115-16 General Thaddeus Kosciusko 2-21-99

The wonderful irritation produced in the minds of our citizens by the X.Y.Z. story, has in great measure subsided. They begin to suspect and to see it coolly in its true light. Mr. Gerry's communications, with other information, prove to them that France is sincere in her wishes for reconciliation; and a recent proposition from that country... puts the matter out of doubt. What course the government will pursue, I know not... . In fine, if war takes place, republicanism has everything to fear; if peace, be assured... that the spirit of our citizens now rising as rapidly as it was then running crazy, and rising with a strength and majesty which show the liveliness of freedom, will make this government in practice, what it is in principle, a model for the protection of men in a state of *freedom* and *order.*

ME X 218-21 James Monroe 3-7-01

You know that the manoeuvers of the year X.Y.Z. carried over from us a great body of the people, real republicans, and honest men under virtuous motives. The delusion lasted a while. At length, the poor arts and tub plots., etc., were repeated till the designs of the party became suspected. From that moment, those who had left us began coming back.

A Terrible But Salutary Lesson

ME X 227-30 Doctor Joseph Priestley 3-21-01

As the storm is now subsiding, and the horizon becoming serene, it is pleasant to consider the phenomenon with attention. We can no longer say there is nothing new under the sun. For this whole chapter in the history of man is new. The great extent of our republic is new. Its sparse habitation is new. The mighty wave of public opinion which has rolled over it is new. But the most pleasing novelty is, its so quietly subsiding over such an extent of surface to its true level again. The order and good sense displayed in this recovery from delusion, and in the momentous crisis which lately arose, really bespeak a strength of character in our nation which augurs well for the duration of our republic; and I am much better satisfied now of its stability than I was before it was tried.

ME X 341-43 Thomas Cooper 11-29-02

I think you will be sensible that our citizens are fast returning from the panic into which they were artfully thrown, to the dictates of their own reason; and I believe the delusions they have seen themselves hurried into will be a useful lesson under similar attempts on them in the future.

The good effects of our late fiscal arrangements will certainly tend to unite them in opinion, and in confidence as to the views of their public functionaries, legislative and executive. The part we have to pursue is so quiet that we have nothing scarcely to propose to our legislature. A noiseless course... unattractive of notice, is going on in happiness... .

Their finances are now under such a course of application as nothing could derange but war or federalism... .

6. A Free Press vs. Libelous Abuse

Commentary

Since freedom, reason, and personal responsibility were among the grand watchwords of Jefferson's lexicon, it was inevitable that he should devote his energies to establish a free press — a thing so novel then as to be almost incredible. Jefferson knew that no dishonest, despotic, and flagitious government could survive the exposes of an untrammelled press; but he did not fear it, because the system established by our Founding Fathers was based on truth, justice, equality, liberty, and the interests of the great majority.

However, this very freedom was to become a thorn in his side; for his many and powerful enemies, among the clergy, the Anglophiles, and the financial community, who abhorred republican principles with a hatred that surpassed all ordinary bounds and comprehension, used their powerful presses to abuse, vilify, and misrepresent every aspect of his ideals and activities. They forged letters and speeches to discredit him; they charged him with misappropriating a widow's estate; of being an avid seeker after the honors and emoluments of office; of giving public funds to political supporters; of lying the Federalists out of office; of favoring France, in spite of her atrocities against the United States; and, when they could find no facts, they simply exhausted their vocabularies in general vituperation and vilification. One of the most blatant charges was his alleged liaison with Sally Hemmings.

In a sense, Jefferson welcomed all this; for he declared that he had offered himself as an experiment — the first of its kind in history — to prove that a free press is compatible with orderly government, and that, in the long run, the people will believe what they see their political servants accomplishing, rather than the lies spewed forth about them by well-financed enemies.

If there was one fact of which Jefferson was more certain than of any other it was that every government, sooner or later, will, unless restrained by a free press, tend and seek to become a tyranny. He therefore wrote to Charles Yancy on June 6, 1816, that

"The functionaries of every government have propensities to command at will the liberty and property of their constituents. There is no safe deposit for

these, but with the people themselves; nor can they be safe with them without information. Where the press is free, and every one can read, all is safe."

There was no field in which Jefferson's glory shines more brightly or permanently than in his advocacy of a free press and in his victory over demogogues who sought its use to destroy him by libel and calumny.

The Crucial Importance of a Free Press

CE VII 452 Proposal for the Virginia Constitution 1781

Printing presses shall be subject to no other restraint than liableness to legal prosecution for false facts printed and published.

FORD VI 521 Notes for a Constitution 1792

Printing presses shall be free except as to false facts published maliciously, either to injure the reputation of another, whether followed by pecuniary damages or not, or to expose him to the punishment of the law.

The First Amendment to the Federal Constitution 1792

Congress shall make no law... abridging the freedom of speech, or of the press... .

ME VIII 394-408 The President of the United States 9-9-92

No government ought to be without censors; and where the press is free, no one ever will. If virtuous, it need not fear the fair operation of attack and defence. Nature has given to man no other means of sifting out the truth, either in religion, law, or politics. I think it as honorable to the government neither to know, nor notice, its sycophants or censors, as it would be undignified and criminal to pamper the former and persecute the latter.

ME X 341-43 Thomas Cooper 11-29-02

The press, the only tocsin of a nation, is completely silenced there [in France], and all means of a general effort taken away.

ME XI 32-35 Judge John Tyler 6-28-04

No experiment can be more interesting than that we are now trying, and which we trust will end in establishing the fact, that men may be governed by reason and truth. Our first object should therefore be, to leave open to him all the avenues to truth. The most effectual hitherto found, is the freedom of the press. It is, therefore, the first shut up by those who fear the investigation of their actions. The firmness with which the people have withstood the late abuses of the press [during the XYZ delusion], the discernment they have manifested between truth and falsehood, show that they may safely be trusted to hear everything true and false, and to form a correct judgment between them... .

I hold it, therefore, certain, that to open the doors of truth, and to fortify the habit of testing everything by reason, are the most effectual manacles we can rivet on the hands of our successors to prevent their manacling the people with their own consent. The panic into which they were artfully thrown in 1798, the frenzy which was excited in them by their enemies against their apparent readiness to abondon all the principles established for their own protection, seemed for awhile to countenance the opinions of those who say they cannot be trusted with their own government. But I never doubted their rallying; and they did rally much sooner than I expected. On the whole, that experiment on their credulity has confirmed my confidence in their ultimate good sense and virtue.

BW 359-63 Second Inaugural Address 3-4-05

Nor was it uninteresting to the world, that an experiment should be fairly and fully made, whether freedom of discussion, unaided by power, is not sufficient for the propagation and protection of truth — whether a government, conducting itself in the true spirit of its constitution, with zeal and purity, and doing no act which it would be unwilling the whole world should witness, can be written down by falsehood and defamation. The experiment has been tried; you have witnessed the scene; our fellow citizens have looked on, cool and collected; they saw the latent source from which these outrages proceeded; they gathered around their public functionaries, and when the constitution called them to the decision by suffrage, they pronounced their verdict, honorable to those who had served them, and consolatory to the friend of man, who believes he may be instrusted with his own affairs.

No inference is here intended, that the laws provided by the States against false and defamatory publications, should not be enforced; he who has time, renders a service to public morals and public tranquillity, in reforming these abuses by the salutary coercions of the law; but the experiment is noted, to prove that, since truth and reason have maintained their ground against false opinions in league with false facts, the press, confined to truth, needs no other legal restraint; the public judgment will correct false reasonings and opinions, on a full hearing of all parties; and no other definite line can be drawn between the inestimable liberty of the press and its demoralizing licentiousness. If there be still improprieties which this rule would not restrain, its supplement must be sought in the censorship of public opinion... .

...our wish... is that the public efforts may be directed honestly to the public good, that peace be cultivated, civil and religious liberty unassailed, law and order preserved, equality of rights maintained, and that state of property, equal or unequal, which results to every man from his own industry, or that of his fathers. When satisfied of these views, it is not in human nature that they should not approve and support them; in the meantime, let us cherish them with patient affection; let us do them justice, and more than justice, in all competitions of interest; and we need not doubt that truth, reason, and their own interests, will at length prevail, will gather them into the fold of their country, and will complete their entire union of opinion, which gives to a nation the blessing of harmony, and the benefit of all its strength.

ME XI 154-56 Thomas Seymour 2-11-07

As to myself, conscious that there was not a *truth* on earth which I feared should it be known, I have lent myself willingly as the subject of a great experiment which was to prove that an administration, conducted with integrity and common understanding, cannot be battered down, even by the falsehoods of a licentious press, and consequently still less by the press restrained by truth. This experiment was wanting for the world to demonstrate the falsehood of the pretext that freedom of the press is incompatible with orderly government. I have never, therefore, even contradicted the thousands of calumnies industriously propagated against myself. But the fact being once established, that the press is impotent when it abandons itself to falsehood, I leave to others to restore it to its strength, by recalling it within the pale of truth. Within that, it is a noble institution, equally the friend of science and of civil liberty.

ME XIV 379-84 Colonel Charles Yancy 1-6-16

If a nation expects to be ignorant and free, in a state of civilization, it expects what never was and never will be... . Where the press is free, and every man able to read, all is safe.

ME XV 480-90 Monsieur Coray 10-31-23

It [the press] is the best instrument for enlightening the mind of man, and improving him as a rational, moral, and social being.

The Libellous and Degenerate Newspapers

ME X 334-37 Robert Livingston 10-10-02

You will have seen by our newspapers... that the federalists have opened all their sluices of calumny. They say we lied them out of power, and openly avow they will do the same by us.

ME X 355-57 Mr. Pictet 2-5-03

I believe you take some interest in our fortune, and [do so] because our newspapers, for the most part, present only the caricatures of disaffected minds. Indeed, the abuses of the freedom of the press have been carried to a length never before known or borne by any civilized nation. But it is so difficult to draw a clear line of separation between the abuse and the wholesome use of the press, that as yet we have found it better to trust the public judgment, rather than the magistrate, with the discrimination between truth and falsehood. And hitherto the public judgment has performed that office with wonderful correctness.

ME X 387-90 Joseph H. Nicholson 5-13-03

While it is best for our own tranquillity to see and hear with apathy the atrocious calumnies of the presses which our enemies support for the purpose of calumny, it is what we have no right to expect; nor can we consider the indignation they excite in others as unjust, or strongly censure those whose temperament is not proof against it.

ME XI 42-45 Mrs. John Adams 7-22-04

With respect to the calumnies and falsehoods which writers and printers at large published against Mr. Adams, I was as far from stooping to any concern or approbation of them, as Mr. Adams was respecting those of Porcupine, Fenno, or Russel, who published volumes against me for every sentence vented by their opponents against Mr. Adams. But I never supposed Mr. Adams had any participation in the atrocities of these editors, or their writers. I knew myself incapable of that base warfare, and believed him to be so. On the contrary, whatever I may have thought of the acts of the administration of that day, I have ever borne testimony to Mr. Adams' personal worth; nor was it ever impeached in my presence without a just vindication of it on my part. I never supposed that any person who knew either of us, could believe that either of us meddled in that dirty work.

ME XI 167-70 James Monroe 3-21-07

I perceive uncommon efforts, and with uncommon wickedness, are making by the federal papers... to irritate the British government by putting a thousand speeches into my mouth, not one word of which I ever uttered.

ME XIII 59-60 James Monroe 5-5-11

Our printers ravin on the agonies of their victims, as wolves do on the blood of the lamb. But the printers and the public see very different personages. The former may lead the latter a little out of the track, while the deviation is insensible; but the moment they usurp their direction and that of their government, they will be reduced to their true places.

ME XIV 46-52 Dr. Walter Jones 1-2-14

I deplore, with you, the putrid state into which our newspapers have passed, and the malignity, the vulgarity, and mendacious spirit of those who write for them; and I enclose you a recent sample, the production of a New England judge, as a proof of the abyss of degradation into which we are fallen. These ordures are rapidly depraving the public taste, and lessening its relish for sound food. As vehicles of information, and a curb on our functionaries, they have rendered themselves useless, by forfeiting all title to belief. That this has, in a great degree, been produced by the violence and malignity of party spirit, I agree with you... .

Libel, Abuse, and Slander

ME IX 424-28 Alexander White 9-10-97

So many persons have of late found an interest, or a passion gratified, by imputing to me sayings and writings which I never said or wrote, or by endeavoring to draw me into newspapers to harass me personally, that I have found it necessary for my own quiet and my other pursuits to leave them in full possession of the field, and not to take the trouble of contradicting them even in private conversation.

ME X 55-59 Samuel Smith 8-22-98

Were I to undertake to answer the calumnies of the newspapers, it would be more than all my own time, and that of twenty aids, could effect. For while answering one, twenty new ones would be invented. I have thought it better to trust to the justice of my countrymen, that they would indulge me by what they see of my conduct on the stage where they have placed me... .

ME X 170-73 Uriah McGregory 8-13-00

From the moment that a portion of my fellow citizens looked towards me with a view to one of their highest offices, the floodgates of calumny have been opened upon me; not where I am personally known, where their slanders would be instantly judged and suppressed, from a general sense of their falsehood; but in the remote parts of the Union, where the means of detection are not at hand, and the trouble of inquiry is greater than would suit the hearers to undertake. I know I might have filled the courts of the United States with actions for these slanders, and have ruined perhaps many persons who are not innocent. But this would be no equivalent to the loss of character. I leave them, therefore, to the reproof of their own consciences.

ME X 376-78 Edward Dowse 4-19-03

Every word which goes from me, whether verbally or in writing, becomes the subject of so much malignant distortion, and perverted construction, that I am obliged to caution my friends against admitting the possibility of my letters getting into the public papers, or a copy of them to be taken under any degree of confidence.

ME XI 38-42 Philip Mazzei 7-18-04

Every word of mine which they can get hold of, however innocent, however orthodox even, is twisted, tormented, perverted, and, like the words of holy writ, are made to mean everything but what they were intended to mean.

ME XII 3-8 James Monroe 3-10-08

If you are less on your guard than we are here, at this moment, the designs of the mischief makers will not fail to be accomplished, and brethren and friends will be made strangers and enemies to each other, without ever having said or thought a thing amiss of each other. I presume that the most insidious falsehoods are daily carried to you, as they are brought to me, to engage us in the passions of our informers, and stated so positively and plausibly as to make even a *doubt* a rudeness to the narrator, who, imposed on himself, has no other than a friendly view of putting us on our guard. My answer is, invariably, that my knowledge of your character is better testimony to me of a negative, than any affirmative which my informant did not hear *from yourself* with his own ears. In fact, when you shall have been a little longer among us, you will find that little is to be believed which interests the prevailing passions, and happens beyond the limits of our own senses... . For myself, I have nothing further to ask of the world, than to preserve in retirement so much of their esteem as I may have fairly earned, and to be permitted to pass in tranquillity, in the bosom of my family and friends, the days which may remain for me.

Reactions to Personal Calumny

ME VIII 394-408 The President of the United States 9-9-92

I am more desirous to predispose everything for the repose to which I am withdrawing, than expose it to be disturbed by newspaper contests. If these, however, cannot be avoided altogether... , I reserve to myself the right of then appealing to my country, subscribing my name to whatever I write, and using with freedom and truth the facts and names necessary to place the cause in its just form before that tribunal.

To a thorough disregard of the honors and emoluments of office, I join as great a value for the esteem of my countrymen, and conscious of having merited it by an integrity which cannot be reproached, and by an enthusiastic devotion to their rights and liberty, I will not suffer my retirement to be clouded by the slanders of a man [Hamilton] whose history, from the moment at which history can stoop to notice him, is a tissue of machinations against the liberty of the country which has not only received and given him bread, but heaped its honors on his head. Still, however, I repeat the hope that it will not be necessary to make such an appeal. Though little known to the people of America, I believe, that, as far as I am known, it is not as an enemy to the Republic, nor an intriguer against it, nor a waster of its revenue, nor prostitutor of it to the purposes of corruption, as the "American" represents me; and I confide that yourself are satisfied that as to dissensions in the newspapers, not a syllable of them has ever proceeded from me, and that no cabals or intrigues of mine have produced those in the legislature, and I hope I may promise both to you and myself, that none will receive aliment from me during the short space I have to remain in office, which will find ample employment in closing the present business of the department.

ME XI 48-53 Mrs. John Adams 9-11-04

I tolerate with the utmost latitude the right of others to differ from me in opinion without imputing to them criminality. I know too well the weakness and uncertainty of human reason to wonder at its different results. Both of our political parties, at least the honest part of them, agree conscientiously in the same object — the public good; but they differ essentially in what they deem the means of promoting that good... . One fears most the ignorance of the people; the other, the selfishness of rulers independent of them. Which is right, time... will tell.

My anxieties on this subject will never carry me beyond the use of fair and honorable means, of truth and reason; nor have they ever lessened my esteem for moral worth, nor alienated my affections from a single friend, who did not first withdraw himself. Whenever this has happened, I confess I have not been insensible to it; yet have ever kept myself open to a return of their justice.

ME XVI 52-69 Martin van Buren 6-29-24

My rule of life has been never to harass the public with fendings and provings of personal slanders... . I have trusted to the justice and consideration of my fellow-citizens, and have no reason to repent it, or to change my course.

7. Jefferson and the Constitution

Commentary

Although Jefferson was in France when the Constitutional Convention met in Philadelphia, we believe that his philosophy was influential in its deliberations; and it is certain that his numerous letters concerning it were significant in fashioning and attaining the Bill of Rights — the first ten amendments — which render the whole document unique in the history of mankind.

After his first reading of the proposed Constitution, he found faults as well as desirable elements. In a long letter to James Madison, dated December 20, 1787, he stated that he liked the organization of the government into legislative, executive, and judicial branches; he was pleased that it would be able to "go on of itself, peaceably, without needing continual recurrence to the State legislatures." He was also happy that all measures for taxation would originate in the House, because this was closest to the electorate. The compromise between the larger and the smaller states met with his approval.

However, there were various features he did not *like: that the senators were not elected by the people directly and that their terms were too long; the re-eligibility of the president for additional terms; and, most of all, the absence of a Bill of Rights, which, in his opinion, was absolutely essential to protect the people from inevitable encroachments by a central government upon their liberties.*

In letter after letter, he emphasized his convictions and spelled out the particulars which should be included: the freedom of religion; freedom of the press; the right to habeas corpus and trial by jury in all civil as well as criminal cases; protection against monopolies; the extreme importance of preserving the rights and powers of the states, in all areas not specifically mandated to the General Government.

Here, as everywhere else, Jefferson's overriding interest was in preserving the freedom and the liberties of the people and to restrict the powers and the activities of the government. Consequently, after accepting almost everything in the original Constitution, there remained two principal objections:

(1) the lack of a Bill of Rights; and (2) the indefinite re-eligibility of the chief magistrate to re-election. Again and again he declared his fear that because of this, such officials could become incumbents for life and might even degenerate into an hereditary position. He declared that unless this possibility were prevented, either by practice or by an amendment to the Constitution, the danger of such perpetuity remained an ever-present threat against the integrity of the republic. He said that we might some day re-elect a man in his dotage. This reads now almost like a prophecy of the fourth election of Franklin D. Roosevelt when he was, in fact, a dying man, so ill that he could not even speak to the convention which nominated him in 1944.

And so Jefferson's hope was at last realized: the Constitution was amended to prevent any president from serving more than two terms.

As Jefferson approached the end of his second term, a great many pleaded with him to accept a third. On December 12, 1807, he wrote to the people of New Jersey, as he did to various others, that short periods in office produce the greatest sum of happiness for mankind; and that he would do nothing to impair that principle.

We should note that under all forms of authoritarian domination, such as exist in labor unions, monarchies, socialist and communist governments, those in control remain there for life. Their practice is the reverse of the Jeffersonian republican principle.

On June 19, 1802, Jefferson wrote to his friend, Joseph Priestley, "that though written constitutions may be violated in moments of passion or delusion," as occurred when the Federalists had power, especially under Adams, "yet they furnish a text to which those who are watchful may again rally and recall the people; they fix too for the people the principles of their political creed." Words to remember!

What Jefferson Approved In It

ME VI 385-93 James Madison 12-20-87

I like much the general idea of framing a government, which should go on of itself, peaceably, without needing continual recurrence to the State legislatures. I like the organization of the government into legislative, judiciary, and executive. I like the power given the legislature to levy taxes, and for that reason solely, I approve of the greater House being chosen by the people directly. For though I think a House so chosen, will be very far inferior to the present Congress, will be very illy qualified to legislate for the Union, for foreign nations, etc., yet this evil does not weigh against the good, of preserving inviolate the fundamental principle, that the people are not to be taxed but by representatives chosen immediately by themselves.

I am captivated by the compromise of the opposite claims of the great and little States, of the latter to equal, and the former to proportional influence. I am much pleased, too, with the substitution of the method of voting by person, instead of that of voting by States; and I like the negative given the Executive, conjointly with a third of either House; though I should have liked it better, had the judiciary been associated for that purpose, or invested separately with a similar power.

There are other good things of less moment.

ME VII 12-15 Count de Moustier 5-17-88

I see in this instrument a great deal of good. The consolidation of our government, a just representation, an administration of some permanence, and other features of great value, will be formed by it. There are, indeed, some faults, which revolted me a good deal in the first moment; but we must be contented to travel on towards perfection, step by step. We must be contented with the ground which this constitution will gain for us, and hope that a favorable moment will come for correcting what is amiss in it.

CE 249-50 Joseph Jones 8-14-87

With all the defects of our Constitution, whether general or particular, the comparison of our governments with those of Europe, is like a comparison of heaven and hell. England, like the earth, may be allowed to take an intermediate station.

ME VII 252-59 Dr. Price 1-8-89

Our new Constitution... has succeeded beyond what I apprehended it would have done: I did not at first believe that eleven States out of thirteen would have consented to the plan consolidating them as much into one. A change in their dispositions, which had taken place since I left them, had rendered this consolidation necessary, that is to say, had called for a federal government which could walk upon its own legs, without leaning for support on the State legislatures. A sense of necessity, and a submission to it, is to me a new and consolatory proof that, whenever the people are well-informed, they can be trusted with their own government; that, whenever things get so far wrong as to attract their notice, they may be relied on to set them to rights.

ME XIII 394-403 John Adams 10-28-13

A constitution has been acquired, which, though neither of us thinks perfect, yet both consider as competent to render our fellow citizens the happiest and the securest on whom the sun has ever shone. If we do not think exactly alike as to its imperfections, it matters little to our country, which, after devoting to it long lives of disinterested labor, we have delivered over to our successors in life, who will be able to take care of it themselves.

Jefferson Magnificent Populist

ME XV 27-31 William Crawford 6-20-16

A government regulating itself by what is wise and just for the many, uninfluenced by the local and selfish views of the few who direct their affairs, has not been seen, perhaps, on earth. Or if it existed, for a moment, at the birth of ours, it would be easy to fix the term of its continuance. Still, I believe it does exist here in greater degree than anywhere else; and for its growth and continuance... , I offer sincere prayers... .

Jefferson's Disapproval

ME VI 385-93 James Madison 12-20-87

I will now tell you what I do not like. First, the omission of a bill of rights, providing clearly, and without the aid of sophism, for freedom of religion, freedom of the press, protection against standing armies, restriction of monopolies, the eternal and unremitting force of the habeas corpus laws, and trials by jury in all matters of fact triable by the laws of the land, and not by the laws of nations. To say, as Mr. Wilson [a Federalist] does, that a bill of rights was not necessary, because all is reserved in the case of the general government which is not given, while in the particular ones, all is given which is not reserved, might do for the audience to which it was addressed; but it is surely a *gratis dictum,* the reverse of which might just as well be said... .

For I consider all the ill as established, which may be established. I have a right to nothing, which another has a right to take away; and Congress will have a right to take away trials by jury in all civil cases.

Let me add that a bill of rights is what the people are entitled to against every government on earth, general or particular; and what no just government should refuse, or rest on inference.

The second feature I dislike, and strongly dislike, is the abandonment, in every instance, of the principle of rotation in office, and most particularly in the case of the President. Reason and experience tell us, that the first magistrate will always be re-elected if he may be re-elected. He is then an officer for life... .

The power of removing every fourth year by the vote of the people, is a power which they will not exercise, and if they were disposed to exercise it, they would not be permitted. The King of Poland is removable every day by the diet. But they never remove him.

I do not pretend to decide, what would be the best method of procuring the establishment of the manifold good things in this constitution, and of getting rid of the bad. Whether by adopting it, in hopes of future amendment; or after it shall have been duly weighed and canvassed by the people... .

I own, I am not a friend to a very energetic government. It is always oppressive. It places the governors indeed more at their ease, at the expense of the people... . [But] say, finally, whether peace is best preserved by giving energy to the government or information to the people... . Educate and inform the whole mass of the people. Enable them to see that it is to their interest to preserve peace and order, and they will preserve them. And it requires no very high degree of education to convince them of this. They are the only sure reliance for the preservation of liberty. After all, it is my principle that the will of the majority should prevail. If they approve the proposed constitution in all its parts, I shall concur in it cheerfully, in hopes they will amend it, whenever they shall find it works wrong... .

ME XIII 368-71 John Adams 11-13-87

How do you like the new Constitution? I confess there are things in it which stagger all my dispositions to subscribe to what such an Assembly has proposed. The House of federal representatives will not be adequate to the management of affairs, either foreign or federal. Their President seems a bad edition of the Polish King. He may be elected from four years to four years for life. Reason and experience prove to us, that a chief magistrate, so continuable, is in office for life. When one or two generations shall have proved that this is an office for life, it becomes, on every occasion, worthy of intrigue, of bribery, of force... . Once in office, and possessing the military force of the Union, without the aid or check of a council, he would not easily be dethroned, even if the people could be induced to withdraw their votes from him. I wish that at the end of four years, they had made him forever ineligible a second time.

ME VI 378-83 William Carmichael 12-11-87

Our new Constitution is powerfully attacked in the American newspapers. The objections are, that its effect would be to form the thirteen States into one; that, proposing to melt all down into a General Government, they have fenced the people by no declaration of rights; they have not renounced the power of keeping a standing army; they have not secured the liberty of the press; they have reserved the power of abolishing trials by jury in civil cases; they have proposed that the laws of the federal legislature shall be paramount to the laws and constitutions of the States; they have abandoned rotation in office; and particularly, their President may be re-elected from four years to four years, for life, so as to render him a King for life, like the King of Poland; they have not given him either a check or a council. To these, they add calculations of expense, etc., etc., to frighten the people. You will perceive that these objections are serious, and some of them not without foundation. The Constitution, however, has been received with a very general enthusiasm, and as far as can be judged from external demonstrations, the bulk of the people are eager to adopt it.

ME XV 32-43 Samuel Kercheval 7-12-16

In truth, the abuses of monarchy had so much filled all the space of political contemplation, that we imagined everything republican which was not monarchy. We had not yet penetrated to the mother principle, that "governments are republican only in proportion as they embody the will of their people, and execute it." Hence, our first constitutions had really no leading principles in them. But experience and reflection have but more and more confirmed me in the particular importance of the equal representation... .

But inequality of representation in both Houses of our legislature, is not the only republican heresy in this first essay of our Revolutionary patriots at forming a Constitution. For let it be agreed that a government is republican in proportion as every member composing it has his equal voice in the direction of its concerns... and let us bring to the test of this canon every branch of our Constitution.

In the legislature, the House of Representatives is chosen by less than half of the people, and not at all in proportion to those who do choose. The Senate are still more disproportionate, and for long terms of irresponsibility... .

But it will be said, it is easier to find faults than to amend them. I do not think their amendment so difficult as is pretended. Only lay down true principles, and adhere to them inflexibly. Do not be frightened into their surrender by the alarms of the timid, or the croakings of wealth against the ascendency of the people. If experience be called for, appeal to that of our fifteen or twenty governments for forty years and show me one where the people have done half the mischief in these forty years, that a single despot would have done in a single year; or show half the riots and rebellions, the crimes and the punishments, which have taken place in any single nation, under kingly government, during the same period.

The Need for a Bill of Rights

ME VII 26-30 William Carmichael 5-27-88

I thought I saw in it [the new Constitution] many faults, great and small. What I have read and reflected has brought me over from several of my objections of the first moment, and to acquiesce under some others. Two only remain, of essential consideration, to wit, the want of a bill of rights, and the expunging the principle of necessary rotation in the offices of President and Senator. At first, I wished that when nine States should have adopted the Constitution, so as to insure us what is good in it, the other four might hold off till the want of a bill of rights, at least, might be supplied. But I am now convinced that the plan of Massachusetts is the best, that is, to accept, and to amend afterwards. If the States which were to decide after her, should all do the same, it is impossible but they must obtain the essential amendments.

ME VII 36-39 Colonel Carrington 5-27-88

There are two amendments only which I am anxious for. 1. A bill of rights, which it is so much the interest of all to have, that I conceive it must be yielded... . The 2nd amendment which appears to me essential is the restoring the principle of necessary rotation, particularly to the Senate and the Presidency; but most of all to the last. Re-eligibility makes him an officer for life, and the disasters inseparable from an elective monarchy, render it preferable if we cannot tread back that step, that we should go forward and take refuge in an hereditary one.

Of the correction of this article, however, I entertain no present hope, because I found it has scarcely excited an objection in America. And if it does not take place erelong, it assuredly never will. The natural progress of things is for liberty to yield, and government to gain ground. And yet our spirits are free. Our jealousy is only put to sleep by the unlimited confidence we all repose in the person to whom we all look as our president. After him, inferior characters may perhaps succeed, and awaken us to the danger which his merit has led us into.

ME VII 93-100 James Madison 7-31-88

I sincerely rejoice at the acceptance of our new Constitution by nine States. It is a good canvass, on which some strokes only want retouching... It seems pretty well understood that this should go to juries, habeas corpus, standing armies, printing, religion, and monopolies. I conceive there may be difficulty in finding general modifications of these, suited to the habits of all the States. But if such cannot be found, then it is better to establish trials by jury, the right of habeas corpus, freedom of the press and freedom of religion, in all cases, and to abolish standing armies in time of peace, and monopolies in all cases, than not to do it in any... .

ME VII 319-24 Colonel Humphreys 3-18-89

There are instruments for administering the government, so peculiarly trustworthy, that we should never leave the legislature at liberty to change them. The new Constitution has secured these in the executive and legislative department; but not in the judiciary. It should have established trials by the people themselves, that is to say, by jury. There are instruments so dangerous to the rights of the nation, and which place them so totally at the mercy of their governors, that these governors, whether legislative or executive, should be restrained from keeping such instruments on foot, but in well-defined cases. Such an instrument is a standing army.

ME VII 338-40 Mr. Littlepage 5-8-89

All our States acceded unconditionally to the new Constitution, except North Carolina and Rhode Island. The latter rejects it in toto. North Carolina neither rejected nor received it, but asked certain amendments before it should receive it. Her amendments concur with those asked by Virginia, New York, and Massachusetts, and consist chiefly in a declaration of rights.

The Danger Inherent in a Constitutional Convention

ME VII 247 William Carmichael 12-25-88

[Explains that New York wants a Constitutional Convention to add a bill of rights — which Jefferson fears, because it may do great harm].

In this way, the whole fabric would be submitted to alteration. Its [the Constitution's] friends, therefore, unite in endeavoring to have the first method [resolution by Congress] adopted, and they seem agreed to concur on adding a bill of rights to the Constitution. This measure will bring over so great a part of the opposition that what will remain after that will have no other than the good effect of watching, as sentinels, the conduct of government, and laying it before the public. Many of the opposition wish to take from Congress the power of internal taxation. Calculation has convinced me this would be very mischievous.

The Value of the Constitution

ME X 324-26 Dr. Joseph Priestley 6-19-02

In the great work which has been effected in America, no individual has a right to take any great share to himself. Our people in a body are wise, because they are under the unrestrained and unperverted operation of their own understanding. Those whom they have assigned to the direction of their affairs, have stood with a pretty even front. If any one of them was withdrawn, many others entirely equal have been ready to fill his place with as good abilities.

A nation, composed of such materials, and free in all its members from distressing wants, furnishes hopeful implements for the interesting experiment of self-government; and we feel that we are acting under obligations not confined to the limits of our own society. It is impossible not to be sensible that we are acting for all mankind; that circumstances denied to others, but indulged to us, have imposed on us the duty of proving what is the degree of freedom and self-government in which a society may venture to have its individual members.

One passage, in the paper you enclosed me, must be corrected. It is the following, "and all say it was yourself more than any other individual, that planned and established it," *i.e.,* the Constitution. I was in Europe when the Constitution was planned... . On receiving it, I wrote strongly to Mr. Madison, urging the want of provision for the freedom of religion, freedom of the press, trial by jury, habeas corpus, the substitution of militia for a standing army, and an express reservation to the States of all rights not specifically granted to the Union. He accordingly moved in the first session of Congress for these amendments, which were agreed to and ratified by the States as they now stand. This is all the hand I had in what related to the Constitution.

Our predecessors [the Federalists] made it doubtful how far even these were of any value; for the very law which endangered your personal safety, as well as that which restrained the freedom of the press, were gross violations of them.

However, it is still certain that though written constitutions may be violated in moments of passion or delusion, yet they furnish a text to which those who are watchful may again rally and recall the people; they fix too for the people the principles of their political creed.

The Term of the Presidency

ME XI 56-58 John Taylor 1-6-05

My opinion originally was that the President of the United States should have been elected for seven years, and forever ineligible afterwards. I have since become sensible that seven years is too long to be irremovable, and that there should be a reasonable way of withdrawing a man in midway who is doing wrong. The service for eight years, with a power to remove at the end of the first four, comes nearly to my principle as corrected by experience; and it is in adherence to that, that I determine to withdraw at the end of a second term.

The danger is that the indulgence and attachments of the people will keep a man in the chair after he becomes a dotard, that re-election through life shall become habitual, and election for life follows that. General Washington set the example of voluntary retirement after eight years. I shall follow it. And a few more precedents will oppose the obstacle of habit to any one after a while who shall endeavor to extend his term.

Perhaps it may beget a disposition to establish it by an amendment of the Constitution. I believe I am doing right therefore in pursuing my principle. I had determined to declare my intention, but I have consented to be silent on the opinion of friends, who think it best not to put a continuance out of my power in defiance of all circumstances. There is, however, but one circumstance which could engage my acquiescence in another election; to wit, such a division about a successor, as might bring in a monarchist. But that circumstance is impossible.

While, therefore, I shall make no formal declaration to the public of my purpose, I have freely let it be understood in private conversation. In this I am persuaded yourself and my friends generally will approve of my views. And should I, at the end of a second term, carry into retirement all the favor which the first has acquired, I shall feel the consolation of having done all the good in my power, and expect with more than composure the termination of a life no longer valuable to others or of importance to myself.

ME XVI 294-97 To the Representatives of the People of New Jersey 12-10-07

If some termination to the services of the chief magistrate be not fixed by the Constitution, or supplied by practice, his office, nominally for years, will, in fact, become for life, and history shows how easily that degenerates into an inheritance. Believing that a representative government, responsible at short periods of election, is that which produces the greatest sum of happiness to mankind, I feel it a duty to do no act which shall essentially impair that principle; and I should unwillingly be the person who, disregarding the sound precedent set by an illustrious predecessor, should furnish the first example of prolongation beyond the second term of office.

The Nature of the Constitution

ME XV 32-44 Samuel Kercheval 7-12-16

Some men look at constitutions with sactimonious reverence, and deem them like the ark of the covenant, too sacred to be touched. They ascribe to the men of the preceding age a wisdom more than human, and suppose what they did to be beyond amendment. I knew that age well; I belonged to it, and labored with it. It deserved well of its country. It was very like the present, but without the experience of the present; and forty years of experience in government is worth a century of book-reading; and this they would say themselves, were they to rise from the dead.

I am certainly not an advocate for frequent and untried changes in laws and constitutions. I think moderate imperfections had better be borne with; because, when once known, we accommodate ourselves to them, and find practical means of correcting their ill effects... .

I know also, that laws and institutions must go hand in hand with the progress of the human mind. As that becomes more developed, more enlightened, and as new discoveries are made, new truths disclosed, and manners and opinions change with the change of circumstances, institutions must advance also, and keep pace with the times. We might as well require a man to wear still the coat which fitted him when a boy, as civilized society to remain ever under the regimen of their barbarous ancestors. It is this preposterous idea which has lately deluged Europe in blood. Their monarchs, instead of yielding wisely to the gradual change of circumstances, of favoring progressive accommodation to progressive improvement, have clung to old abuses, entrenched themselves behind steady habits, and obliged their subjects to seek through blood and violence rash and ruinous innovations, which, had they been referred to the peaceful deliberations and collected wisdom of the nation, would have been put into acceptable and salutary forms. Let us follow no such examples, nor weakly believe that one generation is not as capable as another of taking care of itself, and of ordering its own affairs.

ME XVI 26-30 John Hamblen Pleasants 4-19-24

The present generation has the same right of self-government which the past one has exercised for itself. And those in the full vigor of body and mind are more able to judge for themselves than those who are sinking under the wane of both.

8. Republican Principles: Theory and Practice

Commentary

Jefferson's life and philosophy were governed by a single overwhelming passion: a constant desire to establish a political-economic structure in which the people — the producers of goods and services — would excercise control over the government and, as a result, retain for their own benefit almost all the wealth they created. Against him were arrayed all those whose ambition it was to live in idleness and luxury, battening on the labors of the many; they wished to be the parasites who neither toil nor spin, but who may become veritable Solomons in splendor.

When we consider that Jefferson was himself an aristocrat; that he was the owner of large properties — which deteriorated into bankruptcy because of his public service; that he had nothing to gain except self-respect and the possible approbation of posterity for his self-sacrifice; and that he surrendered everything of personal advantage by the course he pursued, his worth and greatness assume new and herioc dimensions. We can only conclude that he was one of those rare human specimens whose driving force and motivation consist of devotion to truth and justice above all other pursuits and objectives.

Thus it was that he espoused the republican cause, a theory of government which held that men can best be self-governed; that, with some degree of education and information, they can and will establish such administrations of justice as will sustain law and an orderly society. In that day, this was a novel and highly revolutionary concept — unknown in the annals of society, except, perhaps in Athens during its golden age: but this was on a comparatively small scale, and rested on the labor of disenfranchised slaves, who constituted the great majority of the population.

On the other hand, those who opposed Jefferson, had the most compelling motivations imaginable. They *wanted to own nearly all the property; to escape productive labor; to control every element in the government; to keep the producers in ignorance and poverty; to deprive them of any influence in the government; to expropriate the great portion of all wealth produced in the nation; and to become an hereditary aristocracy, modelled primarily on that which had existed in Europe for centuries, and in which only minor reformations had occurred as a result of various violent upheavals.*

Thus it happened that during the early years of our government, titanic forces were joined in battle. Had it not been for Jefferson, we seriously doubt that republicanism could have survived at all; certainly, it could not have emerged victorious as it did with his election to the Presidency in 1800.

To promote his own candidacy, he neither lifted a finger nor uttered a single word. On the one hand, he hoped to escape the terrible ordeal; but, on the other, he believed that when a patriot is called to office by public mandate, it is his duty to accept and perform it to the utmost of his ability and capacity. And this is precisely what Jefferson did; in so doing, he declared that "our Argosy" shall now be placed "on her republican tack, and she will show by the beauty of her motion the skill of her builders... . A just and solid republican government maintained here, will be a standing monument for people in other countries and... will ameliorate the condition of man over a great portion of the globe."

No small accomplishment indeed!

The Price and Benefits of Republicanism

ME VI 63-73 James Madison 1-30-87

I am impatient to learn your sentiments on the late troubles in the Eastern States [Shay's Rebellion, etc.]... . They may conclude too hastily, that nature has formed man unsusceptible of any other government than that of force, a conclusion not founded in truth or experience.

Societies exist under three forms, sufficiently distinguishable. 1. Without government, as among our Indians. 2. Under governments, wherein the will of every one has a just influence; as is the case in England, in a slight degree, and in our States, in a great one. 3. Under governments of force; as is the case in all other monarchies, and in most of the other republics. To have an idea of the curse of existence under the last, they must be seen. It is a government of wolves over sheep. It is a problem, not clear in my mind, whether the first condition is not the best. But I believe it to be inconsistent with any great degree of population. The second state has a great deal of good in it. The mass of mankind under that, enjoys a precious degree of liberty and happiness. It has its evils, too; the principal of which is the turbulence to which it is subject.

But weigh this against the oppressions of monarchy, and it becomes nothing... . Even this evil is productive of good. It prevents the degeneracy of government, and nourishes a general attention to the public affairs. I hold it, that a little rebellion, now and then, is a good thing, and as necessary in the political world as storms in the physical. Unsuccessful rebellions, indeed, generally establish the encroachments on the rights of the people, which have produced them. An observation of this truth should render honest republican governors so mild in their punishment of rebellions, as not to discourage them too much. It is a medicine necessary for the sound health of government.

ME IX 279-301 Monsieur D'Ivernois 2-6-95

We have chanced to live in an age which will probably be distinguished in history, for its experiments in government on a larger scale than has yet taken place. But we shall not live to see the result. The grosser absurdities, such as hereditary magistracies, we shall see exploded in our day, long experience having already pronounced condemnation against them.

But what is to be the substitute? This our children or grandchildren will answer. We may be satisfied with the certain knowledge that none can ever be tried, so stupid, so unrighteous, so oppressive, so destructive of every end for which honest men enter into government, as that which their forefathers had established, and their fathers alone venture to tumble headlong from the stations they have so long abused. It is unfortunate, that the efforts of mankind to recover the freedom of which they have been so long deprived will be accompanied with violence, with errors, and even with crimes. But while we weep over the means, we must pray for the end.

ME X 216-18 John Dickenson 3-6-01

The storm through which we have passed, has been tremendous indeed. The tough sides of our Argosy have been thoroughly tried. Her strength has stood the waves into which she was steered, with a view to sink her. We shall put her on her republican tack, and she will now show by the beauty of her motion the skill of her builders. Figure apart, our fellow-citizens have been led and hoodwinked from their principles, by a most extraordinary combination of circumstances. But the band is removed, and they now see for themselves. I hope to see shortly a perfect consolidation, to effect which, nothing shall be spared on my part, short of the abandonment of the principles of our revolution.

A just and solid republican government maintained here, will be a standing monument and example for the aim and imitation of the people of other countries; and I join with you in the hope and belief that... our revolution and its consequences, will ameliorate the condition of man over a great portion of the globe. What a satisfaction have we in the contemplation of the benevolent effects of our efforts, compared with those of the leaders of the other side, who have discountenanced all advances in science as dangerous innovations, have endeavored to render philosophy and republicanism terms of reproach, to persuade us that men cannot be governed but by the rod, etc., [of iron].

Federalists and Republicans in Office

ME X 199-200 Dr. W. S. Barton 2-14-01

The republicans have been excluded from all offices from the origin of the division into Republican and Federalist. They have a reasonable claim to vacancies till they occupy their due share. My hope, however, is that the distinction will soon be lost, or at most that it will be only of republican and monarchist: that the body of the nation, even that part which French excesses forced over to the federal side, will rejoin the republicans, leaving only those who were pure monarchists, and who will be too few to form a sect.

ME X 241-45 Dr. Benjamin Rush 3-24-01

With regard to appointments, I have so much confidence in the justice and good sense of the federalists, that I have no doubt they will concur in the fairness of the position, that after they have been in the exclusive possession of all offices from the very first origin of party among us, to the 3d of March, at 9 o'clock in the night, no republican ever admitted, and this doctrine newly avowed, it is now perfectly just that the republicans should come in for the vacancies which may fall in, until something like an equilibrium in office be restored.

But the great stumbling block will be removals, which, though made on those just principles only on which my predecessor ought to have removed the same persons, will nevertheless be ascribed to removal on party principles. 1st. I will expunge the effects of Mr. A.'s indecent conduct, in crowding nominations after he knew they were not for himself, till 9 o'clock of the night, at 12 o'clock of which he was to go out of office. So far as they are during pleasure, I shall not consider the persons named, even as candidates of the office, nor pay the respect of notifying them that I consider what was done as a nullity. 2d. Some removals must be made for misconduct... . [But] I see but very few instances where past misconduct has been in a degree to call for notice.

ME X 273-78 Levi Lincoln 8-26-01

I had foreseen, years ago, that the first republican President who should come into office after all the places in the government had become exclusively occupied by federalists, would have a dreadful operation to perform. That the republicans would consent to a continuation of everything in federal hands, was not to be expected, because neither just nor politic. On him, then, was to devolve the office of the executioner, that of lopping off. I cannot say that it has worked harder than I expected. You know the moderation of our views in this business, and that we all concurred in them. We determined to proceed with deliberation. This produced impatience in the republicans, and a belief we meant to do nothing... .

I am satisfied that the heaping of abuse on me, personally, has been with the design and the hope of provoking me to make a general sweep of all federalists out of office. But as I have carried no passion into the execution of this disagreeable duty, I shall suffer none to be excited. The clamor which has been raised will not provoke me to remove one more, nor deter me from removing one less, than if not a word had been said on the subject.

ME X 319 Joseph Barlow 5-3-02

Our majority in the House of Representatives has been about two to one; in the Senate, eighteen to fifteen.

Republican Theory and Principles

FORD VII 14 M. de Meunier 1795

Our public economy is such as to offer drudgery and subsistence only to those entrusted with its administration, — a wise and necessary precaution against the degeneracy of the public servants.

BW 335-42 First Annual Message 12-8-01

Agriculture, manufacture, commerce, and navigation, the four pillars of our prosperity, are the most thriving when left free to individual enterprise... .

I indulge the pleasing persuasion that the great body of our citizens will cordially concur in honest and distinterested efforts which have for their object to preserve the general and State governments in their constitutional form and equilibrium; to maintain peace abroad, and order and obedience to the laws at home; to establish principles and practices of administration favorable to the security of liberty and prosperity, and to reduce expenses to what is necessary for the useful purposes of government... .

Other circumstances, combined with the increase of numbers, have produced an augmentation of revenue arising from consumption, in a ratio far beyond that of population alone; and though the changes of foreign relations now taking place so desirably for the world, may for a season affect this branch of revenue, yet weighing all probabilities of expense, as well as of income, there is reasonable ground of confidence that we may now safely dispense with all the internal taxes, comprehending excises, stamps, auctions, licenses, carriages, and refined sugars, to which the postage on newspapers may be added, to facilitate the progress of information, and that the remaining sources of revenue will be sufficient to provide for the support of government, to pay the interest on the public debts, and to discharge the principals in shorter periods than the laws or the general expectations had contemplated... .

These views, however, of reducing our burdens, are formed on the expectation that a sensible, and at the same time, salutary reduction, may take place in our habitual expenditures. For this purpose, those of the civil government, the army, and navy, will need revisal.

When we consider that this government is charged with the external and mutual relations only of these states; that the states themselves have principal care of our persons, our property, and our reputation, constituting the great field of human concerns, we may well doubt whether our organization is not too complicated, too expensive; whether offices and officers have not been multiplied unnecessarily, and sometimes injuriously to the service they were meant to promote.

I will cause to be laid before you an essay toward a statement of those who, under public employment of various kinds, draw money from the treasury or from our citizens. Time has not yet permitted a perfect enumeration, the ramifications of office being too multiplied and remote to be completely traced in the first trial. Among those who are dependent on executive discretion, I have begun the reduction of what was deemed necessary.

The expenses of the diplomatic agency have been considerably diminished. The inspectors of internal revenue who were found to obstruct the accountability of the institution, have been discontinued. Several agencies created by executive authority, on salaries fixed by that also, have been suppressed and should suggest the expediency of regulating that power by law, so as to subject its exercise to legislative inspection and sanction... .

Considering the general tendency to multiply offices and dependencies, and to increase expense to the ultimate term of burden which the citizen can bear, it behooves us to avail ourselves of every occasion which presents itself of taking off the surcharge; that it never may be seen here that, after leaving to labor the smallest portion of its earnings on which it can subsist, government shall itself consume the residue of what it was instituted to guard.

ME X 301-03 John Dickenson 12-19-01

My great anxiety at present is, to avail ourselves of our ascendency to establish good principles and good practices; to fortify republicanism behind as many barriers as possible, that the outworks may give time to rally and save the citadel, should that be again in danger. On their part, they [the federalists] have retired into the judiciary as a stronghold. There the remains of federalism are to be preserved and fed from the treasury, and from that battery all the works of republicanism are to be beaten down and erased... .

You will perhaps have been alarmed, as some have been, at the proposition to abolish the whole of the internal taxes. But it is perfectly safe... . The impost alone gives us ten or eleven millions annually, increasing at a compound ratio of six and two-thirds per cent. per annum, and consequently doubling in ten years. But leaving that increase for contingencies, the present amount will support the government, pay the interest on the public debt, and discharge the principal in fifteen years.

If the increase proceeds, and no contingencies demand it, it will pay off the principal in a shorter time. Exactly one-half of the public debt, to wit, thirty-seven millions of dollars, is owned in the United States. That capital, then, will be set afloat, to be employed in rescuing our commerce from the hands of foreigners, or in agriculture, canals, bridges, or other useful enterprises. By suppressing at once the whole internal taxes, we abolish three-fourths of the offices now existing, and spread over the land... .

ME XIV 46-52 Dr. Walter Jones 1-2-14

I would say that the people, being the only safe depository of power, should exercise in person every function which their qualifications enable them to exercise, consistently with the order and security of society; that we now find them equal to the election of those who shall be invested with their executive and legislative powers, and to act themselves in the judiciary, as judges in questions of fact; that the range of their powers ought to be enlarged... .

ME XV 46-47 Governor Plumer 7-21-16

I... place economy among the first and most important of republican virtues, and public debt as the greatest of the dangers to be feared. We see in England the consequences of the want of it, their laborers reduced to live on a penny in the shilling of their earnings, to give up bread, and resort to oatmeal and potatoes for food; and their landholders exiling themselves to live in penury and obscurity abroad, because at home the government must have all the clear profits of their land. In fact, they see the fee simple of the island transferred to the public creditors, all its profits going to them for the interest on their debt. Our laborers and landholders must come to this also, unless they severely adhere to the economy you recommend.

ME XV 281-84 Richard Rush 10-20-20

Were we to break [the Union] to pieces, it would damp the hopes and efforts of the good, and give triumph to those of the bad through the whole enslaved world. As members, therefore, of the universal society of mankind, and standing in high and responsible relation with them, it is our sacred duty to suppress passion among ourselves, and not to blast the confidence we have inspired of proof that a government of reason is better than one of force.

ME XV 23-27 Francis W. Gilmer 6-7-16

Our legislators are not sufficiently apprised of the rightful limits of their power; that their true office is to declare and enforce only our natural rights and duties, and to take none of them from us. No man has a natural right to commit aggression on the equal rights of another; and this is all from which the laws ought to restrain him; every man is under the natural duty of contributing to the necessities of the society; and this is all the laws should enforce on him; and, no man having a natural right to be the judge between himself and another, it is his natural duty to submit to the umpirage of an impartial third. When the laws have declared and enforced all this, they have fulfilled their functions; and the idea is quite unfounded, that on entering any society, we give up any natural right.

The trial of every law by one of these texts, would lessen much the labors of our legislators, and lighten equally our municipal codes.

ME XV 17-23 John Taylor 5-28-16

It must be acknowledged that the term *republic* is of very vague application in every language. Witness the self-styled republics of Holland, Switzerland, Genoa, Venice, Poland. Were I to assign to this term a precise and definite idea, I would say, purely and simply, it means a government by its citizens in mass, acting directly and personally, according to rules established by the majority, and that every other government is more or less republican, in proportion as it has in its composition, more or less of this ingredient of the direct action of its citizens.

Such a government is evidently restrained to very narrow limits of space and population. I doubt if it would be practicable beyond the extent of a New England township. The first shade from this pure element, which, like that of pure vital air, cannot sustain life of itself, would be where the powers of the government, being divided, should be exercised each by representatives chosen either *pro hac vice,* or for such short terms as should render secure the duty of expressing the will of their constituents. This I should consider as the nearest approach to a pure republic, which is practicable on a large scale of country or population.

And we have some examples of it in some of our State Constitutions, which, if not poisoned by priest-craft, would prove its excellence over all mixtures with other elements; and, with only equal doses of poison, would still be the best. Other shades of republicanism may be found in other forms of government, where the executive, judiciary, and legislative functions, and the different branches of the latter, are chosen by the people more or less directly, for longer terms of years, or for life, or made hereditary; or where there are mixtures of authorities, some dependent on, and others independent of, the people.

The further the departure from direct and constant control by the citizens, the less has the government of the ingredient of republicanism; evidently none where the authorities are hereditary, as in France, Venice, etc., or self-chosen, as in Holland; and little, where for life, in proportion as the life continues in being after the act of election... .

In our General Government, the House of Representatives is mainly republican; the Senate scarcely so at all, as not elected by the people directly;... the judiciary independent of the nation, their coercion by impeachment being found nugatory.

BW 464 82 Autobiography 1821

It is not by consolidation, or concentration of powers, but by their distribution, that good government is effected. Were not this great country already divided into States, that division must be made, that each might do for itself what concerns itself directly, and what it can do so much better than a distant authority. Every State again is divided into counties, each to take care of what lies within its local bounds; each county again into townships or wards, to manage minuter details; and every ward into farms, to be governed by its individual proprietor. Were we directed from Washington when to sow, when to reap, we should soon want bread.

It is by this partition of cares, descending in gradation from general to particular, that the mass of human affairs may best be measured for the good & prosperity of all.

The Two Parties in Society

ME VII 309-15 James Madison 3-15-89

I know there are some among us, who would now establish a monarchy. But they are inconsiderable in number and weight of character. The rising race are all republicans. We were educated in royalism; no wonder, if some of us retain that idolatry still. Our young people are educated in republicanism; an apostacy from that to royalism, is unprecedented and impossible.

ME IX 335-37 Philip Mazzei 4-24-96

The main body of our citizens, however, remain true to their republican principles; the whole landed interest is republican, and so is the great mass of talents. Against us are the Executive, the Judiciary... all the officers of the government, all who want to be officers, all timid men who prefer the calm of despotism to the boisterous sea of liberty, British merchants and Americans trading on British capital, speculators and holders in the banks and public funds, a contrivance invented for the purposes of corruption, and for assimilating us in all things to the rotten as well as the sound parts of the British model. It would give you a fever were I to name to you the apostates who have gone over to their heresies, men who were Samsons in the field and Solomons in the council, but who have had their heads shorn by the harlot England. In short, we are likely to preserve the liberty we have obtained only by unremitting labors and perils. But we shall preserve it; and our mass of weight and wealth on the good side is so great, as to leave no danger that force will ever be attempted against us. We have only to awake and snap the Lilliputian cords with which they have been entangling us during our first sleep, which succeeded our labors.

ME X 44-47 John Taylor 6-1-98

The republicans... say, that it was the irresistible influence and popularity of General Washington, played off by the cunning of Hamilton, which turned the government over to anti-republican hands, or turned the republicans chosen by the people into anti-republicans... . In every free and deliberating society, there must, from the nature of man, be opposite parties, and violent dissensions and discords; and one of these, for the most part, must prevail over the other for the longer or shorter time.

ME XI 53-54 John P. Mercer 10-9-04

What in fact is the difference of principle between the two parties here? The one desires to preserve an entire independence of the executive and legislative branches on each other, and the dependence of both on the same source — the free election of the people. The other party wishes to lessen the dependence of the Executive and of one branch of the Legislature on the people, some by making them hold for life, some hereditary, and some even for giving the Executive an influence by patronage or corruption over the remaining popular branch, so as to reduce the elective franchise to its minimum.

ME XIV 417-23 Joseph Cabell 2-2-16

What has destroyed liberty and the rights of man in every government which has ever existed under the sun? The generalizing and concentrating all cares and powers in one body, no matter whether of the autocrats of Russia or France, or of the aristocrats of the Venetian Senate.

ME XV 388-90 William T. Barry 7-2-22

I consider the party division of Whig and Tory the most wholesome which can exist in any government, and well worthy of being nourished, to keep out those of a more dangerous character.

ME XVI 73-74 Henry Lee 8-10-24

Men by their constitutions are naturally divided into two parties: 1. Those who fear and distrust the people, and wish to draw all powers from them into the hands of the higher classes. 2. Those who identify themselves with the people, have confidence in them, cherish and consider them as the most honest and safe, although not the most wise depository of the public interests. In every country these two parties exist, and in every one where they are free to think, speak, and write, they will declare themselves. Call them, therefore, Liberals and Serviles, Jacobins and Ultras, Whigs and Tories, Republicans and Federalists, Aristocrats and Democrats, or by whatever name you please, they are the same parties still, and pursue the same object. The last appellation of Aristocrat and Democrat is the true one expressing the essence of all.

ME XVI 92-97 William Short 1-8-25

Men, according to their constitutions, and the circumstances in which they are placed, differ in opinion. Some are Whigs, Liberals, Democrats, call them what you please. Others are Tories, Serviles, Aristocrats, etc. The latter fear the people, and wish to transfer all power to the higher classes of society; the former consider the people as the safest depository of power in the last resort; they cherish them therefore, and wish to leave in them all the powers to the exercise of which they are competent.

This is the division of sentiment now existing in the United States. It is the common division of Whig and Tory, or according to our denominations of republican and federalist; and is the most salutary of all divisions, and ought, therefore, be fostered, instead of being amalgamated. For, take away this, and some more dangerous principle of division will take its place. But there is really no amalgamation. The parties exist now as heretofore. The one, indeed, has thrown off its old name, and has not yet assumed a new one, although obviously consolidationists. And among those in the offices of every denomination, I believe it to be a bare minority.

9. The Federal vs. State Governments

Commentary

If there is a single word which could best characterize Jefferson it is perhaps constitutionalist; *and this was true because in the compact among the States which established the Union, he found — not fully but substantially — the principles necessary to create a true republican government and society, one which would serve principally the self-reliant producers who constituted the great majority of the nation.*

The Federalists or, as Jefferson called them, the Monocrats, wanted no Bill of Rights because, without it, the Constitution could more easily be subverted into an instrument for establishing a centralized and all-powerful autocracy. The same financial interests which conducted their successful assault upon the Constitution in 1913 under Woodrow Wilson and completed their assumption of power under Roosevelt after 1933, were the moving forces pressing for centralization — or consolidation — during Jefferson's lifetime. Under the leadership of Alexander Hamilton and with the acquiescence of Washington and John Adams, the rich and powerful almost succeeded between 1794 and 1800 in accomplishing their nefarious objectives. Had it not been for the fact that in their mad drive for total domination they discredited themselves in the eyes of the people; and had it not been for Jefferson and a few of his loyal friends, the history of this nation would have been totally different.

We quote extensively in another chapter from The Kentucky Resolutions *of 1798; here we reproduce in its entirety the other Jeffersonian declaration, the* Solemn Protest of the Commonwealth of Virginia, *prepared in collaboration with James Madison and adopted by its General Assembly, which sets forth the principles of a limited federal government and the rights and powers of the States reserved by and for them in the Constitution.*

We note elsewhere how, during his presidency, Jefferson rapidly reduced the national debt and why, consequently, the federal government would soon have large surplusses, which he wished to allocate to the States for the purpose of constructing roads, canals, colleges, universities, and libraries. However, he was certain that in order to do this, an amendment to the Constitution would be necessary

Jefferson Magnificent Populist

Under Adams, between 1796 and 1800, the Federalists sought by every possible means to increase federal taxation, the size of the bureaucracy, and the activities which it could perform. In order to justify the pressures for these, it relied on the phrase in the Constitution which empowers Congress to provide for the general welfare — an argument resurrected by the "Liberals" under F. D. Roosevelt. The Federalists cited this authority for building roads and canals; this, however, was only to serve as an entering wedge in a drive to establish a central government without any limitation.

Jefferson opposed all these Federalist policies because he knew that every central government seeks to become a despotism; that it does so by engaging in wars, creating a huge debt, developing large bureaucracies, levying onerous taxes, and finally regimenting and controlling the citizens of the nation.

He therefore declared that although we must suffer many infractions of the Constitution rather than dissolve the Union, there is one calamity that we will not, must not, tolerate: "submission to a government of unlimited power." And he added: "It is only when the hope cf avoiding this shall become absolutely desperate, that further forebearance could not be indulged." In short, should the federal government go to the lengths obviously intended when he wrote The Kentucky Resolutions *and* The Solemn Declaration of the Virginia Assembly, *the only proper recourse for the States would be secession or armed revolt.*

Jefferson declared that these two documents prevented the Federalists from achieving their objectives before 1800. And with his election to the Presidency in that year and an influx of republicans into the Congress, the tide was reversed. The national branch of the government became, as the Constitution intended, the instrument to carry on our foreign and interstate affairs, leaving all others to the States and to the people, as mandated in the 9th and the 10th Amendments.

Under Jefferson, Madison, and Monroe, the ship of state kept on its republican course; but under the administration of John Quincy Adams, beginning in 1825, a strong movement toward consolidation became evident, as Jefferson declared in a letter written only six months before his death. In this, he bemoans the fact that the executive, the courts, and the Congress itself were undermining the Constitution by transferring State powers to the federal government, thus moving closer to unlimited power. "Reason and argument," he declared, would be useless with these proponents of centralization; for "they are joined in a combination, some from incorrect views of government, some from corruption... and bold enough to go forward in defiance."

Should this process continue to the end, "there can be no hesitation" concerning the choice we must make — revolution. "But in the meantime, the States should be watchful to note every usurpation of their rights... ." But, he added, "We must have patience and longer endurance, then, with our brethren, while under delusion . . . and separate from our companions only when the sole alternatives left are the dissolution of our Union with them, or a submission to a government without limitation of power."

We need not doubt that had Jefferson lived during the reign of Franklin Delano Roosevelt, he would have advocated drastic reform; and, had that failed, he would have counselled the dissolution of the government and/or an armed revolt which, under the Constitution would have been possible, since all the States were to have well-armed militias, and the central government was to have no force by which to coerce or overpower them.

The Proper Functions of Federal and State Governments

ME VI 273-73 J. Blair 8-13-87

My idea is that we should be one nation in every case concerning foreign affairs, and separate ones in what is merely domestic... .

ME X 267-68 James Monroe 7-11-01

As to the mode of correspondence between the general and particular executives, [when]... . Comparing the two governments together, it is observable that in all those cases where the independent or reserved rights of the States are in question, the two executives, if they are to act together, must be exactly co-ordinate; they are, in those cases, each the supreme head of an independent government.

ME XV 326-29 Judge Spencer Roane 6-27-21

It is a fatal heresy to suppose that either our State governments are superior to the federal, or the federal to the States. The people... have divided the powers of government into two distinct departments, the leading characters of which are *foreign* and *domestic;* and they have appointed for each a distinct set of functionaries. These they have made co-ordinate, checking and balancing each other like the three cardinal departments in the individual States; each equally supreme as to the powers delegated to itself... or to its co-partner in the government... finally, the peculiar happiness of our blessed system is, that in differences of opinion between these different sets of servants, the appeal is to neither, but to their employers peaceably assembled by their representatives in convention. This is more rational than the *jus fortiores* or the cannon's mouth, the *ultima et sole ratio regum.*

ME XV 439-52 William Johnson 6-12-23

... there are two canons which will guide us safely in most of the cases. 1st. The capital and leading object of the Constitution was to leave with the States all authorities which respected their own citizens only, and to transfer to the United States those which respected citizens of foreign or other States: to make us several as to ourselves, but one as to all others... .

On every question of construction, [let us] carry ourselves back to the time when the Constitution was adopted, recollect the spirit manifested in the debates, and instead of trying what meaning may be squeezed out of the text, or invented against it, conform to the probable one in which it was passed... .

Can it be believed, that under the jealousies prevailing against the General Government, at the adoption of the Constitution, the States meant to surrender the authority of preserving order, of enforcing moral duties and restraining vice, within their own territory?... . Can any good be effected by taking from the States the moral rule of their own citizens, and subordinating it to the general authority, or to one of their corporations, which may justify forcing the meaning of words, hunting after possible constructions, and hanging inference on inference, from heaven to earth, like Jacob's ladder? Such an intention was impossible, and such a licentiousness of construction and inference, if exercised by both governments, as may be done with equal right, would equally authorize both to claim all power, general and particular, and break up the foundations of the union.

Laws are made for men of ordinary understanding, and should, therefore, be construed by the ordinary rules of common sense. Their meaning is not to be sought for in metaphysical subtleties, which may make anything mean everything or nothing, at pleasure. It should be left to the sophisms of advocates, whose trade it is, to prove that a defendant is a plaintiff, though dragged into court, *torto collo,* like Bonaparte's volunteers, into the field in chains, or that a power has been given, because it ought to have been given, *et alia talia.* The States supposed that by their tenth amendment, they had secured themselves against constructive powers... .

I ask for no straining of words against the General Government, nor yet against the States. I believe the States can best govern our home concerns, and the General Government our foreign ones. I wish, therefore, to see maintained that wholesome distribution of powers established by the Constitution for the limitation of both; and never to see all the offices transferred to Washington, where, further withdrawn from the eyes of the people, they may more secretly be bought and sold as at market.

ME VIII 275-78 Archibald Stuart 12-23-91

I wish to preserve the line drawn by the federal Constitution between the general and particular governments as it stands at present, and to take every prudent means of preventing either from stepping over it. Though the experiment has not yet had a long enough course to show us from which quarter encroachments are most to be feared, yet it is easy to foresee, from the nature of things, that the encroachments of the State governments will tend to an excess of liberty which will correct itself, (as in the late instance,) [Shay's Rebellion] while those of the General Government will turn to monarchy, which will fortify itself from day to day, instead of working its own cure, as all experience shows.

I would rather be exposed to the inconveniences attending too much liberty, than those attending too small a degree of it. Then it is important to strengthen the State governments; and as this cannot be done by any change in the federal constitution, (for the preservation of that is all we need contend for,) it must be done by the States themselves, erecting such barriers at the constitutional line as cannot be surmounted either by themselves or by the General Government.

The Proper Distribution of Governmental Powers

ME XVI 42-50 Major John Cartwright 6-5-24

Our Revolution commenced on more favorable ground. It presented us an album on which we were free to write what we pleased. We had no occasion to search into musty records, to hunt up royal parchments, or to investigate the laws and institutions of a semi-barbarous ancestry. We appealed to those of nature, and found them engraved on our hearts.

Yet we did not avail ourselves of all the advantages of our position. We had never been permitted to exercise self-government. When forced to assume it, we were novices in its science. Its principles and forms had entered little into our former education. We established, however, some, although not all its important principles. The constitutions of most of our States assert, that all power is inherent in the people; that they may exercise it by themselves, in all cases to which they think themselves competent... , or they may act by representatives, freely and equally chosen; that it is their right and duty to be at all times armed; that they are entitled to freedom of person, freedom of religion, freedom of property, and freedom of the press... .

Virginia, of which I am myself a native and resident, was not only the first of the States, but, I believe, I may say, the first of the nations of the earth, which assembled its wise men peaceably together to form a fundamental constitution, to commit it to writing, and place it among their archives, where every man should be free to appeal to its text... .

My own State... is now proposing to call a convention for amendment. Among other improvements, I hope they will adopt the subdivision of our counties into wards. The former may be estimated at an average of twenty-four miles square; the latter should be about six miles square each, and would answer to the hundreds of your Saxon Alfred. In each of these might be, 1st, an elementary school; 2d, a company of militia, with its officers; 3d, a justice of the peace and constable; 4th, each ward should take care of their own poor; 5th, their own roads; 6th, their own police; 7th, elect within themselves one or more jurors to attend the courts of justice; and 8th, give in at their folk-house, their votes for all functionaries reserved to their election. Each ward would thus be a small republic within itself... . The wit of man cannot devise a more solid basis for a free, durable, and well-administered republic.

With respect to our State and federal governments, I do not think their relations correctly understood by foreigners. They generally suppose the former subordinate to the latter. But this is not the case. They are coordinate departments of one simple and integral whole. To the State governments are reserved all legislation and administration, in affairs which concern their own citizens only, and to the federal government is given whatever concerns foreigners, or the citizens of other States; these functions being made federal. The one is the domestic, the other the foreign branch of the same government... .

The Limitations Upon Federal Power

ME XV 131-36 Albert Gallatin 6-16-17

You will have learned that an act for internal improvement, after passing both Houses, was negatived by the President [Madison]. The act was founded avowedly, on the principle that the phrase in the Constitution which authorizes Congress "to lay taxes, to pay the debts and provide for the general welfare," was an extension of the powers specifically enumerated to whatever would promote the general welfare; and this, you know, was the federal doctrine. Whereas, our tenet ever was, and, indeed, it is almost the only landmark which now divides the federalists from the republicans, that Congress had no unlimited powers to provide for the general welfare, but were restrained to those specifically enumerated; and that, as it was never meant they should provide for that welfare but by the exercise of the enumerated powers, so it could not have been meant they should raise money for purposes which the enumeration did not place under their action; consequently, that the specification of powers is a limitation of the purposes for which they may raise money.

I think the passage and rejection of this bill a fortunate incident. Every State will certainly concede the power; and this will be a national confirmation of the grounds of appeal to them, and will settle forever the meaning of this phrase, which, by a mere grammatical quibble, has countenanced the General Government in a claim of universal power. For in the phrase, "to lay taxes, to pay the debts and provide for the general welfare," it is a mere question of syntax, whether the two last infinitives are governed by the first or are distinct and co-ordinate powers; a question unequivocably decided by the exact definition of powers immediately following.

It is fortunate for another reason, as the States, in conceding the power, will modify it, either by requiring the federal ratio of expense in each State, or otherwise, so as to secure us against its partial exercise. Without this caution, intrigue, negotiation, and the barter of votes might become as habitual in Congress, as they are in those legislatures which have the appointment of officers, and which, with us, is called "logging," the term of the farmers for their exchanges of aid in rolling together the logs of their newly-cleared grounds.

BW 311-15 Opinion Against the Constitutionality of a National Bank 2-15-93

I consider the foundation of the Constitution as laid on this ground: That all "powers not delegated to the United States, by the Constitution, nor prohibited by it to the States, are reserved to the States or to the people." (Xth Amendment.) To take a single step beyond the boundaries thus specially drawn around the powers of Congress, is to take possession of a boundless field of power, no longer susceptible of any definition... .

Among the powers specially enumerated [are]: A power to lay taxes for the purpose of paying the debts of the United States... [and]

To lay taxes to provide for the general welfare of the United States, that is to say, "to lay taxes for *the purpose* of providing for the general welfare." For the laying of taxes is the *power,* and the general welfare the *purpose* for which the power is to be exercised. They are not to lay taxes *ad libitum for any purpose they please;* but only *to pay the debts or provide for the welfare of the Union.* In like manner, they are not *to do anything they please* to provide for the general welfare, but only to *lay taxes* for that purpose. To consider the latter phrase, not as describing the purpose of the first, but as giving a distinct and independent power to do any act they please, which might be for the good of the Union, would render all the preceding and subsequent enumerations of power completely useless.

It would reduce the whole instrument to a single phrase, that of instituting a Congress with power to do whatever would be for the good of the United States; and, as they would be the sole judges of the good or evil, it would be also a power to do whatever evil they please.

It is an established rule of construction where a phrase will bear either of two meanings, to give it that which will allow some meaning to the other parts of the instrument, and not that which would render all the others useless. Certainly no such universal power was meant to be given them. It was intended to lace them up straitly within the enumerated powers, and those without which, as means, these powers could not be carried into effect... .

The second general phrase is "to make all laws *necessary* and proper for carrying into execution the enumerated powers." But... . If such a latitude of construction be allowed to this phrase as to give any non-enumerated power, it will go to everyone, for there is no one which ingenuity may not torture into a *convenience* in some instance *or other,* to *someone* of so long a list of enumerated powers. It would swallow up all the delegated powers, and reduce the whole to one power, as before observed. Therefore it was that the Constitution restrained them to the *necessary* means, that is to say, to those means without which the grant of power would be nugatory... .

Can it be thought that the Constitution intended that... Congress should be authorized to break down the most ancient and fundamental laws of the several States; such as those against mortmain, the laws of alienage, the rules of descent, the acts of distribution, the laws of escheat and forfeiture, the laws of monopoly? Nothing but a necessity invincible by any other means, can justify such a prostitution of laws, which constitute the pillars of our whole system of jurisprudence. Will Congress be too straight-laced to carry the Constitution into honest effect unless they may pass over the foundation-laws of the State governments... ?

States Rights and Powers

ME IX 422-24 James Monroe 9-7-97

It is of immense consequence that the States retain as complete authority as possible over their own citizens. The withdrawing themselves under the shelter of a foreign [i.e. federal] jurisdiction is so subversive to order and so pregnant of abuse, that it may not be amiss to consider how far a law of *praemunire* [a refusal to obey the law] should be revised and modified, against all citizens who attempt to carry their causes before any other than the State courts, in cases where those other courts have no right to their cognizance. A plea to the jurisdiction of the courts of their State, or a reclamation of a foreign jurisdiction [i.e., the federal], if adjudged valid, would be safe, but if adjudged invalid, would be followed by the punishment of *praemunire* for the attempt.

ME XVII 442-48 The Solemn Declaration and Protest of the Commonwealth of Virginia, on the Principles of the Constitution 1798

We, the General Assembly of Virginia, on behalf, and in the name of the people thereof, do declare as follows:

The States in North America which confederated to establish their independence of the government of Great Britain, of which Virginia was one, became, on that acquisition, free and independent States, and as such, authorized to constitute governments, each for itself, in such form as it thought best.

They entered into a compact, (which is called the Constitution of the United States of America,) by which they agreed to unite in a single government as to their relations with each other, and with foreign nations, and as to certain other articles particularly specified. They retained at the same time, each to itself, the other rights of independent government, comprehending mainly their domestic interests.

For the administration of their federal branch, they agreed to appoint, in conjunction, a distinct set of functionaries, legislative, executive, and judiciary, in the manner settled in that compact: while to each, severally, and of course, remained its original right of appointing, each for itself, a separate set of functionaries, legislative, executive, and judiciary, also, for administering the domestic branch of their respective governments.

These two sets of officers, each independent of the other, constitute thus a *whole* of government, for each State separately; the powers ascribed to the one, as specifically made federal, exercised over the whole, the residuary powers, retained to the other, exercisable exclusively over its particular State, foreign herein, each to the others, as they were before the original compact.

To this construction of government and distribution of its powers, the Commonwealth of Virginia does religiously and affectionately adhere, opposing, with equal fidelity and firmness, the usurpation of either set of functionaries on the rightful powers of the other.

But the federal branch has assumed in some cases, and claimed in others a right of enlarging its own powers by constructions, inferences, and indefinite deductions from those directly given, which this assembly does declare to be usurpations of the powers retained to the independent branches, mere interpolations into the compact, and direct infractions of it.

They claim, for example, and have commenced the exercise of a right to construct roads, open canals, and effect other internal improvements within the territories and jurisdictions exclusively belonging to the several States, which this assembly does declare has not been given to that branch by the constitutional compact, but remains to each State among its domestic and unalienated powers, exercisable within itself and by its domestic authorities alone.

This assembly does further disavow and declare to be most false and unfounded the doctrine that the compact, in authorizing the federal branch to lay and collect taxes, duties, imposts, and excises to pay the debts and provide for the common defence and general welfare of the United States, has given them thereby a power to do whatever they may think, or pretend, would provide for the general welfare, which construction would make that, of itself, a compulsive government, without limitation of powers; but that the plain sense and obvious meaning were, that they might levy the taxes necessary to provide for the general welfare, by the various acts of power therein specified and delegated to them, and by no others.

Nor is it admitted, as has been said, that the people of these States, by not investing their federal branch with all the means of bettering their condition, have denied to themselves any which may effect that purpose; since, in the distribution of these means they have given to that branch those which belong to its department, and to the States have reserved separately the residue which belong to them separately. And thus by the organization of the two branches taken together, have completely secured the first object of human association, the full improvement of their condition, and reserved to themselves all the faculties of multiplying their own blessings.

Whilst the General Assembly thus declares the rights retained by the States, rights which they have never yielded, and which this State will never voluntarily yield, they do not mean to raise the banner of disaffection, or of separation from their compact. They know and value too highly the blessings of their Union as to foreign nations and questions arising among themselves, to consider every infraction as to be met by actual resistance. They respect too affectionately the opinions of those possessing the same rights under the same instrument, to make every difference of construction a ground of immediate rupture. They would, indeed, consider such a rupture as among the greatest calamities which could befall them; but not the greatest.

There is yet one greater, submission to a government of unlimited powers. It is only when the hope of avoiding this shall become absolutely desperate, that further forebearance could not be indulged. Should a majority of the co-parties, therefore, contrary to the expectation and hope of this assembly, prefer, at this time, acquiescence in these assumptions of power by the federal member of the government, we will be patient and suffer much, under the confidence that time, ere it be too late, will prove to them also the bitter consequences in which that usurpation will involve us all.

In the meanwhile, we will breast with them, rather than separate from them, every misfortune, save that only of living under a government of unlimited powers. We owe every other sacrifice to ourselves, to our federal brethren, and to the world at large, to pursue with temper and perseverance the great experiment which shall prove that man is capable of living in society, governing itself by laws self-imposed, and securing to its members the enjoyment of life, liberty, property, and peace; and further to show, that even when the government of its choice shall manifest a tendency to degeneracy, we are not at once to despair but that the will and the watchfulness of its sounder parts will reform its aberrations, recall it to original and legitimate principles, and restrain it within the rightful limits of self-government. And these are the objects of this Declaration and Protest.

Supposing then, that it might be for the good of the whole, as some of its co-States seem to think, that the power of making roads and canals should be added to those directly given to the federal branch, as more likely to be systematically and beneficially directed, than by the independent action of the several States, this commonwealth, from respect to these opinions, and a desire of conciliation with its co-States, will consent, in concurrence with them, to make this addition, provided it be done regularly by an amendment of the compact, in the way established by that instrument, and provided also, it be sufficiently guarded against abuses, compromises, and corrupt practices, not only of possible, but of probable occurrence.

And as a further pledge of the sincere and cordial attachment of this commonwealth to the union of the whole, so far as has been consented to by the compact called "The Constitution of the United States of America," (constructed according to the plain and ordinary meaning of its language, to the common intendment of the time, and of those who framed it;) to give also to all parties and authorities, time for reflection and for consideration, whether, under a temperate view of the possible consequences, and especially of the constant obstructions which an equivocal majority must ever expect to meet, they will still prefer the assumption of this power rather than its acceptance from the free will of their constituents; and to preserve peace in the meanwhile, we proceed to make it the duty of our citizens, until the legislature shall otherwise and ultimately decide, to acquiesce under those acts of the federal branch of our government, which we have declared to be usurpations, and against which, in point of right, we do protest as null and void, and never to be quoted as precedents of right.

We therefore do enact, and be it enacted by the General Assembly of Virginia, that all citizens of this commonwealth, and persons and authorities within the same, shall pay full obedience at all times to the acts which may be passed by the Congress of the United States, the object of which shall be the construction of post roads, making canals of navigation, and maintaining the same in any part of the United States, in like manner as if said acts were, *Totidem verbis,* passed by the legislature of this commonwealth.

The Drift Toward Centralization

ME I 290-92 The Anas

[Under the Treasury run by Hamilton] a system had there been contrived... which had introduced its poison into the government itself... . He [Washington] asked me to what proposition I alluded? I answered, to that in the report on manufactures, which, under the color of giving *bounties* for the encouragement of particular manufactures, meant to establish the doctrine, that the power given by the Constitution to collect taxes and provide for the *general welfare* of the United States, permitted Congress to take everything under their management which *they* should deem for the *public welfare,* and which is susceptible of the application of money; consequently that the enumeration of powers was not the description to which resort must be had, and did not at all constitute the limits of their authority; that this was a very different question from that of the bank, which was thought an incident to an enumerated power... .

ME X 63-67 John Taylor 11-26-98

It is a singular phenomenon, that while our State governments are the very *best in the world,* without exception or comparison, our General Government has, in the rapid course of nine or ten years, become more arbitrary, and has swallowed more of the public liberty than even that of England.

ME XIV 379-84 Charles Yancy 6-6-16

The functionaries of every government have propensities to command at will the liberty and property of their constituents. There is no safe deposit for these, but with the people themselves; nor can they be safe with them without information.

ME XVI 146-50 William B. Giles 12-26-25

I see, as you do, and with the deepest affliction, the rapid strides with which the federal branch of our government is advancing towards the usurpations of all the rights reserved to the States, and the consolidation in itself of all powers, foreign and domestic; and that too, by constructions which, if legitimate, leave no limits to their power.

Take together the decisions of the federal court, the doctrines of the President [John Quincy Adams], and the misconstructions of the constitutional compact acted on by the legislature of the federal branch, and it is but too evident, that the three ruling branches of that department are in combination to strip their colleagues, the State authorities, of the powers reserved by them, and to exercise themselves all functions foreign and domestic. Under the power to regulate commerce, they assume indefinitely that also over agriculture and manufactures, and call it regulation to take the earnings of one of these branches of industry, and that, too, the most depressed, and put them into the pockets of the other, the most flourishing of all. Under the authority to establish post roads, they claim that of cutting down mountains for the construction of roads, of digging canals, and aided by a little sophistry on the words "general welfare," a right to do, not only the acts to effect that, which are specifically enumerated and permitted, but whatsoever they shall think, or pretend, will be for the general welfare.

And what is our resource for the preservation of the Constitution? Reason and argument? You might as well reason and argue with the marble columns encircling them. The representatives chosen by ourselves? They are joined in the combination, some from incorrect views of government, some from corrupt ones, sufficient voting together to outnumber the sound parts; and with majorities only of one, two, or three, bold enough to go forward in defiance.

Are we then *to stand to our arms,* with the hot-headed Georgian? No. That must be the last resource, not to be thought of until much longer and greater sufferings. If every infraction of a compact of so many parties is to be resisted at once, as a dissolution of it, none can ever be formed which would last one year. We must have patience and longer endurance, then, with our brethren, while under delusion; give them time for reflection and experience of consequences; keep ourselves in a situation to profit by the chapter of accidents; and separate from our companions only when the sole alternatives left, are the dissolution of our Union with them, or submission to a government without limitation of powers.

Between these evils, when we must make a choice, there can be no hesitation. But in the meanwhile, the States should be watchful to note every material usurpation on their rights; to denounce them as they occur in the most peremptory terms; to protest against them as wrongs to which our present submission shall be considered, not as acknowledgments or precedents of right, but as temporary yielding to the lesser evil, until their accumulation shall overweigh that of separation.

I would go still further, and give to the federal member, by a regular amendment of the Constitution, a right to make roads and canals of intercommunication between the States, providing sufficiently against corrupt practices in Congress (log-rolling, etc.), by declaring that the federal proportion of each State of the moneys so employed, shall be in works within the State, or elsewhere with its consent, and with a due *salvo* of jurisdiction. This is the course which I think safest and best as yet.

ME XV 325 Judge Spencer Roane 3-9-21

The multiplication of public offices, increase of expense beyond income, growth and entailment of a public debt, are indications soliciting the employment of the pruning-knife; and I doubt not it will be employed; good principles being as yet prevalent enough for that.

10. Jefferson vs. Hamilton

Commentary

Certainly, neither in the career of Jefferson nor during the period in which he lived was there any conflict more fierce or constant than that which raged between the republicans and the Federalists. As Jefferson pointed out again and again, this was a struggle by the wealthy, the "well-born," the privileged, to perpetuate themselves in lives of idleness and luxury at the expense of the producers. They wished to re-create on this continent a socio-economic system like that of Europe; however, the independent proprietors, led by Jefferson, Madison, Monroe, Franklin, and others, were intent on creating what was then a revolutionary form of government, in which the self-reliant, middle-class citizens would create a political form responsible to them; in which its functionaries would be servants *instead of* masters; *which would be thrifty, economical, efficient, financially sound; and which would, above all, permit the producers to retain and enjoy the fruits of their own labor.*

The struggle began the moment the revolutionary war ended; and it boiled with virulence at the Constitutional Convention, where the Federalists, led by Alexander Hamilton, proposed that the president of the new republic should be elected for life and that he *would appoint the governors of all the states, who would likewise hold office for life. These executives were to have absolute veto power over all acts passed by their legislatures. The members of the federal senate were also to hold office for life and were to be elected by the landed aristocracy.*

However, the Convention to which fifty-five delegates had been sent by the states, was dominated by patriots; Hamilton left Philadelphia in frustration; and only thirty-nine individuals finally signed the proposed Constitution.

This defeat did not deter the Federalists from pursuing their objectives; if they could not obtain a king and a house of lords, they would try to prevent a Bill of Rights — which they declared unnecessary — or ignore it if it were added to the Constitution. They continued their machinations to provoke a war with France, colonize South America, increase taxation and the national debt, expand the size of the federal bureaucracy, and, by their own constructions of the Constitution, centralize political power and reduce the states to political nullities. Under Washington and even more under Adams, the Federalists monopolized federal offices, and, under the leadership of Hamilton, moved towards a position of total ascendancy. An excise law was passed, taxing the production of whiskey on individual farms; Pennsylvania was driven to the verge of armed revolt; Jefferson resigned as Secretary of State after writing a long letter to President Washington explaining his differences with Hamilton. Alien and Sedition laws were then passed; the XYZ delusion followed; publishers of republican papers were dragged from their beds in the middle of the night, convicted of sedition for opposing the government, and sentenced to prison.

In all this, the Federalists overreached themselves; and in 1800, the republicans, under the leadership of Jefferson, rode into power. As a reaction against this political development, the Federalists organized what became known as the Essex Junta, centered in Massachusetts, which had as its objective the dismemberment of the Union by the secession of several New England states. These malcontents, led by such men as Timothy Pickering, who had been involved in the X.Y.Z. delusion, Jefferson called traitors subsidized by England; he said that they were "combining with the oppressors of the earth to extinguish the last spark of human hope, that here, at length, will be preserved a model of government, securing to man his rights and the fruits of his own labor, by an organization constantly subject to his own will." This "crime," he continued, "if accomplished, would immortalize its perpetrators, and their names would descend in history with those of Roberspierre and his associates, as the guardian genii of despotism, and demons of human liberty."

However, as the election of 1804 proved, these subverters had little influence among the people; Jefferson was elected by a landslide and even Massachusetts gave him its support.

No matter how often defeated, the Federalists continued, under new names and guises, the pursuit of their objectives. During the war of 1812-14, they made their last determined effort toward nullification and disunion. Under the leadership of the Massachusetts faction, they held a convention in Hartford, Connecticut, which convened on December 15, 1814, where resolutions were passed advocating amendments to the Constitution which would weaken the southern states, reduce the influence of the western, and perhaps lead to actual secession. It also called for a subsequent convention to further their objectives.

However, the defeat of the British at New Orleans, the Peace of Ghent, and the complete victory over the British, spelled a defeat for the Federalists which compelled them to renounce their name and former objectives. Henceforeward they considered it a calumny to be told that they had once favored monarchy or disunion; but they were Federalists still — with new purposes: first, complete control over the judiciary; second, by the process which Jefferson called consolidation, gradually to transfer almost all the political powers of the states to the federal government. They meant also to create banking institutions and other wealthy corporations with an elite aristocracy in control; and thus, in due course, to accomplish the basic Hamiltonian objectives.

All these schemes were defeated under Andrew Jackson, and remained largely in limbo until Woodrow Wilson became president by deceit in 1912; and when, later, by every form of tergiversation, Franklin Delano Roosevelt became president in 1933, he succeeded in establishing the Federalist dreams of 1820-25 under the dictatorship of international financiers.

Rampant Federalism

ME XVI 92-97 William Short 1-8-25

When I arrived in New York in 1790... , I found a state of things, in the general society of the place, which I could not have supposed possible. Being a stranger there, I was feasted from table to table, at large set dinners, the parties generally from twenty to thirty. The revolution I had left, and that we had just gone through in the recent change of our government, being the common topics of conversation, I was astonished to find the general prevalence of monarchical sentiments, insomuch that in maintaining those of republicanism, I had always the whole company on my hands, never scarcely finding among them a single co-advocate in that argument, unless some old member of Congress happened to be present. The furthest that any one would go, in support of the republican features of our new government, would be to say, "the present Constitution is well as a beginning, and may be allowed a fair trial; but it is, in fact, only a stepping-stone to something better."...

... had it not been for the firm and determined stand then made by a counter-party, no man can say what our government would have been at this day. Monarchy, to be sure, is now defeated, and they wish it should be forgotten that it was ever advocated. They see that it is desperate, and treat its imputation to them as a calumny; and I verily believe that none of them have it now in direct aim.

Yet the spirit is not done away. The same party takes now what they deem the next best ground, the consolidation of the government; the giving to the federal member of the government, by unlimited constructions of the Constitution, a control over all the functions of the States, and the concentration of all power ultimately in Washington.

ME X 117-19 Robert R. Livingston 2-28-99

What person... would have believed that within so short a period, not only the jealous spirit of liberty which shaped every operation of our revolution, but even the common principles of English civilization, would be scouted, and the tory principle of passive obedience under the new-fangled names of *confidence* and *responsibility* become entirely triumphant? That the tories, whom in mercy we did not crumble to dust and ashes, could so have entwined us in their scorpion tails, that we cannot now move hand or foot?

Federalist Terrorism

ME I 280-82 The Anas

When General Washington was withdrawn, these *energumeni* of royalism, kept in check hitherto by the dread of his honesty, his firmness, his patriotism, and the authority of his name, now mounted on the car of State and free from control, like Phaeton on that of the sun, drove headlong and wild, looking neither to right nor to left, nor regarding but the objects they were driving at; until, displaying these fully, the eyes of the nation were opened, and a general disbandment of them from the public councils took place.

But... no man who did not witness it can form an idea of their unbridled madness, and the terrorism with which they surrounded themselves. The horrors of the French revolution, then raging, aided them mainly and... they were enabled by their stratagems of X.Y.Z., to which the historian [Marshall] was a leading mountebank, their tales of tub-plots, ocean massacres, bloody buoys, and pulpit lyings and slanderings, and maniacal ravings... to spread alarm into all but the firmest breasts... .

These transactions, now recollected but as dreams of the night, were then sad realities; and nothing rescued us from their liberticide effect, but the unyielding opposition of those firm spirits who sternly maintained their post in defiance of terror, until their fellow citizens could be aroused to their own danger, and rally and rescue the standard of the Constitution... .

Federalism and monarchism have languished from that moment, until their treasonable combinations with the enemies of their country during the late war, their plots of dismembering the Union, and their Hartford Convention, have consigned them to the tomb of the dead... ; and sure I am we may say, that we are indebted for the preservation of this point of ralliance, to that opposition of which so injurious an idea is so artfully insinuated and excited in this history [Marshall's *Life of Washington*].

Kinds of Federalists

ME X 245-48 General Henry Knox 3-27-01

I was always satisfied that the great body of those called federalists were real republicans as well as federalists. I know, indeed, there are monarchists among us. One character of these is in theory only, and perfectly acquiescent in our form of government as it is, and not entertaining a thought of destroying it merely on their theoretical opinions.

The second class, at the head of which is our quondam colleague [Hamilton] are ardently for introduction of monarchy, eager for armies, making more noise for a great naval establishment than better patriots, who wish it on a rational scale only, commensurate to our wants and our means.

This last class ought to be tolerated, but not trusted... .

ME X 319-22 Joel Barlow 5-3-02

The candid federalists acknowledge that their party can never more raise its head... . That [name] of federalism is become so odious that no party can rise under it. As the division into whig and tory is founded in the nature of man, the weakly and nerveless, the rich and the corrupt, see more safety and accessibility in a strong executive; the healthy, firm, and virtuous, feeling a confidence in their physical and moral resources, are willing to part with only so much power as is necessary for their good... .

ME XIII 206-13 John Melish 1-13-13

Among that section of our citizens called federalist, there are three shades of opinion. Distinguishing between the *leaders* and *people* who compose it, the *leaders* consider the English constitution as a model of perfection, some, with a correction of its vices, others, with all its corruptions and abuses. This last was Alexander Hamilton's opinion, which others, as well as myself, have often heard him declare, and that a correction of what are called its vices, would render the English an impracticable government. This government they wished to have established here, and only accepted and held fast, *at first,* to the present constitution, as a stepping stone to the final establishment of their favorite model... .

A weighty MINORITY, however, of these *leaders,* considering the voluntary conversion of our government into a monarchy as too distant, if not desperate, wish to break off from our Union its eastern fragment, as being, in truth, the hot-bed of American monarchism, with a view to a commencement of their favorite government, from whence the other States may gangrene by degrees, and the whole be brought finally to the desired point. For Massachusetts, the prime mover in this enterprise, is the last State in the Union to mean a *final* separation, as being of all the most dependent on the others... . At the head of this MINORITY is what is called the Essex Junto of Massachusetts. But the MAJORITY of these *leaders* do not aim at separation. In this, they adhere to the known principle of General Hamilton, never, under any views, to break the Union.

Anglomany, monarchy, and separation, then, are the principles of the Essex federalists. Anglomany and monarchy, those of the Hamiltonians, and Anglomany alone, that of the portion among the *people* who call themselves federalists. These last are as good republicans as the brethren whom they oppose, and differ from them only in their devotion to England and hatred of France which they have imbibed from their leaders. The moment that these leaders should avowedly propose a separation of the Union, or the establishment of regal government, their popular adherents would quit them to a man, and join the republican standard; and the partisans of this change, even in Massachusetts, would thus find themselves an army of officers without a soldier... .

This I verily believe, after an intimacy of forty years with the public councils and characters, is a true statement of the grounds on which they are at present divided, and that it is not merely an ambition for power.

Federalist Subservience to England

ME IX 75-78 James Monroe 5-5-93

All the old spirit of 1775, rekindling the newspapers from Boston to Charleston, proves this: and even the monocrat papers are obliged to publish the most furious philippics against England... .

In the meantime, H. is panic-struck, if we refuse our breach to every kick which Great Britain may choose to give it. He is for proclaiming at once the most abject principles, such as would merit and invite habitual insults; and indeed every inch of ground must be fought in our councils to desperation, in order to hold up the face of even a sneaking neutrality, for our votes are generally two and a half against one and a half. Some propositions have come from him which would astonish Mr. Pitt himself for their boldness. If we preserve even a sneaking neutrality, we shall be indebted for it to the President, and not to his councellors.

ME IX 419-21 Colonel Arthur Campbell 9-1-97

It is true that a party has risen up among us, or rather has come among us, which is endeavoring to separate us from all friendly connection with France, to unite our destinies with those of Great Britain, and to assimilate our government to theirs. Our lenity in permitting the return of the old tories, gave the first body to this party; they have been increased by large importations of British merchants and factors, by American merchants dealing on British capital, and by stock dealers and banking companies, who, by the aid of a paper system, are enriching themselves to the ruin of our country and swaying the government by their possession of the printing presses, which their wealth commands, and by other means not always honorable to the character of our countrymen. Hitherto, their influence and their system have been irresistible, and they have raised up an executive power which is too strong for the Legislature. But I flatter myself they have passed their zenith... .

All can be done peaceably by the people confining their choice of Representatives and Senators to persons attached to republican government and the principles of 1776, not office-hunters, but farmers, whose interests are entirely agricultural. Such men are the true representatives of the great American interest, and are alone to be relied on for expressing the proper American sentiment. We own gratitude to France, justice to England, good will to all, and subservience to none.

Federalists vs. Republicans

ME VIII 394-408 To the President of the United States 9-9-92

That I have utterly, in my private conversations, disapproved of the system of the Secretary of the Treasury, I acknowledge and avow; and this was not merely a speculative difference. His system flowed from principles adverse to liberty, and was calculated to undermine and demolish the Republic, by creating an influence of his department over the members of the Legislature. I saw this influence actually produced, and its first fruits to be the establishment of the great outlines of his project by the votes of the very persons who, having swallowed his bait, were laying themselves out to profit by his plans; and that had these persons withdrawn, as those interested in a question ever should, the vote of the disinterested majority was clearly the reverse of what they made it. These were no longer the votes then of the representatives of the people, but of deserters from the rights and interests of the people; and it was impossible to consider their decisions, which had nothing in view but to enrich themselves, as the measures of the fair majority, which ought always to be respected.

If, what was actually doing, begat uneasiness in those who wished for virtuous government, what was further proposed was not less threatening to the friends of the Constitution. For, in a report on the subject of manufactures, (still to be acted on,) it was expressly assumed that the General Government has a right to exercise all powers which may be for the *general welfare,* that is to say, all the legitimate powers of government; since no government has a legitimate right to do what is not for the welfare of the governed. There was, indeed, a sham limitation of the universality of this power *to cases where money is to be employed.* But about what is it that money cannot be employed? Thus the object of these plans, taken together, is to draw all the powers of government into the hands of the general Legislature, to establish means for corrupting a sufficient corps in that Legislature to divide the honest votes, and preponderate, by their own, the scale which suited, and to have the corps under the command of the Secretary of the Treasury, for the purpose of subverting, step by step, the principles of the Constitution which he has so often declared to be a thing of nothing, which must be changed.

Such views might have justified something more than mere expressions of dissent, beyond which, nevertheless, I never went... .

He charges me, 1st. With having written letters from Europe to my friends to oppose the present Constitution, while depending. 2d. With a desire of not paying the public debt... .

The first charge is most false. No man in the United States, I suppose, approved more of every tittle in the Constitution; no one, I believe, approved more of it than I did, and more of it certainly was disapproved by my accuser than by me, and of its parts most vitally republican. Of this the few letters I wrote on the subject... will be proof... . You will see there that my objection to the Constitution was, that it wanted a bill of rights securing the freedom of religion, freedom of the press, freedom from standing armies, trial by jury, and a constant habeas corpus act. Colonel Hamilton's was, that it wanted a king and a house of lords. The sense of America has approved my objection and added the bill of rights not the king and the house of lords. I also thought a longer term of service, insusceptible of renewal, would have made a President more independent. My country has thought otherwise; I have acquiesced implicitly. He wishes the General Government should have power to make laws binding the States in all cases whatsoever. Our country has thought otherwise; has he acquiesced?... .

The second charge is equally untrue. My whole correspondence while in France, and every word, letter and act on the subject, since my return, prove that no man is more ardently intent to see the public debt soon and sacredly paid off than I am. This exactly marks the difference between Colonel Hamilton's views and mine, that I would wish the debt paid tomorrow; he wishes it never to be paid, but always to be a thing wherewith to corrupt and manage the legislature.

ME XII 370-73 Doctor Walter Jones 3-5-10

In these discussions, Hamilton and myself were daily pitted in the Cabinet [of General Washington] like two cocks.

ME XV 430-46 William Johnson 6-12-23

The fact is, that at the formation of our government, many had formed their political opinions on European writings and practices, believing the experience of old countries, and especially of England, abusive as it was, to be a safer guide than mere theory. The doctrines of Europe were, that men in numerous associations cannot be restrained within the limits of order and justice, but by forces physical and moral, wielded over them by authorities independent of their will. Hence their organization of kings, hereditary nobles, and priests.

Still further to constrain the brute force of the people, they deem it necessary to keep them down by hard labor, poverty and ignorance, and to take from them, as from bees, so much of their earnings, as that unremitting labor shall be necessary to obtain a sufficient surplus barely to sustain a scanty and miserable life. And these earnings they apply to maintain their privileged orders in splendor and idleness, to fascinate the eyes of the people, and excite in them a humble adoration and submission, as to an order of superior beings.

Although few among us had gone all these lengths of opinion, yet many had advanced, some more, some less, on the way. And in the convention which formed our government, they endeavored to draw the cords of power as tight as they could obtain them, to lessen the dependence of the general functionaries on their constituents, to subject to them those of the States, and to weaken their means of maintaining the steady equilibrium which the majority of the convention had deemed salutary for both branches, general and local. To recover, therefore, in practice the powers which the nation had refused, and to warp to their own wishes those actually given, was the steady object of the federal party.

Ours, on the contrary, was to maintain the will of the majority of the convention, and of the people themselves. We believed, with them, that man was a rational animal, endowed by nature with rights, and with an innate sense of justice; and that he could be restrained from wrong and protected in right, by moderate powers, confided to persons of his own choice, and held to their duties by dependence on his own will. We believed that the complicated organization of kings, nobles, and priests, was not the wisest nor the best to effect the happiness of associated man; that wisdom and virtue were not hereditary; that the trappings of such a machinery, consumed by their expense, those earnings of industry they were meant to protect, and by the inequalities they produced, exposed liberty to sufferance. We believed that men, enjoying in ease and security the full fruits of their own industry, enlisted by all their interests on the side of law and order, habituated to think for themselves, and to follow their reason as their guide, would be more easily and safely governed, than with minds nourished in error, and vitiated and debased, as in Europe, by ignorance, indigence, and oppression.

The cherishment of the people then was our principle, the fear and distrust of them, that of the other party. Composed, as we were, of the landed and laboring interests of the country, we could not be less anxious for a government of law and order than were the inhabitants of the cities, the strongholds of federalism. And whether our efforts to save the principles and form of our Constitution have not been salutary, let the present republican freedom, order, and prosperity of our country determine.

History may distort truth, and will distort it for a time, by the superior efforts at justification of those who are conscious of needing it most... .

I have stated above that the original objects of the federalists were, 1st, to warp our government more to the form and principles of monarchy, and, 2d, to weaken the barriers of the State governments as coordinate powers. In the first they have been so completely foiled by the universal spirit of the nation, that they have abandoned the enterprise, shrunk from the odium of their old appellation, taken to themselves a participation of ours, and under the pseudo-republican mask, are now aiming at their second object, and strengthened by unsuspecting or apostate recruits from our ranks, are advancing fast towards an ascendency. I have been blamed for saying, that a prevalence of the doctrines of consolidation would one day call for reformation or *revolution.* I answer by asking if a single State of the Union would have agreed to the Constitution, had it given all powers to the General Government? If the whole opposition to it did not proceed from the jealousy and fear of every State, of being subjected to the other States in matters merely its own? And if there is any reason to believe the States more disposed now than then, to acquiesce in the general surrender of all their rights and powers to a consolidated government, one and undivided?

ME XV 490-94 Marquis de La Fayette 11-4-23

The Hartford convention, the victory of Orleans, the peace of Ghent, prostrated the name of federalism. Its votaries abandoned it through shame and mortification, and now call themselves republicans. But the name alone is changed, their principles are the same; for in truth, the parties of Whig and Tory, are those of nature. They exist in all countries, whether called by these names, or by those of Aristocrats and Democrats... , Ultras and Radicals, Serviles and Liberals. The sickly, weakly, timid man fears the people, and is a Tory by nature. The healthy, strong, and bold, cherishes them, and is formed a Whig by nature. The line of division now, is the preservation of State rights, as reserved in the Constitution, or, by strained constructions of that instrument, to merge all into a consolidated government. The Tories are for strengthening the Executive and General Government; the Whigs cherish the representative branch, and the rights of the States, as the bulwark against consolidation... .

Federalist Principles

The Original: Monarchist

ME I 284 The Anas

Alexander Hamilton condemning Mr. Adams' writings and most particularly "Davila," as having a tendency to weaken the present government, declared in substance as follows: "I own it is my own opinion... that the present government is not that which will answer the ends of society, by giving stability and protection to its rights, and that it will probably be found expedient to go into the British form."

ME IX 281-83 James Madison 4-3-94

Not that the monocrats and paper men in Congress want war, but they want armies and debts; and though we may hope that the sound part of Congress is now so augmented as to insure a majority in cases of general interest merely, yet I have always observed that in questions of expense, where members may hope either for offices or jobs for themselves or their friends, some few will be debauched, and that is sufficient to turn the decision where a majority is, at most, but small.

ME IX 323-26 James Madison 3-6-96

Hamilton's object from the beginning was to throw them [the finances of the government] into forms which should be utterly undecipherable. I ever said he did not understand their condition himself, nor was he able to give a clear view of the excess of our debts beyond our credits, nor whether we were diminishing or increasing the debt. My own opinion was that from the commencement of this government to the time I ceased to attend to the subject, we had been increasing our debt about a million dollars annually. If Mr. Gallatin would undertake to reduce this chaos to order, present us with a clear view of our finances, and put them into a form as simple as they will admit, he will merit immortal honor. The accounts of the United States ought to be, and may be made, as simple as those of a common farmer, and capable of being understood by common farmers.

ME I 290-92 The Anas

[Under the Secretary of the Treasury] a system had there been contrived... for deluging the States with paper money, instead of gold and silver; for withdrawing our citizens from the pursuits of commerce, manufacture, and other branches of useful industry, to occupy themselves and their capitals in a species of gambling, destructive of morality, which had introduced its poison into the government itself.

ME XII 436-37 David Howell 12-15-10

I have been ever opposed to the party so falsely called federalists because I believe them desirous of introducing into our government authorities hereditary or otherwise independent of the national will. These always consume the public contributions, and oppress the people with labor and poverty.

After Defeat: Consolidation

ME XI 24-26 Gideon Granger 4-16-04

The federalists know, that *eo nomine,* they are gone forever. Their object, therefore, is how to return to power under some other form. Undoubtedly, they have but one means, which is to divide the republicans, join the minority, and barter with them for the cloak of their name. I say *join the minority;* because the majority of the republicans, not needing them, will not buy them. The minority, having no other means of ruling the majority, will give a price for auxiliaries, and that price must be principle... . Thus a bastard system of federo-republicanism will rise on the ruins of the true principles of our revolution.

FORD X 263 Samuel H. Smith 1823

The federalists, baffled in their schemes to monarchise us, have given up their name... taken shelter among us under our name. But they have only changed the point of attack. On every question of the usurpation of State powers by the foreign General Government, the same men rally together, force the line of demarcation, and consolidate our government. The judges are at their head as heretofore, and are their entering wedge. The true republicans stand to the line, and will, I hope, die in it if necessary.

ME XVI 146-51 William B. Giles 11-26-25

Consolidation becomes the fourth chapter of the textbook of their history. But this opens with a vast accession of strength from their younger recruits, who, knowing nothing of them or the feelings or principles of '76, now look to a single and splended government of an aristocracy, founded on banking institutions, and moneyed corporations under the guise and cloak of their favored branches of manufactures, commerce, and navigation, riding and ruling over the plundered ploughman and beggard yeomanry. This will be to them a next best blessing to the monarchy of their first aim, and perhaps the surest stepping stone to it.

Nature of Incurable Federalists

ME X 238-40 William B. Giles 3-23-01

I do not speak of the desperadoes of the quondam faction in and out of the Congress. These I consider as incurables, on whom all attentions would be lost, and therefore will not be wasted. But my wish is, to keep their flock from returning to them.

ME X 273-76 Levi Lincoln 8-26-01

...the moment which should convince me that a healing of the nation into one is impracticable, would be the last moment of my wishing to remain where I am. (Of the monarchical federalists I have no expectations. They are incurables, to be taken care of in a mad house, if necessary, and on motives of charity.) I am much pleased, therefore, with your information that the republican federalists are still coming in to the desired union.

ME X 303-04 Benjamin Rush 12-20-01

Bitter men are not pleased with the suppression of taxes. Not daring to condemn the measure, they attack the motive; and too disingenuous to ascribe it to the honest one of freeing our citizens from unnecessary burdens and unnecessary systems of office, they ascribe it to a desire for popularity. But every honest man will suppose honest acts flow from honest principles, and the rogues may rail without intermission.

ME X 338-40 Levi Lincoln 10-25-02

Their bitterness increases with their desperation. They are trying slanders now which nothing could prompt but a gall which blinds their judgments as well as their consciences. I shall take no other revenge, than by a steady pursuit of economy and peace, and by the establishment of republican principles in substance and in form, to sink federalism into an abyss from which there shall be no resurrection for it.

ME X 443-45 Timothy Bloodworth 1-29-04

I know indeed there are some characters who have been too prominent to retract, too proud and impassioned to relent, too greedy after office and profit to relinquish their longings, and who have covered their devotion to monarchism under the mantle of federalism, who never can be cured of their enmities. These are incurable maniacs, for whom the hospitable doors of Bedlam are ready to open, but they are permitted to walk abroad while they refrain from personal assault.

ME X 334-37 Robert Livingston 10-10-02

You will have seen by our newspapers that... the federalists have opened all their sluices of calumny. They say we lied them out of power, and openly avow they will do the same to us. But it was no lies or arguments on our part which dethroned them, but their own foolish acts, sedition laws, taxes, extravagances and heresies. Porcupine, their friend, wrote them down. Callendar, their new recruit, will do the same. Every decent man among them revolts at their filth; and there cannot be a doubt, that were a Presidential election to come on this day, they would certainly have but three New England States... .

ME XI 15-16 Elbridge Gerry 3-3-04

I sincerely regret that the unbounded calumnies of the federal party have obliged me to throw myself on the verdict of my country for trial, my great desire having been to retire, at the end of the present term, to a life of tranquillity; and this was my decided purpose when I entered into office. They force my continuance. If we can keep the vessel of the State as already in her course for another four years, my earthly purposes will be accomplished, and I shall be free to enjoy, as you are doing, my family, my farm, and my books.

ME XII 9-10 Richard M. Johnson 3-10-08

[After the federalists were defeated], Lamentations and invective were all that remained to them. This last was naturally directed against the agent selected to execute the multiplied reformations which their heresies had rendered necessary. I became, of course, the butt of everything which reason, ridicule, malice, and falsehood could supply. They have concentrated all their hatred on me, till they have really persuaded themselves, that my retirement will abate some of their disaffection to the government of their country, and that my successor will enter on a calmer sea than I did... . Federalism is dead, without even the hope of... resurrection.

ME XIII 72-4 General Henry Dearborn 8-14-11

Tell my old friend, Governor Gerry, that I give him glory for the rasping with which he rubbed down his herd of traitors. Let them [the federalists] have justice and protection against personal violence, but no favor. Powers and preeminences conferred on them are daggers put into the hands of assassins, to be plunged into our own bosoms in the moment the thrust can go home to the heart. Moderation can never reclaim them. They deem it timidity, and despise without fearing, the tameness from which it flows. Backed by England, they never lose the hope that their day is to come, when the terrorism of their earlier power is to be merged in the more gratifying system of deportation and the guillotine.

Federalist Conspiracies and Treason

ME XII 76-77 Doctor Thomas Leib 6-23-08

The other branch of the Federalists who are so in principle as well as in name, disapprove of the republican principle and features of our Constitution, and would, I believe, welcome any public calamity (war with England excepted) which might lessen the confidence of our country in those principles and forms.

ME XII 233-37 Washington Boyd 1-20-09

We know that the government of England, maintaining itself by corruption at home, uses the same means in other countries in which she has any jealousy, by subsidizing agitators and traitors among them to distract and paralyze them. She sufficiently manifests that she has no disposition to spare ours. We see in the proceedings in Massachusetts, symptoms which plainly indicate such a course, and we know as far as such practices can ever be dragged into light, that she has practised and with success on leading individuals of that State. Nay, further, we see those individuals acting on the very plan which our information had warned us was settled between the parties. These elements of explanation, history cannot fail of putting together in recording the crime of combining with the oppressors of the earth to extinguish the last spark of human hope, that here, at length, will be preserved a model of government, securing to man his rights and the fruits of his labor, by an organization constantly subject to his own will.

The crime indeed, if accomplished, would immortalize its perpetrators and their names would descend in history with those of Robespierre and his associates, as the guardian genii of despotism, and demons of human liberty. I do not mean to say that all who are acting with these men are under the same motives. I know some of them personally to be incapable of it. Nor was that the case with the disorganizers and assassins of Paris. Delusions there, and party perversions here, furnish unconscious assistants to the hired actors in these atrocious scenes.

But I have never entertained one moment's fear on this subject. The people of this country enjoy too much happiness to risk it for nothing; and I have never doubted that whenever the incendiaries of Massachusetts should venture openly to raise the standard of separation, its citizens would rise in mass and do justice themselves to their own parricides.

ME XVI 146-51 William Giles 12-26-25

I doubt whether a single fact, known to the world, will carry as clear conviction to it, of the correctness of our knowledge of the treasonable views of the federal party of that day, as that disclosed by this, the most nefarious and daring attempt to dissever the Union, of which the Hartford Convention was a subsequent chapter; and both of these having failed, consolidation became the fourth chapter of the text book of their history.

Unifying the Nation Under Republicanism

ME X 263-66 Levi Lincoln 7-11-01

We are proceeding gradually in the regeneration of offices, and introducing republicans to some share of them. I do not know that it will be pushed further than was settled before you went away, except as to Essex men. I must ask you to make out a list of those in office in yours and neighboring States, and to furnish me with it... amiable monarchists are not safe subjects of republican confidence... .

Our gradual reformations seem to produce good effects everywhere except in Connecticut. Their late session of legislature has been more intolerant than all others... . I am sincerely sorry to see the inflexibility of the *federal* spirit there, for I cannot believe they are all *monarchists.*

ME X 176-80 Robert R. Livingston 12-14-00

The Constitution to which we are all attached was meant to be republican... . Yet we have seen it so interpreted and administered, as to be truly what the French have called, a *monarchie masque.* Yet so long has the vessel run on this way and been trimmed to it, that to put her on her republican tack will require all the skill, the firmness and the zeal of her ablest and best friends. It is a crisis which calls on them, to sacrifice all other objects, and repair to her aid in this momentous operation... . It is essential to assemble in the outset persons to compose our administration, whose talents, integrity, and revolutionary name and principles may inspire the nation at once, with undoubted confidence, and impose an awful silence on all the maligners of republicanism; as may suppress in embryo the purpose avowed by one of their most daring and effective chiefs, of beating down the administration... .

Though I have been too honorably placed in front of those who are to enter the breach so happily made, yet the energies of every individual are necessary, and in the place where his energies can most serve the entire nation.

Come forward then, my dear Sir, and give us the aid of your talents and the weight of your character towards the new establishment of republicanism; I say, for its new establishment; for hitherto we have seen only its travesty.

ME X 245-48 General Henry Knox 3-27-01

I am aware that the necessity of a few removals for legal oppressions, delinquencies, and other official malversations, may be misconstrued as done for political opinions, and produce hesitation in the coalition so much to be desired; but the extent of these will be too limited to make permanent impressions.

In the class of removals, however, I do not rank the new appointments which Mr. A. crowded in with whip and spur from the 12th of December, when the event of the election was known, and, consequently, that he was making appointments, not for himself, but his successor, until 9 o'clock of the night, at 12 o'clock of which he was to go out of office... . I consider the nominations as nullities, and will not view the persons appointed as even candidates for *their* office, much less as possessing it by any title meriting respect.

ME X 387-89 Joseph Nicholson 5-13-03

I have no doubt the agitation of the public mind on the continuance of tories in office is excited in some degree by those who want to get in themselves. However, the mass of those affected by it can have no views of that kind. It is composed of such of our friends as have a warm sense of the former intolerance and present bitterness of our adversaries, and they are not without excuse... .

Nor are they [the Federalists] protected in their places by any right they have to more than a just proportion of them, and still less by their own example while in power; but by considerations respecting the public mind. This tranquillity seems necessary to predispose the candid part of our fellow-citizens who have erred and strayed from their ways, to return again to them, and to consolidate once more that union of will, without which the nation will not stand firm against foreign force and intrigue... .

We laid down our line of proceedings on mature inquiry and consideration in 1801, and have not departed from it. Some removals [have been made] to make room for some participation for the republicans... . Pursuing our object of harmonizing all good people of whatever description, we shall steadily adhere to our rule, and it is with sincere pleasure I learn that it is approved by the more moderate part of our friends.

ME X 360-62 Colonel Benjamin Hawkins 2-18-03

In the public councils, the federal party hold still one-third. This, however, will lessen, but not exactly to the standard of the people; because it will be forever seen that of bodies of men even elected by the people, there will always be a greater proportion aristocratic than among their constituents.

The present administration had a task imposed on it which was unavoidable, and could not fail to exert the bitterest hostility in those opposed to it. The preceding administration left ninety-nine out of every hundred in public offices of the federal sect. Republicanism had been the mark of Cain which had rendered those who bore it exiles from all portion of the trusts and authorities of their country. This description of citizens called imperiously and justly for a restoration of right. It was intended, however, to have yielded to this in so moderate a degree as might conciliate those who had obtained exclusive possession; but as soon as they were touched, they endeavored to set fire to the four corners of the public fabric, and obliged us to deprive of the influence of office several who were using it with activity and vigilance to destroy the confidence of the people in their government, and thus to proceed in the drudgery of removal farther than would have been, had not their own hostile enterprises rendered it necessary in self-defence.

But I think it will not be long before the whole nation will be consolidated in their ancient principles, excepting a few who have committed themselves beyond recall, and who will retire to obscurity and settled disaffection.

11. Subversion of the Judiciary

Commentary

In his discussions concerning the judiciary, Jefferson was always the defender of the people, the producers, the useful citizens of the republic. He declared that they and they alone were entitled to power, for they were the only truly honest and worthy depositories thereof.

Well aware that we must have government with definite powers, he was always extremely jealous of those entrusted to administer it; knowing also that there must be a strong judiciary to prevent injustice, he was — during the earlier phase of his career — more concerned with granting judges independence, firm tenure, and adequate compensation, than over possible dangers resulting from their usurpation of power. He therefore stated that such men as his former mentor, George Wythe, could be entrusted with almost unrestricted authority.

However, the day arrived when his attitude underwent, first, a gradual, then a complete reversal. Not long after the ratification of the Constitution — while Hamilton exercised dominant influence — the federalists crept into the judiciary and Jefferson developed second thoughts concerning the wisdom of giving them independence and life-tenure.

When Jefferson assumed the presidency in 1801, he suffered his first great shock in relation to the judiciary. On his last night in office, as well as during the period preceding, John Adams busied himself appointing leading federalists to high office, especially in the judiciary, including John Marshall as Chief Justice of the Supreme Court. Jefferson condemned this action again and again (cf. letter to Benjamin Rush, 1-16-11 and to William Johnson, 6-12-23). These political enemies, thus entrenched with life-tenure, became and remained a thorn in his side throughout life.

The conflict over the judiciary was simply an integral part of the titanic struggle waged between federalists led by Hamilton, and the republicans, led by Jefferson, the outcome of which determined the fate of the new-born nation. The former wanted a king with a privileged, landed aristocracy in control of the government; the latter wanted a responsible and representative form which would serve the interests of the vast mass of productive citizens. When, as a result of the outrages unsuccessfully attempted to accomplish their objectives, the federalists were thrown out of office in 1800-01, they concentrated their efforts on a single goal: namely, to transfer the powers mandated to the states by the Constitution to the control of the General Government, a process which Jefferson called consolidation and which he dedicated the remainder of his life to combat and prevent. And, since the federalists lost control of the executive and legislative branches after 1800, they retired into the judiciary, where, under the leadership of John Marshall, they attempted by every means conceivable to reduce the states into political non-entities and to increase the income, power, and functions of the federal government far beyond anything contemplated by the Founding Fathers.

"When all government, domestic and foreign," declared Jefferson, "in little as in great things, shall be drawn to Washington as the center of power, it will render powerless the checks provided of one government on another, and will become as venal and oppressive as the government from which we separated." The accessions of the republicans to a power which they held substantially from 1801 to 1912, prevented this disaster; but under Woodrow Wilson and much more under Franklin Delano Roosevelt, virtually all the dreams and purposes of the Hamiltonians were realized for the subversion of Constitutional government in the United States.

Jefferson did not mince words; when the Supreme Court, under John Marshall, effected the acquittal of Aaron Burr, he accused him and it of nothing less than complicity in treason. Jefferson hoped and believed that this would bring about an amendment to the Constitution placing the justices under limited terms and some definite control; in this, he was disappointed, and he predicted a drift of the nation into centralized autocracy.

The Supreme Court, he declared, had become "the subtle corps of sappers and miners constantly working underground to undermine our Constitution from a co-ordinate of a general and special government to a general and supreme one alone. This will lay all things at their feet. ...I will say, that 'against this every man should raise his voice,' and, more, should uplift his arm... ." In short, armed revolution might be necessary as a final solution for this judicial usurpation.

We should note, however, that the spectacular impeachment trial of Samuel Chase in the U.S. Senate in 1804-05, had definite and beneficial results: for since that day, no Supreme Court justice has ever dared to pervert and abuse his position of trust and power in the manner of this contemptuous and contemptible tyrant.

The Jury: Our Rock of Refuge

ME VII 404-08 Thomas Paine 7-11-89

I consider that [the trial by jury] as the only anchor ever yet imagined by man, by which a government can be held to the principles of its constitution.

ME VII 319-24 Colonel Humphreys 3-18-89

[Our new Constitution] should have established trials by the people themselves, that is to say, by jury.

ME XV 480-90 M. Coray 1-31-23

...we call in a jury of the people to decide all controverted matters of fact, because to that investigation, they are entirely competent, leaving thus as little as possible, merely the law of the case, to the decision of the judges. And true it is that the people, especially when moderately instructed, are the only safe, because the only honest, depositories of the public rights... .

Trial by jury is the best of all safeguards for the person, the property, and the fame of every individual.

ME XV 32-44 Samuel Kercheval 7-12-16

The juries [are] our judges of fact, and of law when they choose it... .

ME VII 422-23 M. L'Abbe Arnoud 7-19-89

They [the people] are not qualified to *judge* questions of *law*, but they are very capable of judging questions of *fact*. In the form of juries, therefore, they determine all matters of fact, leaving to permanent judges, to decide the law resulting from those facts. But we all know that permanent judges acquire an *esprit de corps;* that... they are liable to be tempted by bribery; that they are misled by favor, by relationship, by a spirit of party, by a devotion to the executive or legislative power; that it is better to leave a cause to the decision [and to]... the opinion of twelve honest jurymen [than to a biased judge]... . It is in the power, therefore, of the juries, if they think permanent judges are under any bias whatever, in any cause, to take on themselves to judge the law as well as the fact. They never exercise this power but when they suspect partiality in the judges; and by the exercise of this power, they have been the firmest bulwarks of English liberty.

Early Opinions in Regard to the Judiciary

ME IV 258-59 George Wythe July 1776

The dignity and stability of government in all its branches, the morals of the people, and every blessing of society, depend so much upon an upright and skillful administration of justice, that the judicial power ought to be distinct both from the legislature and executive, and independent of both, that so it may be a check on both, as both should be checks on that. The judges, therefore, should always be men of learning and experience in the laws, of exemplary morals, great patience, calmness and attention;... they should not be dependent upon any man or body of men. To these ends, they should hold estates for life in their offices, or, in other words, their commissions should be during good behavior, and their salaries ascertained and established by law.

For misbehavior, the grand inquest of the colony, the house of representatives, should impeach them before the governor and council, when they should have time and opportunity to make their defense; but, if convicted, should be removed from their offices, and subject to such punishment as shall be thought proper.

ME VII 309-15 James Madison 3-15-89

...the judiciary... if rendered independent, and kept strictly to their department, merits great confidence for their learning and integrity. In fact, what degree of confidence would be too much, for a body of such men as composed of Wythe, Blair, and Pendelton?

ME IX 233-36 E. C. Genet 9-9-93

The courts of justice exercise the sovereignty of this country, in judiciary matters; are supreme in these, and liable neither to control nor opposition from any other branch of the government.

ME VIII 275-78 Archibald Stuart 12-23-91

Render the judiciary respectable by every possible means, with firm tenure in office, competent salaries, and reduction in their numbers... . This branch of the government will have the weight of the conflict on their hands, because they are the last appeal to reason.

Federalist Penetration of the Judiciary

ME X 301-03 John Dickenson 12-19-01

...they [the federalists] have retired into the judiciary as a stronghold. There the remains of federalism are to be preserved and fed from the treasury, and from that battery, all the works of republicanism are to be beaten down and erased. By a fraudulent use of the Constitution, which has made judges irremovable, they have multiplied useless judges merely to strengthen their phalanx.

ME XI 49-53 Mrs. John Adams 9-11-04

But the opinion which gives to the judges the right to decide what laws are constitutional, and what not, not only for themselves in their own sphere of action, but for the legislature and executive also, in their spheres, would make the judiciary a despotic branch.

ME XI 185-86 James Bowdoin 4-2-07

The fact is, that the federalists make Burr's cause their own, and exert their whole influence to shield him from punishment... . And it is unfortunate that federalism is still predominant in our judiciary department, which is consequently in opposition to the legislative and executive branches, and is able to baffle their measures often.

ME XI 187-91 William B. Giles 4-20-07

Your favor... on the subject of Burr's offenses, was received... .

The first ground of complaint was the supine inattention of the administration to the treason [Burr's] stalking through the land... . Aided by no process or facilities from the *federal* courts, but frowned on by their new-born zeal for the liberty of those whom we would not permit to overthrow the liberties of their country, we can expect no revealments from the accomplices of the chief offender. Of treasonable intentions, the judges have been obliged to confess there is probable appearance. What loophole they will find in the case, when it comes to trial, we cannot foresee... .

[Chief Justice Marshall refused to indict Burr until legal proofs of his guilt could be obtained, which would require several months. Because of this and later Supreme Court complicity at the trial itself, Burr was acquitted in Richmond, Virginia, where Marshall presided, whom Jefferson accused as equally guilty with the accused. Although there were a hundred prosecution witnesses present, Marshall permitted only one to testify].

If there ever had been an instance in this or the preceding administrations, of federal judges so applying principles of law as to condemn a federal or acquit a republican offender, I should have judged them in the present case with more charity. All this, however, will work well. The nation will judge both the offender and judges for themselves. If a member of the executive or legislature does wrong, the day will never be far distant when the people will remove him. They will see, then, and amend the error in our Constitution, which makes any branch independent of the nation. They will see that one of the great co-ordinate branches of the government, setting itself in opposition to the other two, and to the common sense of the nation, proclaims immunity to that class of offenders which endeavors to overturn the Constitution, and are themselves protected in it by the Constitution itself; for impeachment is a farce which will not be tried again.[a] If their protection of Burr produces this amendment, it will do more good than his condemnation would have done.

On the Separation and Equality of Powers

ME XI 213-16 George Hay 6-2-07

A judge... cannot sit on a bench without a commission, or a record of a commission; and the Constitution having given to the judiciary branch no means of compelling the executive either to *deliver* a commission, or to make a record of it, shows it did not intend to give the judiciary that control over the executive, but that it should remain in the power of the latter to do it or not. Where different branches have to act in their respective lines, finally, and without appeal, under any law, they may give to it different and opposite constructions... . In the cases of Callendar and others, the judges determined the sedition act was valid under the Constitution, and exercised their regular powers of sentencing them to fine and imprisonment. But the executive determined that the sedition act was a nullity under the Constitution, and exercised his regular power of prohibiting the execution of the sentence, or rather of executing the real law, which protected the acts of the defendants... .

On this construction, I have hitherto acted; and on this I shall ever act, and maintain it with the powers of the government, against any control which may be attempted by the judges, in subversion of the independence of the executive and Senate within their peculiar department... . I have long wished for a proper occasion to have the gratuitous opinion in Marbury *v.* Madison brought before the public, and denounced as not law; and I think the present a fortunate one, because it occupies such a place in the public attention.

ME XI 239-42 George Hay 6-20-07

The leading principle of our Constitution is the independence of the legislature, executive, and judiciary of each other, and none are more zealous of these than the judiciary... . The intention of the Constitution, that each branch should be independent of the others, is further manifested

a. This is a reference to the unsuccessful attempt in the United States Senate in 1805 to remove Associate Justice Samuel Chase from the Supreme Court by impeachment because of his outrageous bias and unethical conduct, a procedure which has never been repeated.

by the means it has furnished to each, to protect itself from enterprises of force attempted on them by the others, and to none has it given more effectual or diversified means than to the executive.

ME XV 212-16 Judge Spencer Roane 9-6-19

If [as the Federalists say] "the judiciary is the last resort in relation to the other departments of the government,"... , then indeed is our Constitution a complete *felo de so.* For... . The Constitution, on this hypothesis, is a mere thing of wax in the hands of the judiciary, which they may twist and shape into any form they may please. It should be remembered, as an axiom of eternal truth in politics, that whatever power in any government is independent, is absolute also; in theory only, at first, while the spirit of the people is up, but in practice, as fast as that relaxes. Independence can be trusted nowhere but with the people in mass. They are inherently independent of all but moral law... .

On coming into office, I released these individuals [who had been imprisoned under the Sedition Act], by the power of pardon committed to executive discretion, which could never be more properly exercised than where citizens were suffering without the authority of law, or, which was equivalent, under a law unauthorized by the Constitution, and therefore null.

CE VII 177-79 Mr. Jarvis 9-28-20

You seem... to consider the judges the ultimate arbiters of all constitutional questions; a very dangerous doctrine indeed, and one which would place us under the despotism of an oligarchy. Our judges... and their power [are] the more dangerous as they are in office for life, and are not responsible, as the other functionaries are, to the elective control. The Constitution has erected no such single tribunal, knowing that to whatever hands confided, with the corruptions of time and party, its members would become despots. It has more wisely made all the departments co-equal and co-sovereign within themselves... . When the legislative or executive functionaries act unconstitutionally, they are responsible to the people in their elective capacity. The exemption of the judges from that is quite dangerous enough. I know of no safe depository of the ultimate powers of the society, but the people themselves... .

ME XV 439-52 Judge William Johnson 6-12-23

Among the midnight appointments of Mr. Adams, were commissions to some federal justices of peace for Alexandria. These were signed and sealed by him, but not delivered. I found them on the table of the department of State, on my entrance into office, and I forbade their delivery. Marbury, named in one of them, applied to the Supreme Court for a mandamus to the Secretary of State (Mr. Madison) to deliver the commission intended for him. The Court determined at once, that, being an original process, they had no cognizance of it; and therefore the question before them was ended.

But the Chief Justice went on to lay down what the law would be, had they jurisdiction of the case, to-wit: that they should command the delivery. The object was clearly to instruct any other court having the jurisdiction, what they should do if Marbury should apply to them. Besides the impropriety of this gratuitous interference, could anything exceed the perversion of law? For if there is any principle of the law never yet contradicted, it is that delivery is one of the essentials to the validity of the deed... . Yet this case of Marbury and Madison is continually cited by bench and bar, as if it were settled law, without any animadversions on its being merely an *obiter* dissertation of the Chief Justice... .

But the Chief Justice says, "there must be an ultimate arbiter somewhere." True, there must; but... . The ultimate arbiter is the people of the Union, assembled by their deputies in convention... . Let them decide to which they mean to give an authority claimed by two of their organs. And it has been the peculiar wisdom and felicity of our Constitution, to have provided this peaceable appeal, where that of other nations is at once to force.

The Need for Controls Over the Judiciary

ME XV 32-44 Samuel Kercheval 7-12-16

The judges of Connecticut have been chosen by the people every six months, for nearly two centuries, and I believe there has hardly ever been an instance of change; so powerful is the curb of incessant responsibility...

In the judiciary, the judges of the highest courts are dependent on none but themselves. In England, where judges were named and removable at the will of the hereditary executive, from which branch most misrule was feared, and has flowed, it was a great point gained, by fixing them for life, to make them independent of that executive... . But we have made them independent of the nation itself. They are irremovable, but by their own body, for any depravities of conduct, and even by their own body for the imbecilities of dotage.

ME XV 388-90 William T. Barry 7-2-22

We already see the power, installed for life, responsible to no authority, (for impeachment is not even a scare-crow,) advancing with a noiseless and steady pace to the great object of consolidation. The foundations are already deeply laid by their decisions, for the annihilation of constitutional State rights, and the removal of every check, every counterpoise to the ingulfing power of which themselves are to make a sovereign part. If ever this vast country is brought under a single government, it will be one of the most extensive corruption, indifferent and incapable of a wholesome care over so wide a spread of surface. This will not be borne, and you will have to choose between reformation and revolution. If I know the spirit of this country, the one or the other is inevitable. Before the canker is become inveterate, before its venom has reached so much of the body politic as to get beyond control, remedy should be applied. Let the future appointments of judges be for four or six years, and renewable by the President and Senate. This will bring their conduct, at regular periods, under revision and probation, and may keep them in equipoise between the general and special governments. We have erred in this point, by copying England, where certainly it is a good thing to have the judges independent of the king. But we have omitted to copy their caution also, which makes a judge removable on the address of both legislative Houses. That there should be public functionaries independent of the nation, whatever may be their demerit, is a solecism in a republic, of the first order of absurdity and inconsistency.

The Dangers of Judicial Immunity

ME XV 480-90 M. Coray 10-31-23

At the establishment of our constitutions, the judiciary bodies were supposed to be the most helpless and harmless members of the government. Experience, however, soon showed in what they were to become the most dangerous; that the insufficiency of the means provided for their removal gave them a freehold and irresponsibility in office; that their decisions, seeming to concern individual suitors only, pass silent and unheeded by the public at large; that these decisions, nevertheless, become law by precedent, sapping, by little and little, the foundations of the Constitution, and working its change by construction, before any one has perceived that that invisible and helpless worm has been busily employed in consuming its substance. In truth, man is not made to be trusted for life, or secured against all liability to account.

ME XV 352-2 Judge Spencer Roane 3-9-21

The great object of my fear is the federal judiciary. That body, like gravity, ever acting with noiseless foot, and unalarming advance, gaining ground step by step, and holding what it gains, is ingulfing insidiously the special governments into the maws of that which feeds them.

ME XV 330-33 C. Hammond 7-18-21

It has long, however, been my opinion, and I have never shrunk from its expression... that the germ of dissolution of our federal government is in the constitution of the federal judiciary; an irresponsible body... working like gravity by night and day, gaining a little to-day and a little tomorrow, and advancing its noiseless step like a thief, over the field of jurisdiction, until all shall be usurped from the States, and the government of all be consolidated into one. To this I am opposed; because, when all government, domestic and foreign, in little as in great things, shall be drawn to Washington as the centre of all power, it will render powerless the checks provided of one government on another, and will become as venal and oppressive as the government from which we separated... .

If the States look with apathy on this silent descent of their government into the gulf which is to swallow all, we have only to weep over the human character formed uncontrollable but by a rod of iron, and so the blasphemers of man, as incapable of self-government, become his true historians.

ME XV 295-99 Thomas Ritchie 9-28-20

But it is not from this branch of the government [the legislative] we have the most to fear. Taxes and short elections will keep them right. The judiciary of the United States is the subtle corps of sappers and miners constantly working under ground to undermine the foundations of our confederated fabric. They are construing our Constitution from a co-ordination of a general and special government to a general and supreme one alone. This will lay all things at their feet... . We shall see if they are bold enough to take the daring stride their five lawyers have lately taken. If they do... , I will say, that "against this every man should raise his voice," and more, should uplift his arm... . Having found, from experience, that impeachment is an impracticable thing, a mere scare-crow, they consider themselves secure for life; they skulk from responsibility to public opinion, the only remaining hold on them, under a practice first introduced into England by Lord Mansfield... . A judiciary independent of a king or executive alone, is a good thing; but independence of the will of the nation is a solecism, at least in a republican government... .

ME XV 350-52 Mr. Nicholas 12-11-21

I fear, dear Sir, we are now in such another crisis [as when the Alien and Sedition Laws were enacted], with this difference only, that the judiciary branch is alone and single-handed in the present assaults on the Constitution. But its assaults are more sure and deadly, as from an agent seemingly passive and unassuming.

ME XV 419-23 William Johnson 3-4-23

...there is no danger I apprehend so much as the consolidation of our government by the noiseless, and therefore unalarming, instrumentality of the Supreme Court. This is the form in which federalism now arrays itself, and consolidation is the present principle of distinction between republicans and the pseudo-republicans, but real federalists. I must comfort myself with the hope that the judges will see the importance and the duty of giving their country the only evidence they can give of fidelity to its Constitution and integrity in the administration of the laws... . Let him [a judge] prove by his reasoning... that he has considered the case, that in the application of the law to it, he uses his own judgment independently and unbiased by party views and personal favor or disfavor. Throw himself in every case on God and his country; both will excuse him for error and value him for his honesty... . For in truth there is at this time more hostility to the federal judiciary than to any other organ of the government.

ME XVI 112-15 Edward Livingston 3-25-25

One single object... will entitle you to the endless gratitude of society; that of restraining judges from usurping legislation. And with no body of men is this restraint more wanting than with the judges of what is commonly called our General Government, but what I call our foreign department. They are practising on the Constitution by inferences, analogies, and sophisms, as they would on an ordinary law. They do not seem aware that it is not even a *Constitution,* formed by a single authority, and subject to a single superintendence and control; but that it is a compact of many independent powers, every single one of which claims an equal right to understand it, and to require its observance.

However strong the cord of compact may be, there is a point of tension at which it will break. A few such doctrinal decisions, as barefaced as that of the Cohens, happening to bear immediately on two or three of the large States, may induce them to join in arresting the march of government, and in rousing the co-States to pay some attention to what is passing to bring back the compact to its original principles, or to modify it legitimately by the express consent of the parties themselves, and not by the usurpation of their created agents. They imagine they can lead us into a consolidate government, while their road leads directly to its dissolution. This member of the government was at first considered as the most harmless and helpless of all its organs. But it has proved that the power of declaring what the law is, *ad libitum,* by sapping and mining, slyly, and without alarm, the foundations of the Constitution, can do what open force would not dare to attempt.

12. England, the Enemy

Commentary

It was the tragedy of Jefferson's career — which he would, by preference, have dedicated to science and philosophy — that it was necessarily devoted to the struggle for freedom from England; but it was also his glory, because his everlasting fame emerged from that battle, which consumed his energies for nearly forty years and elevated him to a pinnacle transcending the achievement of any other American.

In this chapter, we trace in his own words the beginning, the development, and the victorious termination of that struggle. We reproduce most of his first great document — The Summary View of British America *— which was actually the preliminary American Declaration of Independence. We then reproduce that immortal proclamation in full as it emerged from his hand and as later amended by the Continental Congress, by alterations, deletions, and additions. We note that the changes gave the Declaration a somewhat more religious complexion, and omitted totally all reference to slavery, which the British had forced upon the Colonies and which Jefferson considered an "infamous practice," — a sentiment with which the representatives of several southern states did not agree.*

Jefferson's activities after his return from France in 1789 and especially during the years of his vice-presidency and chief magistracy, were devoted principally to combatting English aggressions, aided and abetted by a powerful clique of Federalists, led by Alexander Hamilton. After the British were defeated in the War of the Revolution, they had no intention of relinquishing the profits to be had by exploiting the American States. As Jefferson pointed out in a remarkable letter to Elbridge Gerry dated May 13, 1797, the English and their domestic collaborators had entrenched themselves in the trading, shipping, financial, and governmental positions in America; they were the rich, the exploiters, the manipulators, who still sought, without direct foreign authority, to skim off the cream of American production. Under Hamilton, as Secretary of the Treasury, and Washington, under Federalist domination, as John Adams continued to be during his term as president, they filled almost all political and judicial offices, dominated trade and shipping, controlled the banking institutions, and, in general, directed the economic life of the nation. They had one supreme objective: to bring the newly-born nation into complete subservience to England, no matter what method or treason might be necessary to accomplish this nefarious purpose. While Jefferson was vice-president under Adams, the Federalist machinations almost propelled the nation into war against France; it was only his supreme statesmanship which averted this catastrophe. And when they attempted to raise armies to conquer and colonize South America, it was again his wisdom which prevented it.

The constant battle with England is incomprehensible without some understanding of its class structure and government. Among its millions of adults, there were only 160,000 voters; and the members of the Parliament represented the aristocracy and other privileged groups in English society, all of whom lived in luxury, while the masses slaved or starved, or else served in the country's piratical navy and internal standing army. The consumption and the demands of these ruling and parasitical classes were insatiable; and while the Jeffersonian republicans strove to establish here an economy and a government that would serve the interests of the producers, especially the independent farmers, the English government and their American satellites strove fiercely and constantly to reproduce in this country a society and a government created in the image of the British original.

The enmity thus created was deep and irreconcilable; and the American republicans were constantly at swords' points, not only with the foreign tyranny which had been overthrown, but also with a powerful domestic faction. As John Adams remarked tersely in a letter to Thomas Jefferson in 1816: "Britain will never be our friend until we are her master." Even during the Civil War, 1861-65, England committed many hostile acts against our government, for which she was forced to make reparations. It was only in the 20th century that she was forced to come begging her erstwhile colonials for help and salvation when attacked by Germany.

In various letters, Jefferson analyzed the nature of the English government and why it acted as it did. Although its common people were as decent and upright as any in the world, the country exhibited the singular phenomenon of having the worst government in existence — simply because those ordinary and honest citizens had no control thereover. And for that reason, Jefferson was determined that in this country, those who create the wealth shall also control those to whom they entrust political power.

Perhaps the greatest crisis of Jefferson's career occurred with the murderous attack on the Chesapeake in Hampton Roads. The nation teetered on the brink of war; but Jefferson, who desperately wanted peace, and time to prepare for the worst, sent emissaries to London; and while our nation absorbed insults and injuries from both France and England, the President maintained the peace, while he continued to reduce the public debt, increase the military capacities of the nation, develop domestic manufactures, and lay the basis for complete independence. As a substitute for war, he interdicted British warships and established a 15-month embargo; thereby, he procured more time, and avoided the havoc of war; and made the country self-reliant by encouraging domestic manufactures.

At last, however, since English depredations became more outrageous and numerous, Jefferson advocated a declaration of war; and in letter after letter to his associates and friends — written from retirement at his Olympian Mount at Monticello — he analyzed its progress and exulted in the victories of American arms on sea and land; the final expulsion of British power and influence from our continent; and the mastery — or at least a substantial equality — achieved thereby over his lifelong antagonist.

The Declaration of Rights of 1774

(The legislature of Virginia was in session when news arrived from Boston concerning the action taken by the English against the city following the Boston Tea Party; and a day was set aside for fasting and prayer.)

ME I 182 Appendix John Saunderson 8-31-20

The next day, May the 20th, 1774, the Governor dissolved us. We immediately repaired to a room in the Raleigh Tavern, about a hundred paces distant from the Capitol, formed ourselves into a meeting, Peyton Randolph in the chair, and came to resolutions, declaring that an attack on one colony, to enforce arbitrary acts, ought to be considered as an attack on all, and to be opposed by the united wisdom of all. We, therefore, appointed a Committee of Correspondence, to address letters to the Speakers of the several Houses of Representatives of the colonies, proposed the appointment of deputies from each, to meet *annually in a General Congress,* to deliberate their common interests, and on the measures to be pursued in common. The members then separated to their several homes, except those of the Committee, who met the next day, prepared letters according to instructions, and despatched them by messengers express, to their several destinations.

[This was the beginning of the Continental Congress.]

[The following, written by Jefferson as a member of the Committee of Correspondence, was sent to the assemblies of all the Colonies, and made a powerful impression in England, where it was reprinted several times.]

BW 5-19 Summary View of the Rights of British America, May, 1774

Resolved. That it be an instruction to the said deputies, wher assembled in General Congress, with the deputies from the other States.. to propose to the said Congress, that an humble and dutiful address be presented to his Majesty, begging leave to lay before him as Chief Magistrate of the British empire, the united complaints of his Majesty's subjects in America; complaints which are excited by many unwarrantable encroachments and usurpations, attempted to be made by the legislature of one part of the empire, upon the rights which God, and the laws, have given equally and independently to all. To represent to his Majesty that these, his States, have often individually made humble applications to his imperial Throne, to obtain, through its intervention, some redress of their injured rights, to none of which, was ever even an answer condescended. Humbly to hope that this, their joint address, penned in the language of truth, and divested of those expressions of servility, which would persuade his Majesty that we are asking favors, and not rights, shall obtain from his Majesty a more respectful acceptance... .

To remind him that our ancestors, before their emigration to America, were the free inhabitants of the British dominions... [and that] America was conquered, and her settlements made and firmly established, at the expense of individuals, and not of the British public. Their own blood was spilt in acquiring lands for their settlement, their own fortunes expended in making that settlement effectual. For themselves they fought, for themselves they conquered, and for themselves alone they have a right to hold... .

But that not long were they permitted, however far they thought themselves removed from the hand of oppression, to hold undisturbed the rights thus acquired at the hazard of their lives and loss of their fortunes... .

That the exercise of free trade with all parts of the world, possessed by the American colonists, as of natural right, and which no law of their own had taken away or abridged, was next the object of unjust encroachment... Parliament, for the Commonwealth... assumed upon themselves the power of prohibiting their trade with all other parts of the world, except the Island of Great Britain...

Single acts of tyranny may be ascribed to the accidental opinion of the day; but a series of oppressions, begun at a distinguished period, and pursued unalterably through every change of ministers, too plainly prove a deliberate, systematical plan of reducing us to slavery... .

But... one other act... is entitled "an act for suspending the legislature of New York." One free and independent legislature, hereby takes upon itself to suspend the powers of another, free and independent as itself... . Shall these governments be dissolved, their property annihilated, and their people reduced to a state of nature, at the imperious breath of a body of men whom they never saw, in whom they never confided, and over whom they have no powers of punishment or removal, let their crimes against the American people be ever so great?... . Were this to be admitted, instead of being a free people, as we have hitherto supposed, and mean to continue ourselves, we should suddenly be found the slaves, not of one, but of one hundred and sixty thousand tyrants... .

That, by "an act to discontinue... the landing and discharging, lading or shipping of goods, wares, and merchandise, at the town and within the harbor of Boston..." a large and populous town, whose trade was their sole subsistence, was deprived of that trade, and involved in utter ruin... . An act of Parliament had been passed, imposing duties on teas, to be paid in America, against which act the Americans had protested, as inauthoritative... . There are extraordinary situations which require extraordinary interposition. An exasperated people, who feel that they possess power, are not easily restrained within limits strictly regular. A number of them assembled in the town of Boston, threw the tea into the ocean, and dispersed without doing any other act of violence. If in this they did wrong, they were known, and were amenable to the laws of the land... . On the partial representations of a few worthless ministerial dependents... the whole of that ancient and wealthy town, is in a moment reduced from opulence to beggary... . If the pulse of his people shall beat calmly under this experiment, another and another will be tried, till the measure of despotism be filled up... .

That these are the acts of power, assumed by a body of men foreign to our constitutions, and unacknowledged by our laws; against which we do, on behalf of the inhabitants of British America, enter this, our solemn and determined protest... .

For the most trifling reasons, and, sometimes for no conceivable reason at all, his Majesty has rejected laws of the most salutary tendency. The abolition of domestic slavery is the great object of desire in these colonies, where it was, unhappily, introduced in their infant state. But previous to the enfranchisement of the slaves we have, it is necessary to exclude all further importations from Africa. Yet our repeated attempts to effect this, by prohibitions, and by imposing duties which might amount to a prohibition, having been hitherto defeated by his Majesty's negative: thus preferring the immediate advantages of a few African corsairs, to the lasting interests of the American States, and to the rights of human nature, deeply wounded by this infamous practice... .

That, in order to enforce arbitrary measures before complained of, his Majesty has, from time to time, sent among us large bodies of armed forces, not made up of the people here, nor raised by the authority of our laws. Did his Majesty possess such a right as this, it might swallow up all our other rights, whenever he should think proper. But his Majesty has no right to land a single armed man on our shores; and those whom he sends here are liable to our laws, for the suppression and punishment of riots, routs, and unlawful assemblies, or are hostile bodies invading us in defiance of law... .

Every State must judge for itself, the number of armed men which they may safely trust among them, of whom they are to consist, and under what restrictions they are to be laid. To render these proceedings still more criminal against our laws, instead of subjecting the military to the civil power, his Majesty has expressly made the civil subordinate to the military. But can his Majesty thus put down all law under his feet? Can he erect a power superior to that which erected himself? He has done it indeed by force; but let him remember that force cannot give right.

That these are our grievances, which we have thus laid before his Majesty, with that freedom of language and sentiment which becomes a free people, claiming their rights as derived from the laws of nature, and not as a gift of their Chief Magistrate. Let those flatter, who fear: it is not an American art. To give praise where it is not due might be well from the venal, but would ill beseem those who are asserting the rights of human nature. They know, and will, therefore, say, that Kings are the servants, not the proprietors of the people. Open your breast, Sire, to liberal and expanded thought. Let not the name of George the Third, be a blot on the page of history... . It behooves you, therefore, to think and act for yourself and your people. The great principles of right and wrong are legible to every reader; to pursue them, requires not the aid of many counsellors. The whole art of government consists in the art of being honest. Only aim to do your duty, and mankind will give you credit where you fail. No longer persevere in sacrificing the rights of one part of the empire to the inordinate desires of another; but deal out to all, equal and impartial right. Let no act be passed by any one legislature, which may infringe on the rights and liberties of another. This is the important post in which fortune has placed you, holding the balance of a great, if a well-poised empire.

This, Sire, is the advice of your great American council, on the observance of which may perhaps depend your felicity and future fame, and the preservation of that harmony which alone can continue, both to Great Britain and America, the reciprocal advantages of their connection. It is neither our wish nor our interest to separate from her.

We are willing, on our part, to sacrifice everything which reason can ask, to the restoration of that tranquillity for which all must wish. On their part, let them be ready to establish union and a generous plan. Let them name their terms, but let them be just. Accept of every commercial preference it is in our power to give, for such things as we can raise for their use, or they make for ours. But let them not think to exclude us from going to other markets to dispose of those commodities which they cannot use, nor to supply those wants which they cannot supply. Still less, let it be proposed, that our properties, within our own territories, shall be taxed or regulated by any power on earth, but our own. The God who gave us life, gave us liberty at the same time; the hand of force may destroy, but cannot disjoin them.

This, Sire, is our last, our determined resolution. And that you will be pleased to interpose, with that efficacy which your earnest endeavors may insure, to procure redress of these our great grievances, to quiet the minds of your subjects in British America against any apprehensions of future encroachment, to establish fraternal love and harmony through the whole empire, and that that may continue to the latest ages of time, is the fervent prayer of all British America.

The Declaration of Independence

BW 21-28 A Declaration by the Representatives of the United States of America, in General Congress Assembled July 4, 1776

(This includes Jefferson's complete version, before it was altered — to his considerable disappointment — by eliminating certain words and passages, and adding or altering others. The deleted portions are in italics, and those added are in CAPITALS.)

When, in the course of human events, it becomes necessary for one people to dissolve the political bands which have connected them with another, and to assume among the powers of the earth the separate and equal station to which the laws of nature and of nature's God entitle them, a decent respect to the opinions of mankind requires that they should declare the causes which impel them to the separation.

We hold these truths to be self-evident: that all men are created equal; that they are endowed by their creator with CERTAIN *inherent and inalienable* UNALIENABLE rights; that among these are life, liberty, and the pursuit of happiness; that to secure these rights, governments are instituted among men, deriving their just powers from the consent of the governed; that whenever any form of government becomes destructive of these ends, it is the right of the people to alter or to abolish it, and institute new government, laying its foundation on such principles, and organizing its powers in such form, as to them shall seem most likely to effect their safety and happiness. Prudence, indeed, will dictate that governments long established should not be changed for light and transient causes; and accordingly all experience hath shown that mankind are more disposed to suffer while evils are sufferable than to right themselves by abolishing the forms to which they are accustomed. But when a long train of abuses and usurpations *begun at a distinguished period and* pursuing invariably the same object, evinces a design to reduce them under absolute despotism, it is their right, it is their duty, to throw off such government, and to provide new guards for their future security. Such has been the patient sufferance of these Colonies; and such is now the necessity which constrains them to ALTER *expunge* their former systems of government. The history of the present King of Great Britain is a history of REPEATED *unremitting* injuries and usurpations, ALL HAVING *among which appears no solitary fact to contradict the uniform tenor of the rest, but all have* in direct object the establishment of an absolute tyranny over these States. To prove this, let facts be submitted to a candid world *for the truth of which we pledge a faith yet unsullied by falsehood.*

He has refused his assent to laws the most wholesome and necessary for the public good.

He has forbidden his governors to pass laws of immediate and pressing importance, unless suspended in their operation till his assent should be obtained; and, when so suspended, he has utterly neglected to attend to them.

He has refused to pass other laws for the accommodation of large districts of people, unless those people would relinquish the right of representation in the Legislature, a right inestimable to them, and formidable to tyrants only.

He has called together legislative bodies at places unusual, uncomfortable, and distant from the depository of their public records, for the sole purpose of fatiguing them into compliance with his measures.

He has dissolved representative houses repeatedly *and continually* for opposing with manly firmness his invasions on the rights of the people.

He has refused for a long time after such dissolutions to cause others to be elected, whereby the legislative powers, incapable of annihilation, have returned to the people at large for their exercise, the State remaining, in the meantime, exposed to all the dangers of invasion from without and convulsions within.

He has endeavored to prevent the population of these States; for that purpose obstructing the laws for naturalization of foreigners, refusing to pass others to encourage their migration hither, and raising the conditions of new appropriations of lands.

He has suffered the administration of justice *totally to cease in some of these States* refusing his assent to laws for establishing judiciary powers.

He has made *our* judges dependent on his will alone for the tenure of their offices, and the amount and payment of their salaries.

He has erected a multitude of new offices, *by a self-assumed power,* and sent hither swarms of new officers to harass our people and eat out their substance.

He has kept among us in times of peace standing armies *and ships of war* without the consent of our Legislatures.

He has affected to render the military independent of, and superior to, the civil power.

He has combined with others to subject us to a jurisdiction foreign to our constitutions and unacknowledged by our laws, giving his assent to their acts of pretended legislation for quartering large bodies of armed troops among us; for protecting them by a mock trial from punishment for any murders which they should commit on the inhabitants of these States; for cutting off our trade with all parts of the world; for imposing taxes on us without our consent; for depriving us (in many cases) of the benefits of trial by jury; for transporting us beyond seas to be tried for pretended offences; for abolishing the free system of English laws in a neighboring province, establishing therein an arbitrary government, and enlarging its boundaries, so as to render it at once an example and fit instrument for introducing the same absolute rule into these COLONIES *States;* for taking away our charters, abolishing our most valuable laws, and altering fundamentally the forms of our governments; for suspending our own legislatures, and declaring themselves invested with power to legislate for us in all cases whatsoever.

He has abdicated government here by DECLARING US OUT OF HIS PROTECTION AND WAGING WAR AGAINST US. *withdrawing his governors, and declaring us out of his allegiance and protection.*

He has plundered our seas, ravaged our coasts, burnt our towns, and destroyed the lives of our people.

He is at this time transporting large armies of foreign mercenaries to complete the works of death, desolation, and tyranny already begun with circumstances of cruelty and perfidy SCARCELY PARALLELED IN THE MOST BARBAROUS AGES, AND TOTALLY unworthy the head of a civilized nation.

He has constrained our fellow-citizens taken captive on the high seas to bear arms against their country, to become the executioners of their friends and brethren, or to fall themselves by their hands.

He has EXCITED DOMESTIC INSURRECTION AMONG US, AND HAS endeavored to bring on the inhabitants of our frontiers the merciless Indian savages, whose known rule of warfare is an undistinguished destruction of all ages, sexes, and conditions *of existence.*

He has incited treasonable insurrections of our fellow-citizens, with the allurements of forfeiture and confiscation of our property.

He has waged cruel war against human nature itself, violating its most sacred rights of life and liberty in the persons of a distant people who never offended him, captivating and carrying them into slavery in another hemisphere, or to incur miserable death in their transportation thither. This piratical warfare, the oppobrium of INFIDEL powers, is the warfare of the CHRISTIAN King of Great Britain. Determined to keep open a market where MEN should be bought and sold, he has prostituted his negative for suppressing every legislative attempt to prohibit or to restrain this execrable commerce. And that this assemblage of horrors might want no fact of distinguished die, he is now exciting those very people to rise in arms among us, and to purchase that liberty of which he has deprived them, by murdering the people on whom he also obtruded them; thus paying off former crimes committed against the LIBERTIES of one people with crimes which he urges them to commit against the LIVES of another.

In every stage of these oppressions we have petitioned for redress in the most humble terms; our repeated petitions have been answered only by repeated injuries.

A Prince whose character is thus marked by every act which may define a tyrant is unfit to be the ruler of a FREE people *who mean to be free. Future ages will scarcely believe that the hardiness of one man adventured, within the short compass of twelve years only, to lay a foundation so broad and so undisguised for tyranny over a people fostered and fixed in principles of freedom.*

Nor have we been wanting in attentions to our British brethren. We have warned them from time to time of attempts by their legislature to extend AN UNWARRANTABLE *a* jurisdiction over US *these our States.* We have reminded them of the circumstances of our emigration and settlement here, *no one of which could warrant so strange a pretension; that these were effected at the expense of our own blood and treasure, unassisted by the wealth or the strength of Great Britain; that in constituting indeed our several forms of government, we had adopted one common king, thereby laying the foundation for perpetual league and amity with them; but that submission to their parliament was no part of our Constitution, nor ever in idea, if history may be credited; and,* we HAVE appealed to their native justice and magnanimity AND WE HAVE CONJURED THEM BY *as well as to* the ties of our common kindred to disavow these usurpations which WOULD INEVITABLY *were likely to* interrupt our connection and correspondence. They too have been deaf to the voice of justice and of consanguinity, *and when occasions have been given them, by the regular course of their lives, of removing from their councils the disturbers of our harmony, they have, by their free election, re-established them in power. At this very time, too, they are permitting their chief magistrate to send over not only soldiers of our common blood, but Scotch and foreign mercenaries to invade and destroy us. These facts have given the last stab to agonizing affection, and manly spirit bids us to renounce forever those unfeeling brethren. We must endeavor to forget our former love for them, and hold them as we hold the rest of mankind, enemies in war, in peace friends. We might have been a free and great people together; but a communication of grandeur and of freedom, it seems, is below their dignity. Be it so, since they will have it. The road to happiness and to glory is open to us too. We will tread it apart from them, and* WE MUST THEREFORE acquiesce in the necessity which denounces our *eternal* separation. AND HOLD THEM, AS WE HOLD THE REST OF MANKIND, ENEMIES IN WAR, IN PEACE FRIENDS.

We therefore the representatives of the United States of America in General Congress assembled, APPEALING TO THE SUPREME JUDGE OF THE WORLD FOR THE RECTITUDE OF OUR

INTENTIONS do in the name, and by the authority of the good people of these COLONIES *States* SOLEMNLY PUBLISH AND DECLARE, THAT THESE UNITED COLONIES ARE, AND OF RIGHT OUGHT TO BE, FREE AND INDEPENDENT STATES: THAT THEY ARE ABSOLVED FROM ALL ALLEGIANCE TO THE BRITISH CROWN, AND THAT ALL POLITICAL CONNECTION BETWEEN THEM AND THE STATE OF GREAT BRITAIN IS, AND OUGHT TO BE, TOTALLY DISSOLVED: AND THAT, AS FREE AND INDEPENDENT STATES *reject and renounce all allegiance and submission to the kings of Great Britain and all others who may hereafter claim by, through, or under them; we utterly dissolve all political connection which may heretofore have subsisted between us and the people or parliament of Great Britain; and finally we do assert and declare these Colonies to be free and independent States,* and that, as free and independent States, they have full power to levy war, conclude peace, contract alliances, establish commerce, and to do all other acts and things which independent States may of right do.

And for the support of this declaration, WITH A FIRM RELIANCE ON THE PROTECTION OF DIVINE PROVIDENCE we mutually pledge to each other our lives, our fortunes, and our sacred honor.

Post-Revolutionary English Domination

ME IX 380-86 Elbridge Gerry 5-13-97

I do sincerely wish with you, that we could take our stand on a ground perfectly neutral and independent towards all nations. It has been my constant object through my public life; and with respect to the English... they are in possession of several written and formal proofs, in my own hand writing. But they have wished a monopoly of commerce and influence with us; and they have in fact obtained it.

When we take notice that theirs is the workshop to which we go for all we want; that with them centre either immediately or ultimately all the labors of our hands and lands; that to them belongs either openly or secretly the great mass of our navigation; that even the factorage of their affairs here, is kept to themselves by factitious citizenships; that these foreign and false citizens now constitute the great body of what are called our merchants, fill our sea ports, are planted in every little town and district of the interior country, sway everything in the former places by their own votes, and those of their dependants, in the latter, by their insinuations and the influence of their ledgers; that they are advancing fast to a monopoly of our banks and public funds, and thereby placing our public finances under their control; that they have in their alliance the most influential characters in and out of office; when they have shown that by all these bearings on the different branches of the government, they can force it to proceed in whatever direction they dictate, and bend the interests of this country entirely to the will of another; when all this, I say, is attended to, it is impossible for us to say we stand on independent ground, impossible for a free mind not to see and to groan under the bondage in which it is bound.

If anything after this could excite surprise, it would be that they have been able so far to throw dust in the eyes of our own citizens, as to fix on those who wish merely to recover self-government, the charge of subserving one foreign influence, because they resist submission to another. But they possess our printing presses, a powerful engine in their government of us... . After plunging us in all the broils of the European nations, there would remain but one act to close our tragedy, that is, to break up our Union; and even this they have ventured seriously and solemnly to propose and maintain by arguments in a Connecticut paper... .

I have been happy, however, in believing, from the stifling of this effort, that that dose was found too strong, and excited as much repugnance there as it did horror in other parts of our country, and that whatever follies we may be led into as to foreign nations, we shall never give up our Union, the last anchor of our hope, and that alone which is to prevent this heavenly country from becoming an arena of gladiators. Much as I abhor war, and view it as the greatest scourge of mankind, and anxiously as I wish to keep out of the broils of Europe, I would yet go with my brethren into these, rather than separate from them. But I hope we may still keep clear of them.

England: The Permanent Enemy

ME V 129-31 John Langdon 9-11-85

In spite of treaties, England is still our enemy. Her hatred is deep-rooted and cordial, and nothing is wanting with her but the power, to wipe us and the land we live in, out of existence. Her interest, however, is her ruling passion; and the late American measures have struck at that so vitally... that a possibility seems to open of forming some arrangement with her.

ME VI 378-83 William Carmichael 12-11-87

I had never concealed from him [Mr. Eden, English Ambassador] that I considered the British as our natural enemies, and as the only nation on earth who wished us all dead, from the bottom of their souls. And I am satisfied, that were our continent to be swallowed up by the ocean, Great Britain would be in bonfires from one end to the other.

ME XIII 89-92 Clement Caine 9-16-11

What, in short, is the whole system of Europe toward America but an atrocious and insulting tyranny? One hemisphere of the earth, separated from the other by wide seas on both sides, having a different system of interests flowing from different modes of existence, and its local relations and duties, is made subservient to all the petty interests of the other, to *their* laws, *their* regulations, *their* passions, and wars, and interdicted from social intercourse, from the interchange of mutual duties and comforts with their neighbors, enjoined on all men by the laws of nature... . The intention, too which they now formally avow, of taking possession of the ocean as their exclusive domain, and of suffering no commerce on it but through their ports, makes it the interest of all mankind to contrubute their efforts to bring such usurpation to an end... the determination to take all our vessels herself to any other than her ports, amounting to all the war she can make (for we fear no invasion), it would be folly in us to let that war be on one side only, and to make no effort towards indemnification or reprisal.

ME XIV 245-55 La Fayette 2-14-15

I consider it [the treaty of peace with England] as an armistice only, because no security is provided against the impressment of our seamen... . If she thinks the exercise of this outrage is worth eternal war, eternal war it will be... . The first act of impressment she commits on an American will be answered by reprisal, or by a declaration of war here; and the interval must be merely a state of preparation for it. In this, we have much to do, in further fortifying our seaport towns, providing military stores, classing and disciplining our militia, arranging our financial system, and, above all, pushing our domestic manufactures, which have taken such root as never again to be shaken.

CE VII 247-50 Adams to Jefferson 12-16-16

Britain will never be our friend until we are her master. This will happen in less time than we have been struggling with her power, provided we remain united. Aye! there's the rub!

The Nature of the English Government

ME XII 373-79 John Langdon 3-5-10

It may be asked, what in the nature of her government unfits England for the observation of moral duties? In the first place, her king is a cypher; his only function being to name the oligarchy which is to govern her. The parliament is, by corruption, the mere instrument of the will of the administration. The real power and property in the government is in the great aristocractical families of the nation. The nest of office being too small for all of them to cuddle into at once, the contest is eternal, which shall crowd the other out... . Justice, honor, faith, must yield to the necessity of keeping themselves in place. The question, whether a measure is moral, is never asked; but whether it will nourish the avarice of their merchants, or the political spirit of their navy, or produce any other effects which may strengthen them in their places... .

Her good faith! the faith of a nation of merchants! The *Punica Fides* of modern Carthage! Of the friend and protectress of Copenhagen! Of the nation who never admitted a chapter of morality into her political code! And is now boldly avowing that whatever power can make hers, is hers of right... the nature of the English government forbids, of itself, reliance on her engagements... .

This is the true character of the English government in practice, however different its theory; and it presents the singular phenomenon of a nation, the individuals of which are as faithful to their private engagements and duties, as honorable, as worthy, as those of any nation on earth, and whose government is yet the most unprincipled this day known.

ME XIII 68-71 James Ogilvie 8-4-11

The English have been a wise, a virtuous and truly estimable people. But commerce and corrupt government have rotted them to the core. Every generous, nay, every just sentiment, is absorbed in the thirst for gold. I speak of their cities, which we may certainly pronounce to be ripe for despotism, and fitted for no other government. Whether the... agricultural body is sufficient to regenerate the residuary mass... under any reformation of government, may well be doubted.

ME XIII 122-25 John Adams 1-21-12

As for France and England with all their preeminence in science, the one is a den of robbers, and the other of pirates.

ME XIV 245-55 La Fayette 2-14-15

The British ministers find in a state of war rather than peace, by... the vast expenditures of the war supplies that they recruit their broken fortunes, or make new ones, and therefore will not make peace as long as by any delusions they can keep the temper of the nation up to the war point.

ME XIV 306-11 Thomas Leiper 6-12-15

[I consider] the government of England as totally without morality, insolent beyond bearing, inflated with vanity and ambition, aiming at the exclusive dominion of the sea, lost in corruption, of deep-rooted hatred toward us, hostile to liberty wherever it endeavors to show its head, and the eternal disturber of the peace of the world.

ME XV 81-87 John Adams 11-25-16

I consider their government as the most flagitious which has existed... . It is not only founded in corruption itself, but insinuates the same poison into the bowells of every other, corrupts its councils, nourishes factions, stirs up revolutions, and places its own happiness in fomenting commotions and civil wars among others... .

The effect is now coming home to itself. Its first operation will fall on the individuals who have been the chief instruments in its corruptions, and will eradicate the families which have from generation to generation been fattening on the blood of their brethren; and this scoria once thrown off, I am in hopes a purer nation will result, and a purer government instituted, one which, instead of endeavoring to make us their natural enemies, will see in us, what we really are, their natural friends and brethren, and more interested in a fraternal connection with them than with any other nation on earth. I look, therefore, to their revolution with great interest. I wish it to be as moderate and bloodless as will effect the desired object of an honest government, one which will permit the world to live in peace, and under the bonds of friendship and good neighborhood... .

George the Third, then, and his minister Pitt, and successors, have spent the fee simple of the kingdom, under the pretense of governing it; their sinecures, salaries, pensions, priests, prelates, princes, and eternal wars, have mortgaged to its full value the last foot of that soil... . [They should]... Dismiss their parasites, ship off their paupers to this country, let the landholders give half their lands to the money lenders and these last relinquish one-half of their debts. They would still have a fertile island, a sound and effective population to labor it, and would hold that station among political powers, to which their natural resources and faculties entitle them.

They would no longer, indeed, be the lords of the ocean and paymaster of all the princes of the earth. They would no longer enjoy the luxuries of pirating and plundering everything by sea, and of bribing and corrupting everything by land; but they might enjoy the more safe and lasting luxury of living on terms of equality, justice, and good neighborhood with all nations.

As it is, their first efforts will probably be to quiet things awhile by the palliatives of reformation... . The princes and priests will [still] hold the flesh-pots, the empty bellies will seize on them, and these being the multitude, the issue is obvious, civil war, massacre, exile as in France, until the stage is cleaned of everything but the multitude, and the lands get into their hands by such processes as the revolution will engender.

They will then want peace and a government, and what will it be?... . They will probably turn their eyes to us, and be disposed to tread in our footsteps, seeing how safely these have led us into port. There is no part of our model to which they seem unequal, unless perhaps the elective presidency... .

British Atrocities

During the Revolutionary War

BW 237-38 Answers to de Meusnier 1786

M. de Meusnier proposed to mention the facts of cruelty of which he and Mr. Jefferson spoke... . These facts are, 1. The death of upwards of eleven thousand American prisoners in one prison ship (the Jersey), and in the space of three years. 2. General Howe's permitting our prisoners, taken at the battle of Germantown, and placed there under a guard in the yard of the State-house of Philadelphia, to be so long without food furnished them that many perished with hunger. Where the bodies laid, it was seen that they had eaten all the grass around them within their reach, after they had lost the power of rising or moving from their place... . 3. ...they regularly sent our prisoners, taken on the seas and carried to England, to the East Indies. This is so certain, that in the month of November or December, 1785, Mr. Adams having officially demanded a delivery of the American prisoners sent to the East Indies, Lord Caermarthen answered, officially, "That orders were immediately issued for their discharge..."

ME VII 69-70 Doctor Gordon 7-16-88

Wherever he went, the dwelling houses were plundered of everything which could be carried off... . From an estimate I made at that time... , the State of Virginia lost, under Lord Cornwallis' hands, that year, about thirty thousand slaves; and that of these, about twenty-seven thousand died of the small pox and camp fever, and the rest were partly sent to the West Indies, and exchanged for rum, sugar, coffee, and fruit, and partly to New York, from whence they went, at the peace, either to Nova Scotia or England. From the last place, I believe they have been sent to Africa.

History will never relate the horrors committed by the British in the *southern* States of America. They raged in Virginia six months only, from the middle of April to the middle of October, 1781, when they were all taken prisoners... . I suppose their whole devastations during those six months, amounted to about three millions sterling... .

Colonel Tarleton... despatched a troop of his horse, under Captain McLeod, with the double object of taking me prisoner, with two Speakers of the Senate and Delegates, who then lodged with me... . The troop failed... as we had notice of their coming, so that the two Speakers had gone off about two hours before their arrival at Monticello, and myself, with my family, about five minutes.

The Stupidity of English Aggressions

ME XII 291-92 General Henry Dearborn 6-14-09

But her conduct hitherto has been towards us so insulting, so tyrannical, and so malicious, as to indicate a contempt for our opinions or dispositions respecting her. I hope she is now coming over to a wiser conduct, and becoming sensible how much better it is to cultivate the good will of the government itself, than of a faction hostile to it; to obtain its friendship *gratis* than to purchase its enmity by nourishing at great expense a faction to embarrass it, to receive the reward of an honest policy rather than of a corrupt and vexatious one. I trust she has at length opened her eyes to federalist falsehood and misinformation, and learnt, in the issue of the presidential election, the folly of believing them. Such a reconciliation to the government, if real and permanent, will secure the tranquillity of our country, and render the management of our affairs easy and delightful to our successors, for whom I feel as much interest as if I were still in their place. Certainly all the troubles and difficulties in the government during our time proceeded from England; at least all others were trifling in comparison with them.

ME XIV 226-30 James Monroe 1-1-15

It was reserved for England to show that Bonaparte, in atrocity, was an infant to their ministers and their generals.

The Barbaric Raid on Washington

ME XIV 191-94 Samuel H. Smith 9-21-14

I learn from the newspapers that the vandalism of our enemy has triumphed at Washington over science, as well as the arts, by the destruction of the public library with the noble edifice in which it was deposited. Of this transaction, as of that of Copenhagen, the world will entertain but one sentiment. They will see a nation suddenly withdrawn from a great war, full armed and full handed, taking advantage of another whom they had recently forced into it, unarmed, and unprepared, to indulge themselves in acts of barbarism which do not belong to a civilized age. When Van Ghent destroyed their shipping at Chatham, and De Ruyter rode triumphantly up the Thames, he might in like manner, by the acknowledgement of their own historians, have forced all their ships up to London Bridge, and there have burnt them, the Tower, and the city, had these examples been then set... .

...the English have burnt our Capitol and President's house by means of their force. We can burn St. James, and St. Paul's by means of our money, offered to their own incendiaries, of whom there are thousands in London who would do it rather than starve. But it is against the laws of civilized warfare to employ secret incendiaries. Is it not equally so to destroy the works of art by armed incendiaries?

Bonaparte, possessed at times of almost every capital of Europe, and with all his despotism and power, injured no monument of art. If a nation, breaking through all the restraints of civilized character, uses its means of destruction (power for example) without distinction of objects, may we not use our means (*our* money and *their* pauperism) to retaliate their barbarous ravages?... And if we do not carry it into execution, it is because we think it more moral and more honorable to set a good example, than follow a bad one.

The Outrageous Attack on the Chesapeake

ME III 444-53 Seventh Annual Message to Congress 10-27-07

On the 22nd of June last, by a formal order from the British Admiral, the frigate Chesapeake, leaving her port for distant service, was attacked by one of those vessels which had been lying in our harbors under the indulgence of hospitality, was disabled from proceeding, had several of her crew killed, and four taken away... . I immediately by proclamation, interdicted our harbors and waters to all British armed vessels, forbade intercourse with them, and, uncertain how far hostilities were intended, and the town of Norfolk, indeed, being threatened with immediate attack, a sufficient force was ordered for the protection of that place, and such other preparations commenced and pursued as the prospect rendered proper. An armed vessel of the United States was despatched with instructions to our minister at London to call on that government for the satisfaction and security required by the outrage... .

The aggression thus begun has been continued on the part of the British commanders, by remaining within our waters, in defiance of the authority of the country, by habitual violations of its jurisdiction, and at length by putting to death one of the persons they had forcibly taken from on board the Chesapeake.

BW 390-96 Eighth Annual Message to Congress 11-8-08

The communications made to Congress at their last session explained the posture in which the close of the discussion relating to the attack by a British ship of war on the frigate Chesapeake left a subject on which the nation had manifested so honorable a sensibility. Every view of what had passed authorized a belief that immediate steps would be taken by the British government for redressing a wrong, which, the more it was investigated, appeared the more clearly to require what had not been provided for in the special mission. It is found that no steps have been taken for the purpose. On the contrary, it will be seen, in the documents laid before you, that the inadmissible preliminary which obstructed the adjustment is still adhered to... . The instructions which had been given to our ministers at London with a view to facilitate, if necessary, the reparation claimed by the United States, are included in the documents communicated.

War or Embargo (begun on 12-16-07)

ME XII 194-95 Governor Levi Lincoln 11-13-08

The congressional campaign is just opening: three alternatives alone are to be chosen from. 1. Embargo. 2. War. 3. Submission and tribute. And, wonderful to tell, that last will not want advocates. The real question, however, will lie between the two first, on which there is considerable division. As yet the first seems most to prevail; but opinions are by no means yet settled down. Perhaps the advocates of the second may, to a formal declaration of war, prefer *general* letters of mark and reprisal, because, on a repeal of their edicts by the belligerent, a revocation of the letters of mark restores peace without the delay, difficulties, and ceremonies of a treaty.

ME XI 401-02 General John Mason, December 1807

The sum of these mutual enterprises on our national rights is that France, and her allies, reserving for further consideration the prohibiting of our carrying anything to the British territories, have virtually done it, by restraining our bringing a return cargo from them; and Great Britain, after prohibiting a great proportion of our commerce with France and her allies, is now believed to have prohibited the whole. The whole world is thus laid under interdict by these two nations, and our vessels, their cargoes and crews, are to be taken by the one or the other, for whatever place they may be destined, out of our limits. If, therefore, on leaving our harbors, we are certain to lose them, is it not better, as to vessels, cargoes, and seamen, to keep them at home?

ME XII 43-4 General John Armstrong 5-2-08

During the present paroxysm of the insanity of Europe, we have thought it wisest to break off all intercourse with her. We shall, in the course of this year, have all our seaports, of any note, put into a state of defence against naval attacks.

ME XII 232-33 To the Sec. of War 1-17-09

The pressure of the embargo, although sensibly felt by every description of our fellow citizens, has yet been cheerfully borne by most of them, under the conviction that it was a temporary evil, and a necessary one to save us from greater and more permanent evils, — the loss of property and surrender of rights. But it would have been more cheerfully borne, but for the knowledge that, while honest men were religiously observing it, the unprincipled along our seacoast and frontiers were fraudulently evading it; and that in some parts they have even dared to break through it openly, by an armed force too powerful to be opposed by the collector and his assistants. To put an end to this scandalous insubordination to the laws, the Legislature has authorized the President to empower proper persons to employ militia, for preventing or suppressing armed or riotous assemblages of persons resisting the custom house officers in the exercise of their duties, or opposing or violating the embargo laws.

ME XII 248-49 Thomas Mann Randolph 2-7-09

The majority of the Congress... has now rallied to the removing the embargo on the 4th of March, non-intercourse with *France* and *Great Britain,* trade everywhere else, and continuing war preparations. The further details are not yet settled, but I believe it is perfectly certain that the embargo will be taken off the 4th of March.

ME XII 260-62 General John Armstrong 3-5-09

The belligerant edicts rendered our embargo necessary to call home our ships, our seamen, and our property... . After fifteen months' continuance, it is now discontinued, because, losing $50,000,000 of exports annually, by it, it costs more than war... . War must therefore follow if the edicts are not repealed.

The Inescapable Second War with England

ME XIII 71-72 Judge Archibald Stuart 8-8-11

Great Britain has certainly come forward and declared to our government by an official paper, that the conduct of France toward her during this war has obliged her to take possession of the ocean, and to determine that no commerce shall be carried on with the nations connected with France; that, however, she is disposed to relax in this determination so far as to permit the commerce which may be carried on through the British ports. I have, for three or four years, been confident that, knowing that her own resources were not adequate to the maintenance of her present navy, she meant with it to claim the conquest of the ocean and to permit no nation to navigate it, but on payment of a tribute for the maintenance of the fleet necessary to secure the dominion.

ME XVIII 271-72 Charles Pinckney 2-2-12

Every hope from time, patience, and the love of peace, is exhausted, and war or abject submission are the only alternatives left us. I am forced from my hobby, peace, until our revenue is liberated. Then we could make war without either new taxes or loans, and in peace apply the same resources to internal improvements. But they will not give us time to get into this happy state. They will force us, as they have forced France, to become a nation of soldiers, and then more woe to them!

ME XIII 137-39 Hugh Nelson 4-2-12

I think all regret there is cause for war, but all consider it as now necessary.... As to the taxes, they expect to meet them, would be unwilling to have them postponed... .

ME XIII 144-49 James Maury 4-25-12

Surely the world will acquit our government from having sought it [the war]. Never before has there been an instance of a nation's bearing so much as we have borne. Two items alone in our catalogue of wrongs will forever acquit us of being the aggressors: the impressment of our seamen, and the excluding us from the ocean. The first foundations of the social compact would be broken up, were we definitively to refuse to its members the protection of their persons and property, while in their lawful pursuits. I think the war will not be short, because the object of England, long obvious, is to claim the ocean as her domain, and to exact transit duties from every vessel traversing it. This is the sum of her orders of council, which were only a step in this bold experiment never meant to be retracted if it could be permanently maintained. And this object must continue her in war with all the world. To this I see no termination, until her exaggerated efforts, so much beyond her natural strength and resources, shall have exhausted her to bankruptcy... .

We believe that the just standing of all nations is the health and security of all. We consider the overwhelming power of England on the ocean, and of France on the land, as destructive of the prosperity and happiness of the world, and wish both to be reduced only to the necessity of observing moral duties. We believe no more in Bonaparte's fighting merely for the liberty of the seas, than in Great Britain's fighting for the liberties of mankind. The object of both is the same, to draw to themselves the power, the wealth, and the resources of other nations. We resist the enterprises of England first, because they first come vitally home to us. And our feelings repel the logic of bearing the lash of George the III for fear of that of Bonaparte at some future day. When the wrongs of France shall reach us with equal effect, we shall resist them also. But one at a time is enough; and having offered a choice to the champions, England first takes up the gauntlet.

The English newspapers suppose me the personal enemy of their nation. I am not so. I am an enemy to its injuries, as I am to those of France. If I could permit myself to have national partialities, and if the conduct of England would have permitted them to be directed towards her, they would have been so... .

Had I been personally hostile to England, and biased in favor of either the character or views of her great antagonist, the affair of the Chesapeake put war into my hand. I had only to open it and let havoc loose. But if ever I was gratified with the possession of power, and of the confidence of those who had entrusted me with it, it was on that occasion when I was enabled to use both for the prevention of war, towards which the torrent of passion here was directed almost irresistibly, and when not another person in the United States, less supported by authority and favor, could have resisted it.

ME XIII 237-45 Madame La Baronne de Stael-Holstein 5-25-13

The English government, and its piratical principles and practices, have no fixed term of duration. Europe feels, and is writhing under the scorpion whips of Bonaparte. We are assailed by those of England... .

It was not until England had taken one thousand of our ships, and impressed more than six thousand of our citizens; till she had declared, by the proclamation of her Prince Regent, that she would not repeal her aggressive orders *as to us,* until Bonaparte should have repealed his *as to all nations;* till her minister, in formal conference with ours, declared, that no proposition for protecting our seamen from being impressed, under color of taking their own, was practicable or admissible; that, the door to justice and all amicable arrangements being closed, and negotiations become both desperate and dishonorable, we concluded that the war she had for years been waging against us, might as well become a war on both sides. She takes fewer vessels from us since the declaration of war than before, because they venture more cautiously; and we now make full reprisals where before we made none. England is, in principle, the enemy of all maritime nations;... her object is the *permanent dominion of the ocean,* and the *monopoly of the trade of the world.* To secure this, she must keep a larger fleet than her own resources will maintain. The resources of other nations, then, must be impressed to supply the deficiency of her own... .

She first forbade to neutrals all trade with her enemies in time of war, which they had not in time of peace. This deprived them of their trade from port to port of the same nation. Then she forbade them to trade from the port of one nation to that of any other at war with her, although a right fully exercised in time of peace. Next, instead of taking vessels only *entering* a blockaded port, she took them over the whole ocean, if destined to that port, although ignorant of the blockade, and without intention to violate it. Then she took them returning from that port, as if infected by previous infraction of blockade. Then came her paper blockades, by which she might shut up the whole world without sending a ship to sea, except to take all those sailing on it, as they must, of course, be bound to some port. And these were followed by her orders of council, forbidding every nation to go to the port of any other, without coming first to some port of Great Britain, there paying tribute to her, regulated by the cargo, and taking from her a license to proceed to the port of destination; which operation the vessel was to repeat with the return cargo on its way home. According to these orders, we could not send a vessel from St. Mary's to St. Augustine, distant six hours' sail on our own coast, without crossing the Atlantic four times, twice with the outward cargo, and twice with the inward... .

And finally, that her views may no longer rest on inference, in a recent debate her minister declared in open parliament, that the object of the present war is a *monopoly of commerce.*

In some of these atrocities, France kept pace with her fully... . In order, therefore, to single out an enemy, we offered to both, that if either would revoke its hostile decrees, and the other should refuse, we would interdict all intercourse whatever with that other; which would be war of course, as being an avowed departure from neutrality. France accepted the offer, and revoked her decrees as to us. England not only refused, but declared by a solemn proclamation of her Prince Regent, that she would not revoke her orders [of council] even as to us, until those of France should be annulled as to the whole world. We, therefore, declared war.

The sword... can never again be sheathed until the personal safety of an American on the ocean, is completely provided for... . If she thinks it worth eternal war, eternal war we must have.

ME XII 384-87 George Logan 10-3-13

No man on earth has stronger detestation than myself of the unprincipled tyrant who is deluging the continent of Europe with blood. No man was more gratified by his disasters of the last campaign... . But the desire of seeing England forced to just terms of peace with us, make me equally solicitous for her entire exclusion from intercourse with the rest of the world, until by the peaceable engine of constraint, she can be made to renounce her views of the dominion over the ocean... .

How the Americans Won the War

ME XIII 168-70 General Thaddeus Kosciusko 6-28-12

Within these thirty years what a vast course of growth and prosperity have we had! It is not ten years since Great Britain began a series of insults and injuries which would have been met with war in the threshold by any European power. This course has been unremittingly followed up by increasing wrongs, with glimmerings indeed of peaceable redress, just sufficient to keep us quiet... .

The difficulty of selecting a foe between them has spared us many years of war, and enabled us to enter into it with less debt, more strength and preparation. Our present enemy will have the sea to herself, while we shall be equally predominant on land, and shall strip her of all her possessions on this continent. She may burn New York, indeed, by her ships and congreve rockets, in which case we must burn the city of London by hired incendiaries, of which her starving manufacturers will furnish abundance. A people in such desperation as to demand of their government... either bread or the gallows, will not reject the same alternative when offered by a foreign hand. Hunger will make them brave every risk for bread. The partisans of England here have endeavored much to goad us into the folly of choosing the ocean instead of the land, for the theatre of war. This would be to meet their strength with our weakness, instead of their weakness with our strength.

I hope we shall confine ourselves to the conquest of their possessions, and defence of our harbors, leaving the war on the ocean to our privateers. These will immediately swarm in every sea, and do more injury to British commerce than the regular fleets of all Europe would do... .

Some have apprehended we should be overwhelmed by the new improvements of war, which have not yet reached us. But the British possess them very imperfectly, and what are these improvements? Chiefly in the management of artillery, of which our country admits little use. We have nothing to fear from land armies, and shall put nothing in prize to their fleets. Upon the whole, I have known no war entered into under more favorable auspices... .

Nothing is more certain than that, come peace when it will, we shall never again go to England for a shilling where we have gone for a dollar's worth. Instead of applying to her manufacturers there, they must starve or come here to be employed. I give you these details of peaceable operations, because they are within my present sphere. Those of war are in better hands, who know how to keep their own secrets.

ME XIII 180-82 Colonel William Duane 8-4-12

...the seeds of genius which nature sows with even hand through every age and country, and which need only soil and season to germinate, will develop themselves among our military men. Some of them will become prominent, and seconded by the native energy of our citizens, will soon, I hope, to our force add the benefits of skill... .

Their fleet will annihilate our public force on the water, but our privateers will eat out the vitals of their commerce.

Perhaps they will burn New York or Boston. If they do, we must burn the city of London, not by expensive fleets or congreve rockets, but by employing an hundred or two Jack-the-painters, whom nakedness, famine, desperation, and hardened vice, will abundantly furnish from among themselves.

ME XIV 30-33 Don Valentin de Toronda Coruna 12-14-13

We are now at the close of our second campaign with England... this has been more successful... . The two immediate causes of the war were the orders of council and the impressment of our seamen. The first, having been removed after we declared war, the war is continued for the second; and a third has been generated by their conduct during the war, in exciting the Indian hordes to murder and scalp the women and children on our frontier. This renders peace forever impossible but on the establishment of such a meridian boundary to their possessions, as that they never more can have such influence with the savages as to excite again the same barbarities. The thousand ships, too, they took from us in peace, and the six thousand seamen impressed, call for this indemnification. On the water, we have proved to the world the error of their invincibility, and shown that with equal force and well-trained officers, they can be beaten by other nations as brave as themselves.

ME XIV 211-21 William Short 11-28-14

The enemy are... now disgorging what they had so ravenously swallowed... . Our list of captures from them is now one thousand, three hundred, and... we shall probably add one thousand prizes a year to their past losses... the war against us alone cannot cost them less than twenty millions of dollars a year, so that each American impressed has already cost them ten thousand dollars, and every year will add four thousand dollars more to his price. We, I suppose, expend more; but had we adopted the other alternative of submission, no mortal man can tell what the cost would have been. I consider the war, then, as entirely justifiable on our part, although I am sensible it is a deplorable misfortune to us. It has arrested the course of the most remarkable tide of prosperity any nation ever experienced... . Farewell all hopes of extinguishing the public debt! farewell all visions of applying surpluses of revenue to the improvements of peace, rather than the ravages of war. Our enemy indeed has the consolation of Satan of removing our first parents from Paradise; from a peaceable and agricultural nation, he makes us a military and manufacturing one.

We shall indeed survive the conflict. Breeders enough will remain to carry on our population. We shall retain our country, and rapid advances in the art of war will soon enable us to beat our enemy, and drive him from the continent.

ME XIV 226-30 Colonel James Monroe 1-1-15

But, however these difficulties of men and money may be disposed of, it is fortunate that neither of them will affect our war by sea. Privateers will find their own men and money. Let nothing be spared to encourage them. They are the dagger which strikes at the heart of the enemy, their commerce. Frigates and seventy-fours are a sacrifice we must make, heavy as it is, to the prejudices of a part of our citizens. They have, indeed, rendered a great moral service, which has delighted me as much as any one in the United States. But they have had no physical effect sensible to the enemy, and now, while we must fortify them in our harbors and keep armies to defend them, our *privateers* are boarding and blockading the enemy in their own seaports. Encourage them to burn all their prizes, and let the public pay for them. They will cheat us enormously. No matter; they will make the merchants of England feel, and squeal, and cry out for peace.

ME XIV 240-44 William H. Crawford 2-11-15

The victories of the last year at Chippewa, Niagara, Fort Erie, Plattsburg, and New Orleans, the capture of their two fleets on Lakes Erie and Champlain, and repeated triumphs of our frigates over hers... show that we have officers now becoming prominent, and capable of making them feel the superiority of our means in a war on our own soil.

13. France and the U.S.

Commentary

In contemplating the figure of Jefferson, it has been said that he looms majestic with the Declaration of Independence in one hand and the Louisiana Purchase in the other: certainly, these two rank among the most important in American history. And let us review briefly the sequence of events dealing with the acquisition of our west central states.

In 1802, Spain ceded the Port of New Orleans and the Floridas to France, then under the command of Napoleon Bonaparte, whose ambitions envisioned nothing less than a world-embracing empire. Without warning, the Intendant at the Port of New Orleans shut off the passage of American produce. Jefferson was convinced that with Bonaparte astride this crucial passageway, it would have to be acquired peaceably or the issue would soon be left to the arbitrament of war.

This was, to him, an extremely unpleasant prospect; for France had usually been our friend; but with Jefferson, national interests superseded all others; and he was prepared to enter into an alliance with the hated English rather than permit Napoleon to control American destiny.

However, in this crisis, Jefferson again proved himself the ultimate statesman: while ready to enter into alliance with England, he made preparations for war against France as a last resort: but, in the fervent hope that this might be avoided, he first instructed the American ambassador in Paris, Robert Livingston, to feel out the government there as to what might be done; he wrote also to his friend, Dupont de Nemours, seeking his good offices; and he sent James Monroe as Minister Extraordinary, with full discretionary powers, to solve the impasse by a satisfactory agreement. He was to make it clear to Bonaparte that he must cede or sell New Orleans to the United States, or face total war against us in alliance with Great Britain on sea and land.

The prospect of war with France drove the Federalists into deliria of ecstasy; they hoped to increase the public debt, make the new western provinces Federalist, and thus again achieve national power by driving the republicans out of the General Government. However, Jefferson's statesmanship again frustrated and defeated them.

Fortunately, the American position had been strengthened as a result of a French disaster in Santo Domingo; even Napoleon, who needed money badly for his projected conquest of Europe, could see that war on the American continent would not be successful.

Livingston and Monroe carried on their negotiations in Paris between March and May, 1803, not only with great tact, but with extraordinary success. Instead of acquiring merely the Port of New Orleans, they purchased the entire Louisiana Territory — 1,000,000 square miles, about 650,000,000 acres — for $15,000,000, with $2,000,000 down, the rest to be paid after 15 years, which, together with interest, would total $27,000,000, or four cents an acre. Most of this was subsequently obtained from the people in the new territories; and for this reason, they cost the government virtually nothing at all.

This transaction — not strictly legal — was consummated without previous congressional authority or appropriation. But it was a stroke of genius, unparalleled in American history, which more than doubled the area of the United States by adding what became the richest and most productive portion of the nation.

Since Jefferson was stationed in France between August, 1784, and September, 1789, he was able to observe one of the most profound political upheavals that has occurred on the European continent. We consider his letters describing events as they occurred so interesting and important that we quote rather extensively from them. In these, we can trace, step by step, as an eye-witness observed them, the events which finally exploded in a violent revolution by the masses of a major nation.

Among the economic-political revolutions of the western world, that which culminated in France in 1789 and continued for several years thereafter, is the great classic. For a thousand years, the nation — like others in Europe — had been ruled by a church-state coalition, in which the aristocracy and the priesthood — who owned almost all the property, tax-free — were supreme; at the top of this hierarchy stood an absolute and hereditary monarchy, which regarded the peasantry — which had gradually evolved from slavery and serfdom — as no better than cattle, fit only for everlasting labor and slaughter. Kept in ignorance, their production was appropriated by the ruling classes, who lived in a state of luxury and idleness which almost surpass the imagination. Since this production was minimal, the share left for their own sustenance was necessarily at the starvation level.

However, there had been dissident rumblings for decades; and, what was more significant, a middle class, known as the bourgeoisie, had been steadily advancing: shopkeepers, tradesmen, proprietors, and entrepreneurs of many kinds. Their interests were voiced by the Encyclopaedists, headed by Diderot and other scholars; and when Jean Jacques Rousseau published

Le Contrat Social *in 1762, this proved a bombshell which awakened the new class to self-consciousness, and heralded the revolutions in which the old order would perish.*

In 1789, there were four estates or social classes in France: (1) the landed aristocracy; (2) the Church and clergy, who owned nearly one half of the land and exploited millions of peasants; (3) the bourgeoisie, or Tiers Etat, the Third Estate; and (4) the proletarians and peasants, who had no representation in the States General or the National Assembly.

However, when the great explosion came, it was the mobs of Paris principally which accomplished the revolution. They stormed three great prisons, armed themselves with whatever weapons they could find, drove the soldiers out of the city, executed a number of officials, and took actual control. The revolution was established when the armed forces joined the people and became their allies and co-revolutionaries.

Various attempts were made to form a constitutional republic, under which some of the royal prerogatives would remain. However, it was found that the clergy and the aristocracy had no real intention of surrendering their privileges; and during the years after Jefferson left France, the extremists purged the nation by confiscating all the properties of the aristocracy and the Church, executing the King and the Queen, and sending several hundred thousands of the upper classes and their adherents to the guillotine in a bloodbath of the privileged never before equalled in European history.

When the pent-up drive for revenge had run its course, and bankruptcy faced the nation by the issuance of fiat assignats and montats, Napoleon Bonaparte assumed the power, achieved a kind of glory for France, and deluged the Continent with blood and fire — until he too found his ultimate fate on the island of St. Helena.

A Nation on the Verge of Revolution

ME XIX 15-20 James Madison 10-28-85

I fell in with a poor woman [who]... told me she was a day laborer... that she had two children to maintain... that often she could get no employment and of course was without bread.... I gave her, on parting, 24 sous. She burst into tears of a gratitude which I could perceive was unfeigned because she was unable to utter a word... .

This... led me into a train of reflections on that unequal division of property which occasions the wretchedness which... is to be observed all over Europe. The property of this country is absolutely concentred in a very few hands... . These employ the flower of the country as servants, some of them having as many as 200 domestics, not laboring. They employ also a great number of manufacturers and tradesmen, and last a class of laboring husbandmen.

But after all, there comes the most numerous of all classes, that is, the poor who cannot find work. I asked myself what could be the reason so many should be permitted to beg who are willing to work, in a country where there is a very considerable proportion of uncultivated lands? These lands are undisturbed only for the sake of game. It should seem that it must be because of the enormous wealth of the proprietors which places them above attention to the increase of their revenues by permitting these lands to be labored.

CE II 88-92 John Jay 1-9-87

...The King has called an assembly of the Notables of this country. This has not been done for one hundred and sixty years.

ME VI 274-78 General Washington 8-14-87

The Assemblee des Notables has been productive of much good... . Notwithstanding all this, the discovery of abominable abuses of public money by the late Comptroller General, some new expenses of the Court... and the imposition of new taxes, have, in the course of a few weeks, raised a spirit of discontent... so great and so general, as to threaten serious consequences. The parliaments in general, and particularly that of Paris, put themselves at the head of this effervescence, and direct its object to the calling of the Estates General, who have not been assembled since 1614. The object is to fix a constitution, and to limit expenses.

ME VI 285-89 John Adams 8-30-87

It is urged principally against the King that his revenue is one hundred and thirty millions more than that of his predecessor, and yet he demands one hundred and twenty millions further... . In the meantime, all tongues in Paris (and in France as it is said) have been let loose, and never was a license of speaking against the government exercised in London more freely or more universally.

ME VII 112-13 Colonel Monroe 8-9-88

This nation is, at present, under great internal agitation. The authority of the Crown on one part, and that of the parliaments on the other, are fairly at issue... . The government... are yielding daily, one right after another, to the nation. They have acknowledged the King cannot lay a new tax without the consent of the States General; and they will call the States General the next year. The object of this body, when met, will be a bill of rights, a civil list, a national assembly meeting at certain epochs... . So I think it possible, this country will, within two or three years, be in the enjoyment of a tolerably free constitution, and that without its having cost them a drop of blood; for none has yet been spilt, though the English papers have set the whole nation to cutting throats.

BW 467-9 Autobiography 1821

...considerable intervals... gave time for the feelings excited by the proceedings of the Notables to cool off, new claims to be advanced, and a pressure to arise for a fixed constitution, not subject to changes at the will of the King.

Nor should we wonder at this pressure, when we consider the monstrous abuses of power under which this people were ground to powder; when we pass in review the weight of the taxes, and the inequality of their distribution; the oppressions of the tithes, and tailles, the corvees, the gabelles, the farms and the barrier; the shackles on commerce by monopolies; on industry by guilds and corporations; on the freedom of conscience, of thought, and of speech; on the freedom of the press by the Censure; and of the person by Lettres de Cachet; the cruelty of the Criminal code generally; the atrocities of the Rack; the venality of the Judges, and their partialities to the rich; the monopoly of Military honors by the Noblesse; the enormous expenses of the Queen, the Prince and the Court; the prodigalities of pensions; and the riches, luxury, indolence and immorality of the Clergy. Surely, under such a mass of misrule and oppression, a people might justly press for a thorough reformation, and might even dismount their rough-shod riders, and leave them to walk on their own legs... .

...the King... had not a wish but for the good of the nation; and for that object, no personal sacrifice would ever have cost him a moment's regret; but his mind was weakness itself, his constitution timid, his judgment null, and without firmness sufficient even to stand by the faith of his word. His Queen, too, haughty and bearing no contradiction, had an absolute ascendancy over him; and around her were rallied the King's brother d'Artois, the court generally, and the aristocratic part of his Ministers... .

ME VII 223-31 General Washington 12-4-88

The Notables in the true spirit of Priests and Nobles, combining together against the people, have voted, by five *bureaux* out of six, that the people, or Tiers Etat [the Third Estate], shall have no greater number of deputies than each of the other orders separately, and that they shall vote by orders: so that the two orders concurring in a vote, the third will be over ruled... [which] will render the representation of the Tiers Etat nugatory.

ME VII 252-59 Dr. Price 1-8-89

... the American war seems first to have awakened the thinking part of this nation in general from the sleep of despotism in which they were sunk... . Happily for the nation, it happened that, at the same moment, the dissipations of the Court had exhausted the money and credit of the

State... . [It] has no idea of supplying the deficit by economies,... saw no means but by new taxes.

No more can be had from the people. They are squeezed to the last drop. The Clergy and Nobles, by their privileges and influence, have kept their property... untaxed hitherto. They remain to be squeezed, and no agent is powerful enough for this, but the people. But the Notables, consisting mostly of the privileged characters, had proposed a method of compromising the States [General], which would have rendered the voice of the people... inefficient... . The Clergy will move heaven and earth to obtain the suffrage by orders, because that parries the effect of all hitherto done for the people. The people will probably... consent to no tax... unless the voice of the Tiers Etat be equalled to that of the Clergy and Nobles combined.

The Convocation of the States General

(This body finally convened for the first time in 165 years.)

BW 470-71 Autobiography 1821

The States General were opened on the 5th of May, '89... [Its] composition... although equivalent, on the whole, to what had been expected, was something different in its elements. It had been supposed, that a superior education would carry into the scale of the Commons a respectable portion of the Noblesse. It did so as to those of Paris, of its vicinity, and the other considerable cities, whose greater intercourse with enlightened society had liberalized their minds, and prepared them to advance up to the times. But the Noblesse of the country, which constituted two-thirds of that body, were far in their rear. Residing constantly on their patrimonial feuds, and familiarized, by daily habit, with Seigneurial powers and practices, they had not yet learned to suspect their inconsistence with reason and right. They were willing to submit to equality of taxation, but not to descend from their rank and prerogatives to be incorporated in session with the Tiers Etat. Among the Clergy, on the other hand, it had been apprehended that the higher orders of the Hierarchy, by their wealth and connections, would have carried the elections generally; but it turned out, that in most cases, the lower clergy had obtained the popular majorities. These consisted of the Cures, the sons of the peasantry, who had been employed to do all the drudgery of parochial services for ten, twenty, or thirty Louis a year; while their superiors were consuming their princely revenues in palaces of luxury and indolence.

ME VII 356-58 Mr. Jay 5-12-89

The Tiers Etat remain unshaken in their resolution to do no business with the other orders, unless voting by persons. The Nobles are equally determined... to vote only by orders.

ME VII 361-67 Thomas Paine 5-19-89

...the Tiers Etat are immovable. They are not only firm, but a little disdainful. The question is, what will ensue?... As soon as it shall become evident that no amicable determination of the manner of voting can take place, the Tiers Etat will send an invitation to the other two orders to come and take their places in the common chamber. A majority of the lesser Clergy will go, and the minority of the Noblesse. The chamber thus composed will declare that the States General are constituted, will notify it to the King, and that they are ready to proceed to business. If the King refuses to do business with them, and adheres to the Nobles, the common chamber will declare taxes at an end, and will form a declaration of rights, and do such other acts as circumstances will permit, and go home. The tax-gatherers will then be resisted... . But it is more likely that the King will agree to do business with the States General, as constituted... . If the matter takes this turn... no serious difficulty will ensue.

ME VII 367 Monsieur de Crevecoeur 5-20-89

At this moment, however, they are at a dead stand. The great preliminary question, whether they shall vote by orders or persons, seems to threaten a scission.

ME VII 372-76 Monsieur de St. Etienne 6-5-89

A CHARTER OF RIGHTS SOLEMNLY ESTABLISHED BY THE KING AND THE NATION: June, 1789[a]

1. The States General shall assemble, uncalled, on the first day of November, annually...
2. The States General alone shall levy money on the nation, and shall appropriate it.
3. Laws shall be made by the States General only, with the consent of the King.

a.Although this Declaration was composed and proposed early in June, it was not signed by the King; and it was not enacted by the Assembly until the 4th of August, following the capture of the Invalides and the Bastille.

4. No person shall be restrained of his liberty but by regular process from a court of justice, authorized by a general law... . The officer in whose custody the prisoner is, shall obey the orders of the judge; and both the judge and the officer shall be responsible, civilly and criminally, for failure of duty herein.
5. The military must be subordinate to the civil authority.
6. Printers shall be liable to legal prosecution for printing and publishing false facts... ; but they shall be under no other restraint.
7. All pecuniary privileges and exemptions... are abolished.
8. All debts already contracted by the King are hereby made the debts of the nation.
9. Eighty millions of livres are now granted to the King... .
10. The States General shall now separate, and meet again on the first day of November next.

ME VII 375-82 John Jay 6-17-89

The fate of the nation depends on the conduct of the King and his ministers. Were they to side openly with the Commons, the revolution would be completed without convulsions, by the establishment of a constitution, tolerably free, and in which the distinction between noble and commoner would be suppressed. But this is scarcely possible. The King is honest... but the... hereditary aristocracy is too difficult for him... the Commons, after suppressing taxes, and finishing their declaration of rights, would probably go home; if a bankruptcy takes place... and a resistance to the tax-gatherers follows [there will] probably be civil war.

It is a tremendous cloud, indeed, which hovers over this nation... .

National Assembly Established

ME VII 386-90 James Madison 6-18-89

On the 15th [of June] the Commons moved to declare themselves the National Assembly... . We shall know, I think, in a day or two, whether the government will risk a bankruptcy and civil war, rather than see all distinctions of orders done away, which is what the Commons push for... . The Noblesse... are so furious, they can seldom debate at all... . The Clergy are waiting to profit by every incident to secure themselves, and have no other object in view... . The Bishops and Archbishops have been very successful by bribes and intrigues, in detaching the Cures from the Commons... . The Cures form the mass of the Clergy; they are the only part favorably known to the people, because solely charged with the duties of baptism, burial, confession, visitation of the sick, instruction of the children, and aiding the poor; they are themselves of the people, and united with them. The carriages and equipages only of the higher Clergy, not their persons, are known to the people, and are in detestation with them.

ME VII 390 ff. John Jay 6-24-89

[On June 17] the Tiers had declared the illegality of all existing taxes, and their discontinuance from the end of the present session.

[On the 20th, the Tiers found the doors of the House barred and went to another place.] They there bound themselves to each other by an oath, never to separate of their own accord, till they had settled a constitution for the nation on a solid basis, and, if separated by force, that they would re-assemble in some other place. [Describes scencs that followed]. In the afternoon, the people, uneasy, began to assemble in great numbers in the courts and vicinities of the palace. The Queen was alarmed and sent for Mr. Neckar. He was conducted amidst shouts and acclamations of the multitude, who filled all the apartments of the palace.

[On the 25th:] There are now with the Tiers one hundred and sixty-four members of the Clergy, so that the common chamber consists of upwards of eight hundred members. [Describes how the run on the bank continues.]

ME VII 392-99 John Jay 6-29-89

[After the *Seance Royale* on the 23rd, the soldiers began joining the people.] They began to quit their barracks, to assemble in squads, to declare that they would defend the life of the King, but would not cut the throats of their fellow-citizens. [Only the Swiss Guards remained loyal to the King, and even some of them wavered.] They were treated and caressed by the people, carried in triumph through the streets, called themselves the soldiers of the nation, and left no doubt on whose side they would be in case of a rupture... and gave good reason to apprehend that the soldiery, in general, would side with their brothers and fathers, rather than with their officers.

ME VII 404-08 Thomas Paine 7-11-89

The *National Assembly* then (for that is the name they now take), having shown through every stage of these transactions a coolness, wisdom, and resolution to set fire to the four corners of the kingdom and to perish with it themselves, rather than to relinquish an iota from their plan of a total change of government, are now in complete and undisputed possession of the sovereignty. The executive and aristocracy are at their feet; the mass of the nation, the mass of the clergy, and the army are with them; they have prostrated the old government, and are now beginning to build one from the foundation.

Revolution!

ME XIX 62 Nathaniel Cutting 6-7-89

I had high hopes of a favorable issue to the revolution of this country till about ten days ago when there began to be room for fear.

ME XIX 63 Thomas Paine 7-13-89

Mr. Neckar [who advocated compromise] was dismissed from office the evening of the 11th and set out for Geneva.

ME VII 409-22 John Jay 7-19-89

But it was soon observed that troops, and particularly the foreign troops, were on their march towards Paris from various quarters, and that this was against the opinion of Mr. Neckar... . The Marshall de Broglio was appointed to command all the troops... a high-flying aristocrat, cool and capable of everything. Some of the French guards were soon arrested under other pretexts, but in reality, on account of their dispositions in favor of the national cause. The people of Paris forced the prison, released them, and sent a deputation to the States General, to solicit a pardon. The States... recommended these prisoners to the King, and peace to the people of Paris... .

On the 8th day of July, they voted an address to the King to remove the troops. This piece of masculine eloquence, written by Monsieur de Mirabeau, is worth attention on account of the bold matter it expresses and discovers through the whole.

The King refused to remove the troops, and said they might remove themselves, if they pleased... . A declaration of rights, which forms the first chapter of their work, was then proposed by the Marquis de La Fayette. This was on the 11th. In the meantime, troops, to the number of about twenty-five or thirty thousand, had arrived, and were posted in and between Paris and Versailles. The bridges and passes were guarded. At three o'clock in the afternoon, the Count de La Luzerne was sent to notify Mr. Neckar of his dismission, and to enjoin him to retire instantly, without saying a word of it to anybody... .

In the afternoon [of July 12] a body of about one hundred German cavalry were advanced and drawn up in the Place Louis XV and about two hundred Swiss posted at a little distance in their rear. This drew the people to that spot, who naturally formed themselves in front of the troops, at first merely to look at them. But as their numbers increased, their indignation arose; they retired a few steps, posted themselves on and behind large piles of loose stones, collected in that place for a bridge adjacent to it, and attacked the horse with stones. The horse charged, but the advantageous position of the people, and the showers of stones, obliged them to retire, and even to quit the field altogether, leaving one of their number on the ground. The Swiss in their rear were observed never to stir. This was the signal for universal insurrection, and this body of cavalry, to avoid being massacred, retired towards Versailles.

The people now armed themselves with such weapons as they could find in amorers' shops and private houses, and with bludgeons, and were roaming all night through all parts of the city without any decided practicable object.

The next day [the 13th], the States pressed the King to send away the troops, to permit the Bourgeoisie of Paris to arm for the preservation of order in the city, and offered to send a deputation from their body to tranquillize them. He refused all their propositions. A committee of magistrates and electors of the city were appointed by their bodies, to take upon them its government. The mob, now openly joined by the French guards, forced the prison of St. Lazare, released all the prisoners, and took a great store of corn, which they carried to the corn market. Here they got some arms, and the French guards began to form and train them. The committee determined to raise forty-eight thousand Bourgeoisie... . On the 14th, they sent one of their members (Monsieur de Corny, whom we knew in America) to the Hotel des Invalides, to ask arms for their Garde Bourgeoisie. He was followed by, or he found there, a great mob. The Governor of the Invalides came out, and represented the impossibility of his delivering arms, without the orders of those from whom he received them. De Corny advised the people then to retire, and retired himself; and the people took possession of the arms. It was remarkable, that not only the Invalides themselves made no opposition, but that a body of five thousand foreign troops, encamped within four hundred yards, never stirred.

Monsieur de Corny and five others were then sent to ask arms of Monsieur de Launai, Governor of the Bastile. They found a great collection of people already before the place, and they immediately planted a flag of truce which was answered by a like flag hoisted on the parapet. The deputation prevailed on the people to fall back a little, advanced themselves to make their demand of the Governor, and in that instant a discharge from the Bastile killed four people of those nearest to the deputies. The deputies retired; the people rushed against the place, and almost in an instant were in possession of a fortification, defended by one hundred men, of infinite strength, which in other times had stood several regular sieges, and had never been taken. How they got in, has, as yet, been impossible to discover... . They took all the arms, discharged the prisoners, and such of the garrison as were not killed in the first moment of fury, carried the Governor and Lieutenant Governor to the Greve, (the place of public execution,) cut off their heads, and sent them through the city in triumph to the Palais Royal... .

The demolition of the Bastile was now ordered and begun. A body of

Swiss guards of the regiment of Ventimille, and the city horse guards, joined the people. The alarm at Versailles increased, instead of abating. They believed that the aristocrats of Paris were under pillage and carnage, that one hundred and fifty thousand men were in arms, coming to Versailles to massacre the royal family, the court, the ministers, and all connected with them, their practices and principles. The aristocrats of the Nobles and Clergy in the States General, vied with each other in declaring how sincerely they were converted to the justice of voting by persons, and how determined to go with the nation all its lengths. The foreign troops were ordered off instantly. Every minister resigned... .

The King came to Paris, leaving the Queen in consternation for his return... the King's carriage was in the centre, on each side of it the States General, in two ranks, on foot, and at their head the Marquis de La Fayette, as Commander-in-Chief, on horseback, and Bourgeoise guards before and behind. About sixty thousand citizens of all forms and colors, armed with the muskets of the Bastile and the Invalides, as far as they would go, the rest with pistols, swords, pikes, pruning hooks, scythes, etc., lined all the streets through which the procession passed, and, with the crowds of people in the streets, doors and windows, saluted them everywhere with cries of "*vive la nation;*" but not a single "*vive le roy*" was heard. The King stopped at the Hotel de Ville... .

On their return, the popular cries were "*vive le roy et la nation.*" He was conducted by a Garde Bourgeoise to his palace at Versailles, and thus concluded such an *amende honorable,* as no sovereign ever made, and no people ever received. Letters written with his own hand to the Marquis de La Fayette, remove the scruples of his position. Tranquillity is now restored to the capital; the shops are again opened; the people resuming their labors, and if the want of bread does not disturb our peace, we may hope a continuance of it. The demolition of the Bastile is going on, and the Milice Bourgeoisie organizing and training. The ancient police of the city is abolished by the authority of the people, the introduction of the King's troops will probably be proscribed, and a watch or city guards substituted, which shall depend on the city alone. The whole country must pass successively through it, and happy if they get through it as soon and as well as Paris has done.

Facing Counter-Revolution

BW 480-81 Autobiography 1821

In the evening of August 4th, and on the motion of the Viscount de Noailles, brother-in-law of La Fayette, the Assembly abolished all titles of rank, all the abusive privileges of feudalism, the tithes and casuals of the Clergy, all Provincial privileges, and, in fine, the feudal regimen generally... . Many days were employed in putting into the form of laws, the numerous demolitions of ancient abuses; which done, they proceeded to the preliminary work of a Declaration of Rights. There being much concord of sentiment, it was liberally framed, and passed with a very general approbation... .

The aristocracy was cemented by a common principle, of preserving the ancient regime, or whatever should be nearest to it. Making this their polar star, they moved in phalanx, gave preponderance on every question to the minorities of the Patriots, and always to those who advocated the least change. The features of the new constitution were thus assuming a fearful aspect, and great alarm was produced among the honest Patriots by these dissensions in their ranks.

ME VII 432-36 William Carmichael 8-9-89

They [the National Assembly] will distribute the powers of government into three parts, legislative, judiciary, and executive... . There is a considerable division of sentiment whether the executive shall have a negative on the laws... . In the judiciary, the parliaments will be suppressed, less numerous judiciary bodies instituted, and trial by jury established in criminal, if not in civil cases. The executive power will be left entire in the hands of the King. They will establish the responsibility of ministers, gifts and appropriations of money by the National Assembly alone; consequently, a civil list, freedom of the press, freedom of religion, freedom of commerce and industry, freedom of the person against arbitrary arrests, and modifications, if not a total prohibition, of military agency in civil cases.

ME VII 436-45 John Jay 8-27-89

Considerable interval having taken place since any popular execution, the aristocratic party is raising its head. They are strengthened by a considerable defection from the patriots, in consequence of the general supression of the abuses of the 4th of August, in which many acquired strength in the Assembly... .

CE III 96-102 James Madison 8-28-89

That enemy [the aristocracy] begins to raise its head.

ME VII 467-78 John Jay 9-19-89

The patience of the people... is worn threadbare. Time has been given to the aristocrats to recover from their panic, to cabal, to sow dissensions in the Assembly, and distrust out of it... .

The Assembly now consists of four distinct parties. 1. The aristocrats, comprehending the higher members of the clergy, military, nobility, and the parliaments of the whole kingdom... . 2. The moderate royalists who wish for a constitution nearly similar to that of England. 3. The republicans, who are willing to let their first magistracy be hereditary, but to make it very subordinate to the legislature, and to have that legislature consist of a single chamber. 4. The faction of Orleans. The second and third descriptions are composed of honest, well-meaning men, differing in opinion only, but both wishing the establishment of as great a degree of liberty as can be preserved. They are considered together as constituting the patriotic part of the Assembly, and they are supported by the soldiery of the army, the soldiery of the Clergy, that is to say, the Cures and monks, the dissenters, and part of the nobility which is small, and the substantial Bourgeoisie of the whole nation. The part of these collected in the cities, have formed themselves into municipal bodies, have chosen municipal representatives, and have organized an armed corps, considerably more numerous in the whole than the regular army. They have also the ministry, such as it is, and, as yet, the King.

Were the second and third parties, or rather these sections of the same party, to separate entirely, this great mass of power and wealth would be split, nobody knows how. But I do not think they will separate; because they have the same honest views; because... there is no rancor between them... . Another powerful bond of union between these parties, is our friend the Marquis de La Fayette... . His attachment to both is equal, and he labors incessantly to keep them together... . His command of the armed forces of Paris (thirty thousand in number, and comprehending the French guards, who are five thousand regulars), and his influence with the municipality, would secure their city... .

ME VIII 166-74 William Short to T. J. 1-24-91

The resistance of a considerable part of the clergy to a decree of the assembly for their civil organization... has been a matter of uneasiness for some time. By a decree of the assembly all those who, by a given day, had not taken an oath to maintain the civil organization of that body, were to be deprived of their ecclesiastical functions... . In the capital, their [the people's] love of the Revolution so far surpasses every other passion, that all the exertions of the *Garde Nationale* have been necessary to prevent their entering the churches and hanging the curates. They will manifest their dispositions less violently, perhaps, in the provinces, but in general the spirit of the Revolution will certainly predominate even if the clergy succeed to convince them that it is contrary to the spirit of religion.

A King, A Queen, and France

ME VIII 232-34 Edward Rutledge 8-15-91

You will have heard before this reaches you, of the peril into which the French revolution is brought by the flight of their King. Such are the fruits of that form of government, which heaps importance on idiots, and which the Tories of the present day are trying to preach into our favor.

ME IX 33-35 James Madison March, 1793

The death of the king of France has not produced as open condemnation from the monocrats as I expected... . It is certain that the ladies of this city, of the first circle, are open-mouthed against the murderers of a sovereign, and they generally speak those sentiments which the more cautious husbands smother.

ME IX 44-46 3-18-93

We have just received here the news of the decapitation of the king of France. Should the present foment in Europe not produce republics everywhere, it will at least soften the monarchial governments by rendering monarchs amenable to punishment like other criminals, and doing away with that outrage of insolence and oppression, the inviolability of the King's person. We, I hope, shall adhere to our republican government, and keep it to its original principles by narrowly watching it.

ME IX 284-88 Tench Coxe 5-1-94

I hope that the triumph [of the French people] and the consequent disgrace of the invading tyrants, is destined... to kindle the wrath of the people of Europe against those who have dared to embroil them in such wickedness, and to bring at length, kings, nobles, and priests to the scaffolds which they have been so long deluging with human blood. I am still warm whenever I think of those scoundrels, though I do it as seldom as I can, preferring infinitely to contemplate the tranquil growth of my lucerne and potatoes.

BW 478-79 Autobiography 1821

But he had a Queen of absolute sway over his weak and timid virtue... . This angel, as gaudily painted in the rhapsodies of Burke... was proud, disdainful of restraint... eager in the pursuit of pleasure, and firm enough to hold to her desires, or perish in the wreck. Her inordinate gambling and dissipations... had been a sensible item in the exhaustion of the Treasury, which called into action the reforming hand of the nation; and her opposition to it, her inflexible perseverance, and dauntless spirit, led herself to the Guillotine, drew the King on with her, and plunged the world into crimes and calamities which will forever stain the pages of modern history.

I have ever believed, that had there been no Queen, there would have been no revolution. No force would have been provoked or exercised. The King would have gone hand in hand with the wisdom of his sounder counsellors, who, guided by the increasing lights of the age, wished only, with the same pace, to advance the principles of their social constitution...

ME XIV 355-59 Mr. Gallatin 10-16-15

I grieve for France; although it cannot be denied that by the afflictions with which she wantonly and wickedly overwhelmed other nations, she has merited severe reprisals. For it is no excuse to lay the enormities to the wretch who led to them, and who has been the author of more misery and suffering to the world, than any being who ever lived before him. After destroying the liberties of his country, he has exhausted all its resources, physical and moral, to indulge his own maniac ambition, his own tyrannical and overbearing spirit. His sufferings cannot be too great.

CE VII 76-77 M. de Marbois 6-14-17

When I left France at the close of '89, your revolution was, as I thought, under the direction of able and honest men. But the madness of some of their successors, the vices of others, the malicious intrigues of an envious and corrupting neighbor, the tracasserie of the Directory, the usurpations, the havoc, and devastations of your Attila... will form a mournful period of which the last chapter will not be seen in your day or mine, and the one which I still fear is to be written in characters of blood.

Had Bonaparte reflected that each is the moral construction of the world, that no national crime passes unpunished in the long run, he would not now be in the cage of St. Helena, and were your present oppressors to reflect on the same truth, they would spare to their own countries the penalties on their present wrongs which will be inflicted on them in future times... . Like their brother robbers on the highway, they suppose the escape of the moment a final escape, and deem infamy and future risk countervailed by present gain.

Louisiana: Crisis and Solution

(Robert Livingston and James Monroe accomplished the purchase of the entire Louisiana Territory on May 9, 1803; news of the transaction reached Washington on the third of July.)

ME X 311-16 The United States Minister to France 4-18-02

The cession of Louisiana and the Floridas by Spain to France, works most sorely on the United States... . It completely reverses all the political relations of the United States, and will form a new epoch in our political course. Of all nations of any consideration, France is the one which, hitherto, has offered the fewest points on which we could have any conflict of right, and the most points of a communion of interests. From these causes, we have ever looked to her as our *natural friend,* as one with which we never could have an occasion of difference. Her growth, therefore, we viewed as our own, her misfortunes ours.

There is [however] on the globe one single spot, the possessor of which is our natural and habitual enemy. It is New Orleans, through which the produce of three-eighths of our territory must pass to market, and from its fertility it will ere long yield more than half of our whole produce, and contain more than half of our inhabitants. France, placing herself in that door, assumes to us the attitude of defiance. Spain might have retained it quietly for years. Her pacific disposition, her feeble state, would induce her to increase our facilities there, so that her possession of the place would be hardly felt by us, and it would not, perhaps, be very long before some circumstance might arise, which might make the cession of it to us the price of something of more worth to her. Not so can it ever be in the hands of France: the impetuosity of her temper, the energy and restlessness of her character, placed in a point of eternal friction with us, and our character, which, though quiet and loving peace and the pursuits of wealth, is high-minded, despising wealth in competition with insult or injury, enterprising and energetic as any nation on earth; these circumstances render it impossible that France and the United States can continue long friends, when they meet in so irritable a position.

They, as well as we, must be blind if they do not see this; and we must be very improvident if we do not begin to make arrangements on that hypothesis. The day that France takes possession of New Orleans, fixes the sentence which is to restrain her forever within her low-water mark. It seals the union of two nations [the United States and England], who, in conjunction, can maintain exclusive possession of the ocean. From that moment, we must marry ourselves to the British fleet and nation. We must turn all our attention to a maritime force, for which our resources place us on very high ground; and having formed and connected together a power which may render reinforcement of her settlements here impossible to France make the first cannon which shall be fired in Europe the signal for the tearing up any settlement she may have made, and for holding the two continents of America in sequestration for the common purposes of the United British and American nations. This not a state of things we seek or desire. It is one which this measure, if adopted by France, forces on us as necessarily, as any other cause, by the laws of nature, brings on its necessary effect... .

If France considers Louisiana, however, as [not?] indispensable of her views, she might perhaps be willing to look about for arrangements which might reconcile it to our interests. If anything could do this, it would be the ceding to us of the island of New Orleans and the Floridas. This would certainly, in a great degree, remove the causes of jarring and irritation between us, and perhaps for such a length of time, as might produce other means of making the measure permanently conciliatory to our interests and friendships... .

Every eye in the United States is now fixed on the affairs of Louisiana. Perhaps nothing since the revolutionary war, has produced more uneasy sensations through the body of the nation. Notwithstanding temporary bickerings have taken place with France, she has still a strong hold on the affections of our citizens generally. I have thought it not amiss, by way of supplement to the letters of the Secretary of State, to write you this private one, to impress you with the importance we affix to this transaction.

ME X 316-19 Monsieur Dupont de Nemours 4-25-02

...you may be able to impress on the government of France the inevitable consequences of their taking possession of Louisiana; and though, as I here mention the cession of New Orleans and the Floridas to us would be a palliation, yet I believe it would be no more, and that this measure will cost France, and perhaps not very long hence, a war which will annihilate her on the ocean, and place that element under the despotism of two nations, which I am not reconciled to the more because my own would be one of them... . France's possessing herself of Louisiana,... — this speck which now appears as an almost invisible point in the horizon, is the embryo of a tornado which will burst on the countries on both sides of the Atlantic, and involve in its effects their highest destinies.

That it may yet be avoided is my sincere prayer; and if you can be the means of informing the wisdom of Bonaparte of all its consequences, you will have deserved well of both countries. Peace and abstinence from European interferences are our objects, and so will continue while the present order of things in America remain uninterrupted.

ME X 343-46 James Monroe 1-13-03

The agitation of the public mind on occasion of the late suspension of our right of deposit at New Orleans is extreme. In the western country it is natural, and grounded on honest motives. In the seaports it proceeds from a desire for war, which increases the mercantile lottery; in the federalists generally, and especially those of Congress, the object is to force us into war if possible, in order to derange our finances, or if this cannot be done, to attach the western country to them, as their best friends, and thus get again into power... .

The measures we have been pursuing, being invisible, do not satisfy their minds. Something sensible, therefore, has become necessary: and indeed our object of purchasing New Orleans and the Floridas is a measure liable to assume so many shapes, that no instructions could be squared to fit them. It was essential, then, to send a minister extraordinary [Mr. Monroe],... with discretionary powers; first, however, well impressed with all our views, and therefore qualified to meet and modify to these every form of proposition which could come from the other party. This could be done only in full and frequent oral communications. Having determined on this, there could not be two opinions among the republicans as to the person. You possessed the unlimited confidence of the administration and of the western people; and generally of the republicans everywhere... .

On the event of this mission depend the future destinies of this republic. If we cannot by a purchase of the country, insure to ourselves a course of perpetual peace and friendship with all nations, then as war cannot be distant, it behooves us immediately to be preparing for that course, without, however, hastening it; and it may be necessary (on your failure on the continent) to cross the channel. We shall get entangled in European politics, and figuring more, be much less happy and prosperous. This can only be prevented by a successful issue to your present mission.

ME X 347-50 Monsieur Dupont de Nemours 2-1-03

The suspension of the right of deposit at New Orleans, ceded to us by our treaty with Spain, threw our whole country into such a ferment as immediately threatened its peace. This, however, was believed to be the act of the Intendant, unauthorized by his government. But it showed the necessity of making effectual arrangements to secure the peace of the two countries against the indiscreet acts of subordinate agents. The urgency of the case... induced us to [send]... a minister extraordinary... Mr. Monroe... For the occlusion of the Mississippi is a state of things in which we cannot exist. He goes, therefore, joined with Chancellor Livingston, to aid in the issue of a crisis, the most important the United States have ever met since their independence, and which is to decide their future character and career... .

It will often, perhaps, be possible for you, having a freedom of communication... to smooth difficulties by representations and reasonings, which would be received with more suspicion from them. You will thereby render great good to both countries. For our circumstances are so imperious as to admit of no delay as to our course; and the use of the Mississippi so indispensable, that we cannot hesitate one moment to hazard our existence for its maintenance. If we fail in this effort to put it beyond the reach of accident, we see the destinies we have to run, and prepare at once for them. Not but that we shall still endeavor to go on in peace and friendship with our neighbors as long as we can, *if our rights of navigation and deposit are respected;* but as we foresee that the caprices of the local officers, and the abuse of those rights by our boatmen and navigators, which neither government can prevent, will keep up a state of irritation which cannot long be kept inactive, we should be criminally improvident not to take at once eventual measures for strengthening ourselves for the contest.

ME X 402-03 General Horatio Gates 7-11-03

The territory acquired, as it includes all the waters of the Missouri and Mississippi, has more than doubled the area of the United States, and the new part is not inferior to the old, in soil, climate, productions, and important communications.

BW 352 Third Annual Message 10-17-03

Should the acquisition of Louisiana be constitutionally confirmed and carried into effect, a sum of nearly thirteen millions of dollars will then be added to our public debt, most of which is payable after fifteen years; before which term the present existing debts will all be discharged by the established operation of the sinking fund. When we contemplate the ordinary annual augmentation of imposts from increasing population and wealth, the augmentation of the same revenue by its extension to the new acquisition, and the economies which may still be introduced into our public expenditures, I cannot but hope that Congress in reviewing their resources will find means to meet the intermediate interests of this additional debt without recurring to new taxes, and applying to this object only the ordinary progression of our revenue. Its extraordinary increase in times of foreign war will be the proper and sufficient fund for any measure of safety or precaution which that state of things may render necessary in our neutral position.

ME X 443-45 Timothy Bloodworth 1-29-04

To.. purchase a country as large and more fertile than the one we possessed before, yet ask neither a new tax, nor another soldier to be added, but to provide that that country shall by its own income, pay for itself before the purchase money is due... are measures which I think must reconcile the great body of those who thought themselves our enemies; but were in truth only the enemies of certain Jacobinical, atheistical, anarchical, imaginary caricatures, which existed only in the land of raw head and bloody bones, being created to frighten the credulous.

ME X 445-48 Doctor Joseph Priestley 1-29-04

I very early saw that Louisiana was indeed a speck in our horizon which was to burst in a tornado; and the public are unapprized how near this catastrophe was. Nothing but a frank and friendly development of causes and effects on our part, and good sense enough in Bonaparte to see the train was unavoidable, and would change the face of the world, saved us from that storm. I did not expect he would yield till a war took place between France and England, and my hope was to palliate and endure, if Messrs. Ross, Morris, etc., did not force a premature rupture, until that event. I believed the event not very distant, but acknowledge it came on sooner than I had expected. Whether, however, the good sense of Bonaparte might not see the course predicted to be necessary and unavoidable, even before a war should be imminent, was a chance which we thought it our duty to try; but the immediate prospect of rupture brought the case to immediate decision. The *denouement* has been happy; and I confess I look to this duplication of area for the extending a government so free and economical as ours, as a great achievement to the mass of happiness which is to ensue.

ME XI 38-42 Philip Mazzei 7-18-04

The acquisition of Louisiana, besides doubling our extent, and trebling our quantity of fertile country, is of incalculable value, as relieving us from the danger of war. It has also enabled us to do a handsome thing for Fayette. He had received a grant of between eleven and twelve thousand acres north of Ohio, perhaps, a dollar an acre. We have received permission from Congress to locate this in Louisiana.

14. Currency and Monetary Theory

Commentary

If there was one monetary lesson resulting from the Revolutionary war more important than any other, it was that fiat money, no matter by whom issued, in excess of circulation-needs, will result in its depreciation. For this reason, the Founding Fathers attempted to make it certain that this nation would forever maintain a specie currency with coins of a specific weight and fineness. Thus Congress was given the exclusive power to coin money and regulate the value thereof; and the States are forbidden ever *to make anything but gold and silver coin a tender for the payment of debt.*

However, as Jefferson pointed out, the Continental Congress had no money nor did it possess the power to levy taxes; it could, therefore, only issue currency in the hope that before long they would have the power to redeem it, dollar for dollar, in specie. However, as the war dragged on, there were many issues of Continentals; and soon they went 2 for 1; then 5, 10, 15; and by 1779, they were 20 to 1. As they continued to circulate, they depreciated to 40, then 75, and finally 1,000 to one, at which point the whole mass expired. Thereafter, they were purchased by speculators at 5,000 for one silver dollar.

When this currency ceased circulation, the Congress issued certificates of indebtedness which, however, were not circulating currency; and the soldiers, victuallers, and farmers who received them were soon in such distress that they parted with them for as little as one-tenth of their value.

In due course, a contest erupted in Congress so fierce that it threatened the dissolution of the nation: the federal assumption of the State debts, which had been incurred separately during the Revolution. Had Hamilton had his way, the Continentals, the certificates of indebtedness, and the State debts would all have been assumed by the General Government at par, *with a total of at least $400 million, almost all of which would have been net profit to the speculators and jugglers who had obtained it.*

Let us summarize what happened: the $200 million issued by the Continental Congress was worth $36 million at the time of emission. Most of this was in the hands of people who got it almost for nothing. The *certificates of indebtedness, issued to soldiers and suppliers, worth $16 million, were filched from them at drastic discounts. And when Congress decided to assume the State debts to the extent of $20 million, the total funded by the federal government became $72 million; however, since those who finally possessed all this paper, had invested only $6 million, they garnered an ill-gotten loot of $66 million, which became the basis for many new fortunes.*

Jefferson describes poignantly what happened when Congress decided to redeem the certificates of indebtedness at par. Couriers set out on relays of horses and in fast sailing boats to reach every portion of the union before the news of the redemption could reach the people; and by this corruption, Hamilton built a power-base in Congress which enabled him to control every significant vote and — above all else — to achieve the establishment of the First United States Bank.

We never cease to wonder at Jefferson's genius, versatility, and wide-ranging interests: when the time came for Congress in 1790 to consider its First Coinage Act — which was passed in 1792 — the House of Representatives requested that he — then Secretary of State — should prepare coinage and monetary proposals, which he submitted on July 13, 1790. However, six years before, he had submitted to the Federated Congress elaborate Notes *on the same subject — some of which we reproduce in this chapter — and which was basically the same report which he sent to Congress in 1790.*

Thus Jefferson became the Father of our system of coinage, and therefore takes his place once again as the pioneer par excellence. *Ours was the first nation to establish a monetary system based on decimals; the difficult and complicated British system, which had prevailed in the Colonies, was abolished and replaced by the one we have enjoyed for nearly two hundred years.*

Had it been feasible, he would have extended the system to include weights, measures, and capacities: but, as he surmised, the difficulty of so doing might constitute "an insuperable bar to this improvement"; and so it was.

But Jefferson's contribution in this field, as in so many others, stands as an eternal tribute to his towering genius.

Financing the Revolutionary War

BW 205-25 Miscellaneous Papers, Answers to M. de Meusnier 1-24-86

The Issuance of the Continental Currency (214-16)

Previous to the Revolution, most of the States were in the habit, whenever they had occasion for more money than could be raised immediately by taxes, to issue paper notes or bills, in the name of the State, wherein they promised to pay to the bearer the sum named in the note or bill. In some of the States no time of payment was fixed, nor tax laid to enable payment. In these, the bills depreciated. But others of the States named in the bill the day when it should be paid, laid taxes to bring in money enough for that purpose, and paid the bills punctually, on or before the day named. In these States, paper money was in as high estimation as gold and silver.

On the commencement of the late Revolution, Congress had no money. The external commerce of the States being suppressed, the farmer could not sell his produce, and, of course, could not pay a tax. Congress had no resource then but in paper money. Not being able to lay a tax for its redemption, they could only promise that taxes should be laid for that purpose, so as to redeem the bills by a certain day. They did not foresee the long continuance of the war, the almost total suppression of their exports, and other events, which rendered the performance of their engagement impossible.

The paper money continued for a twelvemonth equal to gold and silver. But the quantities which they were obliged to emit for the purpose of the war, exceeded what had been the usual quantity of the circulating medium. It began, therefore, to become cheaper, or, as we expressed it, it depreciated, as gold and silver would have done, had they been thrown into circulation in equal quantities. But not having, like them, an intrinsic value, its depreciation was more rapid and greater than could ever have happened with them. In two years, it had fallen to two dollars of paper money for one of silver; in three years, to four for one; in nine months more, it fell to ten for one; and in the six months following, that is to say, by September, 1779, it had fallen to twenty for one.

Congress, alarmed at the consequences which were to be apprehended, should they lose this resource altogether, thought it necessary to make a vigorous effort to stop its further depreciation. They therefore determined, in the first place, that their emissions should not exceed two hundred millions of dollars, to which term they were then nearly arrived; and though they knew that twenty dollars of what they were then issuing, would buy no more than one silver dollar would buy for their army, yet they thought it would be worth while to submit to the sacrifice of nineteen out of twenty dollars, if they could thereby stop further depreciation.

They, therefore, published an address to their constituents, in which they renewed their original declarations, that this paper money should be redeemed at dollar for dollar. They proved the ability of the States to do this, and that their liberty would be cheaply bought at that price. The declaration was ineffectual. No man received the money at a better rate; on the contrary, in six months more, that is, by March, 1780, it had fallen to forty for one. Congress then tried an experiment of a different kind. Considering their former offers to redeem this money at par, as relinquished by the general refusal to take it, but in progressive depreciation, they required the whole to be brought in, declared it should be redeemed at its present value, of forty for one, and that they would give to the holders new bills, reduced in their denomination to the sum of gold and silver, which was actually to be paid for them. This would reduce the nominal sum of the mass in circulation to the present worth of that mass, which was five millions; a sum not too great for the circulation of the States, and which, they therefore hoped, would not depreciate further, as they continued firm in their purpose of emitting no more.

This effort was as unavailing as the former. Very little of the money was brought in. It continued to circulate and to depreciate, till the end of 1780, when it had fallen to seventy-five for one, and the money circulated from the French army, being by that time, sensible in all the States north of the Potomac, the paper ceased its circulation altogether in those States. In Virginia and North Carolina it continued a year longer, within which time it fell to one thousand for one, and then expired, as it had done in the other States, without a single groan.

Not a murmur was heard on this occasion, among the people. On the contrary, universal congratulations took place on their seeing this gigantic mass, whose dissolution had threatened convulsions which should shake their infant confederacy to its centre, quietly interred in its grave. Foreigners, indeed, who do not, like the natives, feel indulgence for its memory, as of a being which has vindicated their liberties, and fallen in the moment of victory, have been loud, and still are loud, in their complaints. A few of them have reason; but the most noisy are not the best of them. They are persons who have become bankrupt by unskilful attempts at commerce with America. That they may have some pretext to offer to their creditors, they have bought up great masses of this dead money in America, where it is to be had at five thousand for one, and they show the certificates of their paper possessions, as if they had all died in their hands, and had been the cause of their bankruptcy.

Justice will be done to all, by paying to all persons what this money actually cost them, with an interest of six per cent. from the time they received it. If difficulties present themselves in the ascertaining the epoch of the receipt, it has been thought better that the State should lose, by admitting easy proofs, than that individuals, and especially foreigners, should, by being held to such as would be difficult, perhaps impossible.

The Debts of the States (205)

The following is a rough estimate of the particular debts of some of the States as they existed in the year 1784:

New Hampshire	$ 500,000
Rhode Island	5,000,000
Massachusetts	430,000
Connecticut	3,439,063
Virginia	2,300,000

United States' Principal of Foreign Debt Only	$7,000,000
The Principal of the Domestic Debt is somewhere between 27½ and 35½ millions, call it therefore	$31,300,000
Total	$38,300,000

The other States not named here, are probably indebted in the same proportion to their abilities. If so... those eight States will owe about fourteen millions, and consequently the particular debts of all the States will amount to twenty-five or twenty-six millions of dollars... .

Each having their separate debt, and a determinate proportion of the Federal debt, they endeavor to lay taxes sufficient to pay the interest of both of these, and to support their own and the Federal Government. These taxes are generally about one or one and a-half per cent of the value of property; and from two and a-half to five per cent on foreign merchandise imported. But the payment of this interest regularly, is not accomplished in many of the States. The people are as yet not recovered from the depredations of the war. When that ended, their houses were in ruin, their farms waste, themselves distressed for clothing and necessaries for their households. They cannot as yet, therefore, bear heavy taxes. For the payment of the principal no final measures are yet taken. Some States will have land for sale, the produce of which may pay the principal debt. Some will endeavor to have an exceeding of their taxes to be applied as a sinking fund; and all of them look forward to the increase in their population, and of course an increase of production in their present taxes, to enable them to be sinking their debt.

How the Revolutionary Debt was to Be Paid (223-25)

[Some people] suppose, that the several sums emitted by Congress, at different times, amounting nominally to two hundred millions of dollars, had been actually worth that at the time of emission, and, of course, that the soldiers and others had received that sum from Congress. But nothing is further from the truth. The soldier, victualler, or other persons who received forty dollars for a service, at the close of the year 1779, received, in fact, no more than he who received one dollar for the same service, in the year 1775, or 1776; because, in those years, the paper money was at par with silver; whereas, by the close of 1779, forty paper dollars were worth but one of silver, and would buy no more of the necessaries of life. To know what the moneys emitted by Congress were worth to the people, at the time they received them, we will state the date and amount of every several emission, the depreciation of paper money at the time, and the real worth of the emission in silver or gold.

[Here follows a list of 35 emissions, beginning on June 23, 1775, and ending on November 29, 1779; their actual value in specie at the time of emission; and also the face value of each emission, which contributed to the total face value of $200 million].

Thus, it appears, that the two hundred millions of dollars, emitted by Congress, were worth, to those who received them, but about thirty-six millions of silver dollars. If we estimate at the same value, the like sum of two hundred millions, supposed to have been emitted by the States, and reckon the federal debt, foreign and domestic, at about forty-three millions, and the State debts at about twenty-five millions, it will form an amount of one hundred and forty millions of dollars... the total sum which the war has cost the inhabitants of the United States. It continued eight years, from the battle of Lexington to the cessation of hostilities in America. The annual expense, then, was about seventeen millions and five hundred thousand dollars, while that of our enemies was a greater number of guineas.

It will be asked, how will the two masses of Continental and of State money have cost the people of the United States seventy-two millions of dollars, when they are to be redeemed, now, with about six millions? I answer, that the difference, being sixty-six millions, has been lost on the paper bills, separately, by the successive holders of them. Every one, through whose hands a bill passed, lost on that bill what it lost in value, during the time it was in his hands. This was a real tax on him; and in this way, the people of the United States actually contributed those sixty-six millions of dollars, during the war, and by a mode of taxation the most oppressive of all, because the most unequal of all... .

The balances due to the officers and soldiers have been ascertained, and a certificate of the sum given to each; on these, the interest is regularly paid; and every occasion is seized of paying the principal, by receiving these certificates as money, whenever public property is sold, till a more regular and effectual method can be taken, for paying the whole.

The Redemption of the Paper Money (209)

Congress have not yet ultimately decided at what rates they will redeem the paper money in the hands of holders. But a resolution of 1784 has established the principle, so that there can be little doubt that the holders of paper money will receive as much real money as the paper was actually worth at the time they received it, and an interest of six per cent. from the time they received it. Its worth will be found in the depreciation table of the State wherein it was received; these depreciation tables having been formed according to the market price of the paper money at different epochs.

Those who talk of the bankruptcy of the United States, are of two descriptions: 1. Strangers who do not understand the nature and history of our paper money. 2. Holders of that paper money who do not wish that the world should understand it. Thus, when in March, 1780, the paper money being so far depreciated that forty dollars of it would purchase only one silver dollar, Congress endeavored to correct the progress of that depreciation by declaring they would emit no more, and would redeem what was in circulation at the rate of one dollar of silver for forty of paper; this was called by the brokers in paper money, a bankruptcy. Yet these very people who had only given one dollar's worth of provisions, of manufactures, or perhaps of silver, for their forty dollars, were displeased that they could not in a moment multiply their silver into forty.

If it were decided that the United States should pay a silver dollar for every paper dollar they emitted, I am of opinion... that a debt, which in its just amount is no more, perhaps, than six millions of dollars, would amount up to four hundred millions, and instead of assessing every inhabitant with a debt of about two dollars, would fix on him thirty guineas, which is considerably more than the national debt of England affixes on each of its inhabitants, and would make a bankruptcy where there is none. The real just debts of the United States,... will be easily paid by the sale of lands, which were ceded on the fundamental condition of being applied as a sinking fund for this purpose.

The Assumption of the Revolutionary Debts

ME VII 59-62 Edward Rutledge 7-4-90

The general assumption of State debts has been as warmly demanded by some States, as warmly rejected by others. I hope the question may be so divested of the injustice imputed to it as to be compromised.

ME I 271-75 The Anas

It is well known that during the war the greatest difficulty we encountered was the want of money or means to pay our soldiers who fought, or our farmers, manufacturers, and merchants who furnished the necessary supplies of food and clothing for them. After the expedient of paper money had exhausted itself, certificates of debt were given to the individual creditors, with assurance of payment as soon as the United States should be able. But the distresses of these people often obliged them to part with these for the half, the fifth, and even a tenth of their value; and speculators had made a trade of cozening them from the holders by the most fraudulent practices, and persuasions that they would never be paid. In the bill for funding and paying these, Hamilton made no difference between the original holders and the fraudulent purchasers of this paper. Great and just repugnance arose at putting these two classes of creditors on the same footing, and great exertions were used to pay the former the full value, and to the latter, the price only which they had paid, with interest.

But this would have prevented the game which was to be played, and for which the minds of greedy members were already tutored and prepared. When the trial of strength on these several efforts had indicated the form in which the bill would finally pass, this being known within doors sooner than without, and especially, than to those who were in distant parts of the Union, the base scramble began. Couriers and relay horses by land, and swift sailing pilot boats by sea, were flying in all directions. Active partners and agents were associated and employed in every State, town, and country neighborhood, and this paper was bought up at five shillings, and even as low as two shillings in the pound, before the holder knew that Congress had already provided for its redemption at par. Immense sums were thus filched from the poor and ignorant, and fortunes accumulated by those who had themselves been poor enough before. Men thus enriched by the dexterity of a leader [Hamilton], would follow of course the chief who was leading them to fortune, and become the zealous instruments of all his enterprises.

This game was over, and another was on the carpet at the moment of my arrival... . This fiscal manoeuvre is well known by the name of Assumption. Independently of the debts of Congress, the States had during the war contracted separate and heavy debts; and Massachusetts particularly, in an absurd attempt, absurdly conducted, on the British post of Penobscot; and the more debt Hamilton could rake up, the more plunder for his mercenaries. This money, whether wisely or foolishly spent, was pretended to have been spent for general purposes, and ought, therefore, to be paid from the general purse. But it was objected, that nobody knew what these debts were, what their amount, or what their proofs. No matter; we will guess them to be twenty millions. But of these twenty millions, we do not know how much should be reimbursed to one State, or how much to another... . No matter; we will guess. And so another scramble was set on foot among the several States, and some got much, some little, some nothing.

But the main object was obtained, the phalanx of the Treasury was reinforced by additional recruits. This measure produced the most bitter and angry contest ever known in Congress, before or since the Union of the States... .

So high were the feuds excited by this subject, that on its rejection business was suspended. Congress met and adjourned from day to day without doing anything, the parties being too much out of temper to do business together. The western members particularly, who, with Smith from South Carolina, were the principal gamblers in these scenes, threatened a secession and dissolution. Hamilton was in despair... .

ME I 276-77 The Anas

...the Assumption was passed, and twenty millions of stock divided among favored States, and thrown in as a pabulum to the stock-jobbing herd. This added to the number of votaries to the Treasury, and made its chief the master of every vote in the legislature, which might give to the government the direction suited to his political views.

I know well, and so must be understood, that nothing like a majority in Congress had yielded to this corruption. Far from it. But a division, not very unequal, had already taken place in the honest part of that body, between the parties styled republican and federal. The latter being monarchists in principle, adhered to Hamilton of course, as their leader in that principle, and this mercenary phalanx added to them, insured him always a majority in both Houses; so that the whole action of the legislature was now under the direction of the Treasury.

Still the machine was not complete. The effect of the funding system, and of the Assumption, would be temporary; it would be lost with the loss of the individual members whom it has enriched, and some engine of influence more permanent must be contrived while these myrmidons were yet in place to carry it through all opposition. This engine was the Bank of the United States [which was established in 1791].

Barter and Exchange

ME XIII 414-16 John W. Eppes 1-6-13

In the United States it [the need for circulating medium] must be less than in any other part of the commercial world; because the great mass of... exchanges... is effected on credit, in their merchant's ledger, who supplies all their wants through the year... .

It is a fact, that a farmer with a revenue of ten thousand dollars a year, may obtain all his supplies from his merchant, and liquidate them at the end of the year, by the sale of his produce to him, without the intervention of a single dollar of cash. This, then, is merely barter, and in this way of barter a great portion of the annual produce of the United States is exchanged without the intermediation of cash. We might safely, then, state our medium at a minimum of one-thirtieth... .

But suppose that instead of our needing the least circulating medium of any nation, from the circumstances before mentioned, we should place ourselves in the middle term of the calculation, to wit: at thirty-five millions. One-fifth of this, at the least, Smith thinks, should be retained in specie, which would leave twenty-eight millions of specie to be exported in exchange for other commodities; and if fifteen millions of that should be returned in productive goods, and not in articles of prodigality, that would be the amount of capital which this operation would add to the existing mass... .

There is another authority to which we may appeal for the proper quantity of circulating medium for the United States. The old Congress, when we were estimated at about two millions of people, on a long and able discussion, June 22d, 1775, decided the sufficient quantity to be two millions of dollars, which sum they emitted. According to this, it should be eight millions, now that we are eight millions of people. This differs little from Smith's minimum of ten millions, and strengthens our respect for that estimate.

The Theory of Value: Money

ME XIII 404-32 John W. Eppes 11-6-13 Pp. 401-11

Proceeding to reason on this subject [the determinant of value], some principles must be premised as forming its basis. The adequate price of a thing depends on the capital and labor necessary to produce it. Two things requiring the same capital and labor, should be of the same price. If a gallon of wine requires for its production the same capital and labor, with a bushel of wheat, they should be expressed by the same price derived from the application of a common measure to them. The comparative prices of things being thus to be estimated and expressed by a common measure, we may proceed to observe, that were a country so insulated as to have no commercial intercourse with any other, to confine the interchange of all its wants and supplies within itself, the amount of circulating medium, as a common measure for adjusting these exchanges, would be quite immaterial. If their circulation, for instance, were of a million of dollars, and the annual produce of their industry equivalent to ten millions of bushels of wheat, the price of a bushel of wheat might be one dollar. If, then, by a progressive coinage, their medium should be doubled, the price of a bushel of wheat might become progressively two dollars, and without inconvenience.

Whatever be the proportion of the circulating medium to the value of the annual produce of industry, it may be considered as the representative of that industry. In the first case, a bushel of wheat will be represented by one dollar; in the second, by two dollars. This is well explained by Hume, and seems admitted by Adam Smith. But where a nation is in a full course of interchange of wants and supplies with all others, the proportion of its medium to its produce is no longer indifferent. To trade on equal terms, the common measure of values should be as nearly as possible on a par with that of its corresponding nations, whose medium is in a sound state; that is to say, not in an accidental state of excess or deficiency.

A Proposal for a System of Coinage

ME III 32-34 Official Papers 1790

The experiment made by Congress in the year one thousand seven hundred and eighty-six, by declaring there should be one money of account and payment through the United States, and that its parts and multiples should be in a decimal ratio, has obtained such general approbation, both at home and abroad, that nothing seems wanting but the actual coinage, to banish the discordant pounds, shillings, pence, and farthings of the different States, and to establish in their stead the new denominations. Is it in contemplation with the House of Representatives to extend a like improvement to our measures and weights, and to arrange them also in a decimal ratio?... Or, is it the opinion of the Representatives that the difficulty of changing the established habits of a whole nation opposes an insuperable bar to this improvement? Under this uncertainty, the Secretary of State thinks it his duty to submit alternative plans, that the House may, at their will, adopt either the one or the other... .

ME VIII 298 Col. Alexander Hamilton Feb. 1792

With respect to the dollar, it must be admitted by all the world, that there is great uncertainty in the meaning of the term, and therefore all the world will have justified Congress for their first act of removing the uncertainty by declaring what they understand by the term; but the uncertainty once removed, exists no longer, and I very much doubt a right now to change the value, and especially to lessen it. It would lead to so easy a mode of paying off our debts.

ME III 51 Official Papers 1790

Let the money unit, or dollar, contain eleven-twelfths of an ounce of pure silver. This will be 376 troy grains, (or more exactly 375.989343 troy grains,) which will be about a third of a grain more than the present unit. This, with the twelfth of alloy already established, will make the dollar or unit, of the weight of an ounce, or a cubic inch of rain water, exactly. The series of mills, cents, dimes, dollars, and eagles, to remain as already established.

ME XVIII 201-203 John Taylor 10-8-97

By the Constitution, Congress may regulate the value of foreign coin; but if they do not do it, the old power recrues to the States, the Constitution only forbidding them to make anything but gold and silver a tender in payment of debts.

ME III 215-16 Report on Assays at the Mint 1-8-93

The Secretary of State, to whom was referred, by the President of the United States, the resolution of the House of Representatives of the 29th of November, 1792, on the subject of experiments of France, England, Spain, and Portugal reports:

That assays and experiments have been, accordingly, made at the mint, by the director, and under his care and inspection, of sundry gold and silver coins of France, England, Spain, and Portugal, and of the quantity of fine gold and alloy in each of them... .

ME III 47 Official Papers 7-13-90

Plan for Establishing Uniformity in the Coinage, Weights, and Measures of the United States, [is herewith] Communicated to the House of Representatives, July 13, 1790.

ME I 239-57 Notes on the Establishment of a Money Unit and of a Coinage for the United States, Appendix

In fixing the Unit of Money, these circumstances are of principal importance.

I. That it be of convenient size to be applied as a measure to the common transactions of life.

II. That its parts and multiples be in *an easy proportion* to each other, so as to facilitate the money arithmetic.

III. That the Unit and its parts, or divisions, be *so nearly of the value of some of the known coins*, as that they may be of easy adoption for the people... .

I. Taking into our view all money transactions, great and small, I question if a common measure of more *convenient size* than the Dollar could be proposed. The value of 100, 1000, 10,000 dollars is well estimated by the mind; so is that of the tenth or the hundreth of a dollar. Few transactions are above or below these limits. The expediency of attending to the size of the money Unit will be evident, to any one who will consider how inconvenient it would be to a manufacturer or merchant, if, instead of the yard for measuring cloth, either the inch or the mile had been made the Unit of Measure.

II. The most *easy ratio* of multiplication and division is that by ten. Everyone knows the facility of Decimal Arithmetic that, when learning, he used to be puzzled with adding farthings, taking out the fours and carrying them on;... but when he came to the pounds, where he had only tens to carry forward, it was easy and free from error. The bulk of mankind are schoolboys through life. These little perplexities are always great to them. And even mathematical heads feel the relief of an easier, substituted for a more difficult process... . Those who have had occasion to convert the livres, sols, and deniers of the French;... the pounds, shillings, pence, and farthings of these several States, into each other, can judge how much they would have been aided, had their several subdivisions been in a decimal ratio... . If we adopt the dollar as our Unit, we should strike four coins, one of gold, two of silver, and one of copper, viz:

1. A golden piece, equal in value to ten dollars:
2. The Unit or Dollar itself, of silver:
3. The tenth of a Dollar, of silver also:
4. The hundredth of a Dollar, of copper... .

A great deal of small change is useful in a State, and tends to reduce the price of small articles. Perhaps it would not be amiss to coin three more pieces of silver, one of the value of five-tenths, or half a dollar, one of the value of two-tenths, which would be equal to the Spanish pistareen, and one of the value of five coppers, which would be equal to the Spanish half-bit. We should then have five silver coins, viz:

1. The Unit or Dollar:
2. The half-dollar or five-tenths:
3. The double tenth, equal to 2, or one-fifth of a dollar....
4. The tenth, equal to a Spanish bit:
5. The five-copper piece, equal to .05 or one-twentieth of a dollar...

If we determine that a Dollar shall be our Unit, we must then say with precision what a Dollar is... the old Dollar [contained] 376 grains of fine silver, and the new 375 grains. If the Dollars circulating among us be of every date equally, we should examine the quantity of pure metal in each, and from them form an average of our Unit... .

The quantum of alloy is also to be decided. Some is necessary to prevent the coin from wearing too fast; too much, fills our pockets with copper, instead of silver... . [Let a Committee] be instructed... .

To assay and examine... the fineness of all the other coins which may be found in circulation within these States... .

To appoint, also, proper persons to enquire what are the proportions between the values of fine gold, and fine silver, at the markets of the several countries with which we are, or probably may be, connected in commerce; and what would be a proper proportion here, having regard to the average of their values at those markets, and to other circumstances, and to report the same to the Committee, by them to be laid before Congress.

To prepare an Ordinance for establishing the Unit of Money within these States; for subdividing it; and for striking coins of gold, silver, and copper, on the following principles:

That the Money Unit of these States shall be equal in value to a Spanish milled dollar containing so much fine silver as the assay, before directed, shall show to be contained, on an average, in dollars of the several dates in circulation with us.

That this Unit shall be divided into tenths and hundredths; that there shall be a coin of silver of the value of a Unit; one other of the same metal, of the value of one-tenth of a Unit; one other of copper, of the value of the hundredth of a Unit.

That there shall be a coin of gold of the value of ten Units, according to the report before directed, and the judgment of the Committee thereon.

That the alloy of the said coins of gold and silver, shall be equal in weight to one-eleventh part of the fine metal.

That there be proper devices for these coins.

That measures be proposed for preventing their diminution, and also their currency, and that of any others, when diminished.

That the several foreign coins be described and classed in the said Ordinance, the fineness of each class stated, and its value by weight estimated in Units and decimal parts of Units.

And that the said draught of an Ordinance be reported to Congress at their next meeting, for their consideration and determination.

15. Federal Financing

Commentary

Certainly, among all his constant interests, there were none more important to Jefferson than those involving the debt resulting from the Revolutionary war, its funding and repayment, the taxes necessary to accomplish this objective, and an honest and economical federal government, which might meet all its obligations fully and promptly without heavy burdens on the people. That he, and his fellow-Republicans were able to defeat the Federalists, accomplish their purposes, and establish a government which for more than a century substantially observed his principles is, perhaps, his crowning glory.

As he said, the debate over the funding of the colonial debt occasioned greater hostility than any other. On the two extremes of this issue were those who wished to repudiate the debt entirely on the ground that, since both confederate and state currencies had become worthless, the loss had already been sustained by the people, who would receive little reimbursement by federal funding. At the other extreme, stood the Hamiltonian Federalists, representing the financiers and speculators, who had purchased the Continentals at as little as 5,000 to one silver dollar and hoped to be repaid in gold for the entire face of the depreciated currency. This would have created an all-powerful aristocracy, holding federal obligations in the sum of $400 million, on which they would expect to collect interest in perpetuity; and it would have subjected the productive population to burdens so onerous that they must have resulted in destitution or revolution.

Jefferson wished to pursue a middle course: the debt should be funded at the value of the currency when issued; the federal government should assume the State debts, which, combined, totalled about $72 million — a heavy sum, indeed, but within the capacity of the growing and prosperous nation to pay.

However, when the new government was established, the Republicans, who had devised the Constitution, were not in office or power; instead, it was the Federalists, who were determined to undermine and subvert the intentions of the Founding Fathers by a thousand subtle and deceitful methods. Instead of *reducing the debt, they increased it at the rate of approximately $1 million every year. They multiplied offices and departments in every conceivable way; they spent $2 million, where $1 million would have been ample. In order to meet the expenses of the expanding bureaucracy, they devised a multitude of new taxes, which, on one occasion, brought the nation to the verge of civil war. Not satisfied with this, they made two determined attempts to plunge the nation into war, which would, of course, have been the means of doubling or tripling the public debt and creating thousands of additional offices in the federal government. However, it was Jefferson who thwarted the XYZ attempt to make war on France and to raise an army to invade, conquer, and colonize South America.*

The Federalists, as we have noted elsewhere, defeated themselves by overconfidence and the persuasion that the people could be reduced to total subservience under a despotic government. Thus it was that Jefferson was elected president in 1800; that he brought a majority of Republicans with him into office; and that his successors were his intimate friends Madison and Monroe, who continued his beneficent policies and placed the nation solidly on the course of freedom, security, and economic justice for the producing majority.

While the Federalists howled like coyotes in a trap, Jefferson abolished all internal taxes; he dismissed all the officers who had administered and collected them; his Secretary of the Treasury, Albert Gallatin, reorganized the national finances; and so, with only one-half of the former income, he and Madison in ten years reduced the public debt from $83 to $45 million. This was an accomplishment without parallel in the history of central, modern governments.

One of the great objectives of Jefferson's life and fiscal policy was to establish a system under which — when the revolutionary debt was paid — there would always be a substantial federal surplus, ample for all expenses during time of war, which could be applied to domestic improvement in time of peace. Thus, the government could operate in perpetuum *without either new taxes or additional loans.*

As Jefferson saw the day approaching when there would be no public debt and when, therefore, there would be a huge surplus — perhaps of $15 or $20 million a year — he considered what should be done with it. His proposal was an amendment to the Constitution permitting the General Government to distribute its surplus to the states and to be used specifically — not for personal welfare — but for constructive purposes, such as roads, canals, libraries, colleges, education, and other projects which would truly serve the general welfare.

Knowing that it is the nature of all central governments to become despotisms by engaging in wars, making huge expenditures, creating enormous debts, and promoting vast bureaucracies, perhaps the most significant and constant objective of his life was to limit the power of the government to borrow or spend. In one place, he declared for an amendment to the Constitution taking from the government the power to borrow money. If that could not be achieved, he wanted at least to make sure that no appropriation be made or money borrowed without at the same time levying a specific tax to pay the interest thereon and the principal thereof in a period not to exceed the life expectancy of those who incurred the debt. He wrote a long letter to Madison in 1889, setting forth these ideas and advocating them as a part of the Constitution then under consideration; they were the principal subject of three famous letters to his son-in-law, John W. Eppes, then Chairman of the House Finance Committee, in 1813; and in one of his latest letters, to John W. Cartwright, dated June 5, 1824, he reiterated the same philosophy.

What a different nation would be ours today had his advice been followed, especially since 1913, and more particularly since 1933!

The Federal Debt and Its Progression

ME VIII 42-45 James Monroe 6-20-90

Congress has long been embarrassed by [a]... most irritating question:... the funding of the public debt... . I have been and still am of the opinion that Congress should always prefer letting the States raise money in their own way, where it can be done. But in the present instance, I see the necessity of yielding to the cries of the creditors in certain parts of the Union: for the sake of the Union, and to save us from the greatest of all calamities, the total extinction of our credit in Europe.

ME VIII 52-3 Dr. Gilmer 6-27-80

The question for assuming the State debts, has created greater animosity than I ever yet saw take place... . There are three ways in which it may yet terminate... . 1. A rejection of the measure, which will prevent their funding any part of the public debt, and will be something very like a dissolution of the government. 2. A bargain between the eastern members, who have it so much at heart, and the middle members who are indifferent about it, to adopt those debts without any modification... . 3. An adoption of them with this modification, that the whole sum to be assumed shall be divided among the States in proportion to their census; so that each shall receive as much as they are to pay; and perhaps this... is the least bad of all the turns this thing can take.

Historical Statistics, U.S. Dept. of Commerce, p. 306

(Notice that between 1789 and 1801, the debt increased from $72 to $83 million; but under Jefferson and Madison, it fell to $45 million in 1812. However, the Second War with England caused the debts, under banker manipulations, to rise to $127 million; however, under Monroe and Jackson, the entire debt was expunged by 1835.)

1789	$72,000,000	1813	$81,488,000
1795	80,748,000	1816	127,335,000
1801	83,038,000	1820	91,616,000
1806	75,723,000	1830	46,565,000
1812	45,210,000	1835	38,000

The Benefits of Efficient Government

ME X 63-7 John Taylor 11-26-98

I wish it were possible to obtain a single amendment to our Constitution. I would be willing to depend on that alone for the reduction of the administration of our government to the genuine principles of the Constitution: I mean an additional article taking from the federal government the power of borrowing.

ME X 255-56 Walter Jones 3-31-01

[Our purpose] will be chiefly to reform the waste of public money, and thus drive away the vultures who prey upon it... .

ME X 301-03 John Dickenson 12-19-01

The impost alone gives us ten or eleven millions annually, increasing at a compound ratio of six and two-thirds per cent. per annum, and consequently doubling in ten years. But leaving that increase for contingencies, the present amount will support the government, pay the interest on the public debt, and discharge the principal in fifteen years.

ME X 306-09 Albert Gallatin 4-1-02

We shall now get rid of the commissioner of internal revenue... . It remains to amalgamate the comptroller and auditor into one... and then the organization will consist, as it should, of a keeper of money, a keeper of accounts, and the head of the department. This constellation of great men in the treasury department was a piece with the rest of Hamilton's plans. He took his own stand as Lieutenant General, surrounded by his Major Generals, and stationing his Brigadiers and Colonels under the name of Supervisors, Inspectors, etc., in the different States.

ME X 309-10 General Thaddeus Kosciusko 4-2-02

The session of the first Congress convened since republicanism has recovered its ascendancy, is now drawing to a close... . They are disarming executive patronage and preponderance, by putting down one-half the offices of the United States, which are no longer necessary. These economies have enabled them to suppress all the internal taxes, and still to make such provision for the payment of their public debt as to discharge that in eighteen years. They have lopped off a parasite limb, planted by their predecessors on their judiciary body for party purposes; they are opening the doors of hospitality to fugitives from the oppressions of other countries; and we have suppressed all those public forms and ceremonies which tended to familiarize the public eye to the harbingers of another form of government.

The people are nearly all united; their quondam leaders, infuriated with the sense of their impotence, will soon be seen or heard only in the newspapers, which serve as chimneys to carry off noxious vapors and smoke... .

BW 342-46 Second Annual Message 12-15-02

The collection of internal taxes having been completed in some of the States, the officers employed in it are of course out of commission. In others, they will be so shortly... money thus unemployed abroad, shall, in conformity with the law, be faithfully applied here in an equivalent extinction of domestic debt. When effects so salutary result from the plans you have already sanctioned, when merely by avoiding false objects of expense, we are able, without a direct tax, without internal taxes, and without borrowing, to make large and effectual payments toward the discharge of our public debt and the emancipation of our posterity from that moral canker, it is an encouragement, fellow citizens, of the highest order, to proceed, as we have begun, in substituting economy for taxation, and in pursuing what is useful for a nation placed as we are, rather than what is practiced by others under different circumstances.

And whensoever we are destined to meet events which shall call forth all the energies of our countrymen, we have the firmest reliance on those energies, and the comfort of leaving for calls like these the extraordinary resources of loans and internal taxes. In the meantime, by payments of the principal of our debts, we are liberating, annually, portions of the external taxes, and forming from them a growing fund still further to lessen the necessity of recurring to extraordinary resources.

ME X 341-43 Thomas Cooper 12-29-02

If we can prevent the government from wasting the labors of the people, under the pretense of taking care of them, they must become happy. Their finances are now under such a course of application as nothing could derange but war or federalism. The gripe of the latter has shown itself as deadly as the jaws of the former. Our adversaries say we are indebted to their providence for the means of paying the public debt. We never charged them with the want of foresight in providing money, but with the misapplication of it after they had provided it. We say they raised not only enough, but too much, and that after giving back the surplus, we do more with a part than they did with the whole.

BW 359 Second Inaugural Address 3-4-05

These contributions [taxes on imports] enable us to support the current expenses of the government, to fulfill contracts with foreign nations, to extinguish the native right of soil [held by the Indians] within our limits, to extend those limits, and to apply such a surplus to our public debts, as places at a short day their final redemption; and that redemption, once effected, the revenue thereby liberated may, by a just repartition among the States, and a corresponding amendment to the Constitution, be applied *in time of peace,* to rivers, canals, roads, arts, manufactures, education, and other great objects within each State. *In time of war,* if injustice... must sometimes produce war, increased as the same revenue will be increased by population and consumption, and aided by other resources reserved for that crisis, it may meet within the year all the expenses of the year, without encroaching on the rights of future generations, by burdening them with the debts of the past. War will then be but a suspension of useful works, and a return to the state of peace, a return to the progress of improvement.

BW 390-96 Eighth Annual Message 11-8-08

The accounts of the receipts and expenditures during the year [have]... ascertained that the receipts have amounted to near eighteen millions of dollars, which, with the eight millions and a half in the treasury at the beginning of the year, have enabled us, after meeting the current demands and interest incurred, to pay two millions, three hundred thousand dollars of the principal of our funded debts, and left us in the treasury, on that day, near fourteen millions of dollars. Of these, five millions, three hundred and fifty thousand dollars will be necessary to pay what will be due on the first day of January next... .

Debts, Slavery, Thrift and Freedom

ME XI 38-42 Philip Mazzei 7-18-04

Notwithstanding... we pay seven or eight millions of dollars annually on our public debt, and shall completely discharge it in twelve years more. That done, our annual revenue, now thirteen millions of dollars, which by that time will be twenty-five, will pay the expenses of any war we may be forced into, without new taxes or loans.

ME XII 323-25 Albert Gallatin 10-11-09

I consider the fortunes of our republic as depending, in an eminent degree, on the extinguishment of the public debt before we engage in any war: because, that done, we shall have revenue enough to improve our country in peace and defend it in war, without recurring either to new taxes or loans. But if the debt should once more be swelled to a formidable size, its entire discharge will be despaired of, and we shall be committed to the English career of debt, corruption, and rottenness, closing with revolution. The discharge of the debt, therefore, is vital to the destinies of our government... .

ME XV 32-44 Sameul Kercheval 7-12-16

I am not among those who fear the people. They, and not the rich, are our dependence for continued freedom. And to preserve their independence, we must not let our rulers load us with perpetual debt.

We must make our election between *economy and liberty,* or *profusion and servitude.* If we run into such debts, as that we must be taxed in our meat and in our drink, in our necessaries and our comforts, in our labors and our amusements, for our callings and our creeds, as the people of England are, our people, like them, must come to labor sixteen hours in the twenty-four, give the earnings of fifteen of these to the government for their debts and daily expenses; and the sixteenth being insufficient to afford us bread, we must live, as they do now, on oatmeal and potatoes; have no time to think, no means of calling the mismanagers to account; but be glad to obtain subsistence by hiring ourselves [out] to rivet our chains on the necks of our fellow-sufferers.

Our land-holders, too, like theirs... must be contented with penury, obscurity, exile... . And this is the tendency of all human governments. A departure from principle in one instance becomes a precedent for a second; that second for a third; and so on, till the bulk of the society is reduced to be mere automators of misery, and to have no sensibilities left but for sinning and suffering.

Then begins, indeed, the *bellum omnium in omnia,* which some philosophers observing to be so general in this world, have mistaken it for the natural, instead of the abusive state of man. And the fore horse of this frightful team is public debt. Taxation follows that, and in its train wretchedness and oppression.

May One Generation Bind Another?

ME VII 454-62 James Madison 9-6-89

The question whether one generation of men has a right to bind another [is one]... of such consequence as not only to merit decision, but a place also among the fundamental principles of every government.... I set out on this ground, which I suppose to be self-evident, that the *earth belongs in usufruct to the living;* that the dead have neither powers nor rights over it. The portion occupied by any individual ceases to be his when himself ceases to be, and reverts to the society... . Then, no man can, by *natural right,* oblige the lands he occupied, or the persons who succeed him in that occupation, to the payment of debts contracted by him. For if he could, he might during his own life, eat up the usufruct of the lands of several generations to come; and then the lands would belong to the dead, and not to the living, which is the reverse of our principle... .

I suppose that the received opinion, that the public debts of one generation devolve on the next, has been suggested by our seeing, habitually, in private life, that he who succeeds to lands is required to pay the debts of his predecessor; without considering that this requisition is municipal only, not moral, flowing from the will of the society, which has found it convenient to appropriate the lands of a decedent on the condition of a payment of his debts; but that between society and society, or generation and generation, there is no municipal obligation, no umpire but the law of nature... .

But with respect to future debts, would it not be wise and just for that nation to declare in the constitution they are forming, that neither the legislature nor the nation itself, can validly contract more debt than they may pay within their own age, or within the term of thirty-four years? And that all future contracts shall be deemed void, as to what shall remain unpaid at the end of thirty-four years from their date? This would put the lenders, and the borrowers also, on their guard. By reducing, too, the faculty of borrowing within its natural limits, it would bridle the spirit of war, to which too free a course has been procured by the inattention of money lenders to this law of nature, that succeeding generations are not responsible for the preceding... .

It would furnish matter for a fine preamble to our first law for appropriating the public revenue; and it will exclude, at the threshold of our new government, the ruinous and contagious errors of this quarter of the globe, which have armed despots with means which nature does not sanction, for binding in chains their fellow-men. We have already given, in example, one effectual check to the dog of war, by transferring the power of declaring war from the executive to the legislative body, from those who are to spend, to those who are to pay.

ME XIII 269-79 The First Eppes Letter 6-24-13

It is a wise rule, and should be fundamental in a government disposed to cherish its credit, and at the same time restrain the use of it within the limits of its faculties, "never to borrow a dollar without laying a tax in the same instant for paying the interest annually, and the principal within a given term... ." But what limit, it will be asked, does this prescribe to their powers? What is to hinder them from creating a perpetual debt? The laws of nature, I answer. The earth belongs to the living, not to the dead. The will and power of man expire with his life, by nature's law... .

The generations of men may be considered as bodies or corporations. Each generation has the usufruct of the earth during the period of its continuance. When it ceases to exist, the usufruct of the earth passes on to the succeeding generation, free and unincumbered, and so on, successively, from one generation to another forever. We may consider each generation as a distinct nation, with a right, by the will of its majority, to bind themselves, but none to bind the succeeding generation, more than the inhabitants of another country.

Or the case may be likened to the ordinary one of a tenant for life, who may hypothecate the land for his debts, during the continuance of his usufruct; but at his death, the reversioner (who is also for life only) receives it exonerated from all burthen. The period of a generation, or the term of its life, is determined by the laws of mortality, which, varying a little only in different climates, offer a general average, to be found by observation... . At nineteen years, then, from the date of a contract, the majority of the contractors are dead, and their contract with them.

Let this general theory be applied to a particular case. Suppose the annual births of the State of New York to be twenty-three thousand, nine hundred and ninety-four... . Suppose that majority, on the first day of the year 1794, had borrowed a sum of money equal to the fee-simple value of the State, and to have consumed it in eating, drinking, and making merry in their day; or, if you please, in quarrelling and fighting with their unoffending neighbors. Within eighteen years and eight months, one-half of the adult citizens were dead... at that period... a new majority have come into place, in their own right, and not under the rights, the conditions, or laws of their predecessors. Are they bound to acknowledge the debt, to consider the preceding generation as having had a right to eat up the whole soil of their country, in the course of a life, to alienate it from them;... and would they think themselves either legally or morally bound to give up their country and emigrate to another for subsistence? Every one will say no: that the soil is the gift of God to the living, as much as it had been to the deceased generation; and that the laws of nature impose no obligation on them to pay this debt. And although, like some other natural rights, this has not yet entered into any declaration of rights, it is no less a law, and ought to be acted on by honest governments.

It is, at the same time, a salutary curb on the spirit of war and indebtment, which, since the modern theory of the perpetuation of debt, has drenched the earth with blood, and crushed its inhabitants under burthens ever accumulating. Had this principle been declared in the British bill of rights, England would have been placed under the happy disability of waging eternal war, and of contracting her thousand millions of public debt. In seeking then, for an ultimate term for the redemption of our debts, let us rally to this principle, and provide for their payment within the term of nineteen years at the farthest.

Our government has not, as yet, begun to act on the rule of loans and taxation going hand in hand. Had any loan taken place in my time, I should have strongly urged a redeeming tax. For the loan which has been made since the last session of Congress, we should now set the example of appropriating some particular tax, sufficient to pay the interest annually, and the principal within a fixed term, less than nineteen years. And I hope yourself and your committee will render the immortal services of introducing this practice.

ME XIII 353-76 The Second Eppes Letter 9-11-13

The objects of finance in the United States have hitherto been very simple; merely to provide for the support of the government on its peace establishment, and to pay the debt contracted in the Revolutionary war, a war which will be sanctioned by the approbation of posterity through all future ages. The means provided for these objects were simple, and, resting on a consumption which little affected the poor, may be said to have been sensibly felt by none.

The fondest wish of my heart ever was that the surplus portion of these taxes, destined for the payment of that debt, should, when that object was accomplished, be continued by annual or biennial re-enactments, and applied, in time of peace, to the improvement of our country by canals, roads, and useful institutions, literary or others; and in time of war to the maintenance of the war. And I believe that keeping the civil list [the federal employees] within proper bounds, the surplus would have been sufficient for any war, administered with integrity and judgment. For authority to apply the surplus to objects of improvement, an amendment of the Constitution would have been necessary.

I have said that the taxes should be continued by annual or biennial re-enactments, because a constant hold, by the nation, of the strings of the public purse, is a salutary restraint from which an honest government ought not to wish, nor a corrupt one, to be permitted to be free. No tax should ever be yielded for a longer term than that of the Congress wanting it, except when pledged for the reimbursement of a loan. On this system, the standing income being once liberated from the Revolutionary debt, no future loan nor future tax would ever become necessary, and wars would no otherwise affect our pecuniary interests than by suspending the improvement belonging to a state of peace. This happy consummation would have been achieved by another eight years' administration, conducted by Mr. Madison, and executed in its financial department by Mr. Gallatin, could peace have been so long preserved. So enviable a state in prospect for our country, induced me to temporize, and to bear with national wrongs which under no other prospect ought ever to have been unresented or unresisted. My hope ever was, that by giving time for reflection, and retraction of injury, a sound calculation of their own interests would induce the aggressing nations to redeem their own character by a return to a practice of right... .

That we are bound to defray our expenses within our own time, and unauthorized to burthen posterity with them, I suppose to have been proved in my former letter. I will place the question, nevertheless, in one additional point of view. The former regarded their independent right over the earth; this over their own persons. There have existed nations, and civilized and learned nations, who have thought that a father had a right to sell his child as a slave, in perpetuity; that he could alienate his body and industry conjointly, and *a fortiori* his industry separately; and consume its fruits himself.

A nation asserting this fratricide right might well suppose they could burthen with public as well as private debt their *"nati natorum, et qui nascentur at illis."* But we, this age, and in this country especially, are advanced beyond those notions of natural law. We acknowledge that our children are born free; that that freedom is the gift of nature, and not of him who begot them; that though under our care during infancy, and therefore of necessity under a duly tempered authority, that care is confided to us to be exercised for the preservation and good of the child only; and his labors during youth are given as a retribution for the charges of infancy. As he was never the property of his father, so when adult he is *sui juris,* entitled himself to the use of his own limbs and the fruits of his own exertions: so far we are advanced, without mind enough, it seems, to take the whole step.

We believe, or act as if we believed, that although an individual father cannot alienate the labor of his son, the aggregate body of fathers may alienate the labor of all their sons, of their posterity, just or unjust, profitable or ruinous, into which our vices, our passions, or our personal interests may lead us. But I trust that this proposition needs only to be looked at by an American to be seen in its true point of view, and that we shall all consider ourselves unauthorized to saddle posterity with our debts, and morally bound to pay them ourselves; and consequently within what may be deemed the period of a generation, or the life of the majority.

In my former letter, I supposed this to be a little over twenty years. We must raise then ourselves the money for this war, either by taxes within the year, or by loans; and if by loans, we must repay them ourselves, proscribing forever the English practice of perpetual funding; the ruinous consequences of which, putting right out of the question, should be a sufficient warning to a considerate nation to avoid the example... .

Of the modes which are within the limits of right, that of raising within the year its whole expenses by taxation, might be beyond the abilities of our citizens to bear. It is, moreover, generally desirable that the public contributions should be as uniform as practicable from year to year, that our habits of industry and of expense may become adapted to them; and that they may be duly digested and incorporated with our annual economy... .

Ought not then the right of each successive generation to be guaranteed against the dissipations and corruptions of those preceding, by a fundamental provision in our Constitution? And, if that has not been a made, does it exist the less... ?

ME XV 46-47 Governor Plumer 7-21-16

...our lawyers and priests generally inculcate this doctrine, and suppose that preceding generations held the earth more freely than we do; had a right to impose laws on us, unalterable by ourselves, and that we, in like manner, can make laws and impose burthens on future generations which they will have no right to alter; in fine, that the earth belongs to the dead, and not to the living.

16. Bank Paper and Metallic Money

Commentary

Whenever Jefferson uses the word cash, *he means specie, coin, gold or silver money.*

Whenever he refers to bank paper, he means currency issued by private banks far in excess of their reserves and therefore not redeemable in specie.

Whenever he speaks of banks which discount for paper, he means that they advance fiat currency for evidences of debt, collectible against property owned by those signing the promissory notes.

When he says that he approves of banks which discount for cash, he means those buying promissory notes for gold or silver coin.

This chapter deals with a subject of paramount importance to Jefferson; and we can add that his statements apply just as fully to our Federal Reserve system as it did to the First and Second United States Bank and to the state banks established between 1790 and 1820. He recognized in the money-power of his day an implacable enemy of the people and republican government; it was then, as now, an expropriator, deceiver, and oppressor; it was and remains the most powerful and dangerous enemy especially of the middle class producers; it was the most subtle and successful perverter of representative government and that with which he was locked in lifelong combat. Since Alexander Hamilton stood at the head of this consortium, he emerges in Jefferson's writings as the very personification of all that is evil in society. He minced no words: he called the banking manipulators the worst citizens, our bitterest enemies, avaricious jugglers, shavers, swindlers, traitorous — the moneyed aristocracy which sets the government at defiance and uses its profits to live in sumptuous splendor.

We suggest that the reader study this chapter carefully; for it encompasses a wellspring of knowledge on a subject of incomparable significance. Let us, therefore, briefly sketch the basic principles espoused.

Jefferson declared the act establishing the First United States Bank unconstitutional for a variety of reasons, largely because by so doing, Congress exercised a non-enumerated power; furthermore, the Bank would assume one of the principal duties mandated by the Constitution to the federal government —

namely, the issuance and control of money; and it would necessarily trample upon and override the powers conferred upon the states. He declared later that his opposition to it was so warm that he was derided as a maniac by the bank-mongers. However, in spite of his and Madison's pressure to obtain the President's veto, Hamilton prevailed and the bank was established on principles basically similar to those on which the great banks of issue operate today in all the countries of the western world, and especially in the United States.

Those principles are, primarily, as follows: (1) by government authority, a private banking system is created, financed largely by the taxpayers, but completely independent of government control; (2) this bank then issues the currency, sets rates of interest, controls the money supply, and determines the approval or denial of credit; (3) it creates panics, depressions, inflation or deflation at will; (4) it dominates the legislature and all communication medias; and (5) it gradually extends its economic grasp over every segment of society. The bank thus becomes the actual ruler of the nation; it dictates war or peace at will; creates enormous debts, collects fabulous amounts of interest by creating credit out of thin air; reduces every segment of the people into one form or another of intellectual or economic servitude. As alternate deflation follows inflation, it forecloses its liens and mortgages on middle-class property, and revolutions recur every twenty or thirty years.

The essence of the banking swindle consisted then, as now, in what is known as fractional reserve banking: that is, the legal power to create credit far beyond existing capital or reserves, and to issue notes or obtain liens on property by this method. Jefferson said that only those who have money to lend should be permitted to lend it; but even in his day they were permitted to discount obligations with money created out of nothing up to three times their reserves; nor could any one be sure that even this limit was respected or enforced. Thus it was that bank paper increased from about ten or fifteen millions in 1795 to two or three hundred millions in a few years. In the meantime, the price of an acre of land increased at least from $4 to $16 and that of a yard of broadcloth from one to eighteen dollars.

For years, Jefferson had been predicting that the banks would become bankrupt; that a universal "run" upon them would make their paper worthless; and that those holding it would lose hundreds of millions of dollars. The crash did indeed occur in 1819; on the 7th of November of that year, he wrote to Adams that the bubble had burst, the great depression had set in, money had become extremely scarce, prices had fallen, agricultural produce brought almost nothing, and farms were sold under the auctioneer's hammer for less than a year's rent. In short, the Second United States Bank had simply called its loans, restricted credit, repossessed its notes, and created a panic, under which it foreclosed the properties of thousands of middle-class freeholders. Life-savings were confiscated at a few cents on the dollar. A similar tragedy was re-enacted in 1837, 1873, 1893, 1907, 1920-21, 1930-40, and, to a lesser degree, in 1974.

Jefferson warned that unless the country learned how to cope with the banks and place them under a perfect subordination, the condition of this nation would one day become desperate. We are at the mercy of these scoundrels, said Jefferson, who periodically create their flows and ebbs of currency, which result in successive property revolutions. No other nation, he declared, had ever "abandoned to the avarice and jugglings of private individuals to regulate, according to their own interests, the quantum of circulating medium for the nation."

What, then, was Jefferson's proposal? As an immediate solution, he declared that all private emissions of bank paper should be prohibited; that the banks should replace their existing notes with other currency to be redeemed with specie; that this redemption should be completed within a period of five years. As a permanent solution, he proposed:

(1) That the states accede to the national government the sole power to issue money. (this was believed by many to have been accomplished under the National Banking Act of 1863 and the Federal Reserve Act of 1913.)

(2) That the federal government be interdicted forever from establishing any private bank with such power.

(3) That banks in the future be limited to certain functions, such as holding deposits, issuing drafts, and lending at interest only such specie as was actually in their possession.

(4) That all existing paper emissions be withdrawn as rapidly as possible and estopped from further circulation.

(5) That the federal government be empowered during wartime to issue currency of circulating size — such as five- and ten-dollar bills — preferably non-interest-bearing and issued, if necessary, to the limit of acceptable circulation, but not in an amount which could cause substantial inflation.

(6) That, if necessary, such bills could be issued bearing six per cent interest and maturing at the end of a certain number of years; such currency would probably be hoarded, and therefore disappear from circulation, exactly as is the case with government securities at the present time.

(7) That whenever such an emission occurs, a tax must be laid at the same time to redeem all such currency at a stated and not distant time.

(8) That, as soon as a war crisis ends, all such paper emissions will gradually be cancelled and recalled, and specie take their place.

(9) That, after the destructive inflation-deflation cycle of 1812-25 ends and the proper remedies are applied, future congresses must always make certain that a sufficient quantity of gold and silver are on hand so that any war which may arise can be financed without loans or additional taxes.

(10) That, during peacetime, the government surplus will be applied to a variety of national improvements; and, during wartime, to finance current costs without substantial differences in taxation or expenditures.

(11) That a national convention be called to accomplish these objectives.

This was Jefferson's practical plan for financing the government; but neither the republicans of that day nor any subsequent statesmen have been powerful enough to defeat the moneyed interests, who have been in basic control of American destiny since 1791 — and more so than ever since 1913, when the Federal Reserve Act was passed and the 16th Amendment ratified: for these are the twin instruments for reducing the productive American citizens to a state of economic servitude.

There has been some difference of opinion as to what Jefferson taught in regard to currency: whether it should consist of, or be strictly redeemable in, gold and silver; some profess to believe that he supported a national fiat money system because he advocated the issuance of five-and ten-dollar bills, not immediately redeemable, by the federal government in wartime. These emissions, however, were to be temporary expedients and were to be based on immediate taxation; and, as soon as the crisis ended, were to be replaced either by actual coin or by government notes redeemable in specie on demand at any time.

Jefferson emphasized that whenever and wherever a fiat paper currency has been permitted, "it is liable to be abused, has been, is, and forever will be abused, in every country in which it is permitted." It happened in the Roman Empire, in France in 1717-19 and 1792 to 1798, during our Revolution, and was going full blast in 1812-19. And now, in the United States, this abuse is gradually destroying the value of all liquid or intangible assets, and reducing the middle-class, especially the retirees, to a form of pauperism as wards of the state.

Why, asks Jefferson, would the people prefer private bank paper at 13 per cent to finance the war when they could have done it with gold and silver without any interest? He denied that the federal government had power to make anything but gold and silver legal tender, a provision in the Constitution there made specifically applicable to the states. Only England and her copyist, the United States, he declared, tolerate a paper circulation. Specie is the most perfect medium of exchange, because it has universal value, keeps its level at all times, and never depreciates; and it is the only sure resource in time of war. The convenience of paper vs. the investment in coin weighs as nothing against the advantages of specie. It is the best and most perfect medium, because of its intrinsic and universal value; properly used, it will finance any war without the payment of interest or the need for any loans. For these and other reasons, he concluded, we must put down and abolish all private banks of issue and "admit none but a metallic circulation."

We could cite other and similar declarations; but we commit herewith the reader to the following pages, in which he will find a complete exposition of Jefferson's views and principles in regard to finance, bank paper, and the role of gold and silver in an advanced and civilized society.

In 1813, Jefferson wrote three long letters to his son-in-law,

John W. Eppes, who was chairman of the House Committee on Finance. We were tempted to reprint these in full, seriatim, but decided against it, on the ground that these could be difficult, and, at times, uninteresting reading. We have therefore broken them into smaller sections, and used these where they are most relevant. Anyone who wishes to study them as they appear, may do so in any compendium of Jefferson's correspondence.

Revolt or Dismemberment

ME VIII 341-49 The President of the United States 5-23-92

...the public mind is no longer confident and serene... . It has been urged, then, that a public debt, greater than we can possibly pay... has been artifically created...; that this accumulation of debt has taken forever out of our power those easy sources of revenue which, applied to the ordinary necessities and exigencies of government, would have answered them habitually, and covered us from habitual murmurings against taxes and tax-gatherers, reserving extraordinary calls for those extraordinary occasions which would animate the people to meet them... .

They cite propositions in Congress, and suspect other projects on foot still to increase the mass of debt. They say, that by borrowing at two-thirds of the interest, we might have paid off the principal in two-thirds of the time; but that from this we are precluded by its being made irredeemable but in small portions and long terms; that this irredeemable quality was given it for the avowed purpose of inviting its transfer to foreign countries. They predict that this transfer of the principal, when completed, will occasion an exportation of three millions of dollars annually for the interest, a drain of coin, of which, as there has been no example, no calculation can be made of its consequences: that the banishment of our coin will be complicated by the creation of ten millions of paper money, in the form of bank bills now issuing into circulation.

They think the ten or twelve per cent. annual profit paid to the lenders of their paper medium taken out of the pockets of the people, who would have had without interest the coin it is banishing: that all the capital employed in paper speculation is barren and useless, producing, like that on the gambling table, no accession to itself, and is withdrawn from commerce and agriculture, where it would have produced addition to the common mass: that it nourishes in our citizens habits of vice and idleness, instead of industry and morality: that it has furnished effectual means of corrupting such a portion of the legislature as turns the balance between the honest voters, whichever way it is directed: that this corrupt squadron, deciding the voice of the legislature, have manifested their dispositions to get rid of the limitations imposed by the Constitution on the general legislature, limitations, on the faith of which, the States acceded to that instrument... .

So many of them [the Federalists] have got into the Legislature, that aided by the corrupt squadron of paper dealers, who are at their devotion, they make a majority in both houses... .

Of all the mischiefs objected to the system of measures before mentioned, none is so afflicting and fatal to every honest hope, as the corruption of the Legislature... . Withdrawn such a distance from the eye of their constituents, and these so dispersed as to be inaccessible to public information, and particularly to that of the conduct of their own representatives, they will form the most corrupt government on earth, if the means of their corruption be not prevented.

The only hope of safety hangs now on the numerous representation which is to come forward the ensuing year. Some of the new members will be, probably, either in principle or interest, with the present majority; but it is expected that the great mass will form an accession to the republican party. They will not be able to undo all which the preceding Legislatures and especially the first, have done. Public faith and right will oppose this. But some parts of the system may be rightfully reformed, a liberation from the rest unremittingly pursued as fast as right will permit, and the door shut in future against similar commitments of the nation.

Should the next Legislature take this course, it will draw upon them the whole monarchical and paper interest; but the latter, I think, will not go all lengths with the former, because... this is the alternative least likely to produce convulsions. But should the majority of the new members be still in the same principles with the present, and show that we have nothing to expect but a continuance of the same practices, it is not easy to conjecture what would be the result, nor what means would be resorted to for correction of the evil... .

I can scarcely contemplate a more incalculable evil than the breaking of the Union into two or more parts. Yet when we consider the mass which opposed the original coalescence; when we consider that it lay chiefly in the Southern quarter; that the Legislature have availed themselves of no occasion of allaying it, but, on the contrary, whenever Northern and Southern prejudices have come into conflict, the latter have been sacrificed and the former soothed; that the owners of the debt are in the Southern, and the holders of it in the Northern division; that the anti-federal champions are now strengthened in argument by the fulfillment of their predictions; that this has been brought about by the monarchical federalists themselves, who, having been for the new government merely as a stepping stone to monarchy, have themselves adopted the very constructions of the Constitution, of which, when advocating its acceptance before the tribunal of the people, they declared it unsusceptible; that the republican federalists who espoused the same government for its intrinsic merits, are disarmed of their weapons; that which they denied as prophecy, having now become true history, who can be sure that these things may not proselyte the small number which was wanting to place the majority on the other side? And this is the event at which I tremble... .

The First United States Bank

BW 311-15 Opinion Against the Constitutionality of a National Bank 2-15-91

The bill for establishing a National Bank undertakes among other things:

1. To form the subscribers into a corporation.

2. To enable them in their corporate capacities to receive grants of land; and so far is against the laws of *mortmain.*

3. To make alien subscribers capable of holding lands; and so far is against the laws of *alienage.*

4. To transmit these lands, on the death of a proprietor, to a certain line of succession; and so far changes the course of *descents.*

5. To put the lands out of the reach of forfeiture or escheat; and so far is against the laws of *forfeiture* and *escheat.*

6. To transmit personal chattels to successors in a certain line; and so far is against the laws of *distribution.*

7. To give them the sole and exclusive right of banking under the national authority; and so far is against the laws of *monopoly.*

8. To communicate to them a power to make laws paramount to the laws of the States; for so they must be construed, to protect the institution from the control of the State legislatures; and so, probably, they will be construed... .

The incorporation of a bank, and the powers assumed by this bill, have not, in my opinion, been delegated to the United States by the Constitution.

1. They are not among the powers specially enumerated: for these are: 1st. A power to lay taxes for the purpose of paying the debts of the United States; but no debt is paid by this bill, nor any tax laid. Were it a bill to raise money, its origination in the Senate would condemn it by the Constitution.

2nd. "To borrow money." But this bill neither borrows money nor insures the borrowing it. The proprietors of the bank will be just as free as any other money holders, to lend or not to lend their money to the public. The operation proposed in this bill, first, to lend them two millions and then to borrow them back again, cannot change the nature of the latter act, which will still be a payment, and not a loan, call it by any name you please.

3. To "regulate commerce with foreign nations, and among the States, and with the Indian tribes." To erect a bank, and regulate commerce, are very different acts. He who erects a bank, creates a subject of commerce; ...so does he who makes a bushel of wheat, or digs a dollar out of the mines; yet neither of these persons regulates commerce thereby... .

II. Nor are they within either of the general phrases, which are the two following:

1. To lay taxes to provide for the general welfare of the United States, that is to say, "to lay taxes for *the purpose* of providing for the general welfare." For the laying of taxes is the *power*, and the general welfare the *purpose* for which the power is to be exercised... .

It is known that the very power now proposed *as a means* was rejected as *an end* by the Convention which formed the Constitution. A proposition was made to them to authorize Congress to open canals, and an amendatory one to empower them to incorporate. But the whole was rejected, and one of the reasons for rejection urged in debate was, that then they would have a power to erect a bank, which would render the great cities, where there were prejudices and jealousies on the subject, adverse to the reception of the Constitution.

2. The second general phrase is, "to make all laws *necessary* and proper for carrying into execution the enumerated powers." But they can all be carried into execution without a bank. A bank therefore is not *necessary*, and consequently not authorized by this phrase... .

Perhaps, indeed, bank bills may be a more *convenient* vehicle than treasury orders. But a little *difference* in the degree of *convenience*, cannot constitute the necessity which the Constitution makes the ground for assuming any non-enumerated power.

Besides, the existing banks will, without a doubt, enter into arrangements for lending their agency, and the more favorable, as there will be competition among them for it; whereas the bill delivers us up bound to the National Bank, who are free to refuse all arrangements, but on their own terms, and the public not free, on such refusal, to employ any other bank.

ME VIII 206-09 Colonel Monroe 7-10-91

Thus it is that we shall be paying thirteen per cent. per annum for eight millions of paper money, instead of having that circulation of gold and silver for nothing. Experience has proved to us that a dollar of silver disappears for every dollar of paper emitted; and, for the paper emitted from the bank, seven per cent. profit will be received by the subscribers for it as bank paper... and six per cent on the public paper of which it was the representative.

ME VIII 186-87 Edmund Pendleton 7-24-91

You will have seen the rapidity with which the subscriptions to the bank were filled; as yet the delirium of speculation is too strong to admit sober reflections... . I am afraid it is the intention to nourish the spirit of gambling.

ME X 436-39 Albert Gallatin 12-13-03

This institution is one of the most deadly hostility against the principles of our Constitution. The nation is, at this time, so strong... that it cannot be shaken... . But suppose a series of untoward events should occur, sufficient to bring into doubt the competency of a republican government to meet a crisis of great danger, or to unhinge the confidence of the people in the public functionaries; an institution like this, penetrating by its branches, every part of the Union, acting by command and in phalanx, may in a critical moment, upset the government.

I deem no government safe which is under the vassalage of any self-constituted authorities, or any other authority than that of the nation, or its regular functionaries. What an obstruction could not this bank of the United States, with all its branch banks, be in time of war! It might dictate to us the peace we should accept, or withdraw its aids. Ought we then to give further growth to an institution so powerful, so hostile?

That it is so hostile, we know: 1. from a knowledge of the principles of the persons composing the body of directors in every bank, principal or branch; and those of most of the stockholders; 2. from their opposition to the measures and principles of the government, and to the election of those friendly to them; and, 3. from the sentiments of the newspapers they support.

Now, while we are strong, it is the greatest debt we owe to the safety of our Constitution, to bring this powerful enemy to a perfect subordination under its authorities. The first measure would be to reduce them to an equal footing with other banks, as to favors of this government... Could we not make a beginning towards an independent use of our own money, towards holding in our own banks all the deposits where they are received, and letting the treasurer give his draft or note, for payment at any particular place, which, in a well-conducted government, ought to have as much credit as any private draft, or bank note, or bill, and would give us the same facilities which we derive from the banks?

ME XII 230-32 Doctor Maese 1-15-09

It has always been denied by the republican party in this country, that the Constitution had given this power of incorporation to Congress. On the establishment of the Bank of the United States, this was the great ground on which that establishment was combatted; and the party prevailing supported it only on the argument of its being an incident to the power given them for raising money. On this ground, it has been acquiesced in, and will probably be again acquiesced in, as subsequently confirmed by public opinion. But in no other instance have they exercised this power of incorporation out of this district [of Columbia], of which they are the ordinary legislature.

The Currency of Private Banks

ME IX 337-39 James Monroe 6-12-96

You will see further, that we are completely saddled and bridled and that the bank is so firmly mounted on us that we must go where they will guide. They openly publish a resolution, that the national property having increased in value, they must by an increase in circulating medium, furnish an adequate representation of it, and by further additions of active capital, promote the enterprises of our merchants.

ME XIV 179-90 Thomas Cooper 9-10-14

The crisis, then, of the abuses of banking is arrived. The banks have pronounced their own sentence of death. Between two and three hundred millions of dollars of their promissory notes are in the hands of the people, for solid produce and property sold, and they formally declare they will not pay them. This is an act of bankruptcy of course, and will be so pronounced by any court before which it shall be brought.

But... . The law can only uncover their insolvency, by opening to its suitors their empty vaults. Thus by the dupery of our citizens, and tame acquiescence of our legislators, the nation is plundered of two or three hundred millions of dollars, treble the amount of debt contracted in the Revolutionary war, and which, instead of redeeming our liberty, has been expended on sumptuous houses, carriages, and dinners. A fearful tax! if equalized on all; but overwhelming and convulsive by its partial fall.

The crush will be tremendous, very different from that brought on by our paper money. That rose and fell so gradually that it kept all on their guard... . Here the contract of yesterday crushes in an instant the one or the other party. The banks stopping payment suddenly, all their mercantile and city debtors do the same; and all, in short, except those in the country, who, possessing property, will be good in the end. But this resource will not enable them to pay a cent on the dollar.

From the establishment of the United States Bank, to this day, I have preached against this system, but have been sensible no cure could be hoped but in the catastrophe now happening... . Their gossamer castles are dissolved, and they can no longer impede and overawe the salutary measures of the government. Their paper was received on a belief that it was cash on demand. Themselves have declared it was nothing, and such scenes are now to take place as will open the eyes of credulity and of insanity itself, to the dangers of a paper medium abandoned to the discretion of avarice and of swindlers. It is impossible not to deplore our past follies, and their present consequences, but let them at least be warnings against like follies in the future... .

We are now without any medium; and necessity, as well as patriotism and confidence, will make us all eager to receive treasury notes, if founded on specific taxes. Congress may now borrow of the public, and without interest, all the money they may want, to the amount of a competent circulation, by merely issuing their own promissory notes, of proper denominations for the larger purposes of circulation, but not for the small. Leave that door open for the entrance of metallic money... .

The State legislatures should be immediately urged to relinquish the right of establishing banks of discount. Most of them would comply on patriotic principles... and the non-complying may be crowded into concurrence by legitimate devices.

ME XIII 403-32 John W. Eppes 11-6-13

When I speak comparatively of the paper emission of the old Congress and the present banks, let it not be imagined that I cover them under the same mantle. The object of the former was a holy one; for if there ever was a holy war, it was that which saved our liberties and gave us independence. The object of the latter, is to enrich swindlers at the expense of the honest and industrious part of the nation.

ME XIV 355-59 Albert Gallatin 10-16-15

We are undone, my dear Sir, if this banking mania be not suppressed... . The war, had it proceeded, would have upset our government; and a new one, whenever tried, will do it. And so it must be while our money, the nerve of war, is much or little, real or imaginary, as our bitterest enemies choose to make it. Put down the banks, and if this country could not be carried through the longest war against the most powerful enemy, without ever knowing the want of a dollar, without dependence on the traitorous classes of her citizens, without bearing hard on the resources of the people, or loading the public with an indefinite burden of debt, I know nothing of my countrymen.

Not by any novel project, not by any charlatanerie, but by ordinary and well-experienced means; by the total prohibition of all private paper at all times; by reasonable taxes in war aided by the necessary emissions of public paper of circulating size, this bottomed on special taxes, redeemable annually as this special tax comes in, and finally within a moderate period.

Even with the flood of private paper by which we were deluged, if the treasury had ventured its credit in bills of circulating size, as of five or ten dollars, etc., they would have been greedily received by the people in preference to bank paper. But unhappily... the treasury, for want of confidence in the country, delivered itself bound hand and foot to bold and bankrupt adventurers and pretenders to be money-holders, whom it could have crushed at any moment... . For it never was, and is not, any confidence in their frothy bubbles, but the want of all other medium, which induced, or now induces, the *country* people to take their paper; and at this moment, when nothing else is to be had, no man will receive it but to pass it away instantly, none for distant purposes.

We are now without any common measure of the value of property, and private fortunes are up or down at the will of the worst of our citizens. Yet there is no hope of relief from the legislatures who have immediate control over this subject. As little seems to be known of the principles of political economy as if nothing had ever been written or practised on the subject... . It is an evil, therefore, which we must make up our minds to meet and to endure as those of hurricanes, earthquakes, and other casualties... .

ME XV 17-23 John Taylor 5-28-16

The system of banking we have both equally and ever reprobated. I contemplate it as a blot left in all our Constitutions, which, if not covered, will end in their destruction, which is already hit by the gamblers in corruption, and is sweeping away in its progress the fortunes and morals of our citizens... .

I sincerely believe, with you, that banking institutions are more dangerous than standing armies; and that the principle of spending money to be paid by posterity, under the name of funding, is but swindling futurity on a large scale.

ME XV 111-14 Dr. J. Stuart 5-10-17

The bank mania... is raising up a moneyed aristocracy in our country which has already set the government at defiance, and... their principles are unyielded and unyielding.

Banking Trickery and Profits

ME XIII 403-32 John W. Eppes 11-6-13

At the time we were funding our national debt, we heard much about "a public debt being a public blessing;" that the stock representing it was a creation of active capital for the aliment of commerce, manufactures, and agriculture. This paradox was well adapted to the minds of believers in dreams, and the gulls of that size entered *bona fide* into it.

But the art and mystery of banks is a wonderful improvement on that. It is established on the principle that "*private* debts are a public blessing." That the evidences of these private debts, called bank notes, become active capital, and aliment the whole commerce, manufactures, and agriculture of the United States. Here are a set of people, for instance, who have bestowed on us the great blessing of running in our debt about two hundred millions of dollars, without our knowing who they are, where they are, or what property they have to pay this debt when called on; nay, who have made us so sensible of the blessings of letting them run in our debt, that we have exempted them by law from the repayment of these debts beyond a given proportion, (generally estimated at one-third).

And to fill up the measure of blessing, instead of paying, they receive an interest on what they owe from those to whom they owe; for all the notes, or evidences of what they owe, which we see in circulation, have been lent to somebody on an interest which is levied again on us through the medium of commerce. And they... are now willing to let themselves run in our debt ninety millions more, on our paying them the same premium of six or eight per cent. interest, and on the same legal exemption from the repayment of more than thirty millions of the debt, when it shall be called for... . If, then, a *public* debt be no public blessing, we may pronounce *a fortiori*, that a private one cannot be so.

Gold and Silver vs. Bank Paper

FORD V 350 James Madison 1792

Sober thinkers cannot prefer a paper medium at 13 per cent. to gold and silver for nothing.

ME X 63-67 John Taylor 11-26-98

I now deny their power [i.e., the United States Bank] of making paper money... a legal tender.

ME XII 379-80 Abbe Salamankis 3-14-10

That we are overdone with banking institutions, which have banished the precious metals, and substituted a more fluctuating and unsafe medium,... that the wars of the world have swallowed our commerce beyond the wholesome limits of exchanging our own productions for our own wants, and that, for the emolument of a small proportion of our society,... the peace of the whole world is endangered, and all our present difficulties produced, are evils more easily deplored than remedied.

ME XIII 404-32 John W. Eppes 11-6-13

It is a litigated question, whether the circulation of paper, rather than of specie, is a good or an evil. In the opinion of England and of English writers it is a good; in that of all other nations, it is an evil; and excepting England and her copyist, the United States, there is not a nation existing, I believe, which tolerates a paper circulation. The experiment is going on, however, desperately in England, pretty boldly with us, and at the end of the chapter, we shall see which opinion experience approves... .

Now one of the great advantages of specie as a medium is, that being of universal value, it will keep itself at a general level, flowing out from where it is too high, into parts where it is lower. Whereas, if the medium be of local value only, as paper money, if too little, indeed, gold and silver will flow in to supply the deficiency, but if too much, it accumulates, banishes the gold and silver not locked up in vaults and hoards, and depreciates itself; that is to say, its proportion to the annual produce of industry, being raised, more of it is required to represent any particular article of produce than in the other countries... .

[We have in] the United States, a capital of two thousand millions, all in active employment... . Of this, fifteen millions [the value of the gold and silver necessary to carry on business] would be the one hundred and thirty-third part. And it is this petty addition to our capital of the nation, this minimum of one dollar, added to one hundred and thirty-three and a third or three-fourths per cent., that we are to give up our gold and silver medium, its intrinsic solidity, its universal value, and its saving powers in time of war, and to substitute for it paper, with all its train of evils, moral, political, and physical, which I will not pretend to enumerate!... .

If the debt which the banking companies owe be a blessing to anybody, it is to themselves alone, who are realizing a solid interest of eight or ten per cent. on it.[a] As to the public, these companies have banished all our gold and silver medium, which, before their institution, we had without interest, which never could have perished in our hands, and would have been our salvation in the hour of war; instead of which they have given us two hundred millions of froth and bubble, on which we are to pay them heavy interest, until it shall vanish into air... .

There is indeed a convenience in paper; its easy transmission from one place to another. But this may be mainly supplied by bills of exchange, so as to prevent any great displacement of actual coin. Two places trading together balance their dealings, for the most part, by their mutual supplies,

a. *The banks collected 8% interest in gold on money lent in the form of depreciated paper to the government during the war of 1812-14, and thus made a profit of nearly a hundred million dollars on this transaction alone.*

and the debtor individuals of either may, instead of cash, remit the bills of those who are creditors in the same dealings; or may obtain them through some third place with which both have dealings... .

The sum of what has been said is, that... specie is the most perfect medium, because it will preserve its own level; because, having intrinsic and universal value, it can never die in our hands, and it is the surest resource of reliance in time of war; that the trifling economy of paper, as a cheaper medium, or its convenience for transmission, weighs nothing in opposition to the advantages of the precious metals; that it [a paper currency] is liable to be abused, has been, is, and forever will be abused, in every country in which it is permitted; that it is already at a term of abuse in these States, which has never been reached by any other nation, France excepted, whose dreadful catastrophe should be a warning against the instrument which produced it... .

ME XV 27-31 William Crawford 6-20-16

...a third [measure] necessary to ensure our national prosperity, should also insure resources of money by the suppression of all paper circulation during peace, and licensing that of the nation alone during war. The metallic medium of which we should be possessed at the commencement of a war, would be a sufficient fund for all the loans we should need through its continuance; and if the national bills issued, be bottomed (as is indispensable) on pledges of specific taxes for their redemption within certain and moderate epochs, and be of proper denominations for circulation, no interest on them would be necessary or just, because they would answer to every one of the purposes of the metallic money withdrawn and replaced by them.

ME XV 279-81 Charles Pinckney 9-30-20

I should say, put down all banks, admit none but a *metallic circulation* that will take its proper level with the like circulation in other countries, and then our manufacturers may work in fair competition with those of other countries... .

Federal Finances

Hamilton's Manipulation of the Treasury

ME X 306-09 Albert Gallatin, Sec. of the Treasury 4-1-02

I think it an object of great importance... to simplify our system of finance, and bring it within the comprehension of every member of Congress. Hamilton set out on a different plan. In order that he might have the entire government of his machine, he determined to complicate it so that neither the President nor Congress should be able to understand it, or to control him. He succeeded in doing this, not only beyond their reach, but so that he at length could not unravel it himself. He gave to the debt, in the first instance, in funding it, the most artificial and mysterious form he could devise. He then moulded up his appropriations of a number of scraps and remnants, many of which were nothing at all, and applied them to different objects in reversion and remainder, until the whole system was involved in impenetrable fog; and while he was giving himself the airs of providing for the payment of the debt, he left himself free to add to it continually, as he did in fact, instead of paying it... .

But there is a point beyond this on which I should wish to keep my eye... . That is, to form into one consolidated mass all the moneys received into the treasury, and to the several expenditures... . [This] would furnish a simple measure by which every one... could decide when taxes were deficient or superabundant. If to this can be added a simplification of the form of accounts in the treasury department, and in the organization of its officers, so as to bring everything to a single centre, we might hope to see the finances of the Union as clear and intelligible as a merchant's books, [and]... to bring things back to that simple and intelligible system on which they should have been organized at first.

What the Fiscal Policies of the Government Should Be

ME XIII 269-79 The First Eppes Letter 6-24-13

It is a wise rule... "never to borrow a dollar without laying a tax in the same instant for paying the interest annually, and the principal within a given term; and to consider that tax as pledged to the creditors on the public faith." On such a pledge as this, sacredly observed, a government may always command, on a *reasonable interest,* all the lendable money of their citizens, while the necessity of an equivalent tax is a salutary warning to them and their constituents against oppressions, bankruptcy, and its inevitable consequence, revolution... .

The fund I mean is the *mass of circulating coin.* Every one knows that, although not literally, it is nearly true, that every paper dollar emitted banishes a silver one from the circulation. A nation, therefore, making its purchases and payments with bills fitted for circulation, thrusts an equal sum of coin out of circulation. This is equivalent to borrowing that sum, and yet the vendor receiving payment in a medium as effectual as coin for his purchases or payments, has no claim to interest. And so the nation may continue to issue its bills as far as its wants require, and the limits of the circulation will admit... .

But this, the only resource which the government could command with certainty, the States have unfortunately fooled away, nay corruptly alienated to swindlers and shavers, under the cover of private banks. Say, too, as an additional evil, that the disposal funds of individuals, to this great amount, have thus been withdrawn from improvements and useful enterprise, and employed in the useless, usurious and demoralizing practices of bank directors and their accomplices... .

In the revolutionary war, the old Congress and the States issued bills without interest, and without tax. They occupied the channels of circulation very freely, till those channels were overflowed by an excess beyond all the calls of circulation. But although we have so improvidently suffered the field of circulating medium to be filched from us by private individuals, yet I think we may recover it in part, and even in the whole, if the States will co-operate with us. If treasury bills are emitted on a tax appropriated for their redemption in fifteen years, and (to insure preference in the first moments of competition) bearing an interest of six per cent. there is no one who would not take them in preference to the bank paper now afloat, on a principle of patriotism as well as interest; and they would be withdrawn from circulation into private hoards to a considerable amount. Their credit once established, others might be emitted, bottomed also on a tax, but not bearing interest; and if ever their credit faltered, open public loans, on which these bills alone should be received as specie. These, operating as a sinking fund, would reduce the quantity in circulation, so as to maintain that in an equilibrium with specie... .

It is not easy to estimate the obstacles which, in the beginning, we should encounter in ousting the banks from their possession of the circulation; but a steady and judicious alternation of emissions and loans, would reduce them in time. But, while this is going on, another measure should be pressed, to recover ultimately our right to the circulation. The States should be applied to, to transfer the right of issuing circulating paper to Congress exclusively, *in perpetuum,* if possible; but during the war at least, with a saving of charter rights. I believe that every State west and south of Connecticut river, except Delaware, would immediately do it; and the others would follow in time. Congress would, of course, begin by obliging unchartered banks to wind up their affairs within a short time, and the others as their charters expired, forbidding the subsequent circulation of their paper. This they would supply with their own, bottomed, every emission, on an adequate tax, and bearing or not bearing interest, as the state of the public pulse should indicate. Even in the non-complying States, these bills would make their way, and supplant the unfunded paper of their banks, by their solidity, by the universality of their currency, and by their receivability for customs and taxes. It would be in their power, too, to curtail those banks to the amount of their actual specie, by gathering up their paper, and running it constantly on them. The national paper might thus take place even in the non-complying States.

In this way, I am not without hope, that this great, this sole resource for loans in an agricultural country, might yet be recovered for the use of the nation during war; and, if obtained *in perpetuum,* it would always be sufficient to carry us through any war; provided that in the interval between war and war, all the outstanding paper should be called in, coin be permitted to flow in again, and to hold the field of circulation until another war should require its yielding place again to the national medium.

But it will be asked, are we to have no banks? Are merchants and others to be deprived of the resource of short accommodations, found so convenient? I answer, let us have banks; but let them be such as are alone to be found in any country on earth, except Great Britain. There is not a bank of discount on the continent of Europe, (at least there was not one when I was there,) which offers anything but cash in exchange for discounted bills.

No one has a natural right to the trade of money lender, but he who has the money to lend. Let those then among us, who have a moneyed capital, and who prefer employing it in loans rather than otherwise, set up banks, and give cash or national bills for the notes they discount. Perhaps, to encourage them, a larger interest than is legal in the other cases might be allowed them, on the condition of their lending for short periods only. It is from Great Britain we copy the idea of giving paper in exchange for discounted bills; and while we have derived from that country some good principles of government and legislation, we unfortunately run into the most servile imitation of all her practices, ruinous as they prove to her, and with the gulf yawning before us into which these very practices are precipitating her.

The unlimited emission of bank paper has banished all her specie, and is now, by a depreciation acknowledged by her own statesmen, carrying her rapidly to bankruptcy, as it did France, as it did us, and will do us again, and every country permitting paper to be circulated, other than that by public authority, rigorously limited to the just measure for circulation.

Private fortunes, in the present state of our circulation, are at the mercy of those self-created money lenders, and are prostrated by the floods of nominal money with which their avarice deluges us. He who lent his money to the public or to an individual, before the institution of the United States Bank, twenty years ago, when wheat was well sold at a dollar a bushel, and receives now his nominal sum when it sells for two dollars, is cheated of half his fortune; and by whom? By the banks, which, since that, have thrown into circulation ten dollars of their nominal money where was one at that time.

...[these ideas]... comfort me in the belief, that they point out a resource ample enough, without overwhelming war taxes, for the expense of the war, and possibly still recoverable; and that they hold up to all future time a resource within ourselves, ever at the command of government, and competent to any wars into which we may be forced. Nor is it a slight object to equalize taxes through peace and war.

Financing the Government in Peace and War

ME XIII 353-68 John W. Eppes 9-11-13

There remains for us the method of limited anticipation, the laying taxes for a term of years within that of our right, which may be sold for a present sum equal to the expenses of the year... . This is, in fact, what has been called raising money on the sale of annuities for years. In this way, a new loan, and of course a new tax, is requisite every year during the continuance of the war... . This method of anticipating our taxes... insures repayment to the lender, guards the rights of posterity, prevents a perpetual alienation of the public contributions, and consequent destitution of every resource even for the ordinary support of the government... .

The question will be asked and ought to be looked at, what is to be the resource if loans cannot be obtained? There is but one, "*Carthago delenda est.*" Bank paper must be suppressed, and the circulating medium must be restored to the nation to whom it belongs. It is the only fund on which they can rely for loans; it is the only resource which can never fail them, and it is an abundant one for every necessary purpose. Treasury bills, bottomed on taxes, bearing or not bearing interest, as may be found necessary, thrown into circulation will take the place of so much gold and silver, which last, when crowded, will find an efflux into other countries, and thus keep the quantum of medium at its salutary level... .

But this view, being in prospect only, should not affect the quantum of tax which the former circulation pronounces necessary. Our creditors have a right to certainty, and to consider these political speculations as make-weights only to that, and at our risk, not theirs. To us belongs only the comfort of hoping an earlier liberation than that calculation holds out, and the right of providing expressly that the tax hypothecated shall cease so soon as the debt it secures shall be actually reimbursed; and I will add that to us belongs also the regret that improvident legislators should have exposed us to twenty years' thraldom of debts, and taxes, for the necessary defence of our country, where the same contributions would have liberated us in eight or nine years... .

But our business being to make every loan tax a sinking fund for itself, no general one will be wanting; and if my confidence is well founded that our original import, when freed from the revolutionary debt, will suffice to embellish and improve our country in peace, and defend her in war, the present may be the only occasion of perplexing ourselves with sinking funds... .

My original disapprobation of banks' circulating paper is not unknown, nor have I since observed any effects either on the morals or fortunes of our citizens, which are any counterbalance for the public evils produced; and a thorough conviction that, if this war continues, that circulation must be suppressed, or the government shaken to its foundation by the weight of taxes, and impracticability to raise funds on them, renders duty to that paramount... .

Plan for Amortizing the Federal Debt

ME XIV 202-07 President James Madison 10-15-14

Suppose we require, to carry on the war, an annual loan of twenty millions, then I propose that, in the first year, you shall lay a tax of ten millions, and emit twenty millions of treasury notes, of a size proper for circulation, and bearing no interest, to the redemption of which the proceeds of that tax shall be inviolably pledged and applied, by recalling annually their amount of the identical bills funded on them. The second year lay another tax of ten millions and emit twenty millions more. The third year the same, and so on, until you have reached the maximum of taxes which ought to be imposed... . It would be in thirty years, then, prima facie, that you would reach the present circulation of three hundred millions, or the ultimate term to which we might adventure.

But observe, also, that in that time we shall have become thirty millions of people, to whom three hundred millions of dollars would be no more than one hundred millions are to us now... All we should have to do would be, when the war should be ended, to leave the gradual extinction of these notes to the operation of the taxes pledged for their redemption; not to suffer a dollar of paper to be emitted either by public or private authority, but let the metallic medium flow back into the channels of circulation, and occupy them until another war should oblige us to recur, for its support, to the same resource, and the same process, on the circulating medium.

ME XIV 211-21 William Short 11-28-14

I am in hopes the present session of Congress will provide... a better train of finance. Their banking projects are like dosing dropsy with more water. If anything could revolt our citizens against the war, it would be the extravagance with which they are about to be taxed... . How can a people who cannot get fifty cents a bushel for their wheat, while they pay twelve dollars a bushel for their salt, pay five times the amount of taxes they ever paid before?

ME XIV 221-25 M. Correa de Serra 12-27-14

M. Say will be surprised to find that... instead of funding issues of paper on the redeeming taxes... , we are trusting to the tricks of jugglers on the cards, the illusions of banking schemes for the resources of the war, and for the cure of colic by inflations of more wind.

ME XIV 226-30 Colonel James Monroe 1-1-15

Although a century of British experience has proved to what a wonderful extent the funding on specific redeeming taxes enables a nation to anticipate in war the resources of peace, and although the other nations of Europe have tried and trodden every path of force and folly in fruitless quest of the same object, yet *we* still expect to find in juggling tricks and banking dreams, that money can be made out of nothing, and in sufficient quantity to meet the expenses of a heavy war by sea and land.

It is said, indeed, that money cannot be borrowed from our merchants as from those of England. But it can be borrowed from our people. They will give you all the necessaries of war they produce, if, instead of the bankrupt trash they now are obliged to receive for want of any other, you will give them a paper promise funded on a specific pledge, and of a size for common circulation.

But you say the merchants will not take this paper. What the people take, the merchants must take, or sell nothing. All these doubts and fears prove only the extent of the dominion which the banking institutions have obtained over the minds of our citizens, and especially of those inhabiting cities or other banking places; and this dominion must be broken, or it will break us.

But here, as in the other case, we must make up our minds to suffer yet longer before we can get right. The misfortune is, that in the meantime we shall plunge ourselves in unextinguishable debt; and entail on our posterity an inheritance of eternal taxes, which will bring our government and people into the condition of those of England, a nation of pikes and gudgeons, the latter bred merely as food for the former.

The Destructive Financial Panic

ME XIII 404-32 The Third Eppes Letter 11-6-13

It is said that our paper is as good as silver, because we may have silver for it at the bank where it issues. This is not true. One, two, or three persons might have it; but a general application would soon exhaust their vaults, and leave a ruinous proportion of their paper in its intrinsic worthless form.

It is a fallacious pretence, for another reason. The inhabitants of the banking cities might obtain cash for their paper, as far as the cash in the vaults would hold out, but distance puts it out of the power of the country to do this. A farmer having a note of a Boston or Charleston bank distant hundreds of miles, has no means of calling for the cash. And while these calls are impracticable for the country, the banks have no fear of their being made from the towns; because their inhabitants are mostly on their books, and there on sufferance only, and during good behavior.

In this state of things, we are called on to add ninety millions more to the circulation. Proceeding in this career, it is infallible, that we must end where the revolutionary paper ended. Two hundred millions was the whole amount of all the emissions of the old Congress, at which point their bills ceased to circulate. We are now at that sum, but with treble the population, and of course a longer tether. Our depreciation is, as yet, but about two for one. Owing to the support its credit receives from the small reservoirs of specie in the vaults of the banks, it is impossible to say at what point their notes will stop. Nothing is necessary to effect it but a general alarm, and that may take place whenever the public shall begin to reflect on, and perceive, the impossibility that the banks should repay this sum.

At present, caution is inspired no farther than to keep prudent men from selling property on long payments. Let us suppose the panic to arise at three hundred millions, a point to which every session of the legislatures hasten us by long strides. Nobody dreams that they would have three hundred millions of specie to satisfy the holders of their notes. Were they even to stop now, no one supposes they have two hundred millions in cash, or even the sixty-six and two third millions, to which amount alone the law compels them to repay.

One hundred and thirty-three and one-third millions of loss, then, is thrown on the public by law; and as the sixty-six and two-thirds, which they are legally bound to pay, and ought to have in their vaults, every one knows there is no such amount of cash in the United States; and what would be the course with what they really have there? Their notes are refused. Cash is called for. The inhabitants of the banking towns will get what is in the vaults, until a few banks declare their insolvency; when, the general crush becoming evident, the others will withdraw even the cash they have, declare their bankruptcy at once, and leave an empty house and empty coffers for the holders of their notes.

In this scramble of creditors, the country gets nothing, the towns but little. What are they to do? Bring suits? A million of creditors to bring a million of suits against John Nokes and Robert Styles, wheresoever to be found? All nonsense. The loss is total. And a sum is thus swindled from our citizens, of seven times the amount of the real debt, and four times that of the fictitious one of the United States, at the close of the war.

All this they will justly charge on their legislatures; but this will be poor satisfaction for the two or three hundred millions they will have lost. It is time, then, for the public functionaries to look to this. Perhaps it may not be too late. Perhaps, by giving time to the banks, they may call in and pay off their paper by degrees. But no remedy is ever to be expected while it rests with the State legislatures. Personal motive can be excited through so many avenues to their will, that, in their hands, it will continue to go on from bad to worse, until the catastrophe overwhelms us.

I still believe, however, that on proper representations of the subject, a great proportion of these legislatures would cede to Congress their power of establishing banks, saving the charter rights already granted. And this should be asked, not by way of amendment to the Constitution, because until three-fourths should consent, nothing could be done; but accepted from them one by one, singly, as their consent might be obtained.

The Ravages of Inflation

The Mississippi Bubble

ME XIII 404-32 The Third Eppes Letter 11-6-13

Smith again says "that the industry of Scotland languished for want of money to employ it, was the opinion of the famous Mr. Law. By establishing a bank of a particular kind, which, he seems to have imagined might issue paper to the amount of the whole value of all the lands in the country, he proposed to remedy this want of money. It was afterwards adopted, with some variations, by the Duke of Orleans, at that time Regent of France. The idea of the possibility of multiplying paper to almost any extent, was the real foundation of what is called the Mississippi scheme, the most extravagant project both of banking and stock jobbing, that perhaps the world ever saw. The principles upon which it was founded are explained by Mr. Law himself, in a discourse concerning money and trade, which he published in Scotland when he first proposed his project. The splendid but visionary ideas which are set forth in that and some other works upon the same principles, still continue to make an impression upon many people, and have perhaps, in part, contributed to that excess of banking which has of late been complained of both in Scotland and in other places."

The Mississippi scheme, it is well known, ended in France in the bankruptcy of the public treasury; the crush of thousands and thousands of private fortunes, and scenes of desolation and distress equal to those of any invading army, burning and laying waste all before it.

The State of Monetary Insecurity

ME XIII 404-32 The Third Eppes Letter 11-6-13

We are already at ten or twenty times the due quantity of medium; insomuch, that no man knows what his property is now worth, because it is bloating while he is calculating; and still less what it will be worth when the medium shall be relieved from its present dropsical state; and that it is a palpable falsehood to say we can have specie for our paper whenever demanded. Instead, then, of yielding to the cries of scarcity of medium set up by speculators, projectors, and commercial gamblers, no endeavors should be spared to begin the work of reducing it by such gradual means as may give time to private fortunes to preserve their poise, and settle down with the subsiding medium; and that, for this purpose, the States should be urged to concede to the General Government, with a saving of chartered rights, the exclusive power of establishing banks of discount for paper.

To the existence of banks of *discount for cash,* as on the continent of Europe, there can be no objection... . Even banks of deposit, where cash should be lodged, and a paper acknowledgement taken out as its representative, entitled to a return of the cash on demand, would be convenient for remittances, travelling persons, etc. But, liable as its cash would be to be pilfered and robbed, and its paper to be fradulently re-issued, or issued without deposit, it would require skilful and strict regulation.

The Deluge of Bank Paper

ME XIV 54-63 Thomas Cooper 1-16-14

Everything predicted by the enemies of banks, in the beginning, is now coming to pass. We are to be ruined now by the deluge of bank paper, as we were formerly by the old Continental paper. It is cruel that such revolutions in private fortunes should be at the mercy of avaricious adventurers, who, instead of employing their capital, if any they have, in manufactures, commerce, and other useful pursuits, make it an instrument to burden all the interchanges of property with their swindling profits, profits which are the price of no useful industry of theirs. Prudent men must be on their guard in this game of *Robin's alive,* and take care that the spark does not extinguish in their hands. I am an enemy of all banks discounting bills or notes for anything but coin. But our whole country is so fascinated by this Jack-lantern wealth, that they will not stop short of its total and fatal explosion.

FORD X 116 Albert Gallatin 1818

The flood with which the bankers are deluging us of nominal money has placed us completely without any certain measure of value, and, by interpolating a false measure, is deceiving and ruining multitudes of our citizens.

ME XV 179-81 Nathaniel Macon 1-12-19

There is indeed one evil which wakens me at times, because it jostles me at every turn. It is that we now have no measure of value. I am asked eighteen dollars for a yard of broadcloth, which, when we had dollars, I used to get for eighteen shillings; from this, I can only understand that a dollar is now worth but two inches of broadcloth, but broadcloth is no standard or measure of value. I do not know, therefore, whereabouts I stand in the scale of property, nor what to ask, or what to give for it... . I see nothing... but a general demoralization of the nation, a filching from industry its honest earnings, wherewith to build up palaces, and raise gambling stock for swindlers and shavers, who are to close their career of piracies by fraudulent bankruptcies.

Bank Paper vs. Treasury Notes

ME XIV 258-67 Jean Batiste Say 3-2-15

And at this time, we have probably one hundred banks, with capitals amounting to one hundred millions of dollars, on which they are authorized by law to issue notes to three times that amount, so that our circulating medium may now be estimated at from two to three hundred millions of dollars, on a population of eight and a half millions. The banks were able, for awhile, to keep this trash at par with metallic currency... by keeping deposits of cash sufficient to exchange for such of their notes as they were called on to pay in cash.

But the circumstances of the war draining away all our specie, all these banks have stopped payment, but with a promise to resume specie exchanges whenever circumstances shall produce a return of the metals. Some of the most prudent and honest will possibly do this; but the mass of them never will nor can. Yet, having no other medium, we take their paper, of necessity, for purposes of the instant, but never to lay by us.

The government is now issuing treasury notes for circulation, bottomed on solid funds, and bearing interest. The banking confederacy (and the merchants bound to them by their debts) will endeavor to crush the credit of these notes; but the country is eager for them, as something they can trust to, and so soon as a convenient quantity of them can get into circulation, the bank notes die... .

I will state to you the progressive prices which have been paid for particular parcels of land for some years back, which may enable you to distinguish between the real increase of value regularly produced by our advancement in population, wealth, and skill, and the bloated value arising from the present disordered and dropsical state of our medium. [He then gives an example of land worth $4 an acre in 1795 which sold for $12 in 1812 and $16 in 1815].

The Delusions of Inflation

ME XIV 379-84 Colonel Charles Yancy 1-6-16

Like a dropsical man calling out for water, water, our deluded citizens are clamoring for more banks, more banks. The American mind is now in that state of fever which the world has so often seen in the history of other nations. We are under the bank bubble, as England was under the South Sea bubble, France under the Mississippi bubble, and as every nation is liable to be, under whatever bubble, design, or delusion may puff up in moments when off their guard. We are now taught to believe that legerdemain tricks upon paper can produce as solid wealth as hard labor in the earth. It is vain for common sense to urge that *nothing* can produce but *nothing;* that it is an idle dream to believe in a philosopher's stone which is to turn everything into gold... .

Not Quixote enough, however, to attempt to reason Bedlam to rights, my anxieties are turned to the most practicable means of withdrawing us from the ruin into which we have run. Two hundred millions of paper in the hands of the people... is a fearful tax to fall at haphazard on their heads. The debt which purchased our independence was but of eighty millions, of which twenty years of taxation had in 1809 paid but one half. And what have we purchased with this tax of two hundred millions which we are to pay by wholesale but usury, swindling, and new forms of demoralization? Revolutionary history has warned us of the probable moment when this baseless trash is to receive its fiat. Whenever so much of the precious metals shall have returned into the circulation as that every one can get some in exchange for his produce, paper, as in the Revolutionary war, will experience at once an universal rejection.

When public opinion changes, it is with the rapidity of thought.

Confidence is already on the totter, and every one now handles this paper as if playing at Robin's alive. That in the present state of the circulation, the banks should resume payments in specie, would require their vaults to be like the widow's cruse... . The difficulty is indeed great; and the greater, because the patient revolts against all medicine. I am far from presuming to say that any plan can be relied on with certainty, because the bubble may burst from one moment to another... .

Opinion On Second United States Bank

ME XIII 404-12 The Third Eppes Letter 11-6-13

I have received... a paper [which] contains two propositions: the one for issuing treasury notes, bearing interest, and to be circulated as money: the other for the establishment of a national bank... .

The scheme is for Congress to establish a national bank, suppose of thirty millions capital, of which they shall contribute ten millions in new six per cent. stock, the States ten millions, and individuals ten millions, one-half of the two last contributions to be of similar stock, for which the parties are to give cash to Congress; the whole, however, to be under the exclusive management of the individual subscribers, who are to name all the directors; neither Congress nor the States having any power of interference in its administration.... The charter is proposed to be for forty or fifty years, and if any future augmentation should take place, the individual proprietors are to have the privilege of being the sole subscribers for that... .

After the solemn decision of Congress against the renewal of the charter of the Bank of the United States, and the grounds of that decision, (the want of constitutional power,) I had imagined that question at rest, and that no more applications would be made to them for the incorporation of banks. The opposition on that ground to its first establishment, the small majority by which it was overborne, and the means practised for obtaining it, cannot already be forgotten. The law having passed, however, by a majority, its opponents true to the sacred principle of submission to a majority, suffered the law to flow through its term without obstruction.

During this, the nation had time to consider the constitutional question, and when the renewal was proposed, they condemned it, not by their representatives in Congress only, but by express instructions from different organs of their will. Here then we might stop, and consider the memorial as answered. But, setting authority aside, we will examine whether the legislature ought to comply with it, even if they had the power. [Here, Jefferson goes to great length to show that the Bank would not only be unconstitutional, but also economically undesirable.]

The Inflation-Deflation Cycle

How the States Could Deal With the Problem

ME XIII 404-32 John W. Eppes 11-6-13

Any single state, even if no other should come into the measure, would find its interest in arresting foreign bank paper immediately, and its own by degrees. Specie would then flow in on them as paper disappeared. Their own banks would call in and pay off their notes gradually, and their constituents would be saved from the general wreck.

Should the greater part of the States concede, as is expected, their power over banks to Congress, besides insuring their own safety, the paper of the non-conceding States might be so checked and circumscribed, by prohibiting its receipt in any of the conceding States, and even in the non-conceding as to duties, taxes, judgments, or other demands of the United States, or of the citizens of other States, that it would soon die of itself, and the medium of gold and silver be universally restored. This is what ought to be done.

But it will not be done. *Carthago non delibutur.* The overbearing clamor of merchants, speculators, and projectors, will drive us before them with our eyes open, until, as in France, under the Mississippi bubble, our citizens will be overtaken by the crush of this baseless fabric, without other satisfaction than that of execrations on the heads of those functionaries, who, from ignorance, pusillanimity, or corruption, have betrayed the fruits of their industry into the hands of projectors and swindlers.

ME XIV 67-69 Joseph Cabell 1-17-14

I enclose *for your own perusal,* therefore, three letters which I wrote to him [Mr. Eppes] on the course of our finances... .

Until the gigantic banking propositions of this winter had made their appearance in the different legislatures, I had hoped that the evil might still be checked; but I see now that it is desperate... . I had been in hopes that good old Virginia... would have set the example... by passing a law that, after a certain time, suppose six months, no bank bill of less than ten dollars should be permitted. That after some other reasonable term, there should be none less than twenty dollars, and so on, until those only should be left... whose size would be above the common transactions... .

This would ensure to us an ordinary circulation of metallic money, and would reduce the quantum of paper within the bounds of moderate mischief... . Such a mode of doing it, too, would give less alarm to the bankholders, the discreet part of whom must wish to see themselves secured by some circumscription... . But I now give up all hope. After producing the same revolutions in private fortunes as the Continental paper did, it will die like that, adding a total incapacity to raise resources for the war.

ME XIV 71-79 John Adams 1-24-14

I have been the enemy of banks... foisting their own paper into circulation, and thus banishing our cash. My zeal against these institutions was so warm and open at the establishment of the Bank of the United States, that I was derided as a maniac by the tribe of bank-mongers, who were seeking to filch from the public their swindling and barren gains.

But the errors of that day cannot be recalled. The evils they have engendered are now upon us, and the question is how are we to get out of them?... . The mania is too strong. It has seized, by its delusions and corruptions, all the members of our governments, general, special, and individual. Our circulating paper of the last year was estimated at two hundred millions of dollars. The new banks now petitioned for, to the several legislatures, are for about sixty millions additional capital, and of course one hundred and eighty millions of additional circulation, nearly doubling that of the last year, and raising the whole mass to near four hundred millions, or forty for one, of the wholesome amount of circulation for a population of eight millions circumstanced as we are; and you remember, how rapidly our money went down after our forty for one establishment in the Revolution. I doubt if the present trash can hold as long... .

Citizens Must Be Informed

ME XV 181-86 John Adams 3-21-19

The evils of this deluge of paper money are not to be removed until our citizens are generally and radically instructed in their cause and consequences, and silence by their authority the interested clamors and sophistry of speculating, shaving, and banking institutions. Till then, we must be content to return, *quond hoc,* to the savage state, to recur to barter in the exchange of our property, for want of a stable, common measure of value, that now in use being less fixed than the beads of wampum of the Indian, and to deliver up our citizens, their property, and their labor, passive victims, to the swindling tricks of bankers and mountebanks.

The Money Withdrawn: Prices Plummet

ME XV 224-25 John Adams 11-7-19

The paper bubble then is burst. This is what you and I, and every reasoning man... have long foreseen; yet its disastrous effects are not the less for having been foreseen. We were laboring under a dropsical fulness of circulating medium. Nearly all of it is now called in by the banks, who have the regulation of the safety-valves of our fortunes, and who condense and explode them at their will. Lands in this State cannot now be sold for a year's rent; and unless our legislature have wisdom enough to effect a remedy by a gradual diminution only of the medium, there will be a general revolution of property in this State.

Over our own paper and that of other States coming among us, they have competent powers; over that of the Bank of the United States there is doubt... . That bank will probably conform voluntarily to such regulations as the legislature may prescribe for the others. If they do not, we must shut their doors, and join the other States which deny the right of Congress to establish banks, and solicit them to agree to some mode of settling this constitutional question. They have themselves twice decided against their right and twice for it. Many of the States have been uniform in denying it, and between such parties the Constitution has provided no umpire. I do not know particularly the extent of this distress in the other States; but southwardly and westwardly, I believe all are involved in it.

ME XVII 437-38 Miscellaneous Papers 1822

That a fair price cannot be obtained by sale in the ordinary way, and in the present depressed state of agricultural industry, is well known.

Lands in the State will now sell for not more than a third or fourth of what they would have brought a few years ago; perhaps at the very time of the contraction of the debts for which they are now to be sold. The low price in foreign markets, for a series of years past, of agricultural produce, of wheat generally, of tobacco most commonly, and the accumulation of duties on the articles of consumption not produced within our State, not only disable the farmer or planter from adding to his farm by purchase, but reduces him to sell his own, and remove to the western country, glutting the market he leaves, while he lessens the number of bidders.

ME XIX 273-74 Elijah Griffith 5-15-20

The distresses you describe in your section of the Union have been bitterly felt here. They are not greater than I had always expected and freely expressed in the creation of the first bank by the new government. Mr. Madison and myself left nothing untried to obtain General Washington's negative of the law, but after a long struggle in his mind, Hamilton prevailed in the last hour and let in a torrent of swindling institutions which have spread ruin and wretchedness over the face of our country. And what is the most disheartening, it has still left such a hankering after these allusive establishments that no hope remains of their proscription in future. Their fatal effect has been greatly aggravated in this State by an unexampled drought which, having prevailed from June last to this time, destroyed the bread of that year and threatens that of the present.

Jefferson's Plan for Reducing the Circulation

ME XV 229-32 William C. Rives 11-28-19

The distresses of our country, produced first by the flood, then by the ebb, of bank paper, are such as cannot fail to engage the interposition of the legislature... . If we suffer the moral of the present lesson to pass away without improvement by the eternal suppression of bank *paper,* then indeed is the condition of our country desperate, until the slow advance of public instruction shall give to our functionaries the wisdom of their station... .

The plethory of circulating medium which raised the prices of everything to several times their ordinary and standard value, in which state of things many and heavy debts were contracted; and the sudden withdrawing too great a proportion of that medium, and reduction of prices far below that standard, constitute the disease under which we are now laboring, and which must end in a general revolution of property, if some remedy is not applied. That remedy is clearly a gradual reduction of the medium to its standard level, that is to say, to the level which a metallic medium will always find for itself, so as to be in equilibrio with that of the nations with which we have commerce.

To effect this,

Let the whole of the present paper medium be suspended in its circulation after a certain and not distant day.

Ascertain by proper inquiry the greatest sum of it which has at any time been in actual circulation.

Take a certain term of years for its gradual reduction, suppose it to be five years; then let the solvent banks issue 5/6 of that amount in new notes... . Let 1/5 of these notes bear on their face that the bank will discharge them with specie at the end of one year; another 5th at the end of two years; a third 5th at the end of three years; and so of the 4th and 5th. They will be sure to be brought in at their respective periods of redemption.

Make it a high offense to receive or pass within this State a note of any other.

There is little doubt that our banks will agree readily to this operation; if they refuse, declare their charters forfeited by their former irregularities and give summary process against them for the suspended notes.

The bank of the United States will probably concur also; if not, shut their doors and join the other States in respectful, but firm applications to Congress, to concur in constituting a tribunal (a special convention, e.g.) for settling amicably the question of their right to institute a bank, and that also of the States to do the same... .

Interdict forever to both the State and national governments, the power of establishing any paper bank; for without this interdiction, we shall have the same ebbs and flows of medium, and the same revolutions of property to go through every twenty or thirty years.

In this way the value of property, keeping pace nearly with the sum of circulating medium, will descend gradually to its proper level, at the rate of about 1/5 every year, the sacrifices of what shall be sold for payment of the first instalments of debts will be moderate, and time will be given for economy and industry to come in aid of those subsequent.

Certainly, no nation ever before abandoned to the avarice and jugglings of private individuals to regulate, according to their own interests, the quantum of circulating medium for the nation, to inflate, by deluges of paper, the nominal prices of property, and then to buy up that property at 1 shilling in the pound, having first withdrawn the floating medium which might endanger a competition in purchase.

Yet this is what has been done, and will be done, unless stayed by the protecting hand of the legislature. The evil has been produced by the error of their sanction of this ruinous machinery of banks; and justice, wisdom, duty, all require that they should interpose and arrest it before the schemes of plunder and spoliation desolate the country. It is believed that harpies are already hoarding their money to commence these scenes on the separation of the legislature; and we know that lands have been already sold under the hammer for less than a year's rent.

17. A Pioneer in Education

Commentary

As we contemplate Jefferson's passion for education and the increase of knowledge among the people, we realize that in this he had a dual objective: first, to enable them to preserve their republican heritage and so prevent the development of autocratic and despotic government; and, second, perhaps even more important, to enable the gifted and ambitious children of those too poor to send them to schools and colleges, to obtain the very best education available. Thus would emerge an aristocracy of virtue and talent, independent of birth or social position, who would achieve a merited economic success and be entrusted with the most influential positions in society. They, and not the pampered scions of privilege, would be the elite of future generations.

History, said Jefferson, demonstrates that those entrusted with power always pervert it into tyranny if they can; there is no sure foundation for the preservation of happiness except an educated common people, who will preserve order when it is to their interest. Let the youth absorb as much knowledge as their drives and capacities make possible; they will be the sole depositories of political and religious freedom. In a state of civilization, freedom cannot co-exist with ignorance; but wherever people in general are enlightened, tyranny and oppression vanish like ghosts before the rising sun.

In 1779, during the height of the Revolutionary War, Jefferson introduced into the Virginia Assembly a Bill for the More General Diffusion of Knowledge; although the proposals therein were not enacted until 1817, this established the first free, public, non-sectarian school system in the world, available to everyone.

Jefferson wanted every child, male and female, to receive gratis three years of education, during which the pupils would become proficient in reading, writing, and arithmetic; they would also learn geography, and study Greek, Roman, English, and American history. Thus, three years of schooling would provide a solid elementary education, which would probably compare favorably with or exceed the progress made by those graduating from the eighth grade in the public schools today.

The brightest and most ambitious of those completing this course would then, if from families too poor to pay for their education, be given five or six years of free board, lodging, and tuition at what Jefferson called colleges or grammar schools; here the curriculum resembled a mixture of what students now obtain in high schools and junior college.

Under the Bill of 1779, the very best graduates of the grammar schools who came from poor families would be given three-year scholarships at William and Mary in Williamsburg; those from wealthy families would pay all expenses beyond the first three grades.

We should note that while all girls would attend the ward schools, only boys were eligible for the grammar schools, or colleges, and the university.

When Jefferson prepared the expanded Bill which became law in 1817, it is significant that no minister of the gospel could serve as a Visitor; that the Christian Scriptures would not be used in the classrooms; and that "no religious reading, instruction, or exercise shall be prescribed or practiced inconsistent with the tenets of any religious sect... ." In short, virtually no religious doctrine could be taught.

We should note also that the same Bill which established the free three-year ward schools, also provided, not only for five-year colleges or grammar schools, but also for the establishment of his beloved University of Virginia at Charlottesville, situated at the base of Monticello. In this, there would be no department or professorship of divinity, or even one of theoretical medicine, which he called the "charlatanerie of the body" as the doctrines of the priests were those of the mind. Although he advocated facilities near the University in which the various sects could conduct classes in their specific tenets, in the University itself, religious sources and moral principles would be treated and taught objectively, like any other science. In fact, one of the crucial reasons for establishing this new university was that it would be a secular institution, the only one then of higher learning in the nation, dedicated to the "illimitable freedom of the human mind. For here we are not afraid to follow truth wherever it may lead, or to tolerate error so long as reason is left free to combat it."

We should not be surprised, therefore, that the clergy fulminated against it, and forced the dismissal of Thomas Cooper, on the ground that he was a Unitarian and could, therefore, not be trusted to teach such a subject as minerology. Jefferson did not want the youth of Virginia to go to Yale, Harvard, Princeton, Columbia, or others in New England, or even to William and Mary, where they would imbibe "opinions and principles in discord with those of their own country." All of these had been founded by religious denominations and existed largely or primarily to prepare graduates for the ministry. At that time, Jefferson's was the first publicly owned American university.

Jefferson secured the lands for his University, laid out the campus, designed the buildings, superintended their construction, procured the professors, prepared the curriculum, served from the beginning not only as one of the Visitors (comparable to a modern Board of Regents), but also as its Rector, responsible for keeping the minutes of all meetings and making reports — which fill about 140 pages in the Supplementary Manuscripts *of Jefferson's works. For all of his efforts, which must have consumed most of his life force during his last ten years, he received no monetary compensation whatever. As he declared on his tombstone, he was indeed the Father of the University of Virginia.*

To bring this great project to completion was a herculean task. At times, he despaired of success; there were long and frustrating delays. Its completion, he wrote in 1821, "is the last act of usefulness I can render; and could I see it open, I would not ask an hour more of life." It was years later, March 25, 1825, before he was able to announce in a letter to Edward Livingston that "The institution is at length happily advanced to completion, and has commenced under auspices as favorable as I could expect.... It is the last object for which I shall obtrude myself on the public observation." On May 2, 1826, he wrote a long letter to Doctor John P. Emmett, explaining its operation. This was one of his last epistles, for two months later, he went "to the land of dreams, to sleep with the dreamers of all past and future times."

Does he, from wherever he may be dreaming, today contemplate the institution he founded, which now has more than 1,300 instructors and in excess of 16,000 students?

The Importance of General Knowledge

BW 40-46 A Bill for the More General Diffusion of Knowledge 1779

...experience hath shown, that even under the best forms, those entrusted with power have, in time, and by slow operations, perverted it into tyranny; and... that the most effectual means of preventing this would be to illuminate, as far as practicable, the minds of the people at large, and more especially to give them knowledge of those facts which history exhibiteth, that, possessed thereby of the experience of other ages and countries, they may be enabled to know ambition under all its shapes, and prompt to exert their natural powers to defeat its purposes... whence it becomes expedient for promoting the public happiness that those persons, whom nature hath endowed with genius and virtue, should be rendered by liberal education worthy to receive, and able to guard, the sacred deposit of the rights and liberties of their fellow citizens, and that they should be called to that charge without regard to wealth, birth, or other accidental condition or circumstance... it is better that such should be sought for and educated at the common expence of all, than that the happiness of all should be confined to the weak or wicked... .

ME V 394-98 George Wythe 8-19-86

No other sure foundation can be devised for the preservation of freedom and happiness. If anybody thinks that kings, nobles, and priests are good conservators of the public happiness, send him here [France]. It is the best school in the universe to cure him of that folly... . Preach... a crusade against ignorance; establish and improve the law for educating the common people. Let our countrymen know that the people alone can protect us against these evils [of tyrannical government].

ME VI 385-93 James Madison 12-20-87

And say, finally, whether peace is best preserved by giving energy to the government, or information to the people... . Educate and inform the mass of the people. Enable them to see that it is to their interest to preserve peace and order, and they will preserve them. And it requires no very high degree of education to convince them of this. They are the only sure reliance for the preservation of liberty.

ME IX 306-07 Mann Page 8-30-95

I do most anxiously wish to see the highest degree of education given to the higher degrees of genius, and to all degrees of it so much as may enable them to read and understand what is going on in the world, and to keep their part of it going right; for nothing can keep it right but their own vigilant and distrustful superintendence... the higher orders... rising above the swinish multitude, always continue to nestle themselves into the places of power and profit. These rogues set out with stealing the people's good opinion, and then steal from them the right of withdrawing it, by contriving laws and associations against the power of the people... .

ME XII 282-83 John Wythe 5-19-09

I always hear with pleasure of institutions for the promotion of knowledge among my countrymen. The people of every country are the only safe guardians of their own rights, and are the only instruments which can be used for their destruction.

ME XII 413-17 William Duane 9-16-10

...the information of the people at large can alone make them safe, as they are the sole depository of our political and religious freedom.

ME XIV 487-92 Dupont de Nemours 4-24-16

Enlighten the people generally, and tyranny and oppressions of body and mind will vanish like evil spirits at the dawn of day. Although I do not, with some enthusiasts, believe that the human condition will ever advance to such a state of perfection as that there shall no longer be pain or vice in the world, yet I believe it susceptible of much improvement, and, most of all, in matters of government and religion... .

ME XIV 379-84 Colonel Yancy 1-16-16

If a nation expects to be ignorant and free, in a state of civilization, it expects what never was and never will be. The functionaries of every government have propensities to command at will the liberty and property of their constituents. There is no safe deposit for these but with the people themselves; nor can they be safe with them without information. Where the press is free, and every man is able to read, all is safe.

Jefferson's Legislative Measures

BW 40-46 A Bill for the More General Diffusion of Knowledge 1779

SECTION II. Be it therefore enacted by the General Assembly, that in every county within this commonwealth, there shall be chosen annually... three of the most honest and able men of their country, to be called Aldermen of the county... .

SECTION IV. The said Aldermen... shall... divide their said county into hundreds... so that... all the children within each hundred may daily attend the school to be established therein... .

SECTION VI. At every of those schools shall be taught reading, writing, and common arithmetick, and the books which shall be used therein for instruction shall be such as will at the same time make them acquainted with Graecian, Roman, English, and American history. At these schools, all the free children, male and female, resident within the respective hundred, shall be entitled to receive tuition gratis, for the term of three years and as much longer, at their private expense, as their parents, guardians, or friends shall think proper... .

SECTION IX. And in order that grammar schools may be rendered convenient to the youth in every part of the commonwealth, be it therefore enacted that... the said overseers... shall fix on such place in... the counties in their district as shall be most proper for situating a grammar school-house, endeavoring that the situation be as central as may be to the inhabitants of the said counties... .

SECTION XVI. Every overseer of the hundred schools shall, in the month of September annually, after the most diligent and impartial examination and inquiry, appoint from the among the boys who shall have been two years at the least at some of the schools under his superintendence, and whose parents are too poor to give them farther education, some one of the best and most promising genius and disposition, to proceed to the grammar school of his district... .

SECTION XVII. Every boy so appointed shall be authorized to proceed to the grammar school of his district, there to be educated and boarded during such time as is hereafter limited; and his quota of the expences of the house together with a compensation to the master or usher for his tuition, at the rate of twenty dollars by the year, shall be paid by the Treasurer quarterly on warrant from the Auditors... .

SECTION XIX. The visitors for the districts... after diligent examination and enquiry as before directed, shall chuse one among the said seniors, of the best learning and most hopeful genius and disposition, who shall be authorized by them to proceed to William and Mary College; there to be educated, boarded, and clothed, three years; the expence of which annually shall be paid by the Treasurer on warrant from the Auditors.

BW 150-52 Notes on Virginia 1781

Another object... is to diffuse knowledge more generally through the mass of the people... .

The general objects of this law are to provide an education adapted to the years, to the capacity, and the condition of every one, and directed to their freedom and happiness... . Instead, therefore, of putting the Bible and Testament into the hands of the children at an age when their judgments are not sufficiently matured for religious inquiries, their memories may here be stored with the most useful facts from Grecian, Roman, European, and American history. The first elements of morality too may be instilled into their minds; such as, when further developed as their judgments advance in strength, may teach them how to work out their own greatest happiness, by showing them that it does not depend on the condition of life in which chance has placed them, but is always the result of a good conscience, good health, occupation, and freedom in all just pursuits.

Those whom either the wealth of their parents or the adoption of the State shall destine to higher degrees of learning, will go on to the grammar schools, which constitute the next stage... .

An amendment of our constitution must here come in aid of the public education. The influence over government must be shared among all the people. If every individual which composed their mass participates of the ultimate authority, the government will be safe, because corrupting the whole mass will exceed any private resource of wealth; and public ones cannot be provided but by levies on the people. In this case, every man would have to pay his own price.

The government of Great Britain has been corrupted, because but one man in ten has a right to vote for members of parliament. The sellers of the government, therefore, get nine-tenths of their price clear. It has been thought that corruption is restrained by confining the right to suffrage to a few of the wealthier of the people; but it would be more effectually restrained by an extension of that right to such numbers as would bid defiance to the means of corruption.

The Education Act, Passed in 1817

An Act for Establishing Elementary Schools and a University

ME XVII 418-41

1. Be it enacted by the General Assembly of Virginia, that at the first session of the Superior Court... the judge thereof shall appoint three discreet and well-informed persons, residents of the county, and not being ministers of the gospel of any denomination, to serve as Visitors of the Elementary Schools of the said county... .

2. The said Visitors shall... proceed to divide their county into wards... which division into wards shall... be completely designated, published, and reported, by their metes and bounds, to the office of the clerk of the Superior Court... .

3. The original division into wards being made, the Visitors shall appoint days for the first meeting of every ward and shall propose to them to decide by a majority of their votes, — 1. The location of a school-house for the ward, and a dwelling-house for the teacher... . 2. The size and structure of the said houses; and 3. Whether the same shall be built by the joint labor of the warders, or by their pecuniary contributions; and also 4. To elect by a plurality of their votes a warden, resident, who shall direct and superintend the said buildings, and be charged with their future care.

4. And if they decide that the said buildings shall be erected by the joint labor of the warders, then all persons within the said ward liable to work in the highways, shall attend at the order of the warden, and, under this direction, shall labor thereon until completed, under the same penalties as provided by law to enforce labor on the highways. And if they decide on erection by pecuniary contributions, the residents and owners of property within the ward shall contribute toward the cost, each in proportion to the taxes they last paid to the State for their persons and for the same property... .

5. It shall be the duty of the said Visitors to seek and to employ for every ward, whenever the number and ages of its children require it, a person of good moral character, qualified to teach reading, writing, numeral arithmetic and geography, whose subsistence shall be furnished by the residents and proprietors of the ward, either in money or in kind, at the choice of each contributor, and in the ratio of their public taxes, to be

apportioned and levied as on the failures before provided for. The teacher shall also have the use of the house and accommodations provided for him, and shall moreover receive annually such standing wages as the Visitors shall have determined to be proportioned on the residents and proprietors of the ward, and to be paid, levied and applied as before provided in other cases of pecuniary contribution.

6. At this school shall be received and instructed gratis, every infant of competent age who has not already had three years schooling. And it is declared and enacted, that no person unborn or under the age of twelve years at the passing of this act, and who is *compos mentis,* shall, after the age of fifteen years, be a citizen of this commonwealth until he or she can read readily in some tongue, native or acquired... .

11. The said teachers shall, in all things relating to the education and government of their pupils, be under the direction and control of the Visitors; but no religious reading, instruction or exercise, shall be prescribed or practiced inconsistent with the tenets of any religious sect or denomination.

12. Some one of the Visitors, once in every year at least... shall examine the progress of the pupils, and give to those who excel in reading, in writing, in arithmetic, or in geography, such honorary marks and testimonies of approbation, as may encourage and excite to industry and emulation... .

14. Be it further enacted as follows: The several counties of this commonwealth shall be distributed into nine collegiate districts... .

17. Within seven months after the passing of this act the said Board of Public Instruction shall determine on such of the sites reported as they shall think most eligible for the college of each district... .

18. On each of the sites so located shall be erected one or more substantial buildings — the walls of which shall be of brick or stone, with two school rooms, and four rooms for the accommodation of the professors, and with sixteen dormitories in or adjacent to the same, each sufficient for two pupils, and in which no more than two shall be permitted to lodge, with a fire place in each, and the whole in a comfortable and decent style, suitable to their purpose... .

22. To each of the said colleges shall be appointed two professors, the one for teaching Greek, Latin, and such other branches of learning, before described, as he may be qualified to teach, and the other for the remaining branches thereof, who shall be allowed the use of the apartments provided for him, and a standing salary of $500 yearly... .

28. Some member, or members, of the Board of Visitors, to be nominated by the said Board, or such other persons as they shall nominate, shall, once in every year, at least, visit the college of their district, enquire into the proceedings and practices thereat, examine the progress of the pupils, and give to those who excel in any branch of learning prescribed

for the college, such honorary marks and testimonies of approbation as may encourage or excite to industry and emulation... .

30. And for establishing in a central and healthy part of the State an University wherein all the branches of useful science may be taught, Be it further enacted as follows:

31. Whensoever the Visitors of the Central College... shall convey or cause to be conveyed to the Board of Public Instruction, for the use of this commonwealth, all the lands, buildings, property, and rights of the said college... the same shall be thereupon vested in this commonwealth, and shall be appropriated to the institution of an University to be called the University of Virginia, which shall be established on the said lands. The said Board of Public Instruction shall thereupon forthwith appoint eight fit persons who shall compose the Board of Visitors for the government of the University, notifying thereof the persons so appointed, and prescribing to them a day for their first meeting at Charlottesville... .

34. In the said University shall be taught history and geography, ancient and modern; natural philosophy, agriculture, chemistry, and the science of medicine, anatomy, zoology, botany, minerology and geology; mathematics, pure and mixed; military and naval science; ideology, ethics, the law of nature and of nations; law, municipal and foreign; the science of civil government and political economy; languages, rhetoric, belles lettres, and the fine arts generally; which branches of science shall be so distributed and under so many professorships, not exceeding ten, as the Visitors shall think most proper.

35. Each professor shall be allowed the use of the apartments and accommodations provided for him, and such standing salary, not exceeding $1,000 yearly, as the Visitors shall think proper, to be drawn from the literary fund, with such tuition fees from the students as the Visitors shall establish... .

41. And to avail the commonwealth of those talents and virtues which nature has sown as liberally among the poor as rich, and which are lost to their country by the want of means for their cultivation, Be it further enacted as follows:

42. On the 29th day of February... the Visitors of the ward-schools in every county shall meet at the court-house of their county and, after the most diligent and impartial observation and enquiry of the boys who have been three years at the ward-schools, and whose parents are too poor to give them a collegiate education, shall select from among them some one of the most promising and sound understanding, who shall be sent to the first meeting of the Visitors of their collegiate district, with such proofs as the case requires and admits, for the examination and information of that Board; who, from among the candidates so offered from the several counties of their district, shall select two of the most sound and promising understanding, who shall be admitted to their college, and there be

maintained and educated five years at the public expense, under such rules and limitations as the Board of Public Instruction shall prescribe; and at the end of the said five years the said Collegiate Visitors shall select that one of the two who shall, on their most diligent and impartial enquiry and best information, be adjudged by them to be of the most sound and promising understanding and character, and most improved by their course of education, who shall be sent on immediately thereafter to the University, there to be maintained and educated in such branches of the sciences taught there as are most proper to qualify him for the calling to which his parents or guardians may destine him; and to continue at the said University three years at the public expense, under such rules and limitations as the Board of Public Instruction shall prescribe. And the expenses of the persons so to be publicly maintained and educated at the colleges and University shall be drawn by their respective Visitors from the literary fund.

The Progress of the University

ME XIV 446-56 Governor Wilson C. Nicholas 4-2-16

Education. The President and Directors of the Literary Fund are desired to digest and report on a system of public education... .

As the buildings [of the University] to be erected will also enter into their report, I would strongly recommend to their consideration, instead of one immense building, to have a small one for every professorship, arranged at proper distances around a square, to admit extension, connected by a piazza... .

This village form is preferable to a single great building for many reasons... and should the idea be approved by the Board, more may be said hereafter on the opportunity these small buildings will afford of exhibiting models of architecture of the purest forms of antiquity, furnishing to the student examples of the precepts he will be taught in that art.

The Elementary or Ward Schools are the last branch of the subject... [here follows a discussion of the middle schools or colleges].

My partiality for that division is not founded in views of education solely, but infinitely more as the means of a better administration of our government, and the eternal preservation of its republican principles... . Should the Board of Directors approve the plan, and make ward divisions the substratum of their elementary schools, their report may furnish a happy occasion of introducing them, leaving all their other uses to be adapted from time to time hereafter as occasion shall occur.

ME XIX 385-86 Supplementary Manuscripts 10-4-19

...the Visitors trust that they could have in place, by the autumn or winter of the coming year, the complement of professors contemplated by the law, and open the institution at that epoch with the distinction called for by the interests of this State...

But this urgency they leave with confidence... to the wiser judgment of the legislature, with assurance, on the part of the Visitors, that... they will omit nothing which may hasten the desirable moment when the youth of their country may find at home those resources of instruction which they have so long been in the habit of seeking elsewhere, and when, by a sound education, a wholesome direction may be given to *public opinion,* the safest guide and guardian of the public morals and welfare, the arbitress, in every nation, of its destinies to happiness or wretchedness.

ME XV 219-24 William Short 10-31-19

Come, too, and see our incipient University, which has advanced with great activity this year. By the end of next, we shall have elegant accommodations for seven professors, and the year following the professors themselves. No secondary character will be received among them. Either the ablest, which America or Europe can furnish, or none at all.

ME XV 243-46 William Short 4-13-20

The history of our University you know so far. Seven of the ten pavilions destined for the professors, and about thirty dormitories, will be completed this year; and three others, with six hotels for boarding, and seventy other dormitories, will be completed the next year, and the whole be in readiness then to receive those who are to occupy them... .

But in despite of their [the clergy's] fulminations against endeavors to enlighten the general mind, to improve the reason of the people, and encourage them in the use of it, the liberality of this State will support this institution and give fair play to the cultivation of reason.

ME XII 359-61 Rev. Mr. Knox 2-24-10

Truth and reason are eternal. They have prevailed. And they will eternally prevail, however in times and places they may be overborne for a while by violence, military, civil, or ecclesiastical.

ME XV 302-04 William Roscoe 12-27-20

This institution will be based on the illimitable freedom of the human mind. For here we are not afraid to follow truth wherever it may lead, nor to tolerate any error so long as reason is left free to combat it.

ME XVIII 312-13 John Taylor 2-14-21

Our University labors hard to come into existence... We shall receive only those subjects who desire the highest degree of instruction, for which they now go to Harvard, Princeton, New York, and Philadelphia. These seminaries are no longer proper for Southern or Western students. The signs of the times admonish us to call them home. If knowledge is power, we should look to its advancement at home, where no resource of power will be wanting. This may not be in my day; but probably will be in yours. God send our country [Virginia] a happy deliverance.

ME XV 314-15 General James Breckenridge 2-15-21

I learn, with deep affliction, that nothing is likely to be done for our University this year. So near it is to the shore that one shove more would land it there... . The reflections that the boys of this age are to be the men of the next; that they should be prepared to receive the holy charge which we are cherishing to deliver over to them; that in establishing an institution of wisdom for them, we secure it to all our future generations; that in fulfilling this duty, we bring home to our own bosoms the sweet consolation of seeing our sons rising under a luminous tuition, to destinies of high promise... .

If, as has been estimated, we send three hundred thousand dollars a year to the Northern seminaries, for the instruction of our own sons, then we must have there five hundred of our sons, imbibing opinions and principles in discord with those of their own country. This canker is eating on our vitals... and if not arrested at once, will be beyond remedy.

ME XV 325-26 Judge Spencer Roane 3-9-21

The University will give employment to my remaining years, and quite enough for my senile faculties. It is the last act of usefulness I can render, and could I see it open, I would not ask an hour more of life.

Whitman Collection 362 William Short 11-24-21

You enquire also about our University. All its buildings except the Library will be finished by the ensuing spring. It will be a splendid establishment, would be thought so in Europe, and for the chastity of its architecture and classical taste leaves everything in America far behind it. But the Library, not yet begun, is essentially wanting to give it unity and consolidation as a single object. It will have cost in the whole but 250,000 dollars. The Library is to be on the principle of the Pantheon, a sphere within a cylinder of 70 feet diameter, — to wit, one-half only of the dimensions of the Pantheon, and of a single order only. When this is done you must come and see it.

ME XV 403-06 Doctor Thomas Cooper 11-2-22

The time of opening our University is still... uncertain... . All the pavilions, boarding-houses, and dormitories are done. Nothing is now wanting but the central building for a Library and other general purposes.

ME XVI 31-35 Richard Rush 4-26-24

We have been four or five years engaged in erecting our buildings... we propose to open it [the University] the beginning of the next year. We require the intervening time for seeking out and engaging Professors... .

But how to find out those who are of the first grade of science, of sober, correct habits and morals, harmonizing tempers, talents for communication, is the difficulty... .

From our information of the character of the different Universities, we expect we should go to Oxford for our classical professor, to Cambridge for those of Mathematics, Natural Philosophy, and Natural History, and to Edinburg for a professor of Anatomy and the elements or outlines only of Medicine... .

We can place in Mr. Gilmer's hands but a moderate sum at present for merely text-books to begin with, and for indispensable articles of apparatus, Mathematical, Astronomical, Physical, Chemical, and Anatomical. We are in the hope of a sum of $50,000, as soon as we can get a settlement passed through the public offices... .

Mr. Gilmer takes... with him plans of our establishment, which we think it may be encouraging to show to the persons to whom he will make propositions, as well to let them see the comforts provided for themselves, as to show by the extensiveness and expense of the scale, that it is no emphemeral thing to which they are invited.

ME XVI 112-15 Edward Livingston 3-25-25

Seven years ago, indeed, I embarked in an enterprise, the establishment of an University, which placed and keeps me still under the public eye. The call was imperious, the necessity urgent, and the hazard of titubation less, by these seven years, than it now is. The institution is at length happily advanced to completion, and has commenced under auspices as favorable as I could expect. I hope it will prove a blessing to my own State, and not unuseful perhaps to some others. At all hazards, and seconded by the aid of my able coadjutors, I shall continue, while I am in being, to contribute to it whatever my weakened and weakening powers can. But assuredly, it is the last object for which I shall obtrude myself on the public observation.

Theology, Religion and Medicine

ME XV 403-406 Doctor Thomas Cooper 11-2-22

In our university you know there is no Professorship of Divinity. A handle has been made of this, to disseminate an idea that this is an institution, not merely of no religion, but against all religion. Occasion was taken at the last meeting of the Visitors, to bring forward an idea that might silence this calumny, which weighed on the minds of some honest friends to the institution. In our annual report to the legislature, after stating the constitutional reasons against a public establishment of any religious instruction, we suggest the expediency of encouraging the different religious sects to establish, each for itself, a professorship of their own tenets, on the confines of the university, so near as that their students may attend the lectures there, and have the free use of our library, and every other accommodation we can give them; preserving, however, their independence of us and of each other.

ME XIV 199-202 Thomas Cooper 2-7-14

I agree with you... that a professorship of Theology should have no place in our institution... . Perhaps I should concur with you also in excluding the *theory* (not the practice) of medicine. This is the charlatanerie of the body, as the other is of the mind.

ME XIX 413-16 Supplementary Manuscripts 10-7-22

In the same report of the commissioners of 1818, it was stated by them that "in conformity with the principles of constitution, which place all sects of religion on an equal footing, with the jealousies of the different sects in guarding that equality from encroachment or surprise, and with the sentiments of the legislature in freedom of religion, manifested on former occasions, they had not proposed that any professorship of divinity should be established in the University; that provision, however, was made for giving instruction in the Hebrew, Greek, and Latin languages, and depositories of the originals, and of the earliest and most respected authorities of the faith of every sect, and for courses of ethical lectures, developing those moral obligations in which all sects agree. That, proceeding thus far, without offence to the constitution, they had left, at this point, to every sect, to take into their own hands, the office of further instruction in the peculiar tenet of each.

It was not, however, to be understood that instruction in religious opinion and duties was meant to be precluded by the public authorities, as indifferent to the interests of society. On the contrary, the relations which exist between man and his Maker, and the duties resulting from these relations, are the most interesting and important to every human being, and the most incumbent on his study and investigation. The want of instruction in the various creeds of religious faith existing among our citizens presents, therefore, a chasm in a general institution of the useful sciences. But it was thought that this want, and the entrustment to each society of instruction in its own doctrine, were evils of less danger than a permission to the public authorities to dictate modes or principles of religious instruction, or than opportunities furnished them by giving countenance or ascendancy to any one sect over another.

A remedy, however, has been suggested of promising aspect, which, while it excludes the public authorities from the domain of religious freedom, will give to the sectarian schools of divinity the full benefit of the public provisions made for instruction in the other branches of science. These branches are equally necessary to the divine as to the other professional or civil characters, to enable them to fulfill the duties of their calling with understanding and usefulness. It has, therefore, been in contemplation, and suggested by some pious individuals, who perceive the advantages of associating other studies with those of religion, to establish their religious schools on the confines of the University, so as to give to their students ready and convenient access and attendance on the scientific lectures of the University; and to maintain, by that means, those destined for the religious professions on as high a standing of science, and of personal weight and respectability, as may be obtained by others from the benefits of the University. Such establishments would offer the further and greater advantage of enabling the students of the University to attend religious exercises with the professor of their particular sect, either in the rooms of the building still to be erected, and destined to that purpose under impartial regulations, as proposed in the same report of the commissioners, or in the lecturing room of such professor.

To such propositions the Visitors are disposed to lend a willing ear, and would think it their duty to give every encouragement, by assuring to those who might choose such a location for their schools, that the regulations of the University should be so modified and accommodated as to give every facility of access and attendance to their students, with such regulated use also as may be permitted to the other students, of the library which may hereafter be acquired, either by public or private munificence. But always understanding that these schools shall be independent of the University and of each other.

Such an arrangement would complete the circle of the useful sciences embraced by this institution, and would fill the chasm now existing, on the principles which would leave inviolate the constitutional freedom of religion, the most inalienable and sacred of all human rights, over which the people and authorities of this State, individually and publicly, have ever manifested the most watchful jealousy: and could this jealousy be now alarmed, in the opinion of the legislature, by what is here suggested, the idea will be relinquished on any surmise of disapprobation which they might think proper to express.

ME XIX 489 Supplementary Manuscripts 4-7-26

There shall be established in the University a dispensary, which shall be attached to the medical school, and shall be under the sole direction and government of the professor of medicine, who shall attend personally to the anatomical theatre, or such other place as he shall notify, from half after one to two o'clock on every Tuesday, Thursday, and Saturday, for the purpose of dispensing medical advice, vaccination, and aid in surgical cases or ordinary occurrences, to applicants needing them.

18. Estimates of Contemporaries

Commentary

Since Jefferson's friends and correspondents were, to a large extent, the Olympians of his era, his evaluations of them and his pronouncements to them, are fascinating and significant.

It is interesting indeed to note that the highest accolade of all went to Joseph Priestley, the English scientist and expatriate, the philosopher, the scientist, the theologian, and Unitarian iconoclast. The sheer admiration contained in Jefferson's letters to and about him, are without limit or circumspection.

Extremely significant are Jefferson's opinions concerning Washington, which, though unbounded in devotion, are always spiced with criticism or indicative of limitations: his education was elementary; he could display a fearful temper; he was of a gloomy disposition; he had little confidence in the people or our republican experiment; he was given to ceremonial displays; he believed that eventually, we would retrograde into an English constitution. Especially after Jefferson left the government at the end of 1793 following the ghastly military invasion of Pennsylvania — at the head of which rode Hamilton and Washington — the latter succumbed entirely to Federalist control, and he wrote letters which stand as monuments to mortal decay. His seduction was such that during his declining days, he became alienated from Jefferson and the Republicans, and so remained until his death.

Yet, in remembrance of his greatness, his incomparable services, his personal devotion to duty, his memory was enshrined and embalmed forever in the hearts of his countrymen.

The Madison-Monroe phenomenon remains as one of the most touching in Jeffersonian lore. These were his closest friends; both became two-term presidents; both were without taint in character, principle, elevation, and constant devotion to Republican principles. However, we have a definite feeling that Jefferson's love and admiration for Madison exceeded all others: here was the one soul that he wished to grapple to his own with hoops of steel; next to Priestley, this was the man whom he admired above all others in the world.

Perhaps no other human relationship in Jefferson's life compared with that which existed between him and John Adams, whom he replaced in the Presidency in 1800. In the early days, these two were among the outstanding gladiators who fought for a solid republican constitution. But when Adams was ambassador to England, his political philosophy underwent a radical transformation; and, flattered and seduced by the Federalists, he became their instrument during his four years in the White House; however, as Jefferson points out, he simply prepared his own political suicide by being their tool. The most contemptible thing he ever did was to appoint a great many extreme Federalists to office — especially in the permanent judiciary, including John Marshall — at the very end of his incumbency.

As a result, and in spite of Jefferson's fervent wishes to continue and renew the friendship, it was broken from 1796 to 1812 — when it was restored and blossomed into one of the most interesting correspondences in American history. The Memorial Edition of Jefferson's Writings *includes 35 letters from Adams to Jefferson between 1813 and 1826 (he wrote many more). In addition to several letters from or to Mrs. Adams in 1804, 86 more by Jefferson are included, of which 46 are dated between 1812 and 1825. There are none between 1796 and 1811, which may be called the period of the Interregnum.*

Most of the letters beginning in 1812 deal with science, philosophy, and religion, the latter being a field in which Adams became deeply engrossed and in which he developed a position even more rationalistic than Jefferson's.

Jefferson was deeply impressed by Patrick Henry's oratory and diction; for Franklin he felt a veneration approaching mingled love and awe; for La Fayette, he felt an unbounded debt of gratitude, and rejoiced in the fact that, when he became bankrupt, the United States could come to his relief; for the Prince of Wales and the Kings of France and England, he felt little emotion except contempt; and for Marie Antoinette — discussed elsewhere — and Bonaparte — although for entirely different reasons — he had little else than unqualified condemnation: for the one as the fierce and domineering profligate adulteress and gamester who led her nation into ruin; and for the other, as the unparalleled maniac butcher and murderer of the modern world.

The relationship between Paine and Jefferson was surely unique. Paine had endeared himself to the American patriots in 1775-83 by writing Common Sense *and* The Crisis, *which many believe propelled the Revolution to victory. Returning to England in 1787, he became involved in socio-economic issues; and when Edmund Burke wrote his fierce* Reflections on the French Revolution *in 1790, Paine replied with his classic and extremely popular* Rights of Man, *for which he was indicted for treason and condemned to death. Escaping to France, he became a member of the Estates General, but was condemned to death and saved only by the interposition of James Monroe, the American ambassador to France. While there, Paine wrote* The Age of Reason, *1794-96, begun while in prison, a book which remains to this day as perhaps the most scathing critique of orthodox Christianity ever published.*

In spite of this, however, upon his return to America in 1802, Jefferson invited him to the White House and procured for him a house and a plot of land, where he spent his remaining days, sometimes working on inventions, until 1809; he lived there under constant attack and derision as a reputed atheist, which he certainly was not, and an enemy of God, religion, and common morality.

Joseph Priestley

ME X 227-30 Joseph Priestley 3-21-01

Yours is one of the few lives precious to mankind, and for the continuance of which every thinking man is solicitous. Bigots may be an exception. What an effort, my dear Sir, of bigotry in politics and religion, have we gone through! The barbarians really flattered themselves they should be able to bring back the times of Vandalism, in which ignorance put everything into the hands of power and priestcraft. All advances in science were proscribed as innovations. They pretended to praise and encourage education, but it was to be the education of our ancestors. We were to look backwards, not forwards, for improvement;... we were never to expect to go beyond them in real science. This was the real ground of all the attacks upon you... .

Our countrymen have recovered from the alarm into which art and industry had thrown them [during the XYZ delusion]; science and honesty are replaced on their high ground; and you, as their great apostle, are on its pinnacle. It is with heartfelt satisfaction that, in the first moments of my public action, I can hail you with welcome to our land, tender to you the homage of its respect and esteem, cover you under the protection of those laws which were made for the wise and good like you, and disclaim the legitimacy of that libel on legislation, which, under the form of law [the Alien Act], was for some time placed among them.

ME XI 265-66 Thomas Cooper 7-9-07

I had not before learned, that a life of Priestley had been published, or I should certainly have procured it; for no man living had a more affectionate respect for him. In religion, in politics, in physics, no man has rendered more service.

ME XI 351-52 Thomas Cooper 9-1-07

Your favor of the 9th is received and with it the copy of Dr. Priestley's Memoirs, for which I return you many thanks. I shall read them with great pleasure, as I revered the character of no man living more than his.

George Washington

ME I 278 Anas

General Washington... was true to the republican charge confided to him; and has solemnly and repeatedly protested to me, in our conversations, that he would lose the last drop of his blood in support of it; and he did this the oftener and with the more earnestness, because he knew my suspicions of Hamilton's designs against it, and wished to quiet them. For he was not aware of the drift, or of the effect, of Hamilton's schemes. Unversed in financial projections and calculations and budgets, his approbation of them was bottomed on his confidence in the man.

ME I Anas 282-83 2-4-18

From the moment... of my retiring from the administration [in 1794], the federalists got unchecked hold of General Washington. His memory was already sensibly impaired by age, the firm tone of mind for which he had been remarkable, was beginning to relax, its energy was abated, a listlessness of labor, a desire for tranquillity, had crept over him, and a willingness to let others act and even think for him. Like the rest of mankind, he was disgusted with the atrocities of the French Revolution, and was not sufficiently aware of the difference between the rabble who were used as instruments of their perpetration, and the steady and rational character of the American people in which he had not sufficient confidence. The opposition too of the republicans to the British treaty, and the zealous support of the federalists in that unpopular but favorite measure of theirs, had made him all their own. Understanding, moreover, that I disapproved of that treaty, and copiously furnished with falsehoods... , he had become alienated from myself personally, as from the republican body generally of his fellow-citizens; and he wrote letters to Mr. Adams and Mr. Carroll, over which, in devotion to his imperishable fame, we must forever weep as monuments of mortal decay.

ME XIV 46-52 Dr. Walter Jones 1-2-14

His mind was great and powerful, without being of the very first order; his penetration strong... ; and, as far as he saw, no judgment was ever sounder. It was slow in operation, being little aided by invention or imagination, but sure in conclusion. Hence the common remark of his officers, of the advantage he derived from councils of war, where hearing all suggestions, he selected whatever was best; and certainly no general ever planned his battles more judiciously. But if deranged during the course of action, if any member of his plan was dislocated by sudden circumstances, he was slow in re-adjustment... .

His temper was naturally irritable and high-toned; but reflection and resolution had obtained a firm and habitual ascendancy over it. If ever, however, it broke its bonds, he was most tremendous in his wrath. In his expenses he was honorable, but exact; liberal in contributions to whatever promised utility; but frowning and unyielding on all visionary projects, and all unworthy calls on his charity. His heart was not warm in its affections; but he exactly calculated every man's value, and gave him a solid esteem proportioned to it.

His person, you know, was fine, his stature exactly what one would wish, his deportment easy, erect and noble; the best horseman of his age, and the most graceful figure that could be seen on horseback. Although in the circle of his friends, where he might be unreserved with safety, he took a free share in conversation, his colloquial talents were not above mediocrity, possessing neither copiousness of ideas, nor fluency of words. In public, when called on for a sudden opinion, he was unready, short, and embarrassed. Yet he wrote readily, rather diffusely, in an easy and correct style. This he had acquired by conversation with the world, for his education was merely reading, writing and common arithmetic, to which he added surveying at a later day. His time was employed in action chiefly, reading little, and that only in agriculture and English history. His correspondence became necessarily extensive, and, with journalizing his agricultural proceedings, occupied most of his leisure hours within doors.

On the whole, his character was, in its mass, perfect, in nothing bad, in few points indifferent; and it may truly be said, that never did nature and fortune combine more perfectly to make a man great, and to place him in the same constellation with whatever worthies have merited from man an everlasting remembrance. For his was the singular destiny and merit, of leading the armies of his country successfully through an arduous war, for the establishment of its independence; of conducting its councils through the birth of a government, new in its forms and principles, until it had settled down into a quiet and orderly train; and of scrupulously obeying the laws... .

He has often declared to me that he considered our new Constitution as an experiment on the practicability of republican government, and with what dose of liberty man could be trusted for his own good; that he was determined the experiment should have a fair trial, and would lose the last drop of his blood in support of it... .

I do believe that General Washington had not a firm confidence in the durability of our government. He was naturally distrustful of men, and inclined to gloomy apprehensions; and I was ever persuaded that a belief that we must at length end in something like a British constitution, had some weight in the adoption of the ceremonies of levees, birthdays, pompous meetings with Congress, and other forms of the same character, calculated to prepare us gradually for a change which he believed possible, and to let it come on with as little shock as might be to the public mind... .

During the war and after it we corresponded occasionally, and in the four years of my continuance in the office of Secretary of State, our intercourse was daily, confidential and cordial. After I retired from that office, great and malignant pains were taken by our federal monarchists, and not entirely without effect, to make him view me as a theorist, holding principles of government which would lead infallibly to licentiousness and anarchy. And to this he listened more easily, from my known disapprobation of the British treaty. I never saw him afterwards, or these malignant insinuations would have been dissipated before his just judgment, as mists before the sun. I felt on his death, with my countrymen, that "verily a great man hath fallen this day in Israel."

ME XVI 52-69 Martin van Buren 6-29-24

General Washington was himself sincerely a friend to the republican principles of our Constitution. His faith, perhaps, in its duration, might not have been as confident as mine; but he repeatedly declared to me that he was determined it should have a fair chance for success, and that he would lose the last drop of his blood in its support... .

He lived too short a time after, and too much withdrawn from information, to correct the views into which he had been deluded; and the continued assiduities of the party drew him into the vortex of their intemperate career; separated him still farther from his real friends, and excited him to actions and expressions of dissatisfaction, which grieved them, but could not loosen their affections from him. They would not suffer the temporary aberration to weigh against the immeasurable merits of his life; and although they tumbled his seducers from their places, they preserved his memory embalmed in their hearts, with undiminished love and devotion; and there it forever will remain embalmed, in entire oblivion of every temporary thing which might cloud the glories of his splendid life.

It is vain for Mr. Pickering and his friends to endeavor to falsify his character, by representing him as an enemy to republicans and republican principles, and as exclusively the friend of those who were so; and had he lived longer, he would have returned to his ancient and unbiased opinions, would have replaced his confidence in those whom the people approved and supported, and would have seen that they were only restoring and acting on the principles of his own first administration.

Patrick Henry

ME I 5 and 55 Autobiography 1781

When the famous Resolutions of 1765 against the Stamp-act were proposed, I was yet a student of law at Williamsburg. I attended the debate, however,... and heard the splendid display of Mr. Henry's talents as a popular orator. They were great indeed; such as I have never heard from any other man. He appeared to me to speak as Homer wrote... .

[I remember] his sublime imagination, his lofty and overwhelming diction,... .

ME XIV 162-72 William Wirt 8-14-14

I well remember the cry of treason, the pause of Mr. Henry at the name of George the III., with which he closed his sentence, and baffled the charge vociferated.

ME XIII 434-37 John Adams to Thomas Jefferson 11-12-13

In the Congress of 1774, there was not one member, except Patrick Henry, who appeared to me sensible of the precipice, or rather, the pinnacle, on which we stood, and had candor and courage enough to acknowledge it.

ME VII 282-84 William Short 2-9-89

A vast majority of anti-federalists have got into the Assembly of Virginia, so that Mr. Henry is omnipotent there...

ME XV 162-65 Benjamin Waterhouse 3-1-18

Mr. Wirt... in his Life of Patrick Henry, quotes me as saying that "Mr. Henry certainly gave the first impulse to the ball of revolution." I well recollect to have used some such expression in a letter to him, and am tolerably certain that our State being then the subject under contemplation, I must have used it with respect to that only... . Whether he has given it a more general aspect, I cannot say... . But the question, who commenced the Revolution? is as difficult as that of the first inventors of a thousand good things... .

James Madison and James Monroe

ME V 312-14 W. T. Franklin 5-7-86

You have formed a just opinion of Monroe. He is a man whose soul might be turned wrong side outward, without discovering a blemish to the world.

ME IX 293-97 James Madison 12-28-94

Hold on, then, my dear friend, that we may not shipwreck in the meanwhile. I do not see, in the minds of those with whom I converse, a greater affliction than the fear of your retirement; but this must not be, unless to a more splendid and more efficacious post. There I should rejoice to see you; I hope I may say, I shall rejoice to see you. I have long had much in my mind to say to you on that subject. But double delicacies have kept me silent. I ought perhaps to say, while I would not give up my own retirement for the empire of the universe, how can I justify wishing one whose happiness I have so much at heart as yours, to take the front of the battle which is fighting for my security.

ME IX 301-04 James Madison 4-27-95

I expressed my hope of the only change of position I ever wished to see you make, and I expressed it with entire sincerity; because there is not another person in the United States, who, being placed at the helm of our affairs, my mind would be so completely at rest for the fortune of our political bark.

FORD VII 322 John Taylor 1799

Many points in Monroe's character would render him the most valuable acquisition the republican interest in the Congress could make.

ME XI 443-45 James Monroe 2-18-08

I see with infinite grief a contest arising between yourself and another who have been very dear to each other, and equally so to me... . But my wish for retirement itself is not stronger than that of carrying into it the affections of all my friends. I have ever viewed Mr. Madison and yourself as two principal pillars of my happiness. Were either to be withdrawn, I should consider it as among the greatest calamities which could assail my future peace of mind. I have great confidence that the candor and high understanding of both will guard me against this misfortune, the bare possibility of which has so far weighed on my mind, that I could not be easy without unburdening it.

ME XII 330-33 James Madison 11-30-09

Everything from him [Monroe] breathed the purest patriotism, involving, however, a close attention to his own honor and grade. He expressed himself with the utmost devotion to the interests of our country, and I am satisfied he will pursue them with honor and zeal in any character in which he shall be willing to act.

ME XII 404-09 Colonel William Duane 8-12-10

Anxious in my retirement, to enjoy undisturbed repose, my knowledge of my successor [Mr. Madison] and late coadjutors, and my entire confidence in their wisdom and integrity, were assurances to me that I might sleep in security with such watchmen at the helm, and that whatever difficulties or dangers should assail our course, they would do what could be done to avoid or surmount them. In this confidence I envelope myself, and hope to slumber to my last sleep.

ME XIII 190-91 Thomas C. Flourney 10-1-12

I have known him [Mr. Madison] from 1779, when he first came into the public councils, and from three and thirty years' trial, I can say conscientiously that I do not know in the world a man of purer integrity, more dispassionate, distinterested, and devoted to genuine republicanism; nor could I, in the whole scope of America and Europe, point out an abler head... what man can do will be done by Mr. Madison. I hope, therefore, there will be no difference among republicans as to his re-election, and we shall know his value when we have to give him up, and look at large for his successor.

ME XIII 186-89 Colonel William Duane 10-1-12

I clearly think with you on the competence of Monroe to embrace great views of action. The decision of his character, his enterprise, firmness, industry, and unceasing vigilance, would, I believe, secure, as I am sure they would merit, the public confidence and give us all the success which our means can accomplish.

ME XV 179-81 Nathaniel Macon 1-12-19

I have had, and still have, such entire confidence in the late and present presidents [Madison and Monroe] that I willingly put both soul and body into their pockets.

ME I 61 Autobiography 1821

Mr. Madison came into the House in 1776... his extreme modesty prevented his venturing himself for debate before his removal to the Council of State in November, 1777... where he acquired a habit of self-expression, which placed at ready command the rich resources of his luminous and discriminating mind, and of his extensive information, and rendered him the very first of every assembly afterwards of which he became a member. Never wandering from his subject into vain declamation, but pursuing it closely, in language pure, classical, and copious, soothing always the feelings of his adversaries, by civilities and softness of expression — he rose to the eminent station he held in the Great Convention of 1787; and in that of Virginia, which followed, he sustained the new constitution in all its parts, bearing off the palm against the logic of George Mason and the fervid declamations of Mr. Henry. With these consummate powers were united a pure and spotless virtue, which no calumny has ever attempted to sully. Of the powers and polish of his pen and wisdom of his administration in the highest office of the nation, I need say nothing.

ME XVI 155-59 James Madison 2-17-26

It has also been a great solace to me, to believe that you are engaged in vindicating to posterity the course we have pursued for preserving to them, in all their purity, the blessings of self-government, which we had assisted too in acquiring for them. If ever the earth has beheld a system of administration conducted with a single and steadfast eye to the general interest and happiness of those committed to it, one which, protected by truth, can never know reproach, it is that to which both our lives have been devoted. To myself, you have been a pillar of support through life. Take care of me when I am dead, and be assured that I shall leave with you my last affections.

Benjamin Franklin

ME XVIII 166-72 Anecdotes of Benjamin Franklin 12-4-18

When Dr. Franklin went to France on his revolutionary mission, his eminence as a philosopher, his venerable appearance, and the cause on which he was sent, rendered him extremely popular. For all ranks and conditions of men there, entered warmly into the American interest.

ME VIII 128-31 To 2-19-91

I can testify... that there appeared to me more respect and veneration to the character of Doctor Franklin in France, than to that of any other person in that country, foreign or native.

ME II 94-95 Notes on Virginia 1781

In physics, we have produced a Franklin, than whom no one of this present age has made more important discoveries, no one has enriched philosophy with more, or more ingenious solutions of the phenomena of nature.

ME X 55-59 Samuel Smith 8-22-98

Dr. Franklin, the greatest man and ornament of the age and country in which he lived.

ME XII 413-17 Colonel William Duane 9-16-10

I... believe that a greater or better character rarely existed.

ME XIII 176-78 Thomas Cooper 7-10-12

You know the just esteem which attested itself to Dr. Franklin's science, because he always endeavored to direct it to something useful in private life.

ME VIII 23-25 Mr. Grand 4-23-90

The good old Dr. Franklin, so long the ornament of our country, and, I may say, of the world, has at length closed his eminent career. He died on the 17th instant... . Congress wear mourning for him... .

ME VIII 128-31 To 2-19-91

His death was an affliction which was to happen to us at some time or other. We have reason to be thankful that he was so long spared, that the most useful life should be the longest also, that it was protracted so far beyond the ordinary span attached to man, as to avail us of his wisdom in the establishment of our own freedom... .

Alexander Hamilton

ME IX 309-11 James Madison 9-21-95

Hamilton is really a colossus... he is an host within himself... . We have had only middling performances to oppose him. In truth, when he comes forward, there is no one but yourself who can meet him. His adversaries having begun the attack, he has the advantage of answering them, and remains unanswered himself. A solid reply might yet completely demolish what was too feebly attacked, and has gathered strength from the weakness of the attack... .

Thus it is that Hamilton, Jay, etc., in the boldest act they ever ventured to undermine the government, have the address to screen themselves, and direct the hue and cry against those who wish to drag them into light. A bolder party stroke was never struck. For it certainly is an attempt of a party who find they have lost their majority in one branch of the Legislature to make a law by the aid of the other branch [the Senate] and of the executive under color of a treaty [with England], which shall bind up the adverse branch from ever restraining the commerce of their patron-nation.

ME XIII 1-9 Benjamin Rush 1-16-11

Another incident took place... which will further delineate Mr. Hamilton's political principles. The room being hung around with a collection of the portraits of remarkable men, among them were those of Bacon, Newton, and Locke, Hamilton asked me who they were. I told him they were my trinity of the three greatest men the world had ever produced, naming them. He paused for some time: "the greatest man," said he, "that ever lived, was Julius Caesar."

ME I 278-79 Anas

Hamilton was not only a monarchist, but for a monarchy bottomed on corruption... . [He] was indeed, a singular character. Of acute understanding, disinterested, honest, and honorable in all private transactions, amiable in society, and duly valuing virtue in private life, yet so bewitched and perverted by the British example, as to be under thorough conviction that corruption was essential to the government of a nation.

Adams and Hamilton

ME I 278-79 Anas

Some occasion for consultation arising, I invited [several] gentlemen... to dine with me, in order to confer on the subject. After the cloth was removed, and our question agreed and dismissed, conversation began on other matters, and by some circumstance, was led to the British constitution, on which Mr. Adams observed, "purge that constitution of its corruption, and give to its popular branch equality of representation, and it would be the most perfect constitution ever devised by the wit of man." Hamilton paused and said, "purge it of its corruption, and give to its popular branch equality of representatuon, and it would become an *impracticable* government; as it stands at present, with all its supposed defects, it is the most perfect government which ever existed."

And this was assuredly the exact line which separated the political creeds of these two gentlemen. The one was for two hereditary branches and an honest elective one; the other, for an hereditary king, with a House of Lords and Commons corrupted to his will, and standing between him and the people.

John Adams

ME VI 63-75 James Madison 1-30-87

You know the opinion I formerly entertained of my friend, Mr. Adams... . I afterward saw proofs which convicted him of a degree of vanity, and of blindness to it, of which no germ [had] appeared [previously]... . That is all of the ill which can possibly be said of him. He is as disinterested as the being who made him: he is profound in his views; and accurate in his judgement, except where knowledge of the world is necessary to form a judgment. He is so amiable, that I promise you will love him, if ever you become acquainted with him. He would be, as he was, a great man in Congress.

ME VIII 192-95 The President of the United States 5-8-91

...Mr. Adams, for whom, as one of the most honest and disinterested men alive, I have a cordial esteem, increased by long habits of concurrence in opinion in the days of his republicanism; and even since his apostacy to hereditary monarchy and nobility, though we differ, we differ as friends should.

ME IX 355-57 John Adams 12-28-96

I have no ambition to govern men. It is a painful and thankless office. Since the day, too, on which you signed the treaty of Paris, our horizon has never been so overcast. I devoutly wish you may be able to shun for us the contest by which our agriculture, commerce, and credit will be destroyed. If you are, the glory will be all your own; and that your administration may be filled with glory, and happiness to yourself and advantages to us, is the sincere wish of one who, though in the course of our voyage through life, various little incidents have happened or been contrived to separate us, retains still for you the solid esteem of the moments when we were working for our independence, and sentiments of respect and affectionate attachment.

ME IX 375-76 James Madison 1-30-97

Mr. Adams and myself were cordial friends from the beginning of the revolution. Since our return from Europe, some little incidents have happened, which were capable of affecting a jealous mind like his. His deviation from that line of politics on which we had been united, has not made me less sensible of the rectitude of his heart; and I wished him to know this, and also another truth, that I am sincerely pleased at having escaped the late draught for the helm, and have not a wish which he stands in the way of. That he should be convinced of these truths, is important to our mutual satisfaction, and perhaps to the harmony and good of the public service [during the coming years in wiich T. J. would be Vice-President under Adams].

ME XI 28-30 Mrs. John Adams 6-13-04 (in response to a letter of condolence received upon the death of his daughter)

Mr. Adams' friendship and mine began at an earlier date. It accompanied us through long and important scenes. The different conclusions we had drawn from our political reading and reflections, were not permitted to lessen personal esteem; each party being conscious they were the result of honest conviction in the other. Like differences of opinion existing among our fellow-citizens, attached them to one or the other of us, and produced a rivalship in their minds which did not exist in ours. We never stood in one another's way... .

This consideration was sufficient to keep down all jealousy between us, and to guard our friendship from any disturbance by sentiments of rivalship; and I can say with truth, that one act of Mr. Adams' life, and only one, ever gave me a moment's personal displeasure. I did consider his last appointments to offices as personally unkind. They were from among my most ardent political enemies, from whom no faithful co-operation could ever be expected; and laid me under the embarrassment of acting through men whose views were to defeat mine, or to encounter the odium of putting others in their places. It seems but common justice to leave a successor free to act by instruments of his own choice. If my respect for him did not permit me to ascribe the whole blame to the influence of others, it left something for friendship to forgive; and after brooding over it for some little time, and not always resisting the expression of it, I forgave it cordially, and returned to the same state of esteem and respect for him which had so long existed... .

I have thus, my dear Madam, opened myself to you without reserve, which I have long wished an opportunity of doing; and without knowing how it will be received, I feel relief from being unbosomed.

ME XIII 1-9 Doctor Benjamin Rush 1-16-11

I receive with sensibility your observations on the discontinuance of friendly correspondence between Mr. Adams and myself, and the concern you take in its restoration. This discontinuance has not proceeded from me, nor from the want of sincere desire and of effort on my part, to renew our intercourse. You know the perfect coincidence of principle and action in the early part of our revolution, which produced a high degree of mutual respect and esteem between Mr. Adams and myself. Certainly, no man was ever truer than he was, in that day, to those principles of rational republicanism which, after the necessity of throwing off our monarchy, dictated all our efforts in the establishment of a new government. And, although he swerved, afterwards, toward the principles of the English constitution, our friendship did not abate on that account... .

Mr. Adams, you know, was overwhelmed with feverish addresses, dictated by the fear, and often by the pen, of the *bloody buoy,* and was seduced by them into some open indications of his new principles of government, and, in fact, was so elated as to mix with his kindness a little superciliousness towards me. Even Mrs. Adams, with all her good sense and prudence, was sensibly flushed... .

The nation at length passed condemnation on the political principles of federalism, by refusing to continue Mr. Adams in the Presidency. On the day on which we learned in Philadelphia the vote of the city of New York, which it was well known would decide the vote of the State, and that, again, the vote of the Union, I called on Mr. Adams on some official business. He was very sensibly affected, and accosted me with these words: "Well, I understand that you are to beat me in this contest, and I will only say that I will be as faithful a subject as any you will have."

"Mr. Adams," said I, "this is no personal contest between you and me. Two systems of principles on the subject of government divide our fellow citizens into two parties. With one of these you concur, and I with the other. As we have been longer on the public stage than most of those now living, our names happen to be more generally known. One of these parties, therefore, has put your name at its head, the other mine. Were we both to die to-day, to-morrow two other names would be in the place of ours, without any change in the motion of the machinery. Its motion is from its principle, not from you or myself."

"I believe you are right," said he, "that we are but passive instruments, and should not suffer this matter to affect our personal dispositions... ."

A little time and reflection effaced in my mind this temporary dissatisfaction with Mr. Adams, and I... did not cease to wish for some opportunity of renewing our friendly understanding. Two or three years later, having had the misfortune to lose a daughter, between whom and Mrs. Adams there had been a considerable attachment, she made it the occasion of writing me a letter, in which, with the tenderest expressions of concern at this event, she carefully avoided a single one of friendship towards myself... .

I determined to make an effort towards removing the cloud between us... . Indeed, I thought it highly disgraceful to us both, as indicating minds not sufficiently elevated to prevent a public competition from affecting our personal friendship. I soon found from the correspondence that conciliation was desperate, and, yielding to an intimation in her last letter, I ceased from further explanation.

I have the same good opinion of Mr. Adams which I ever had. I know him to be an honest man, an able one with his pen, and he was a powerful advocate on the floor of Congress. He has been alientated from me, by belief in the lying suggestions contrived for electioneering purposes, that I perhaps mixed in the activity and intrigues of the occasion. My most intimate friends can testify that I was perfectly passive... and I am satisfied Mr. Adams' conduct was equally honorable towards me. But I think it part of his character to suspect foul play in those of whom he is jealous, and not easily to relinquish his suspicions.

ME I 279-80 Anas

Mr. Adams had originally been a republican. The glare of royalty and nobility, during his mission in England, had made him believe their fascination a necessary ingredient in government; and Shay's Rebellion, not sufficiently understood where he then was, seemed to prove that the absence of want and oppression, was not a sufficient guarantee of order. His book on the American constitutions having made known his political bias, he was taken up by the monarchical federalists in his absence, and on his return to the United States, he was by them made to believe that the general disposition of our citizens was favorable to monarchy. He here wrote his "Davila," as a supplement to a former work, and his election to the Presidency confirmed him in his errors. Innumerable addresses too, artfully and industriously poured in upon him, deceived him into a confidence that he was on the pinnacle of popularity, when the gulf was yawning at his feet, which was to swallow up him and his deceivers... .

Mr. Adams, I am sure, has long since been convinced of the treacheries with which he was surrounded during his administration. He has since thoroughly seen, that his constituents were devoted to republican government, and whether his judgment is re-settled on its ancient basis, or not, he is confirmed as a good citizen to the will of the majority, and would now, I am persuaded, maintain its republican structure with the zeal and fidelity belonging to his character. For even an enemy has said, "he is always an honest man, and often a great one." But in the fervor of the fury and follies of those who made him their stalking horse, no man who did not witness it can form an idea of their unbridled madness, and the terrorism with which they surrounded themselves.

The Marquis De La Fayette

ME IV 370-71 de La Fayette 3-2-81

...it gives me great pleasure that we shall be so far indebted... to a nobleman who has already so much endeared himself to the citizens of these States by his great exertions and the very effectual aids he has been the means of procuring them.

ME V 428-29 Prevot des Marchands et Echevins 9-27-86

The commonwealth of Virginia, in gratitude for the services of Major-General the Marquis de La Fayette, have determined to erect his bust in their capitol. Desirous to place a like monument of his worth... in the country to which they are indebted for his birth, they have hoped the city of Paris will consent to become the depository of the second testimony of their gratitude.

ME VI 63-72 James Madison 1-30-87

The Marquis de La Fayette is a most valuable auxilliary to me. His zeal is unbounded, and his weight with those in power, great. His... good sense enabling him to comprehend perfectly whatever is explained to him, his agency has been very efficacious. He has a great deal of sound genius, is well remarked by the King, and rising in popularity. He has nothing against him, but the suspicion of republican principles. I think he will one day be of the ministry. His foible is a canine appetite for popularity and fame; but he will get above this.

ME VII 231-34 John Adams 12-5-88

We are greatly indebted to the Marquis de La Fayette for his aid on this, as on every other occasion. He has paid the closest attention to it, and combatted for us, with the zeal of a native.

ME XIX 280-81 de La Fayette 1-16-25

I congratulate you on the testimony of gratitude you have lately received from Congress, and that it was with scarcely a shadow of opposition. The relief from your debts will give you nights of sound sleep and the surplus I hope days of ease and comfort through the rest of your life.

The Heir to the English Throne

ME VII 259-67 John Jay 1-11-89

..the Prince of Wales... has taken no pains to hide himself from the world... . He happened, when last in London, to be invited to a dinner... . He ate half a leg of mutton; did not taste of small dishes, because small; drank Champagne and Burgundy, as small beer during dinner, and Bordeaux after dinner, as the rest of the company. Upon the whole, he ate as much as the other three, and drank about two bottles of wine without seeming to feel it... .

His education... was the learning a little Latin. He has not a single element of Mathematics, of Natural or Moral Philosophy, or of any other science on earth, nor has the society he has kept been such as to supply the void of education. It has been that of the lowest, the most illiterate and profligate persons of the kingdom, without choice of rank or mind, and with whom the subjects of conversation are only horses, drinking-matches, bawdy houses, and in terms the most vulgar... . In fact, he never associated with a man of sense. He has not a single idea of justice, morality, religion, or of the rights of man, or any anxiety for the opinion of the world. He carries that indifference for fame so far, that he would probably not be hurt were he to lose his throne, provided he could be assured of having always meat, drink, horses, and women... . He had a fine person, but it is becoming coarse... . The Duke of York, who was for some time cried up as the prodigy of the family, is as profligate, and of less understanding... .

Thomas Paine

ME VIII 206-09 Colonel Monroe 7-10-91

The papers... will have shown you what a dust Paine's pamphlet [The Rights of Man] has kicked up here... . A writer, under the name of Publicola, in attacking Paine's principles, is very desirous of involving me in the same censure with the author. I certainly merit the same, for I profess the same principles; but it is equally certain I never meant to have entered as a volunteer into the cause... . A host of writers have risen in favor of Paine, and prove that in this quarter, at least, the spirit of republicanism is sound.

ME X 3-18-01 and VIII 223-25 7-29-91 Thomas Paine

I am indeed glad you did not come away till you had written your "Rights of Man." That has been much read here with avidity and pleasure... .

Your letters were... published in the newspapers, and under your own name. These papers contain precisely our principles, and I hope will be generally recognized here... . [When you return], I am in hopes you will find us returned generally to sentiments worthy of former times. In these, it will be your glory to have steadily labored, and with as much effect as any man living. That you may long live to continue your useful labors, and to reap their reward in the thankfulness of nations, is my sincere prayer.

ME XV 304-06 Francis Eppes 1-19-21

You ask my opinion of Lord Bolingbroke and Thomas Paine. They were alike in making bitter enemies of the priests and pharisees of their day. Both were honest men; both advocates of human liberty. Paine wrote for a country [America] which permitted him to push his reasoning to whatever length it would go... . No writer has exceeded Paine in ease and familiarity of style, in perspicuity of expression, happiness of elucidation, and in simple and unassuming language. In this he may be compared with Dr. Franklin; and indeed his Common Sense was, for a while, believed to have been written by Dr. Franklin... .

Napoleon Bonaparte

ME X 396-98 Sir John Sinclair 6-30-03

Bonaparte has produced such a state of things in Europe as it would seem difficult for him to relinquish in any sensible degree, and equally dangerous for Great Britain to suffer to go on, especially if accompanied by maritime preparations on his part... .

ME XII 274-77 James Madison 4-19-09

As to Bonaparte, I should not doubt the revocation of his edicts, were he governed by reason. But his policy is so crooked that it eludes conjecture... . He may fear that opening the ports of Europe to our vessels will open them to an inundation of British wares. He ought to be satisfied with having forced her to revoke the orders on which he pretended to retaliate, and to be particularly satisfied with us, by whose unyielding adherence to principle she has been forced into the revocation. He ought the more to conciliate our good will, as we can be such an obstacle to the new career opening on him in the Spanish colonies. That he would give us the Floridas to withhold intercourse with the residue of these colonies, cannot be doubted. But that is no price; because they are ours in the first moment of the first war; and, until a war, they are of no particular necessity to us.

ME XII 370 William Duane 3-5-10

Bonaparte hates our government because it is a living libel on his.

ME XII 370-73 Dr. Walter Jones 3-5-10

A conqueror roaming over the earth with havoc and destruction.

ME XII 373-79 Governor John Langdon 3-5-10

The fear that Bonaparte will come over to us and conquer us also, is too chimerical to be genuine. Supposing him to have finished Spain and Portugal, he has yet England and Russia to subdue... .

When all this is done and settled... will he attack us first, from whom he will get but hard knocks and no money? Or will he first lay hold of the gold and silver of Mexico and Peru, and the diamonds of Brazil?...

ME XII 357-59 Caesar A. Rodney 2-10-10

The death of Bonaparte would, to be sure, remove the first and chiefest apostle of desolation of man and morals, and might withdraw the scourge from the land.

ME XIII 237-45 Madame Baronne de Stael-Holstein 5-24-13

Robespierre met his fate, and his memory the execration, he so justly merited. The rich were his victims, and perished by the thousands. ...It is by the millions that Bonaparte destroys the poor... having been the greatest destroyer of the human race. What year of his military life has not consigned a million of human beings to death, to poverty, and wretchedness! What field in Europe may not raise a monument of the murders, the burnings, the desolations, the famines and miseries it had witnessed from him!

ME XIV 306-10 Thomas Leiper 6-12-15

I view him [Bonaparte] as a political engine only, and a very wicked one... obeying, as an instrument, an unseen hand. I still deprecate his becoming sole lord of the continent of Europe, which he would have been, had he reached in triumph the gates of St. Petersburg. The establishment in our day of another Roman Empire, spreading vassalage and depravity over the face of the globe, is not, I hope, within the purposes of heaven.

Nor does the return of Bonaparte give me pleasure unmixed; I see in his expulsion of the Bourbons, a valuable lesson to the world, as showing that its dynasties may be changed for their misrule. Should the allied powers presume to dictate a ruler and government to France, and follow the example he had set of parcelling and usurping to themselves their neighbor nations, I hope he will give them another lesson in vindication of the rights of independence and self-government, which himself had heretofore so much abused, and that in this contest he will wear down the maritime power of England to limitable and safe dimensions.

So far, good. It cannot be denied, on the other hand, that... his restless spirit leaves no hope of peace to the world; and his hatred of us is only a little less than that he bears to England, and England to us. Our form of government is odious to him, as a standing contrast between republican and despotic rule; and as much from that hatred, as from ignorance in political economy, he had excluded intercourse between us and his people by prohibiting the only articles they wanted from us... .

ME XIV 435-37 Benjamin Austin 1-9-16 and XIV 387-93

[Bonaparte] saw nothing in the world but himself, and looked on the people under him as cattle, beasts of burthen and slaughter. Instead of the parricide treason of Bonaparte, in perverting the means confided to him as a republican magistrate, to the subversion of that republic and erection of a military despotism for himself and his family, had he used it honestly for the establishment and support of a free government in his own country, France would now have been in freedom and rest; and her example operating in a contrary direction, every nation in Europe would have had a government over which the will of the people would have had some control. His atrocious egotism has checked the salutary progress of principle, and deluged it with rivers of blood, which are not yet run out. To the vast sum of devastations and human misery, of which he has been the guilty cause, much is still to be added.

19. The Indian Problem

Commentary:

We will search in vain in the archives of American literature to find the writings of another statesman so deeply concerned over the Indians, their problems, sufferings, and destiny, as was Jefferson. No one else was so sympathetic over their plight or tried to do so much for their welfare.

Although he was well aware of their communal social structure, it is apparent that he never fully understood their organization into clans and the sexual relationships based thereon. It was not until Henry Lewis Morgan — who lived for many years among the Six Nations and who was made a member of the Iroquois tribe, published his epoch-making Ancient Society *in 1877, that a clear understanding of tribal mores became available to the public.*

Jefferson's knowledge of Indian life was, nevertheless, almost on the par with his interest. He declared that they were the physical and intellectual equals of the whites; and, realizing that time was rapidly running out on their ability to live by hunting and fishing, he exerted every effort within his power to induce and encourage their transition from savegery into civilization. Again and again, he expressed his wish and belief that in the not-too-distant future, the blood of the red and the white races would intermingle so that a single people would emerge. Had he understood what Morgan revealed, he would have known what difficulties stood in the way of such a denouement.

Hoping to discover the truth concerning Indian origins, Jefferson became deeply interested in their languages and vocabularies. Although he believed that migrations might have come from northern Europe in the distant past, his conclusion was that our aborigines had probably come from Asia. Although he had no way of determining the length of their habitation on this continent, he was certain that its duration must have encompassed thousands of years, for otherwise languages so radically different could not have developed.

As Secretary of State under Washington and even more as President, Jefferson was deeply involved with the Indian problem: how to deal with them when, egged on by British or others, they attacked the American settlements, massacred men, women, and children, burned and looted wherever they could, and then fled before superior armed forces. There is no doubt that Jefferson felt the white man's guilt for taking the red man's land and depriving him of his ancient means of livelihood. But what could he do? No one could stem the tide of European migration; the lost hunting grounds could not be restored; in short, the clock of history could not be reversed in motion. He therefore used every means at his disposal to civilize his red children and brethren, teach them to till the soil, own separate properties, establish monogamous families — in short, persuade them in one generation to achieve a development which had required thousands of years for the whites themselves to accomplish.

There is no doubt that one Indian weakness contributed to his decimation and degeneracy: although he would not work to produce the goods and comforts of civilized life he had an inordinate desire to obtain them: and especially one destructive item — whiskey. Thus, the red men were constantly running into debt, which they could pay only by the loss of their lands, which left them in steadily more deplorable conditions.

We note that the Cherokees, and, to a lesser extent, some others, had made progress toward civilization; and it is possible, had Jefferson's statesmanship — his altruistic policies — been pursued, that definitive results might have been achieved. However, this was not to be; for, as the whites proliferated, their attitudes hardened; as the Indians retaliated in the only manner they understood, the whites killed their buffalo, pushed them from their lands, drove them into the deserts, and caused a gradual decimination which bade fair by the end of the nineteenth century to accomplish their actual extermination.

And to this day, while the black man has sought to integrate with white society in one way or another, the red man stands largely aloof. He rejects the white man's religion, his family structure, and his way of life. Even when relegated to the most uninhabitable areas — like the Hopis and the Navajos in Arizona — he prefers this existence to accepting the white man's responsibilities. Although there are schools dedicated to their education, as in Phoenix, Arizona, and in Gallup, New Mexico; and although some individuals have "made it" in the White Man's World, the squaw is still the principal laborer; the man avoids the joys or burdens of monogamic family life. The communal-tribal ties are still of overwhelming strength and duration.

Perhaps nowhere else — at least in America — has the White Man's Burden been more palpable than in his relation to the Red Man. The Red Woman did the work; the Red Man was the Warrior-Hunter. They practiced a syndiasmian form of marriage, in which all the males of one clan were collectively the husbands of all the females of another. Thus, as Jefferson observes in one passage, the Indian languages had no word for father; for no child could know the identity of his sire, but only the tribe or clan to which he belonged. Descent was through the female, as Morgan demonstrated that it was under matriarchies in all ancient societies. Under this type of socio-economic organization, three million square miles hardly sufficed to sustain a million people: the tribes were therefore almost constantly at war with one another to prevent them from encroaching upon their hunting grounds. Thus, all the males were non-productive warriors; the women were forced to do the work of the clan, the tribe, the nation. Actually, warfare served also as a means of limiting any potential increase in population.

Under such conditions, life could continue indefinitely without basic alteration or progress. Shall we say that one of the great tragedies of human history occurred when the White Man, by the compulsion of fate, was compelled to fullfil his destiny by driving the Red Man from his hunting grounds and into the limbo of desert-privation?

We note, finally, that Jefferson's solution for the Red Man was basically the same as for American society in general: he wanted him to settle on his individual farm, own and operate it with his own labor, and by so doing learn the value of private property, from which he would create an ample livelihood for himself and his family. He would thus become a law-abiding citizen, since it would be in his interest and advantage to protect his economic stake in the nation. And his blood would commingle with that of the American people as a whole.

We need not wonder that even Jefferson was unable to solve the problems posed by the Indians, which still hang like a somber cloud over the records of American history.

Government and Social Structure

ME II 128-29 Notes on Virginia 1781

Very possibly there may have been anciently three different stocks, each of which multiplying in a long course of time, had separated into so many little societies.

ME VI 55-59 Colonel Edward Carrington 1-16-87

I am convinced that those societies (as the Indians) which live without government, enjoy in their general mass an infinitely greater degree of happiness than those who live under the European governments. Among the former, public opinion is in the place of law, and restrains morals as powerfully as laws ever did anywhere. Among the latter, under pretence of governing, they have divided their nations into two classes, wolves and sheep. I do not exaggerate. This is a true picture of Europe.

ME XV 23-27 Francis W. Gilmer 6-7-16

Our Indians are evidently in that state of nature which has passed the associating of a single family, and not yet submitted to the authority of positive laws, or of any acknowledged magistrate. Every man, with them, is perfectly free to follow his own inclinations. But if, in doing this, he violates the rights of another, if the case be slight, he is punished by the disesteem of his society, or, as we say, by public opinion; if serious, he is tomahawked as a serious enemy. Their leaders conduct them by the influence of their character only; and they follow, or not, as they please, him of whose character for wisdom or war they have the highest opinion.

ME XVII 280 Miscellaneous Papers

Among the Indians, this indication [that the sexes try to please each other], fails from a particular cause: every Indian man is a soldier or warrior, and the whole body of warriors constitute a standing army, always employed in war or hunting. To support that army, there remain no laborers but the women. Here, then, is so heavy a military establishment, that the civil part of the nation is reduced to women only. But this is a barbarous perversion of the natural distinctions of the two sexes. Women are formed by nature for attentions, not for hard labor. A woman never forgets one of the numerous train of little offices which belong to her. A man forgets often.

ME II 272-73 Appendix

Their government is a kind of patriarchal confederacy. Every town or family has a chief, who is distinguished by a particular title, and whom we commonly call "Sachem." The several towns or families that compose a tribe, have a chief who presides over it, and the several tribes composing the nation have a chief who presides over the whole nation. These chiefs are generally men advanced in years, and distinguished by their prudence and abilities in council. The matters which merely regard a town or family are settled by the chief and principal men of the town; those which regard a tribe, such as the appointment of head warriors or captains, and settling differences between different towns and families, are regulated at a meeting or council of the chiefs from the several towns; and those which regard the whole nation, such as the making war, concluding peace, or forming alliances with the neighboring nations, are deliberated on and determined in a national council composed of the chiefs of the tribe attended by the head warriors and a number of the chiefs from the towns, who are his counsellors.

In every town, there is a council house, where the chief and old men of the town assemble, when occasion requires, and consult what is proper to be done. Every tribe has a fixed place for the chiefs of the towns to meet and consult on the business of the tribe; and in every nation there is what they call the central council house, or central council fire, where the chiefs of the several tribes, with the principal warriors, convene to consult and determine on their national affairs. When any matter is proposed in the national council, it is common for the chiefs of the several tribes to consult thereon apart with their counsellors, and when they have agreed, to deliver the opinion of the tribe at the national council; and, as their government seems to rest wholly on persuasion, they endeavor by mutual concessions, to obtain unanimity.

Indian Qualities and Capacities

ME V 1-7 General Chastellux 6-7-85

I am safe in affirming, that the proofs of genius given by the Indians of North America place them on a level with whites in the same uncultivated state... .

ME II 82-89 Notes on Virginia 1781

The Indian of North America... is neither more defective in ardor, nor more impotent with his female, than the white reduced to the same diet and exercise; that he is brave, when an enterprise depends on bravery; education with him making the point of honor consist in the destruction of an enemy by stratagem, and in the preservation of his own person free from injury;... that he will defend himself against a host of enemies, always choosing to be killed, rather than to surrender;... that... he meets death with more deliberation, and endures tortures with a firmness unknown almost to religious enthusiasm with us; that he is affectionate to his children, careful of them, and indulgent in the extreme;... that his friendships are strong and faithful to the uttermost extremity; that his sensibility is keen, even the warriors weeping most bitterly on the loss of their children, though in general they endeavor to appear superior to human events; that his vivacity and activity of mind is equal to ours in the same situation; hence his eagerness for hunting, and for games of chance.

The women are submitted to unjust drudgery. This I believe is the case with every barbarous people. With such, force is law. The stronger sex imposes on the weaker. It is civilization alone which replaces women in the enjoyment of their natural equality... .

An Indian man is small in the hand and wrist, for the same reason for which a sailor is large and strong in the arms and shoulders, and a porter in the legs and thighs. They raise fewer children than we do. The causes of this are to be found, not in a difference of nature, but of circumstance. The women very frequently attending the men in their parties of war and hunting, child-bearing becomes extremely inconvenient to them... .

No wonder, then, if they multiply less than we do. Where food is regularly supplied, a single farm will show more of cattle, than a whole country of forests can of buffaloes. The same Indian women, when married to white traders, who feed them and their children plentifully and regularly, who exempt them from excessive drudgery, who keep them stationery and unexposed to accident, produce and raise as many children as the white women... .

The principles of their society forbidding all compulsion, they are to be led to duty and to enterprise by personal influence and persuasion. Hence eloquence in council, bravery and address in war, become the foundations of all consequence with them. To these acquirements all their faculties are directed. Of their bravery and address in war we have multiplied proofs, because we have been the subjects on which they were exercised. Of their eminence in oratory we have fewer examples, because it is displayed chiefly in their own councils. Some, however, we have, of very superior lustre.

ME II 267-74 Appendix

It is true they do not indulge those excesses [sexual activities] nor discover that fondness which is customary in Europe; but this is not owing to a defect in nature but to manners. Their soul is wholly bent upon war. This is what procures them glory among the men, and makes them the admiration of the women. To this, they are educated from their earliest youth. When they pursue game with ardor, when they bear the fatigues of the chase, when they sustain and suffer patiently hunger and cold; it is not so much for the sake of the game they pursue, as to convince their parents and the council of the nation that they are fit to be enrolled in the number of the warriors. The songs of the women, the dance of the warriors, the sage counsel of the chiefs, the tales of the old, the triumphal entry of the warriors returning with success from battle, and the respect paid to those who distinguish themselves in war, and in subduing their enemies; in short everything they see or hear tends to inspire them with an ardent desire for military fame... .

All the nations of Indians in North America lived in the hunter state, and depended for subsistence on hunting, fishing, and the spontaneous fruits of the earth, and a kind of grain which was planted and gathered by the women, and is now known by the name of Indian corn. Long potatoes, pumpkins of various kinds, and squashes, were also found in use among them. They had no flocks, herds, or tamed animals of any kind.

Indian History and Origins

ME II 131-40 Notes on Virginia 1781

What would be the melancholy sequel of their history [that of the American Indian tribes], may, however, be argued from the census of 1669; by which we discover that the tribes therein enumerated were, in the space of sixty-two years, reduced to about one-third of their former numbers. Spiritous liquors, the small-pox, war, and an abridgement of territory... had committed terrible havoc among them... .

That the lands... were taken from them by conquest, is not so general a truth as is supposed. I find in our historians and records, repeated proofs of purchase... . The upper country, we know, has been acquired — altogether acquired by purchase made in the most unexceptionable form... .

I know of no such thing existing as an Indian monument... unless indeed it would be the barrows, of which many are to be found all over this country... . Some ascribed them to the custom... of collecting, at certain periods, the bones of all their dead, wheresoever deposited at the time of death. Others again supposed them the general sepulchres for towns, conjectured to have been on or near these grounds; and this opinion was supported by the quality of the lands in which they are found. (those constructed of earth being generally in the softest and most fertile meadow-grounds on river sides,) and by a tradition, said to be handed down from the aboriginal Indians, that, when they settled in a town, the first person who died was placed erect, and earth put about him, so as to cover and support him; that when another died, a narrow passage was dug to the first, the second reclined against him, and the cover of earth replaced, and so on... .

Great question has arisen from whence came these aboriginals of America?... the late discoveries of Captain Cook, coasting from Kamchatka to California, have proved that if the two continents of Asia and America be separated at all, it is only by a narrow strait. So that from this side also, inhabitants may have passed into America; and the resemblance between the Indians of America and the eastern inhabitants of Asia, would induce us to conjecture that the former are the descendants of the later, or the latter of the former... .

Languages and Vocabularies

BW 153 Notes on Virginia 1781

The purposes of the Brafferton Institution [at William and Mary College] would be better answered by maintaining a perpetual mission among the Indian tribes, the object of which, besides instructing them in the principles of Christianity, as the founder requires, should be to collect their traditions, laws, customs, languages, and other circumstances which might lead to a discovery of their relations with one another, or descent from other nations.

ME II 141 Notes on Virginia 1781

But imperfect as our knowledge of the tongues in America, it suffices to discover the following remarkable fact: Arranging them under the radical ones to which they may be palpably traced, and doing the same by those of the red men of Asia, there will be found probably twenty in America, for one in Asia, of those radical languages, so called, because if they were ever the same, they have lost all resemblance to one another. A separation into dialects may be the work of a few ages only, but for two dialects to recede from one another till they have lost all vestiges of their common origin, must require an immense course of time; perhaps not less than many people give to the age of the earth. A greater number of those radical changes of language having taken place among the red men of America, proves them of greater antiquity than those of Asia.

ME X 160-61 Colonel Benjamin Hawkins 3-14-00

I have long believed we can never get any information of the ancient history of the Indians, of their descent and filiation, but from a knowledge and comparative view of their languages.

ME XV 3-8 Monsieur Correa de Serra 4-26-16

I had myself made a collection of about forty vocabularies of Indians on this side of the Mississippi, and Captain Lewis was instructed to take those of every tribe beyond, which he possibly could. The intention was to publish the whole, and leave the world to search for affinities between them and the languages of Europe and Asia. He was furnished with a number of printed vocabularies of the same words and forms I had used, with blank spaces for the Indian words.

ME XVI 107-10 To 2-20-25

I thank you for the copy of your Cherokee Grammar... your analysis... adds valuable matter for reflection, and strengthens our desire to see more of these languages as scientifically elucidated. Their grammatical devices... prove that if man came from one stock, his languages did not... .

I am persuaded that among the tribes on our two continents a great number of languages radically different, will be found... . It will be curious to consider how so many radically different have been preserved by such small tribes in coterminous settlements of moderate extent.

Wars, Depredations, and Retaliation

ME IX 148-51 Messrs. Carmichael and Short 6-30-93

At the commencement of the late war, the United States laid it down as a rule of their conduct, to engage the Indian tribes within their neighborhood to remain strictly neutral. They accordingly strongly pressed it on them, urging that it was a family quarrel with which they had nothing to do, and in which we wished them to take no part; and we strengthened these recommendations by doing them every act of friendship and good neighborhood, which circumstances left in our power. With some, these solicitations prevailed; but the greater part of them suffered themselves to be drawn into the war against us. They waged it in their usual cruel manner, murdering and scalping men, women, and children, indiscriminately, burning their houses, and desolating the country. They put us to vast expense, as well by the constant force we were obliged to keep up in that quarter, as by the expeditions of considerable magnitude which we were under the necessity of sending into their country from time to time.

Peace being at length concluded with England, we had it also to conclude with them. They had made war on us without the least provocation or pretence of injury. They had added greatly to the cost of that war. They had insulted our feelings by their savage cruelties. They were by our arms completely subdued and humbled. Under all these circumstances, we had a right to demand substantial satisfaction and indemnification. We used that right, however, with real moderation.

Their limits with us under the former government were generally ill-defined, questionable, and the frequent cause of war. Sincerely desirous of living in their peace, of cultivating it by every act of justice and friendship, and of rendering them better neighbors by introducing among them some of the most useful arts, it was necessary to begin by a precise definition of boundary. Accordingly, at the treaties held with them, our mutual boundaries were settled; and notwithstanding our just right to concessions adequate to the circumstances of the case, we required such only as were inconsiderable; and for even these, in order that we might place them in a state of perfect conciliation, we paid them a valuable consideration, and granted them annuities in money which have been regularly paid, and were equal to the prices for which they have usually sold their lands... .

The... Shawanese and other tribes, acknowledging control from none, and never in a state of peace, have readily engaged in the hostilities against us to which they were encouraged. But what was much more important, great numbers of the Creeks, chiefly their young men, have yielded to these incitements, and have now, for more than a twelvemonth, been committing murders and desolations on our frontiers. Really desirous of living in peace with them, we have redoubled our efforts to produce the same dispositions in them. We have borne with their aggressions, forbidden all returns of hostility against them, tied up the hands of our people, inasmuch that few instances of retaliation have occurred even from our suffering citizens; we have multiplied our gratifications to them, fed them when starving, from the produce of our own fields and labor. No longer ago than the last winter, when they had no other resource against famine, and must have perished in great numbers, we carried into their country and distributed among them, gratuitously, ten thousand bushels of corn; and that, too, at the same time, when their young men were daily committing murders on helpless women and children on our frontiers. And though these depredations now involve more considerable parts of the nation, we are still demanding punishment of the guilty individuals only, and shall be contented with it... .

If we cannot otherwise prevail on the Creeks to discontinue their depredations, we will attack them in force.

ME XII 37-38 Colonel Thomas Worthington 4-24-08

I have now addressed a message to the Indians from the northwest, in which I inform them of our differences with England, and of the uncertainty how they will issue. Assure them of the continuance of our friendship, and advise them in any event to remain quiet at home, taking no part in our quarrel, and declaring unequivocally that if any nation takes up the hatchet against us, we will drive them from the land of their fathers and never permit them to return.

English Conspiracies With the Indians

ME IV 301-10 Sir Guy Carleton 8-22-79

Those who act together in war are answerable for each other. No distinction can be made between principal and ally... . He who employs another to do a deed, makes the deed his own. If he calls in the hand of the assassin or murderer, he himself becomes the assassin or murderer.

The known rule of warfare of the Indian savages is an indiscriminate butchery of men, women, and children. These savages, under this well-known character, are employed by the British Nation as allies in the war against the Americans. Governor Hamilton undertakes to be the conductor of the war. In the execution of that undertaking, he associates small parties of the whites under his immediate command with large parties of the savages, and sends them to act, sometimes jointly, and sometimes separately, not against our forts or armies in the field, but the farming settlements on our frontiers. Governor Hamilton is himself the butcher of men, women, and children.

ME XIV 20-25 Alexander von Humboldt 12-6-13

The confirmed brutalization, if not the extermination of this race in our America, is therefore to form an additional chapter in the English history of the same colored men in Asia, and of the brethren of their own color in Ireland, and wherever else Anglo-mercantile cupidity can find a two-penny interest in deluging the earth with human blood.

The Wabash Prophet

ME XIII 241-44 John Adams 4-20-12

You wish to know something of the... Wabash prophet... more rogue than fool, if to be a rogue is not the greatest of all follies. He arose to notice while I was in the administration, and became, of course, a proper subject of inquiry for me... . His declared object was the reformation of his red brethren, and their return to their pristine manner of living. He pretended to be in constant communication with the Great Spirit; that he was instructed by him to make known to the Indians that they were created by him distinct from the whites, of different natures, for different purposes, and placed under different circumstances, adapted to their nature and destinies; that they must return from all the ways of the whites to the habits and opinions of their forefathers; they must not eat the flesh of hogs, of bullocks, or sheep, etc., the deer and the buffalo having been created for their food; they must not make bread of wheat, but of Indian corn; they must not wear linen or woolen, but dress like their fathers in the skins and furs of animals; they must not drink ardent spirits, and I do not remember whether he extended his inhibitions to the gun and gunpowder, in favor of the bow and arrow.

I concluded from all this, that he was a visionary, enveloped in the clouds of their antiquities, and vainly endeavoring to lead back his brethren to the fancied beatitudes of their golden age. I thought there was little danger of his making many proselytes from the habits and comforts they had learned from the whites, to the hardships and privations of savagism and no great harm if he did. We let him go on, therefore, umolested. But his followers increased till the English thought him worth corruption, and found him corruptible. I suppose his views were then changed; but his proceedings in consequence of them were after I left the administration, and are, therefore, unknown to me; nor have I ever been informed what were the particular acts on his part, which produced an actual commencement of hostilities on ours. I have no doubt, however, that his subsequent proceedings are but a chapter... in the Book of the Kings of England.

ME XI 324-25 Secretary of War Henry Dearborn 8-12-07

With respect to the [Wabash] prophet, if those who are in danger from him would settle it in their own way, it would be their affair. But we should do nothing towards it. That kind of policy is not in the character of our government, and still less of the paternal spirit we wish to show towards that people.

But could not Harrison gain over the prophet, who no doubt is a scoundrel, and only needs his price? The best conduct we can pursue to countervail these movements among the Indians, is to confirm our friends by redoubled acts of justice and favor, and to endeavor to draw over the individuals indisposed toward us. The operations we contemplate, should there be occasion for them, would have an imposing effect on their minds, and, if successful, will indeed put them entirely in our power; if no occasion arises for carrying these operations into effect, then we shall have time enough to get the Indian mind to rights.

ME XI 342-43 Secretary of War Henry Dearborn 8-28-07

While it appeared that the workings among the Indians of that neighborhood proceeded from their prophet chiefly, and that his endeavors were directed to the restoring them to their ancient mode of life, to the feeding and clothing themselves with the produce of the chase, and refusing all those articles of meat, drink, and clothing, which they can only obtain from the whites, and are now rendered necessary by habit, I thought it a transient enthusiasm, which, if let alone, would evaporate innocently of itself; although visibly tinctured with a partiality against the United States. But the letters and documents now enclosed give to the state of things there a more serious aspect; and the visit of the Governor of Upper Canada, and assembling of the Indians by him, indicate the object to which these movements are to point. I think, therefore, we can no longer leave them to their own course, but that we should immediately prepare for war in that quarter, and at the same time redouble our efforts for peace.

Policy Toward the Indians

ME V 390-92 Mr. Hawkins 8-13-86

The attention you pay to their [the Indians'] rights, also, does you great honor, as the want of that is a principal source of dishonor to the American character. The two principles on which our conduct towards the Indians should be founded, are justice and fear. After the injuries we have done them, they cannot love us, which leaves us no alternative but that of fear to keep them from attacking us. But justice is what we never lose sight of, and in time it may recover their esteem.

ME VIII 178-82 The President of the United States 4-17-91

General Knox expressed an apprehension that the Six Nations might be induced to join our enemies... . As to myself, I hope we shall give the Indians a thorough drubbing this summer, and I should think it better afterwards to take up the plan of liberal and repeated presents to them. This would be much the cheapest in the end, and would save all the blood which is now spilt; in time, too, it would produce a spirit of peace and friendship between us. The expense of a single expedition would last a very long time for presents.

ME IX 326-39 Gouvernor Morris 9-11-93

The north western Indians have refused to meet our commissioners unless they would agree to the Ohio as our boundary by way of preliminary articles; and this being impossible on account of army locations, and particularly sales on that side of the river, the war will go on.

ME X 357-59 General Andrew Jackson 2-16-03

In keeping agents among the Indians, two objects are principally in view: 1. The preservation of peace; 2. The obtaining lands. Towards effecting the latter object, we consider the leading the Indians to agriculture as the principal means from which we can expect much effect in the future. When they shall cultivate small spots of earth, and see how useless their extensive forests are, they will sell, from time to time, to help out their personal labor in stocking their farms, and procuring clothes and comforts from our trading houses... .

I am myself alive to the obtaining lands from the Indians by all *honest* and *peaceable means*, and I believe that the honest and peaceable means adopted by us will obtain them as fast as the expansion of our settlements, with due regard to compactness, will require.

ME X 368-73 Governor William H. Harrison 2-27-03

Our system is to live in perpetual peace with the Indians, to cultivate an affectionate attachment from them, by everything just and liberal which we can do for them within the bounds of reason... . In this way, they will in time either incorporate with us as citizens of the United States, or remove beyond the Mississippi.

ME XI 342-46 Secretary of War Henry Dearborn 8-28-07

Governors Hull and Harrison [should] be instructed to have interviews by themselves or well-chosen agents, with the chiefs of the several tribes in that quarter, to recall to their minds the paternal policy pursued towards them by the United States, and still meant to be pursued. That we never wished to do them an injury, but on the contrary, to give them all the assistance in our power towards improving their condition, and enabling them to support themselves and their families; that a misunderstanding having arisen between the United States and the

English, war may possibly ensue. That in this war it is our wish the Indians should be quiet spectators, not wasting their blood in quarrels which do not concern them; that we are strong enough to fight our own battles, and therefore ask no help; and if the English should ask theirs, it should convince them that it proceeds from a sense of their own weakness which would not augur success in the end; that at the same time, as we have learnt that some tribes are already expressing intentions hostile to the United States, we think it proper to apprise them of the ground on which they now stand; for which purpose we make to them this solemn declaration of our unalterable determination, that we wish them to live in peace with all nations as well as with us, and we have no intention ever to strike them or to do them an injury of any sort, unless first attacked or threatened; but that learning that some of them meditate war on us, we too are preparing for war against those; and those only who shall seek it; and that if ever we are constrained to lift the hatchet against any tribe, we will never lay it down till that tribe is exterminated, or driven beyond the Mississippi. Adjuring them, therefore, if they wish to remain on the land which covers the bones of their fathers, to keep the peace with a people who ask their friendship without needing it, who wish to avoid war without fearing it.

In war, they will kill some of us; but we shall destroy all of them. Let them then continue quiet at home, take care of their women and children, and remove from among them the agents of any nation persuading them to war... .

ME XIV 20-25 Alexander von Humboldt 12-6-13

You know, my friend, the benevolent plan we were pursuing here for the happiness of the aboriginal inhabitants in our vicinities. We spared nothing to keep them at peace with one another, to teach them agriculture and the rudiments of the most necessary arts, and to encourage industry by establishing among them separate property. In this way, they would have been enabled to subsist and multiply on a moderate scale of landed possessions. They would have mixed their blood with ours, and been amalgamated and identified with us within no distant period of time.

Civilizing the Indians

ME X 261-65 Colonel Benjamin Hawkins 2-18-03

I consider the business of hunting as already become insufficient to furnish clothing and subsistence to the Indians. The promotion of agriculture, therefore, and household manufacture, are essential to their preservation... . While they are learning to do better on less land, our increasing numbers will be calling for more land, and thus a coincidence of interests will be produced between those who have lands to spare and want other necessaries, and those who have such necessaries to spare and want lands. This commerce, then, will be for the good of both... .

In truth, the ultimate point of rest and happiness for them is to let our settlements and theirs meet and blend together, to intermix and become one people... .

And we have already had an application from a settlement of Indians to become citizens of the United States...; convinced of its soundness, I feel it consistent with pure morality to lead them towards it, to familiarize them to the idea that it is for their interest to cede lands at times to the United States, and for us to procure gratifications to our citizens, from time to time, by new acquisitions of land.

ME XI The Society of Friends 11-13-07

They are our brethren, our neighbors; they may be valuable friends, and troublesome enemies. Both duty and interest then enjoin, that we should extend to them the blessings of civilized life, and prepare their minds for becoming useful members of the American family.

ME XI 394-95 James Pemberton, Society of Friends 11-16-07

It is evident that your society has begun at the right end for civilizing these people. Habits of industry, easy subsistence, attachment to property, are necessary to prepare their minds for the first elements of science, and afterwards for moral and religious instruction. To begin with the last has ever ended either in effecting nothing, or ingrafting bigotry on ignorance, and setting them to tomahawking and burning old women and others as witches, of which we have seen a commencement among them.

ME XII 74-75 James Pemberton 6-21-08

The four great Southern tribes are advancing hopefully. The foremost are the Cherokees [who] have made a formal application to be received into the Union as citizens of the United States, and to be governed by our laws. If we can form for them a simple and acceptable plan of advancing by degrees to a maturity for receiving our laws, the example will have a powerful effect towards stimulating the other tribes to the same progression... .

ME XII 270-71 James Jay 4-7-09

The plan of civilizing the Indians is undoubtedly a great improvement on the ancient and totally ineffectual one of beginning with religious missionaries. Our experience has shown that this must be the last step in the process. The following is what has been successful: 1st, to raise cattle, etc., and thereby acquire a knowledge of the value of property; 2d, arithmetic, to calculate that value; 3rd, writing, to keep accounts, and here they begin to enclose farms, and the men to labor, the women to spin and weave... .

Excerpts From Presidential Addresses

ME XVI 390-91 Brothers of the Miamis, Powtewatamies, and Weeauks 1-7-02

Peace, brothers, is better than war. In a long and bloody war, we lose many friends, and gain nothing. Let us then live in peace and friendship together, doing to each other all the good we can. The wise and good on both sides desire this, and we must take care that the foolish and wicked among us shall not prevent it.

On our part, we shall endeavor in all things to be just and generous towards you, and to aid you in meeting these difficulties which a change of circumstances is bringing on. We shall, with great pleasure, see your people become disposed to cultivate the earth, to raise herds of the useful animals, and to spin and weave for their food and clothing. These resources are certain; they will never disappoint you: while those of hunting may fail, and expose your women and children to the miseries of hunger and cold. We will with pleasure furnish you with implements for the most necessary arts, and with persons who may instruct you how to make and use them.

ME XVI 393-95 Brother Handsome Lake 11-3-02

I am happy to learn you have been so far favored by the Divine Spirit as to be made sensible of those things which are for your good and that of your people, and of those which are hurtful to you; and particularly that you and they see the ruinious effects which the abuse of spiritous liquors have produced upon them. It has weakened their bodies, enervated their minds, exposed them to hunger, cold, nakedness, and poverty, kept them in perpetual broils, and reduced their population... .

You remind me, brother, of what I said to you, when you visited me the last winter, that the lands you then held would remain yours, and shall never go from you but when you should be disposed to sell. This I now repeat, and will ever abide by... .

Nor do I think, brother, that the sale of lands is, under all circumstances, injurious to your people. While they depended on hunting, the more extensive the forest around them, the more game they would yield. But going into a state of agriculture, it may be as advantageous to a society, as it is to an individual, who has more land than he can improve, to sell a part, and lay out the money in stocks and implements of agriculture, for the better improvement of the residue. A little land, well stocked and improved, will yield more than a great deal without stock or improvement.

ME XVI 405-10 My Children, White-Hairs, Chiefs and Warriors of the Osage Nation 7-16-04

By late arrangements with France and Spain, we now take their place as your neighbors, friends, and fathers; and we hope you will have no cause to regret the change. It is so long since our forefathers came from beyond the great water, that we have lost the memory of it, and seem to have grown out of this land, as you have done. Never more will you have occasion to change your fathers. We are all now of one family, born in the same land, and bound to live as brothers; and the strangers from beyond the great water are gone from among us. The Great Spirit has given you strength, and has given us strength; not that we might hurt one another, but to do each other all the good in our power. Our dwellings, indeed, are very far apart, but not too far to carry on commerce and useful intercourse. You have furs and peltries which we want, and we have clothes and other useful things which you want. Let us employ ourselves, in mutually accommodating each other.

ME XVI 410-12 My Children, Chiefs of the Chickasaw Nation 3-7-05

We have been told that you have contracted a great debt to some British traders, which gives you uneasiness, and which you honestly wish to pay by the sale of some of your lands. Whenever you raise food from the earth, and make your own clothing, you will find that you have a great deal of land more than you can cultivate... and that it will be better for you to sell some of that to pay your debts, and to have something over to be paid to you annually to aid you in feeding and clothing yourselves.

Your lands are your own, my children, they shall never be taken from you by our people or any others. You will be free to keep or to sell as yourselves shall think most for your own good. If at this time, you think it will be better for you to dispose of some of them to pay your debts, and to help your people to improve the rest, we are willing to buy on reasonable terms. Our people multiply so fast that it will suit us to buy as much as you wish to sell, but only according to your good will.

ME XVI 421-23 Chiefs of the Shawanee Nation 2-10-07

You say that you like our mode of living, that you wish to live as we do, to raise a plenty of food for your children, and to bring them up in good principles; that you adopt our mode of living, and ourselves as your brothers. My children, I rejoice to hear this; it is the wisest resolution you have ever formed, to raise corn and domestic animals, by the culture of the earth, and to let your women spin and weave clothes for you all, instead of depending for these on hunting... .

You ask for instruction in our manner of living, for carpenters and blacksmiths. My children, you shall have them. We will do everything in our power to teach you to take care of your wives and children, that you may multiply and be strong. We are sincerely your friends and brothers, we are as unwilling to see your blood spilt in war, as our own. Therefore, we encourage you to live in peace with all nations, that your women and children may live without danger, and without fear. The greatest honor of a man is in doing good to his fellow men, not in destroying them.

ME XVI 450-54 Captain Hendrick, the Delawares, Mohicans and Munries 12-21-08

Let me entreat you, therefore, on the lands now given you to begin to give every man a farm; let him enclose it, cultivate it, build a warm house on it, and when he dies, let it belong to his wife and children after him. Nothing is so easy as to learn to cultivate the earth; all your women understand it, and to make it easier, we are always ready to teach you how to make ploughs, hoes, and necessary utensils. If the men will take the labor of the earth from the women, they will learn to spin and weave and to clothe their families. In this way, you will also raise many children, you will double your numbers every twenty years, and soon fill the lands your friends have given you, and your children will never be tempted to sell the spot on which they have been born, raised, and have labored and called their own.

When once you have property, you will want laws and magistrates to protect your property and persons, and to punish those among you who commit crimes. You will find that our laws are good for this purpose; you will wish to live under them, you will unite yourselves with us, join in our Great Councils and form one people with us, and we shall all be Americans; you will mix with us by marriage, your blood will run in our veins, and will spread with us over this great island.

Instead, then, my children, of the gloomy prospect you have drawn of your total disappearance from the face of the earth, which is true, if you continue to hunt the deer and buffalo and go to war, you see what a brilliant aspect is offered to your future history, if you give up war and hunting. Adopt the culture of the earth and raise domestic animals; you see how from a small family you may become a great nation by adopting the course, which, from the small beginning you describe, has made us a great nation.

20. The Negro Emancipation

Commentary

Jefferson's inflexible position and conviction concerning human comparisons, racial and otherwise, constitute so sensitive an area that most writers choose either to ignore or misrepresent them. When he declared that all men are created equal, he meant simply that they are entitled to equality before the law. The fact is that he saw infinite gradations of worth, from the lowest to the highest, even among the whites; and he never swerved from his belief that the Negro race was inferior intellectually, genetically, artistically, and creatively to other races. These conclusions resulted from first-hand observation and experience; and, if anything, became more fixed with advancing years.

We would say that in respect to American Negroes and slavery, three convictions remained uppermost with him throughout his life: (1) that slavery is an abhorrent evil and injustice; (2) that, no matter what the cost might be, the Negroes in the United States must be given their freedom, the sooner the better; and (3) that, since egalitarian and peaceful integration with the whites would certainly prove impractical, if not impossible — at least for many generations — their expatriation and recolonization were social, economic, and political imperatives. He declared that "Nothing is more certainly written in the book of fate than that these people are to be free; nor is it less certain that the two races, equally free, cannot live in the same government."

Perhaps Jefferson was wrong, but let us consider this: that, had his proposals been adopted and implemented, there would have been no civil war, which took the lives of several times as many white men as there were black male adults in 1800; that the cost of this conflict to the North alone was several billion dollars; that the devastation and losses to the South were almost beyond comprehension and threatened almost to exterminate the masters, a tragedy which Jefferson foresaw but hoped would not accompany emancipation. His humane plan would have compensated the owners fully for their property and would have settled the blacks in congenial conditions with full complements of necessary tools and equipment costing only a fraction of $900 million. Furthermore, had it been adopted, there would not now be several million *illegitimate Negro children to be supported by the taxpayers at an expense that staggers the imagination; and we would not have the riot-torn and burned-out cities which constitute an inherited curse in American society.*

Briefly stated, Jefferson's plan, first outlined in the Notes on Virginia *in 1781, and repeated in a letter to Jared Sparks in 1824, was simply to transport all the males upon reaching the age of 21 and the females at 18 to some suitable place; their owners to be fully compensated and the blacks themselves to be placed under the protection of our government and supplied with everything necessary to establish themselves in comfortable circumstances. A fleet of ships would be prepared to carry the blacks to their destination and to bring back an equal number of whites from England and the European continent.*

He urged that his plan be put into operation without delay; for the 650,000 blacks of 1786 had increased to 1.5 million in 1824 and would become 6 million before the then-existing generation had passed and would include 1 million fighting men who might well engage the country in a fearful civil war after declaring "We will not go!"

After Banneker, a Negro, and the French Bishop Henri Gregoire, wrote, extolling the intelligence and the accomplishments of the blacks, Jefferson wrote to Joel Barlow criticizing the latter very severely and declaring that the former "had a mind of very common stature indeed." The fact is that in spite of his most sincere efforts to find contravening evidence and his desire to show not only compassion, but also respect and admiration for creativity, he never found any substantive basis for such esteem among the blacks.

We should note that one of Jefferson's bitterest condemnations of the British government was that it insisted on the slave trade instead of permitting its own starving unemployed to emigrate, since these served as potential manpower for their commercial and piratical ships and to quell domestic riots and insurrections. Jefferson states that these charges were deleted from the Declaration of Independence because of certain southern gentlemen "whose reflections were not yet matured to the full abhorrence of that traffic."

At this point, we feel we should take note of Callendar and others who vilified him by declaring that Sally Hemmings, a mulatto slave, who accompanied his two daughters to Europe as their nurse, was his mistress for many years and bore him several children. Since his wife is reputed to have exacted from him a deathbed promise not to remarry and since he is not known to have engaged in an affair with a woman of his own social position, this alleged liaison has been given some credence. Sally was manumitted after his death, as he had promised; and her children, probably fathered by several different men, were given their freedom in his will. We have found no evidence which we consider acceptable, that they were his. Nevertheless, in 1974, Fawn Brodie published a biography of Jefferson subtitled An Intimate History, *in which she focuses on his friendship with Maria Cosway, a woman he met in Europe; and much more on his alleged "affair" with his slave-mistress, which was denied by his family as a vicious libel.*

Jefferson himself simply ignored all the gossip and calumnies which filled the Federalist papers of the time and which were intended to destroy him as a proponent of thrifty and republican government.

To us, the story of Jefferson's liaison is incredible; not only because of his general and known attitude toward Negroes, but much more because of his sterling honesty. Never in his life was it ever proven that he told a lie or made the slightest attempt to conceal any truth concerning himself; and yet he addressed a letter to Thomas Seymour on February 11, 1807 — four years after the Callendar libels were published — in which he declared: "As for myself, conscious that there was not a truth *on earth, which I feared, should it be known, I have lent myself willingly as the subject of a great experiment, which was to prove..." that the lies and calumnies of a licentious press could not batter down one who, like himself, had led a blameless life and had nothing to hide. How could he have made such a statement so confidently if Sally's children were also his? or if, as his libellers maintained, she continued as his mistress without interruption from 1787 until the very end of his life? And how could such a relationship have continued and been maintained in secrecy over a period of nearly four decades?*

There are people in the world who find delight in the destruction of the characters and reputations of the great and good; and such, we think, are those who obviously take pleasure in maligning the personal honesty and integrity of Thomas Jefferson.

The First Disquisitions

BW 144-149 Notes on Virginia 1781

To emancipate all slaves born after the passing the Act. The bill reported by the revisers does not itself contain this proposition; but an amendment containing it was prepared, to be offered to the legislature whenever the bill should be taken up, and further directing, that they should continue with their parents to a certain age, then be brought up, at the public expense, to tillage, arts, or sciences, according to their geniusses till the females should be eighteen, and the males twenty-one years of age, when they should be colonized to such place as the circumstances of the time should render most proper, sending them out with arms, implements of household and of the handicraft arts, seeds, pairs of the useful domestic animals, etc., to declare them a free and independent people, and extend to them our alliance and protection, till they shall have acquired strength; and to send vessels at the same time to other parts of the world for an equal number of white inhabitants; to induce whom to migrate hither, proper encouragements were to be proposed.

It will probably be asked, Why not retain and incorporate the blacks into the state, and thus save the expence of supplying by importation of white settlers, the vacancies they will leave? Deep rooted prejudices entertained by the whites; ten thousand recollections, by the blacks, of the injuries they have sustained; new provocations; the real distinctions which nature has made; and many other circumstances will divide us into parties, and produce convulsions which will probably never end but in the extermination of the one or the other race.

To these objections, which are political, may be added others, which are physical and moral. The first difference which strikes us is that of colour. Whether the black of the negro resides in the reticular membrane... the difference is fixed in nature, and is as real as if its seat and cause were better known... The circumstance of superior beauty in the white race, is thought worthy of attention in the propagation of our horses, dogs, and other domestic animals; why not in that of man? Besides those of colour, figure, and hair, there are other physical distinctions proving a difference of race. They have less hair on the face and body. They secrete less by the kidnies, and more by the glands of the skin, which gives them a very strong and disagreeable odour... .

They are more ardent after their female; but love seems with them to be more an eager desire, than a tender delicate mixture of sentiment and sensation. Their griefs are transient. Those numberless afflictions, which render it doubtful whether heaven has given life to us in mercy or in wrath, are less felt, and sooner forgotten with them. In general, their existence appears to participate more of sensation than reflection. To this must be ascribed their disposition to sleep when abstracted from their diversions, and unemployed in labour. An animal whose body is at rest, and who does not reflect, must be disposed to sleep of course. Comparing them by their faculties of memory, reason, and imagination, it appears to me that in memory they are equal to the whites; [but] in reason much inferior, as I think one could scarcely be found capable of tracing and comprehending... Euclid; and that in imagination they are dull, tasteless, and anomalous... .

It will be right to make great allowances for the difference of condition, of education, of conversation, of the sphere in which they move. Many millions of them have been brought to, and born in America. Most of them, indeed, have been confined to tillage, to their own homes, and their own society: yet many have been so situated, that they might have availed themselves of the conversation of their masters; many have been brought up to the handicraft arts, and from that circumstance have always been associated with the whites. Some have been liberally educated, and all have lived in countries where the arts and sciences are cultivated to a considerable degree, and have had before their eyes samples of the best works from abroad... .

Misery is often the parent of the most affecting touches in poetry. — Among the blacks is misery enough, God knows, but no poetry. Love is the peculiar oestrum of the poet. Their love is ardent, but it kindles the senses only, not the imagination... .

The improvement of the blacks in body and mind, in the first instance of their mixture with the whites, has been observed by every one, and proves that their inferiority is not the effect merely of their condition of life. We know that among the Romans, about the Augustan age especially, the condition of their slaves was much more deplorable than that of the blacks on the continent of America... . [For] in this country the slaves multiply as fast as the free inhabitants. Their situation and manners place the commerce between the two sexes almost without restraint. Cato, on the principle of economy, always sold his sick and superannuated slaves... . The American slaves cannot enumerate this among the injuries and insults they receive. It was common practice to expose in the island of Aescalapius... diseased slaves whose cure was like to become tedious... . The exposing of them in the United States is a crime of which no instance has existed with us; and were it to be followed by death, it would be punished capitally... .

With the Romans, the regular method of taking the evidence of slaves was under torture. Here is has been thought better never to resort to their evidence... . Yet notwithstanding these and other discouraging circumstances among the Romans, their slaves were often their rarest artists. They excelled too in science, insomuch as to be usually employed as tutors to their master's children... . But they were of the race of whites. It is not their condition, then, but nature, which has produced the distinction.

Whether further observation will or will not verify the conjecture, that nature has been less bountiful to them in their endowments of the head, I believe that in those of the heart she will be found to have done them justice. That disposition to theft with which they have been branded, must be ascribed to their situation, and not to depravity of the moral sense. The man in whose favour no laws of property exist, probably feels himself less bound to respect those made in favour of others. When arguing for ourselves, we lay it down as fundamental, that laws, to be just, must give reciprocation of right: that, without this, they are mere arbitrary rules of conduct, founded in force, and not in conscience; and it is a problem which I give to the master to solve, whether the religious precepts against the violation of property were not framed for him as well as his slave? And whether the slave may not as justifiably take a little from one who has taken all from him, as he may slay one who would slay him? That a change in the relations in which a man is placed should change his ideas of moral right and wrong, is neither new, nor peculiar to the colour of the blacks... .

Notwithstanding these considerations which must weaken their respect for the laws of property, we find among them instances of the most rigid integrity, and as many as among their better instructed masters, of benevolence, gratitude, and unshaken fidelity. The opinion that they are inferior in the faculties of reason and imagination, must be hazarded with great diffidence. To justify a general conclusion, requires many observations... .

I advance it, therefore, as a suspicion only, that the blacks, whether originally a distinct race, or made distinct by time and circumstances, are inferior to the white in the endowments both of body and mind. It is not against experience to suppose that different species of the same genus, or varieties of the same species, may possess different qualifications. Will not a lover of natural history, then, one who views the gradations in all the races of animals with the eye of philosophy, excuse an effort to keep those in the department of man as distinct as nature has formed them? This unfortunate difference in colour, and perhaps of faculty, is a powerful obstacle to the emancipation of these people... . Some of these, embarrassed by the question, 'What is to be done with them?' join themselves in opposition with those who are actuated by sordid avarice only. Among the Romans emancipation required but one effort. The slave, when made free, might mix with, without staining the blood of his master. But with us a second is necessary, unknown in history. When freed, he is to be removed beyond the reach of mixture.

The Inquity of Slavery

ME V 56-57 Dr. Price 8-7-85

In that part of America the [North] there being but a few slaves, they can easily disencumber themselves of them; and emancipation is put into such a train, that in a few years, there will be no slaves northward of Maryland. In Maryland, I do not find as much of a disposition to begin the redress of this enormity, as in Virginia. This is the next State to which we may turn our eyes for the interesting spectacle of justice, in conflict with avarice and oppression... .

ME XVII 103 Miscellaneous Papers

But we must await, with patience, the workings of an overriding Providence, and hope that that is preparing the deliverance of these, our suffering brethren. When the measure of their tears shall be full, when their groans shall have involved heaven itself in darkness, doubtless, a God of justice will awaken to their distress and by diffusing light and liberality among their oppressors, or, at length, by his exterminating thunder, manifest His attention to the things of this world, and that they are not left to the guidance of a blind fatality.

ME XVIII 166-72 Anecdotes of Benjamine Franklin

When the Declaration of Independence was under the consideration of Congress... . Severe strictures on the conduct of the British king, in negotiating our repeated appeals of the law which permitted the importation of slaves, were disapproved by some Southern gentlemen, whose reflections were not yet matured to the full abhorrence of that traffic.

BW 422 Autobiography 1821

The pusillanimous idea that we still had friends in England worth keeping terms with, still haunted the minds of many [when the Declaration of Independence was prepared and signed]. For this reason, those passages which conveyed censures on the people of England were struck out, lest they should give them offence. The clause, too, reprobating the enslaving the inhabitants of Africa, was struck out, in complaisance to South Carolina and Georgia, who had never attempted to restrain the importation of slaves, and who, on the contrary, still wished to continue it. Our northern brethren also, I believe, felt a little tender under these censures; for though their people had very few slaves themselves, yet they had been pretty considerable carriers of them to others.

BW 431 Autobiography 1821

The first establishment in Virginia which became permanent, was made in 1607. I have found no mention of negroes in the colony until about 1650. The first brought here as slaves were by a Dutch ship after which the English commenced the trade, and continued it until the revolutionary war. That suspended, *ipso facto,* their further importation for the present, and the business of the war pressing constantly on the legislature, this subject was not acted on finally until the year '78 when I brought in a bill to prevent their further importation. This passed without opposition, and stopped the increase of the evil by importation, leaving to future efforts its final eradication.

ME XV 467-70 William Short 9-8-23

Our only blot is becoming less offensive by the great improvement in the condition and civilization of that race who can now more advantageously compare their situation with that of laborers of Europe. Still, it is a hideous blot, as well from the heteromorph peculiarities of the race, as that, with them, physical compulsion to action must be substituted for the moral necessity which constrains the free laborers to work equally hard. We feel and deplore it morally and politically, and we look without despair to some redeeming means not yet specifically foreseen. I am happy in believing that the conviction of the necessity of removing this evil gains ground with time... .

BE 160-61 Notes on Virginia 1781

There must doubtless be an unhappy influence on the manners of our people produced by the existence of slavery among us. The whole commerce between master and slave is a perpetual exercise of the most boisterous passions, the most unremitting despotism on the one part, and degrading submissions on the other... .

The man must be a prodigy who can retain his manners and morals undepraved by such circumstances. And with what execration should the statesman be loaded, who, permitting one half the citizens thus to trample on the rights of the other, transforms those into despots, and these into enemies, destroys the morals of the one part, and the *armor patriae* of the other. For if a slave can have a country in this world, it must be any other in preference to that in which he is born to live and labor for another; in which he must lock up the faculties of his nature, contribute as far as depends on his individual endeavors to the evanishment of the human race, or entail his own miserable condition on the endless generations proceeding from him.

With the morals of the people, their industry is destroyed. For in a warm climate, no man will labor for himself who can make another labor for him... . Indeed, I tremble for my country when I reflect that God is just; that his justice cannot sleep forever; that considering numbers, nature and natural means only, a revolution of the wheel of fortune, an exchange of situation is among possible events; that is, may become probable by supernatural interference!

The Almighty has no attribute which can take side with us in such a contest. But it is impossible to be temperate and to pursue this subject through the various considerations of policy, or morals, or history, natural and civil. We must be contented to hope they will force their way into everyone's mind. I think a change already perceptible, since the origin of the present revolution. The spirit of the master is abating, that of the slave rising from the dust, his condition mollifying, the way I hope preparing, under the auspices of heaven, for a total emancipation, and that this is disposed, in the order of events, to be with the consent of the masters, rather than by their extirpation.

Desire for Negro Equality

ME VIII 241-42 Benjamin Banneker 8-30-91

Nobody wishes more than I do to see such proofs as you exhibit, that nature has given to our black brethren, talents equal to those of the other colors of men, and that the appearance of a want of these is owing merely to the degraded condition of their existence, both in Africa and America.

I can add with truth, that nobody wishes more ardently to see a good system commenced for raising the condition both of their body and mind to what it ought to be, as fast as the imbecility of their present existence, and other circumstances, will permit.

ME XII 254-55 M. Henri Gregoire 2-25-09

Be assured that no person living wishes more sincerely than I do, to see a complete refutation of the doubts I have myself entertained and expressed on the grade of understanding allotted to them by nature, and to find that in this respect they are on a par with ourselves. My doubts were the result of personal observation on the limited sphere of my own State, where the opportunities for the development of their genius were not favorable; and those of exercising it still less so. I expressed them therefore with great hesitation; but whatever be their degree of talent it is no measure of their rights... . On this subject they are gaining daily in the opinions of nations, and hopeful advances are making towards their re-establishment on an equal footing with the other colors of the human family. I pray you therefor to accept my thanks for the many instances you have enabled me to observe of respectable intelligence in that race of men, which cannot fail to have effect in hastening the day of their relief... .

ME XII 321-23 Joel Barlow 10-8-09

You have done right in giving him [Bishop Gregoire] a sugary answer. But he did not deserve it... . I believe him a very good man, with imagination enough to declaim eloquently, but without judgment to decide. He wrote to me also on the doubts I had expressed five or six and twenty years ago in the Notes on Virginia, as to the grade of understanding of the negroes, and he sent me his book on the literature of the negroes. His credulity has made him gather up every store he could find of men of color, (without distinguishing whether black, or of what degree of mixture,) however slight the mention, or light the authority on which they are quoted. The whole do not amount, in point of evidence, to what we know ourselves of Banneker. We know he had spherical trigonometry enough to make almanacs, but not without the suspicion of aid from Ellicot, who was his neighbor and friend, and never missed an opportunity of puffing him. I have a long letter from Banneker, which shows him to have had a mind of very common stature indeed. As to Bishop Gregoire, I wrote him, as you have done, a very soft answer. It was impossible for doubt to have been more tenderly or hesitatingly expressed than that in the Notes on Virginia, and nothing was or is farther from my intentions than to enlist myself as the champion of a fixed opinion, where I have only expressed a doubt.

ME V 3-7 General Chastellux 6-7-85

I believe the Indian, then, to be, in body and mind, equal to the white man. I have supposed the black man, in his present state, might not be so...

ME XIX 41-44 Edward Bancroft 1-26-88

I can judge from the experiments which have been made to give liberty to, or rather abandon, persons whose habits have been formed in slavery, is like abandoning children. Many Quakers in Virginia seated their slaves on their lands as tenants... . I remember that the landlord was obliged to plan their crops for them, to direct all their operations during every season and according to the weather; but what is more afflicting, he was obliged to watch them daily and almost constantly to make them work and even to whip them... . These slaves chose to steal from their neighbors, rather than work; they became public nuisances and in most instances were reduced to slavery again... .

Conditions of American Slavery

BW 110 Notes on Virginia 1781

Under the mild treatment our slaves experience, and their wholesome, though coarse, food, this blot in our country increases as fast, or faster than, the whites. During the regal government we had at one time obtained a law which imposed such a duty on the importation of slaves as amounted nearly to a prohibition, when one inconsiderable assembly, placed under a peculiarity of circumstances, repealed the law. This repeal met a joyful sanction from the then reigning sovereign, and no devices, no expedients, which could ever be attempted by subsequent assemblies, and they seldom met without attempting them, could succeed in getting the royal assent to a renewal of the duty. In the very first session held under the republican government, the assembly passed a law for the perpetual prohibition of the importation of slaves. This will, in some measure, stop the increase of this great political and moral evil, while the minds of our citizens may be ripening for a complete emancipation of human nature.

ME XIV 179-91 Thomas Cooper 9-10-145

Even these are better fed in these States, warmer clothed, and labor less than the journeymen or day laborers of England. They have the comfort, too, of numerous families, in the midst of whom they live without want, or fear of it; a solace which few of the laborers of England possess.

Proposals for Emancipation and Removal

ME XVII 119 Answers to Questions from M. de Meusnier 2-24-86

I conjecture there are six hundred and fifty thousand negroes in the five southernmost States, and not fifty thousand in the rest. In most of the latter, effectual measures have been taken for their future emancipation.... The disposition to emancipate is strongest in Virginia.... I flatter myself it will take place there at some period not very distant.... South Carolina and Georgia... and North Carolina, continue importations of negroes. These have long been prohibited in other States.

ME X 294-297 Governor James Monroe 11-24-01

I have not been unmindful... of a resolution of the House of Representatives of Virginia [to emancipate and colonize the slaves].... The idea seems to be to provide for these people by a purchase of lands; and it is asked whether such a purchase can be made of the United States in their western territory?.... Questions would arise whether the establishment of such a colony within our limits... would be desirable... ?

The West Indies offer a more probable and practicable retreat for them. Inhabited already by a people of their own race and color; climates congenial with their natural constitution; insulated from the other descriptions of men; nature seems to have formed these islands to become the receptacle of the blacks transplanted into this hemisphere.... The most promising portion of them is the island of St. Domingo, where the blacks are established into a sovereignty *de facto,* and have organized themselves under regular laws and government. I should conjecture that their present ruler might be willing, on many considerations, to receive [them... .

Africa would offer a last and undoubted resort, if all others more desirable should fail us.

ME X 326-30 Rufus King (English Ambassador) 7-13-02

The course of things in the neighboring islands of the West Indies, appear to have given a considerable impulse to the minds of the slaves in different parts of the United States... . The Legislature [of Virginia] at a subsequent meeting took the subject into consideration, and have communicated to me through the Governor of the State, their wish that some place could be provided, out of the limits of the United States, to which slaves... might be transported... .

ME XIII 10-13 John Lynch 1-21-11

Going from a country possessing all the useful arts, they might be the means of transplanting them among the inhabitants of Africa, and would thus carry back to the country of their origin, the seeds of civilization which might render their sojournment and sufferings here a blessing in the end to that country... .

Indeed, nothing is more to be wished than that the United States would themselves undertake to make such an establishment on the coast of Africa. Exclusive of motives of humanity, the commercial advantages to be derived from it might repay all its expenses... the proposition should be made with all the prudent cautions and attentions requisite to reconcile it to the interests, safety, and prejudices of all parties.

ME XVI 8-13 Jared Sparks 2-4-24

The article on the African colonization of the people of color... . I have read with great consideration... In the disposition of these unfortunate people, there are two rational objects to be distinctly kept in view. First. The establishment of a colony on the coast of Africa, which may introduce among the aborigines the arts of cultivated life, and the blessings of civilization and science. By doing this, we may make to them some retribution for the long course of injuries we have been committing on their population... . Under this view, the colonization... is to be considered as a missionary society, having in view, however, objects more humane, more justifiable,... than the others of that appellation.

The second object... is to provide an asylum to which we can, by degrees, send the whole of that population from among us, and establish them under our patronage and protection, as a separate, free and independent people, in some country and climate friendly to human life and happiness. That any place on the coast of Africa should answer [at once] the latter purpose, I have ever deemed entirely impossible... . I will appeal to figures only, which admit of no controversy... . There are in the United States a million and a half of people of color in slavery. To send off the whole of these at once, nobody conceives to be practicable for us, or expedient for them. Let us take twenty-five years for its accomplishment, within which time they will be doubled. Their estimated value as property... would amount to six hundred millions of dollars, which must be paid or lost by somebody. To this, add the cost of their transportation by land and sea... a year's provision of food and clothing, implements of husbandry and their trades, which will amount to three hundred millions more, making thirty-six millions of dollars a year for twenty-five years... . I do not say this to induce an inference that the getting rid of them is forever impossible. For that is neither my opinion nor my hope. But only that it cannot be done in this way. There is, I think, a way in which it can be done; that is by emancipating the afterborn, leaving them, on due compensation, with their mothers, until their services are worth their maintenance, and then putting them to industrious occupations, until a proper age for deportation. This was the result of my reflections on the subject five and forty years ago, and I have never yet been able to conceive any other practicable plan... .

And from what fund are these expenses to be furnished? Why not from the lands which have been ceded by the very States now needing this relief?... The slave States, too, if more interested, would also contribute more by their gratuitous liberation, thus taking on themselves alone the first and heaviest item of expense.

In the plan sketched in the Notes on Virginia, no particular place of asylum was specified; because it was thought possible, that in the revolutionary state of America, then commenced, events might open to us some one within practicable distance. This has now happened. St. Domingo has become independent, and with the population of that color only; and if the public papers are to be credited, their Chief offers to pay their passage, to receive them as free citizens, and to provide them employment. This leaves, then, for the general confederacy, no expense but of nurture with the mother for a few years, and would call, of course, for a very moderate appropriation of the vacant lands. Suppose the whole annual increase to be of sixty thousand effective births, fifty vessels, of four hundred tons burden each, constantly employed in that short run, would carry off the increase of every year, and the old stock would die off in the ordinary course of nature, lessening from the commencement until its final disappearance. In this way no violation of private right is proposed... .

And who could estimate its blessed effects? I leave this to those who will live to see their accomplishment, and to enjoy a beatitude forbidden to my age. But I leave it with this admonition, to rise and be doing. A million and a half are within their control; but six millions, (which a majority of those now living will see them attain,) and one million of these fighting men, will say, "we will not go."

I am aware that this subject involves some constitutional scruples. But a liberal construction, justified by the object, may go far, and an amendment to the Constitution, the whole length necessary. The separation of infants from their mothers, too, would produce some scruples of humanity. But this would be straining at a gnat, and swallowing a camel.

ME XVI 120-21 Mrs. Frances Wright 8-7-25

The abolition of the evil is not impossible; it ought never therefore to be despaired of. Every plan should be adopted, every experiment tried, which may do something towards the ultimate object [to emancipate and re-colonize the blacks]... . An opinion is hazarded by some, but proved by none, that moral urgencies are not sufficient to induce them to labor; that nothing can do this but physical coercion. But this is a problem which the present age alone is prepared to solve by experiment. It would be a solecism to suppose a race of animals created, without sufficient foresight and energy to preserve their own existence. It is disproved, too, by the fact that they exist, and have existed through all the ages of history. We are not sufficiently acquainted with all the nations of Africa, to say that there may not be some in which habits of industry are established, and the arts practised which are necessary to render life comfortable. The experiment now in progress in St. Domingo, those of Sierra Leone and Cape Mesurado, are but beginnings... . These, however, I must leave to another generation.

ME I 72-73 Autobiography 1821

The principles of the amendment [to the Bill to Emancipate the Slaves in Virginia], however, were agreed on, that is to say, the freedom of all born after a certain day, and deportation at a proper age. But it was found that the public mind would not yet bear the proposition, nor will it bear it even at this day. Yet the day is not distant when it must bear and adopt it, or worse will follow. Nothing is more certainly written in the book of fate, than that these people are to be free; nor is it less certain that the two races, equally free, cannot live in the same government. Nature, habit, opinion, have drawn indelible lines of distinction between them. It is still in our power to direct the process of emancipation and deportation, peaceably, and in such slow degree, as that the evil will wear off insensibly, and their place be, *pari passu,* filled up by free white laborers. If, on the contrary, it is left to force itself on, human nature must shudder at the prospect held up. We should in vain look for an example in the Spanish deportation or deletion of the Moors. This precedent would fall far short of our case.

21. Jefferson on Religion

Commentary

Although Jefferson stands incomparably as the greatest American statesman and Founding Father, it was almost by accident that he achieved this status: for his most profound interests were in other fields, one of which was religion. When he prepared the inscription to be placed on his tombstone, he never even mentioned that he had been President: instead, he proclaimed that he was the author of the Declaration of Independence, that he wrote the Bill for Establishing Religious Freedom in Virginia, and that he was the father of the University in that State.

He was a thinker, a scientist, a philosopher, a determined exponent of equality, justice, and the rights of the productive citizen. Beyond that, his entire career was a tribute to that sacred human element, Individual Reason, the sole source of dependable authority, the only ineluctable guide of conscience, the one supreme and undeniable determinant of truth.

It is only by comprehending this unchanging basis for Jefferson's principles that we can appreciate fully the constant battles he fought. Throughout life, his political and ideological opponents were the Federalists and the clergy: the former, because they wished to establish an economic and political system in which privileged classes would batten in luxurious idleness on the labors of the productive citizens; and the latter because, in their arrogance and contempt for others, they preached a system of theology and morals which Jefferson considered an insult to human reason and sought thereby to achieve wealth and power for themselves.

At least, in one respect, the American complex was a fortunate basis for Jefferson's advocacy of religious freedom and church-state separation. As more and more refugees of various religious persuasions fled from European tyranny to enjoy freedom of conscience in America, whenever they had the power, they sought to establish an intolerance almost as great as that from which they had fled. However, as the number and variety of such dissidents increased, it became obvious that no one of them could become the established church: they therefore agreed, reluctantly enough, that each would relinquish dominion over all the others in return for complete freedom to operate as separate private entities. But this movement was not led by clerics; it was powered by men like Franklin, Madison, Washington, and Morris, but most of all by Jefferson, who were themselves without definite theological commitments but who were determined to achieve religious freedom for themselves and all their compatriots.

Jefferson's charges against the priesthoods which had ruled Europe for so many centuries were various and definitive: by controlling civil governments, they had drowned the continent in blood over speculative doctrines and disputes which defied every effort of intelligence to comprehend them; they had prevented the advancement of science; they had prostituted education to the purposes of an insane theology; they had kept the people in ignorance and virtual slavery; and, most terrible of all, they had denied Reason any role in human affairs. Because of this and more, religious societies were forced to become and remain private entities with untrammeled rights to believe and teach their own creeds, but without power to force their will or opinions on any one else.

It was therefore no accident that when a law was proposed in New York aimed against the Shakers — a bizarre communal-celibate cult, which had gathered a considerable following — Jefferson came to their defence. He declared that this attempt to annul their marriages, confiscate their properties, and take their children from them "will carry us back to the times of darkest bigotry and barbarism, to find a parallel." There should be no interference on the part of the civil magistrate with any religious activity.

Two of Jefferson's bete noirs *were the dreadful God of Calvin and the doctrine of the Trinity: the one because it postulated a deity so horrible that he became the real Anti-Christ, as he stated in a letter to Samuel Kercheval; the other because it constituted a total negation of human reason.*

Because of his determined opposition to clerical advantages and special privileges, the hatred and calumny visited upon Jefferson are probably without parallel in American history. He was called an atheist, a devil, an enemy of God, religion, and decency; he was often called an *anti-Christ and sometimes even* the *Anti-Christ. But he never made any public reply to these attacks; and even in private correspondence, he enjoined the strictest confidence. When Banjamin Waterhouse asked permission to publish a letter, he answered: "No, my dear Sir, not for the world. Into what a nest of hornets would it thrust my head!" To John Mercer, he wrote: "I should as soon think of writing for the reformation of Bedlam, as for the world of religious sects." For himself, he desired only privacy: "Our particular principles of religion," he declared in a letter to Miles King, "are the subject of accountability to our God alone. I inquire after no man's, and trouble none with mine..." . Referring specifically to the Episcopalians and the Congregational Calvinists, he stated in a letter to Benjamin Rush, that he would oppose any efforts by them to establish theirs as the form of Christianity to prevail throughout the country: "they believe that any portion of power confided to me, will be exerted in opposition to their schemes. And they believe rightly: for I have sworn upon the altar of God, eternal hostility against every form of tyranny over the mind of man."*

Reason was ever the beacon light of Jefferson's mind. In 1887, he wrote his young nephew, Peter Carr: "you must lay aside all prejudice... and neither believe nor reject anything because any other person, or description of persons, have rejected or believed it. Your own reason is the only oracle given you by heaven, and you are answerable, not for the rightness, but the uprightness of the decision." In a letter to Miles King, he iterated: "For dispute as long as we will on religious tenets, our reason at last must ultimately decide, as it is the only oracle which God has given us to determine what comes from Him and the phantasms of a disordered or deluded imagination."

Despite his rejection of church dogma, we cannot doubt that Jefferson was deeply religious. He certainly believed in a Creator-God, the benevolent Ruler of the Universe, who had ordered and designed all things as they are. He believed also with realizing faith that a good and moral life, following the basic precepts of Jesus, was not only infinitely desirable, but also the only possible highway to a happy immortality. He declared himself an Epicurean, a philosophy which postulated a creator-God, but denied the existence of providence or an after-life: however, it would seem that Jefferson subscribed rather to its morality than to its declarations concerning the soul.

He emphasized that the moral teachings of Jesus require only a good life and that speculative doctrines and a belief in miracles are not only worthless, but totally destructive. No one else can atone for our *sins — we must love our neighbor and make restitution for every wrong-doing. Reason and conscience are dependable guides; again and again, he declared that anyone who leads a good life must be actuated by a good religion; and, conversely, that a correct religion will cause a good life — which will, at last, be the determinant of a blessed immortality.*

Whatever else we may say about Jefferson's religion, he was certainly an uncompromising Unitarian, who proclaimed constantly his belief in the "one only God." We should not be surprised, therefore, that his admiration for Joseph Priestley — the great English scientist and Unitarian theologian and minister, whose home and laboratory had been burned by a native mob — exceeded that which he felt for any other man in the world. So far as is recorded, he never attended any religious services except those at which this eloquent preacher presided; in welcoming him as an exile from his own country, Jefferson wrote that "Yours is one of the few lives precious to mankind;" and we "cover you with the protection of those laws which were made for the wise and good like you..." . However, the American Unitarians, as we have noted, developed creeds of their own: and the doctrine of the Unal and uncredalized God did not achieve the prevalence or success which Jefferson hoped for and expected even in their *denomination until about 1926.*

Dedicated to these convictions, he lived a long and extraordinarily useful and constructive life, at the close of which he fell quietly into his final and blissful sleep.

Commentaries and Religious Legislation

PE I 544-48 Notes on Religion Cir. 1774

No man has power to let another prescribe his faith. Faith is not faith without believing. No man can conform his faith to the dictates of another.

The life and essence of religion consist in the internal persuasion of belief of the mind. External forms of worship, when against our belief, are hypocrisy and impiety.

If it be said the magistrate may make use of arguments and so draw the heterodox to truth, I answer every man has a commission to admonish, exhort, convince another of error.

The people have not given the magistrate the care of souls because they could not. They could not, because no man has the right to abandon the care of salvation to another... .

Compulsion in religion is distinguished peculiarly from compulsion in every other thing. I may grow rich by the art I am compelled to follow; I may recover my health by medicine I am compelled to take against my own judgment; but I cannot be saved by a *worship* I disbelieve and abhor... .

Why have Christians been distinguished above all people who have ever lived, for persecutions? Is it because it is the genius of their religion? No, its genius is the reverse. It is the refusing of *toleration* to those of a different opinion which has produced all the bustles and wars on account of religion.

It was the misfortune of mankind that during the darker centuries, the Christian priests, following their ambition and avarice, combining with the magistrate to divide the spoils of the people, could establish the notion that schismatics might be ousted of their possessions and destroyed. This notion we have not yet cleared ourselves from. In this case, no wonder the oppressed should rebel, and they will continue to rebel, and raise disturbances until their civil rights are fully restored to them, and all partial distinctions, exclusions, and incapacitations are removed.

BW 48-49 A Bill for Establishing Religious Freedom 1779

Section I. Well aware that... Almighty God hath created the mind free;... that all attempts to influence it by temporal punishments or burthens, or by civil incapacities, tend only to beget habits of hypocrisy and meanness, and are a departure from the plan of the Holy Author of our religion, who being Lord both of body and mind, yet chose not to propagate it by coercions on either, as was in his Almighty power to do;...

that the impious presumption of legislators and rulers, civil as well as ecclesiastical, who, being themselves but fallible and uninspired men, have assumed dominion over the faith of others, setting up their own opinions and modes of thinking as the only true and infallible, and as such endeavoring to impose them on others, hath established and maintained false religions over the greatest part of the world, and through all time; that to compel a man to furnish contributions of money for the propagation of opinions which he disbelieves and abhors, is sinful and tyrannical; that even forcing him to support this or that teacher of his own religious persuasion, is depriving him of the comfortable liberty of giving his contributions to the particular pastor whose morals he would make his pattern, and whose powers he feels most persuasive to righteousness; and is withdrawing from the ministry those temporal rewards, which proceeding from an approbation of their personal conduct, are an additional excitement to earnest and unremitting labours for the instruction of mankind; that our civil rights have no dependence on our religious opinions, more than our opinions in physics or geometry; that, therefore, the proscribing any citizen as unworthy the public confidence by laying upon him an incapacity of being called to offices of trust and emolument, unless he profess or renounce this or that religious opinion, is depriving him injuriously of those privileges and advantages to which in common with his fellow citizens he has a natural right; that it tends also to corrupt the principles of that very religion it is meant to encourage, by bribing, with a monopoly of worldly honors and emoluments, those who will externally profess and conform to it; that though indeed these are criminals who do not withstand such temptation, yet neither are those innocent who lay the bait in their way; that to suffer the civil magistrate to intrude his powers into the field of opinion and to restrain the profession or propagation of principles, on the supposition of their ill tendency, is a dangerous fallacy, which at once destroys all religious liberty, because he being of course judge of that tendency, will make his opinions the rule of judgment, and approve or condemn the sentiments of others only as they shall square with or differ from his own; that it is time enough for the rightful purposes of civil government, for its officers to interfere when principles break out into overt acts against peace and good order; and finally, that truth is great and will prevail if left to herself, that she is the proper and sufficient antagonist to error, and has nothing to fear from the conflict, unless by human interposition disarmed of her natural weapons, free argument and debate; errors ceasing to be dangerous when it is permitted freely to contradict them.

Section II. *Be it therefore enacted by the General Assembly,* That no man shall be compelled to frequent or support any religious worship, place or ministry whatsoever, nor shall be enforced, restrained, molested, or burthened in his body or goods, nor shall otherwise suffer on account of his religious opinions or belief; but that all men shall be free to profess, and by argument to maintain, their opinions in matters of religion, and that the same shall in nowise diminish, enlarge, or affect their civil capacities.

Section III. And though we well know this Assembly, elected by the people for the ordinary purposes of legislation only, have no power to restrain the acts of succeeding Assemblies, constituted with the powers equal to our own, and that therefore to declare this act irrevocable, would be of no effect in law, yet we are free to declare, and do declare, that the rights hereby asserted are of the natural rights of mankind, and that if any act shall hereafter be passed to repeal the present or to narrow its operation, such act will be an infringement of natural right.

BW 156-59 Notes on Virginia 1781

The first settlers in this country were emigrants from England, of the English Church, just at a point of time when it was flushed with complete victory over the religious of all other persuasions. Possessed, as they became, of the powers of making, administering, and executing the laws, they showed equal intolerance in this country with their Presbyterian brethren, who had emigrated to the northern government.

The poor Quakers were flying from persecution in England. They cast their eyes on these new countries as asylums of civil and religious freedom; but they found them free only for the reigning sect. Several acts of the Virginia assembly of 1639, 1662, and 1693, had made it penal in parents to refuse to have their children baptized; had prohibited the unlawful assembling of Quakers; had made it penal for any master of a vessel to bring a Quaker into the State; had ordered those already here, and such as should come thereafter, to be imprisoned till they should abjure the country; provided a milder punishment for their first and second return, but death for their third; had inhibited all persons from suffering their meetings in or near their houses, entertaining them individually, or disposing of books which supported their tenets... .

The Anglicans retained full possession of the country about a century. Other opinions began then to creep in, and the great care of the government to support their own church, having begotten an equal degree of indolence in the clergy, two-thirds of the people had become dissenters at the commencement of the present revolution... .

The [Virginia] convention of May 1776, in their declaration of rights, declared it to be the truth, and a natural right, that the exercise of religion should be free... . The same convention... in October, 1776, repealed all *acts of parliament* which had rendered criminal the maintaining any opinions in matters of religion, the forbearing to repair to church, and the exercise of any mode of worship; and suspended the laws giving salaries to the clergy, which suspension was made perpetual in October, 1779... .

At the common law, *heresy* was a capital offence, punishable by burning. Its definition was... that nothing should be deemed heresy, but what had been so determined... by the express and plain words of the scriptures... . By our own act of assembly of 1705, if a person brought up to the Christian religion denies the being of a God, or the Trinity, or asserts there are more gods than one, or denies the Christian religion to be true, or the scriptures to be the divine authority, he is punishable on the first offence by incapacity to hold any office, or employment ecclesiastical, civil, or military; on the second, by disability to sue, to take any gift or legacy, or be guardian, executor, or administrator, and by three years' imprisonment without bail. A father's right to the custody of his own children being founded in law on his right of guardianship, this being taken away, they may of course be severed from him and put by the authority of a court into more orthodox hands.

This is a summary view of that religious slavery under which a people had been willing to remain, who had lavished their lives and fortunes for the establishment of their civil freedom... . The rights of conscience we never submitted, we could not submit. We are answerable for them to our God. The legitimate powers of government extend to such acts only as are injurious to others. But it does me no injury for my neighbor to say there are twenty gods, or no God. It neither picks my pocket nor breaks my leg. If it be said, his testimony in a court of justice cannot be relied on, reject it then, and be the stigma on him. Constraint may make him worse by making him a hypocrite, but it will never make him a truer man. It may fix him obstinately in his errors, but will not cure them.

Reason and free inquiry are the only effectual agents against error. Give a loose to them, they will support the true religion by bringing every false one to their tribunal, to the test of their investigation. They are the natural enemies of error, and of error only. Had not the Roman government permitted free inquiry, Christianity could never have been introduced. Had not free inquiry been indulged at the era of the Reformation, the corruptions of Christianity could not have been purged away. If it be restrained now, the present corruptions will be protected, and new ones encouraged. Was the government to prescribe to us our medicine and diet, our bodies would be in such keeping as our souls are now... . Galileo was sent to the Inquisition for affirming that the earth was a sphere; the government had declared it to be as flat as a trencher, and Galileo was obliged to abjure his error. This error, however, at length prevailed, the earth became a globe, and Descartes declared it was whirled round on its axis by a vortex... the Newtonian principle of gravitation is now more firmly established on the basis of reason, than it would be were the government to step in, and to make it an article of necessary faith. Reason and experiment have been indulged, and error has fled before them. It is error alone which needs the support of government. Truth can stand by itself... .

Difference of opinion is advantageous in religion. The several sects perform the office of a *censor morum* over each other. Is uniformity attainable? Millions of innocent men, women, and children, since the introduction of Christianity have been burnt, tortured, fined, imprisoned; yet we have not advanced one inch towards uniformity. What has been the effect of coercion? To make one half the world fools, and the other half hypocrites. To support roguery and error all over the earth. Let us reflect that it is inhabited by a thousand millions of people. That these profess probably a thousand different systems of religion. That ours is but one of that thousand. That if there be but one right, and ours that one, we should wish to see the nine hundred and ninety nine wandering sects gathered into the fold of truth. But against such a majority we cannot effect this by force. Reason and persuasion are the only practicable instruments. To make way for these, free inquiry must be indulged; and how can we wish others to indulge it while we refuse it ourselves?

But every State, says an inquisitor, has established some religion. No two, say I, have established the same. Is this a proof of the infalibility of establishment? Our sister States of Pennsylvania and New York, however, have long subsisted without any establishment at all. The experiment was new and doubtful when they made it. It has answered beyond conception. They flourish infinitely. Religion is well supported; of various kinds, indeed, but all good enough; all sufficient to preserve peace and order; or if a sect arises, whose tenets would subvert morals, good sense and fair play, then reason laughs it out of doors, without suffering the State to be troubled with it. They do not hang more malefactors than we do. They are not disturbed with religious dissensions. On the contrary, their harmony is unparalleled, and can be ascribed to nothing but their unbounded tolerance, because there is no other circumstance in which they differ from every nation on earth. They have made the happy discovery, that the way to silence religious disputes is to take no notice of them. Let us too give this experiment fair play, and get rid, while we may, of these tyrannical laws... .

I doubt whether the people of this country would suffer an execution for heresy, or a three years' imprisonment for not comprehending the mysteries of the Trinity. But is the spirit of the people an infallible... reliance? Is it government? Is this the kind of protection we receive in return for the rights we give up? Besides, the spirit of the time may alter, will alter. Our rulers will become corrupt, our people careless. A single zealot may commence persecutor, and better men be his victims. It can never be too often repeated, that the time for fixing every essential right on a legal basis is while our rulers are honest, and ourselves united. From the conclusion of this war, we shall be going down hill. It will not then be necessary to resort every moment to the people for support. They will be forgotten, therefore, and their rights disregarded. They will forget themselves, but in the sole faculty of making money, and will never think of uniting to effect a due respect for their rights. The shackles, therefore, which shall not be knocked off at the conclusion of this war, will remain on us long, will be made heavier and heavier, till our rights shall revive or expire in a convulsion.

Bigotry, Intolerance, and Persecution

ME X 273-76 Levi Lincoln 8-26-01

The Palladium is understood to be the *clerical* paper, and from the clergy I expect no mercy. They crucified their Saviour, who preached that their kingdom was not of this world; and all who practice on that precept must expect the extreme of their wrath. The laws of the present day withhold their hands from blood; but lies and slander still remain to them.

ME X 376-78 Edward Dowse 4-19-03

I never will, by any word or act, bow to the shrine of intolerance, or admit a right of enquiry into the religious opinions of others. On the contrary, we are bound, you, I, and every one, to make common cause, even with error itself, to maintain the common right of freedom of conscience. We ought with one heart and one hand to hew down the daring and dangerous efforts of those who would seduce the public opinion to substitute itself into that tyranny over religious faith which the laws have so justly abdicated.

ME I 433-34 Anas 2-1-00

Doctor Rush tells me that... when the clergy addressed General Washington on his departure from the government, it was observed in their consultation that he had never, on any occasion, said a word to the public which showed a belief in the Christian religion; and they thought they should so pen their address, as to force him at length to declare publickly whether he was a Christian or not. They did so. However, he observed, the old fox was too cunning for them. He answered every article of their address particularly, except that, which he passed over without notice. Rush observed, he never did say a word on the subject in any of his public papers... .

ME X 236-37 Moses Robinson 3-25-01

The Eastern States will be the last to come over [to republicanism], on account of the domination of the clergy, who had got a smell of union between Church and State, and began to indulge reveries which can never be realized in the present state of science. If, indeed, they could have prevailed on us to view all advances in science as dangerous innovations, and to look back to the opinions and practices of our forefathers, instead of looking forward, for improvement, a promising groundwork would have been laid. But I am in hopes that their good sense will dictate to them, that since the mountain will not come to them, they had better go to the mountain; that they will find their interest in acquiescing in the liberty and science of their country, and that the Christian religion, when divested of the rags in which they have enveloped it, and brought to the original purity and simplicity of its benevolent institutor, is a religion of all others most friendly to liberty, science, and the freest expansion of the human mind.

ME XIV 126-129 N. G. DuFief 4-19-14

I am really mortified to be told that, in the *United States of America,* a fact like this [the publication of a scientific work] can become a subject of inquiry, and of criminal inquiry too, as an offence against religion; that a question about the sale of a book can be carried before the civil magistrate. Is this then our freedom of religion? and are we to have a censor whose imprimatur shall say what books may be sold, and what we may buy? And who is thus to dogmatize religious opinions for our citizens? Whose foot is to be the measure to which ours are to be cut or stretched? Is a priest to be our inquisitor, or shall a layman, simple as ourselves, set up his reason as the rule for what we are to read, and what we must believe? It is an insult to our citizens to question whether they are rational beings or not, and blasphemy against religion to suppose it cannot stand the test of truth and reason. If M. De Becourt's book be false in its facts, disprove them; if false in its reasoning, refute it. But, for God's sake, let us freely hear both sides, if we choose... .

I have just been reading the new constitution of Spain. One of its fundamental bases is expressed in these words: "The *Roman Catholic* religion, the only true one, is, and always will be, that of the Spanish nation. The government protects it by wise and just laws, and prohibits the exercise of any other whatever." Now I wish this presented to those who question what you may sell, or we may buy, with a request to strike out the words, "Roman Catholic," and to insert the denomination of their own religion. This would ascertain the code of dogmas which each wishes should domineer over the opinions of all others, and be taken, like the Spanish religion, under the "protection of wise and just laws." It would show to what they wish to reduce the liberty for which one generation has sacrificed life and happiness. It would present our boasted freedom of religion as a thing of theory only, and not of practice.

ME XIV 118-20 Horatio Spafford 3-17-14

In every country and in every age, the priest has been hostile to liberty. He is always in alliance with the despot, abetting his abuses in return for protection to his own. It is easier to acquire wealth and power by this combination than by deserving them... .

FORD X 13 Horatio Gates Spafford 1816

The sway of the clergy in New England is indeed formidable. No mind beyond mediocrity dares there develop itself. If it does, they excite against it the public opinion which they command, and by little, but incessant and tearing persecutions, drive it out from among them. Their present emigrations to the western country are real flights from persecution, religious and political... .

ME XVIII 286-87 William Short 5-15-15

Among the victims of his [Bonaparte's] return to power, I contemplate but one with pleasure: that is the Pope. The insult which he and the bigot of Spain have offered to the lights of the nineteenth century by the reestablishment of the Inquisition admits no forgiveness. How happily distant are we from the Bedlam of Europe!

ME XV 131-35 Albert Gallatin 6-16-17

...an act of the legislature of New York... will carry us back to the times of the darkest bigotry and barbarism, to find a parallel. Its purport is, that all those who shall *hereafter* join in communion with the religious sect of Shaking Quakers, shall be deemed civilly dead, their marriages dissolved, and all their children and property taken out of their hands. This act... contrasts with a contemporary vote of the Pennsylvania legislature, who, on a proposition to make the belief in God a necessary qualification for office, rejected it by a great majority, although assuredly there was not a single atheist in their body.

ME XV 241-48 William Short 4-13-20

The serious enemies [of our University] are the priests of the different religious sects, to whose spells on the human mind its improvement is ominous. Their pulpits are now resounding with denunciations against the appointment of Doctor Cooper, whom they charge as a monotheist in opposition to their tritheism. Hostile as these sects are, in every other point, to one another, they unite in maintaining their mystical theogony against those who believe there is one God only. The Presbyterian clergy are loudest; the most intolerant of all sects, the most tyrannical and ambitious; ready at the word of the lawgiver, if such a word could be now obtained, to put the torch to the pile, and to rekindle in this virgin hemisphere, the flames in which their oracle Calvin consumed the poor Servetus, because he could not find in his Euclid the proposition which has demonstrated that three are one and one is three, nor subscribe to that of Calvin, that magistrates have a right to exterminate all heretics to the

Calvinistic Creed. They pant to re-establish, *by law,* that holy inquisition, which they can now only infuse into *public opinion.* We have unwisely committed to the hierophants of our particular superstition, the direction of public opinion, that lord of the universe. We have given them stated and privileged days to collect and catechise us, opportunities of delivering their oracles to the people in mass, and of moulding their minds as wax in the hollow of their hands.

ME XV 252-56 General Robert Taylor 5-16-20

You may have heard of the hue and cry raised from the different pulpits on our appointment of Dr. Cooper, whom they charge with Unitarianism as boldly as if they knew the fact, and as presumptuously as if it were a crime, and one for which, like Servetus, he should be burned; and perhaps you may have seen the particular attack made on him in the Evangelical magazine. For myself, I was not disposed to regard the denunciations of these satellites of religious inquisition; but our colleagues, better judges of popular feeling, thought... it might be better to relieve Dr. Cooper, ourselves, and the institution from this crusade. I had received a letter from him expressing his uneasiness, not only for himself, but lest this persecution should become... injurious to the institution; with an offer to resign, if we had the same apprehensions... .

"I regret [he wrote] the storm that has been raised on my account; for it has separated me from many fond hopes and wishes. Whatever my religious creed may be, and perhaps I do not exactly know it myself, it is a pleasure to reflect that my conduct has not brought, and is not likely to bring, discredit to my friends."

ME XV 403-406 Doctor Thomas Cooper 11-2-22

The atmosphere of our country is unquestionably charged with a threatening cloud of fanaticism, lighter in some parts, denser in others, but too heavy in all. I had no idea, however, that in Pennsylvania, the cradle of toleration and freedom of religion, it could have risen to the height you describe. This must be owing to the growth of Presbyterianism. The blasphemy and absurdity of the five points of Calvin and the impossibility of defending them, render their advocates impatient of reasoning, irritable, and prone to denunciation... .

Their ambition and tyranny would tolerate no rival if they had power. Systematical in grasping at an ascendency over all other sects, they aim, like the Jesuits, at engrossing the education of the country, are hostile to every institution which they do not direct, and jealous at seeing others begin to attend at all to that object.

ME XIV 20-25 Baron Alexander von Humboldt 12-6-13

History, I believe, furnishes no example of a priest-ridden people maintaining a free civil government. This marks the lowest grade of ignorance, of which their civil as well as religious leaders will always avail themselves for their own purposes.

Clerical Enmity

ME XV 59-61 Mrs. M. Harrison Smith 8-6-16

...the priests indeed have heretofore thought proper to ascribe to me religious, or rather anti-religious sentiments, of their own fabric, but such as soothed their resentments against the act of Virginia for establishing religious freedom. They wished him to be thought atheist, deist, or devil, who could advocate freedom from their religious dictations. But I have ever thought religion a concern purely between our God and our consciences, for which we were accountable to Him, and not to the priests. I never told my own religion, nor scrutinized that of another. I never attempted to make a convert, nor wished to change another's creed. I have ever judged of the religion of others by their lives, and by this test, my dear Madam, I have been satisfied yours must be an excellent one, to have produced a life of such exemplary virtue and correctness. For it is in our lives, and not from our words, that our religion must be read. By the same test the world must judge me.

But this does not satisfy the priesthood. They must have a positive, a declared assent to all their interested absurdities. My opinion is that there never would have been an infidel, if there had never been a priest. The artificial structures they have built on the purest of all moral systems, for the purpose of deriving from it pence and power, revolt those who think for themselves, and who read in that system only what is really there. These, therefore, they brand with such nick-names as their enmity chooses gratuitously to impute. I have left the world, in silence, to judge of causes from their effects; and I am consoled in this course, my dear friend, when I perceive the candor with which I am judged by your justice and discernment; and that, notwithstanding the slanders of the saints, my fellow citizens have thought me worthy of trusts. The imputations of irreligion having spent their force... , I shall leave them, as heretofore, to grope on in the dark.

ME XIII 252-56 John Adams 6-15-13

This letter will gratify the priesthood with new occasions for repeating their comminations against me. They wish it to be believed that he can have no religion who advocates its freedom.

Jefferson in Power, by Claude Bowers 145, 265, 361

Jefferson, who, more than any other single man, had insisted on the separation of Church and State and had fought a successful battle on the issue in the Virginia Assembly, had been habitually denounced as an anti-Christ by the political preachers of his time. He was still hated in Virginia for breaking the connection, and in the New England States, where the greater part of the ministers were militant Federalists, he was hated with an unholy hate. More false witness had been borne by the ministers of New England and New York against Jefferson than had ever been borne against any other American... . History has shown that on no subject can human passions be aroused to such a murderous frenzy as on that of man's relation to his Maker.

And what a dreadful man was Jefferson! Had he not invited Tom Paine to the White House? Was he not an anti-Christ?

Throughout New England, the Jeffersonian fight against the political domination of the clergy was pronounced as an attack on 'religion' under the direction of the 'Anti-Christ' in the White House.

ME X 173-76 Benjamin Rush 9-23-00

I promised you a letter on Christiantiy... the *genus irritabile vatum...* are all in arms against me. Their hostility is on too interesting ground to be softened. The delusion into which the X.Y.Z. plot showed it possible to push the people; the successful experiment made under the prevalence of that delusion on the clause of the Constitution, which, while it secured the freedom of the press, covered also the freedom of religion, had given to the clergy a very favorite hope of obtaining an establishment of a particular form of Christianity throughout the United States; and as every sect believes its own form the true one, every one perhaps hoped for his own, but especially the Episcopalians and Congregationalists [Calvinists].

The returning good sense of our country threatens abortion to their hopes, and they believe that any portion of power confided to me, will be exerted in opposition to their schemes. And they believe rightly: for I have sworn upon the altar of God, eternal hostility against every form of tyranny over the mind of man. But this is all they have to fear from me: and enough too in their opinion. And this is the cause of their printing lying pamphlets against me, forging conversations for me... which are absolute falsehoods without a circumstance of truth to rest on... .

The Subversion of Christianity

ME VII 252-59 Dr. Price 1-8-89

I concur with you strictly in your opinion of the comparative merits of atheism and daemonism, and really see nothing but the latter in the Being worshipped by many who think themselves Christians.

ME X 251-55 Elbridge Gerry 3-29-01

..the clergy live by the zeal they can kindle, and the schisms they can create. It is contest of opinion... which makes us take great interest in them, and bestow our money liberally on those who furnish aliment to our appetite. The mild and simple principles of the Christian philosophy would produce too much calm, too much regularity of good, to extract from its disciples a support for a numerous priesthood, were they not to sophisticate it, ramify it, split it into hairs, and twist its texts till they... require a priesthood to explain them. The Quakers... have no priests, therefore no schisms.

ME XV 425-30 John Adams 4-11-23

I can never join Calvin in addressing *his God.* He was indeed an atheist, which I can never be; or rather his religion is daemonism. If ever man worshipped a false God, he did.. a daemon of malignant spirit. It would be more pardonable to believe in no God at all, than to blaspheme Him by the atrocious attributes of Calvin.

ME XII 345-47 Samuel Kercheval 1-19-10

Nothing can be more exactly or more seriously true than... that but a short time elapsed after the death of a great reformer of the Jewish religion, before his principles were departed from by those who professed to be his special servants, and perverted into an engine for enslaving mankind... a mere contrivance to filch wealth and power to themselves: that rational man, not being able to swallow their impious heresies, in order to force them down their throats, they raise the hue and cry of infidelity, while themselves are the greatest obstacles to the advancement of the real doctrines of Jesus, and do, in fact, constitute the real Anti-Christ.

ME XIV 144-51 John Adams 7-5-14

In truth he [Plato] is one of the race of genuine sophists, who has escaped the oblivion of his brethren... chiefly, by the adoption and incorporation of his whimsies into the body of artificial Christianity... . Yet this, which should have consigned him to early oblivion, really procured him immortality of fame and reverence. The Christian priesthood, finding the doctrines of Christ levelled to every understanding, and too plain to need explanation, saw in the mysticism of Plato, materials with which they might build up an artificial system, which might, from its indistinctness, admit everlasting controversy, give employment for their order, and introduce it to profit, power, and pre-eminence.

ME XV 202-04 Ezra Stiles 6-25-19

You say you are a Calvinist. I am not. I am a sect by myself, as far as I know. I am not a Jew, and therefore do not adopt their theology, which supposes the God of infinite justice to punish the sins of the fathers upon their children unto the third and the fourth generation; and the benevolent and sublime Reformer of that religion has told us only that God is good and perfect, but has not defined him.

ME XIV 232-34 Charles Clay, Esq. 1-29-05

I abuse the priests, indeed, who have so much abused the pure and holy scriptures of their Master... to make them the instruments of wealth,... and power and pre-eminence to themselves. And while I have classed them with soothsayers and necromancers, I place Him among the greatest... scourges of priestcraft that have ever existed. They felt Him as such, and never rested until they had silenced Him by death. But His heresies against Judaism prevailing in the long run, the priests have tacked about and rebuilt upon them the temple which he destroyed, as splendid, as profitable, and as imposing as that.

ME XVI 42-48 Major John Cartwright 6-5-24

I was glad to find in your book a formal contradiction of the judiciary usurpation of legislative powers; for such the judges have usurped in their repeated decisions, that Christianity is a part of the common law. The proof to the contrary, which you have adduced, is incontrovertible: to wit, that the common law existed while the Anglo Saxons were yet pagans, at a time when they had never yet heard the name of Christ... .

ME XVI 100-01 General Alexander Smyth 1-17-25

It is between fifty and sixty years since I read it [the Apocalypse], and I then considered it as merely the ravings of a maniac, no more worthy nor capable of explanation than the incoherences of our own nightly dreams. ...I do not consider them as revelations of the Supreme Being, whom I would not so far blaspheme as to impute to Him a pretension of revelation, couched at the same time in terms which, He would know, were never to be understood by those to whom they were addressed.

ME XV 373-74 Rev. Thomas Whittemore 6-5-22

I have never permitted myself to meditate a specified creed. These formulas have been the bane and ruin of the Christian Church..., which, through so many ages, made of Christendom a slaughter-house, and at this day divides it into castes of inextinguishable hatred to one another. Witness the present internecine rage of all other sects against the Unitarian. The religions of antiquity had no particular formulas or creed... the Quakers have none. And hence, alone, the harmony, the quiet, and brotherly affections... of the Society of Friends, and I hope the Unitarians will follow their happy example.

Theology and Religious Theory

ME XV 425-30 John Adams 4-11-23

I think that every Christian sect gives a great handle to atheism by their general dogma, that, without revelation, there would not be sufficient proof of the being of a God. Now one-sixth of mankind only are supposed to be Christians; the other five-sixths, then, who do not believe in the Jewish and Christian revelation, are without knowledge of the existence of God! That gives [a basis for the hypothesis]... that it is more simple to believe at once in the eternal pre-existence of the world, as it is now going on, and may forever go on, by the principle of reproduction which we see and witness, than to believe in the eternal pre-existence of an ulterior cause, or Creator of the world, a Being whom we see not and know not, of whose form, substance, and mode, or place of existence, or of action, no sense informs us, no power of the mind enables us to delineate or comprehend.

On the contrary, I hold, (without appeal to revelation) that when we take a view of the universe, in its parts, general or particular, it is impossible for the human mind not to perceive and feel a conviction of design, consummate skill, and indefinite power in every atom of its composition. The movements of the heavenly bodies, so exactly held in their course by the balance of centrifugal and centripetal forces; the structure of our earth itself, with its distribution of lands, waters, and atmosphere; animal and vegetable bodies, examined in all their minutest particles; insects, mere atoms of life, yet as perfectly organized as man or mammoth; the mineral substances, their generation and uses; it is impossible, I say, for the human mind not to believe, that there is in all this, design, cause, and effect, up to an ultimate cause, a Fabricator of all things from matter and motion, their Preserver and Regulator while permitted to exist in their present forms, and their regeneration into new and other forms.

We see, too, evident proofs of the necessity of a superintending power, to maintain the universe in its course and order... . So irresistible are these evidences of an intelligent and powerful Agent, that, of the infinite numbers of men who have existed through all time, they have believed, in the proportion of a million at least to unit, in the hypothesis of an eternal pre-existence of a Creator, rather than in that of a self-existent universe.

Reason and Morality vs. Clerical Dogma

ME VI 256-62 Peter Carr 8-10-87

Religion. Your reason is now mature enough to examine this object. In the first place, divest yourself of all bias in favor of novelty and singularity of opinion. Indulge them in any other subject rather than that of religion. It is too important and the consequences of error may be too serious. On the other hand, shake off all the fears and servile prejudices, under which weak minds are servilely crouched. Fix reason firmly in her seat, and call to her tribunal every fact, every opinion. Question with boldness even the existence of God; because, if there be one, he must more approve of the homage of reason, than that of blindfolded fear.

You will naturally examine first, the religion of your own country. Read the Bible, then, as you would read Livy or Tacitus. The facts which are within the ordinary course of nature, you will believe on the authority of the writer, as you do those of the same kind in Livy and Tacitus. The testimony of the writer weighs in their favor in one scale; and their not being against the laws of nature, does not weigh against them. But those facts in the Bible which contradict the laws of nature, must be examined with more care, and under a variety of faces. Here you must recur to the pretensions of the writer to inspiration from God. Examine upon what evidence his pretensions are founded, and whether that evidence is so strong, as that its falsehood would be more improbable than a change in the laws of nature, in the case he relates. For example, in the book of Joshua, we are told, the sun stood still several hours. Were we to read that fact in Livy or Tacitus, we should class it with their showers of blood, speaking of statues, beasts, etc. But it is said, that the writer of that book was inspired. Examine, therefore, candidly, what evidence there is of his having been inspired. The pretension is entitled to your enquiry, because millions believe it. On the other hand, you are astronomer enough to know how contrary it is to the law of nature that a body revolving on its axis, as the earth does, should have stopped, should not, by that sudden stoppage, have prostrated animals, trees, buildings, and should after a certain time have resumed its revolution, and that without a second general prostration. Is this arrest of the earth's motion, or the evidence which affirms it, most within the law of probabilities?

You will read next the New Testament. It is the history of a personage called Jesus. Keep in your eye the opposite pretensions: 1, of those who say he was begotten by God, born of a virgin, suspended and reversed the laws of nature at will, and ascended bodily into heaven; and 2, of those who say he was a man of illegitimate birth, of a benevolent heart, enthusiastic mind, who set out without pretensions to divinity, ended in believing them, and was punished capitally for sedition, by being gibbeted, according to Roman law... .

These questions are examined in the books I have mentioned, under the head of Religion, and several others. They will assist you in your enquiries; but keep your reason firmly on the watch in reading them all. Do not be frightened from this inquiry by any fear of its consequences. If it ends in a belief that there is no God, you will find incitements to virtue in the comfort and pleasantness you feel in its exercise, and the love of others which it will procure you. If you find reason to believe there is a God, a consciousness that you are acting under his eyes, and that he approves you, will be a vast additional incitement; if that there be a future state, the hope of a happy existence in that increases the appetite to deserve it; if that Jesus was also a God, you will be comforted by a belief of his aid and love.

In fine, I repeat, you must lay aside all prejudice on both sides, and neither believe nor reject anything, because any other persons, or descriptions of persons, have rejected or believed it. Your own reason is the only oracle given you by heaven, and you are answerable, not for the rightness, but the uprightness of the decision. I forgot to observe, when speaking of the New Testament, that you should read all the histories of Christ [including] those which a council of ecclesiastics have decided for us, to be Pseudo-evangelists... . Because those Pseudo-evangelists pretended to inspiration, as much as the others, you are to judge their pretensions by your own reason, and not by the reason of those ecclesiastics.

ME VI 154-56 Thomas Seymour 2-11-07

It would seem impossible that an intelligent people, with the faculty of reading and the right of thinking, should continue much longer to slumber under the pupilage of an interested aristocracy of priests and lawyers, persuading them to distrust themselves, and to let them think for them. I sincerely wish that your efforts may awaken them from this voluntary degradation of mind, restore them to a due estimate of themselves and their fellow citizens, and a just abhorrence of the falsehoods and artifices which have seduced them.

Ford IX 410 John Adams 1813

If thinking men would have the courage to think for themselves, and to speak what they think, it would be found that they do not differ in religious opinions as much as is supposed.

ME XV 97-100 John Adams 1-11-17

The result of your fifty or sixty years of religious reading, in the four words, "Be just and good," is that in which all our inquiries must end... . What we all agree in, is probably right. What no two agree in, most probably wrong.

ME XIV 196-97 Miles King 9-26-14

Hitherto, I have been under the guidance of that portion of reason which He had thought proper to deal out to me. I have followed it faithfully in all important cases, to such degree at least as leaves me without uneasiness; and if on minor occasions I have erred from its dictates, I have trust in Him who made us what we are, and know it was not His plan to make us always unerring. He has formed us moral agents. Not that, in the perfection of His state, He can feel pain or pleasure in anything we may do. He is far above our power; but that we may promote the happiness of those with whom He has placed us in society, by acting honestly towards all, benevolently to those who fall within our way, respecting sacredly their rights, bodily and mental, and cherishing especially their freedom of conscience, as we value our own.

I must ever believe that religion substantially good which produces an honest life; and we have been authorized by One whom you and I equally respect, to judge of the tree by its fruit. Our particular principles of religion are a subject of accountability to our God alone. I inquire after no man's, and trouble none with mine; nor is it given to us in this life to know whether yours, or mine, our friends or our foes, are exactly the right. Nay, we have heard it said that there is not a Quaker, or a Baptist, a Presbyterian, or an Episcopalian, a Catholic or a Protestant in heaven; that, on entering that gate, we leave these badges of schism behind, and find ourselves united in those principles only in which God has united us all. Let us not be uneasy then about the different roads we may pursue, as believing them the shortest, to that last abode; but, following the guidance of a good conscience, let us be happy in the hope that by these different paths we shall all meet in the end. And that you and I may meet there and embrace, is my earnest prayer.

Epicureanism

ME XIV 385-87 Charles Thompson 1-9-16

The doctrine of Epicurus... is the most rational system remaining of the philosophy of the ancients... frugal of vicious indulgence, and fruitful of virtue...

ME XV 219-24 William Short 10-31-19

As you say of yourself, I too am an Epicurean.

The Quakers

ME XII 345-47 Samuel Kercheval 1-19-10

You expect that your book will have some effect on the prejudices which the Society of Friends entertain against the present and late administrations. In this I think you will be disappointed. The Friends are men formed with the same passions, and swayed by the same natural principles and prejudices as others. In cases where the passions are neutral, men will display their respect for the religious *professions* of their sect. But where their passions are enlisted, these *professions* are no obstacle. You observe very truly, that both the late and present administration conducted the government on principles *professed* by the Friends. Our efforts to preserve peace, our measures as to the Indians, as to slavery, as to religious freedom, were all in consonance with their *profession.* Yet I never expected we should get a vote from them, and in this I was neither deceived nor disappointed. There is no riddle in this to those who do not suffer themselves to be duped by the *professions* of religious sectaries. The theory of American Quakerism is a very obvious one. The mother society is in England. Its members are English by birth and residence, devoted to their own country as good citizens ought to be. The Quakers of these States are colonies or filiations from the mother society, to whom that society sends its yearly lessons. On these, the filiated societies model their opinions, their conduct, their passions and attachments. A Quaker is essentially an Englishman, in whatever part of the earth he is born or lives. The outrages of Great Britain on our navigation and commerce, have kept us in perpetual bickerings with her. The Quakers here have taken sides against their own government, not on their profession of peace, for they saw that peace was our object also, but from devotion to the views of the mother society. In 1797-8, when an administration sought war with France, the Quakers were the most clamorous for war. The principle of peace, as a secondary one, yielded to the primary one of adherence to the Friends in England, and what was patriotism in the original, became treason in the copy. On that occasion, they obliged their good old leader, Mr. Pemberton, to erase his name from a petition to Congress against war, which had been delivered to a Representative of Pennsylvania, a member of the late and present administration; he accordingly permitted the old gentleman to erase his name. You must not therefore expect that your book will have any more effect on the Society of Friends here, than on the English merchants settled among us. I apply this to the Friends in general, not universally. I know some individuals among them as good patriots as we have.

ME XV 114-18 de La Fayette 5-14-17

Little Delaware... is essentially a Quaker State, the fragments of a religious sect which there, as in the other States, and in England, are a homogeneous mass, acting with one mind, and that directed by the Mother Society in England. Dispersed, as the Jews, they still form, as those do, one nation, foreign to the land they live in. They are Protestant Jesuits, implicitly devoted to the will of their superior, and forgetting all duties to their country in the execution of the policy of their order. When war is proposed with England, they have religious scruples; but when with France, these are laid by, and they become clamorous for it. They are, however, silent, passive, and give no other trouble... .

Desire for Religious Privacy

ME XI 53-4 John Mercer 10-9-04

...with a Quaker or a Catholic, I would avoid speaking on religion.

ME XIV 232-34 Charles Clay, Esq. 1-29-15

Of publishing a book on religion, my dear Sir, I never had an idea. I should as soon think of writing for the reformation of Bedlam, as of the world of religious sects. Of these, there must be, at least, ten thousand, every individual of every one of which believes all wrong but his own. To undertake to bring them all right, would be like undertaking single-handed, to fell all the forests of America... .

I not only write nothing on religion, but rarely permit myself to speak on it, and never but in a reasonable society. I have probably said more to you than to any other person, because we have had more hours of conversation *in duetto* in our meetings at the Forest.

FORD IX 238 Thomas Leiper 1809

Neither of us knows the religious opinions of the other; that is a matter between our Maker and ourselves.

CE VII 55 John Adams 1817

...priests... I certainly never made the confidants of my creed... my religion... is known to my God and myself alone. Its evidence before the world is to be sought in my life; if that has been honest and *dutiful* to society, the religion which has regulated it, cannot be a bad one.

ME XV 390-92 Dr. Benjamin Waterhouse 8-19-22

I should not so soon have troubled you with an acknowledgement of your favor of the 8th, but for the request it contained of my consent to the publication of my letter of June the 26th. No, my dear Sir, not for the world. Into what a nest of hornets would it thrust my head! the *genus irritable vatum*, on whom argument is lost, and reason is, by themselves, disclaimed in matters of religion. Don Quixote undertook to redress the bodily wrongs of the world, but the redressment of mental vagaries would be an enterprise more than Quixotic. I should as soon undertake to bring the crazy skulls of Bedlam to sound understanding, as inculcate reason into that of an Athanasian. I am old, and tranqullity is now my *summom bonum*. Keep me, therefore, from the fire and fagots of Calvin and his victim Servetus.

Hope or Expectation of Immortality

ME XIII 394-403 John Adams 10-28-13

I hope your quiet is not to be affected at this day by the rudeness or intemperance of scribblers, but that you may continue in tranqulllity to live and to rejoice in the prosperity of our country, until it shall be your own wish to take your seat among the aristoi who have gone before you.

CE VII 108 John Adams 1818

The term is not very distant, at which we are to deposit in the same cerement, our sorrows and suffering bodies, and to ascend in essence to an ecstatic meeting with the friends we have loved and lost, and whom we shall still love and never lose again.

ME XVIII 308-10 Maria Cosway 12-27-20

...the religion you so sincerely profess tells us we shall meet again; and we have all so lived as to be assured it will be in happiness. Mine is the next turn, and I shall meet it with good will, for after one's friends are all gone before them, and our faculties leaving us, too, one by one, why wish to linger in mere vegetation — as a solitary trunk in a desolate field, from which all its former companions have disappeared?

ME XVI 42-52 Major John Cartwright 6-5-24

Your age of eighty-four and mine of eighty-one years, insure us of a speedy meeting. We may then commune at leisure, and more fully, on the good and evil which, in the course of our long lives, we have both witnessed; and, in the meantime, I pray you to accept assurance of my high veneration and esteem for your person and character.

Joseph Priestley and Unitarianism

ME XIII 349-53 John Adams 8-22-13

I remember to have heard Dr. Priestley say, that if all England would candidly examine themselves, and confess, they would find that Unitarianism was really the religion of all; and I observe a bill is now depending in parliament for the relief of Anti-Trinitarians. It is too late in the day for men of sincerity to pretend they believe in the Platonic mysticisms that three are one, and one is three; and yet that the one is not three, and three are not one; to divide mankind by a single letter into *homoousian* and *homoiousian*. But this constitutes the craft, the power, and the profit of the priests. Sweep away their gossamer fabrics of factitious religion, and they would catch no more flies. We should all then, like the Quakers, live without an order of priests, moralize for ourselves, follow the oracle of conscience, and say nothing about what no man can understand, nor therefore believe... .

ME XV 390-92 Dr. Benjamin Waterhouse 8-19-22

I am not unaware of the peculiar resistance to Unitarianism... . When I lived in Philadelphia, there was a respectable congregation of that sect, with a meeting-house and regular service which I attended, and in which Doctor Priestley officiated to numerous audiences... . That doctrine has not yet been preached to us; but the breeze begins to be felt which precedes the storm; and fanaticism is all in a bustle, shutting its doors and windows to keep it out... .

A bold and eloquent preacher would be nowhere listened to with more freedom than in this State, nor with more firmness of mind. They might need a preparatory discourse on the text of "prove all things, hold fast that which is good," in order to unlearn the lesson that reason is an unlawful guide in religion... . The preacher might be excluded by our hierophants from their churches and meeting-houses, but would be attended in the fields by whole acres of hearers and thinkers. Missionaries from Cambridge would soon be greeted with more welcome, than from the tritheistic school of Andover.

ME XV 403-406 Doctor Thomas Cooper 11-2-22

In Boston, however, and its neighborhood, Unitarianism has advanced to so great strength, as now to humble this haughtiest of all religious sects [the Presbyterian]; insomuch, that they condescend to interchange with them and the other sects, the civilities of preaching freely and frequently in each others' meeting-houses. In Rhode Island, on the other hand, no sectarian preacher will permit an Unitarian to pollute his desk... .

The diffusion of instruction, to which there is now so growing an attention, will be the remote remedy to this fever of fanaticism; while the more proximate one will be the progress of Unitarianism. That this will, ere long, be the religion of the majority from North to South, I have no doubt.

ME XV 408-10 James Smith 12-8-22

I have to thank you for your pamphlets on the subject of Unitarianism, and to express my gratification with your efforts for the revival of primitive Christianity in your quarter. No historical fact is better established, than that the doctrine of one God, pure and uncompounded, was that of the early ages of Christianity; and was among the efficacious doctrines which gave it triumph over the polytheism of the ancients, sickened with the absurdities of their own theology. Nor was the unity of the Supreme Being ousted from the Christian creed by the force of reason, but by the sword of the civil government, wielded at the will of the fanatic Athanasius. The hocus-pocus phantasm of a God like another Cerberus, with one body and three heads, had its birth and growth in the blood of thousands and thousands of martyrs. And a strong proof of the solidity of the primitive faith, is its restoration, as soon as a nation arises which vindicates to itself the freedom of religious opinion, and its external divorce from the civil authority. The pure and simple unity of the Creator of the universe, is now all but ascendant in the Eastern States; it is dawning in the West, and advancing towards the South; and I confidently expect that the present generation will see Unitarianism become the general religion of the United States. The Eastern presses are giving us many excellent pieces on the subject, and Priestley's learned writings on it are, or should be, in every hand. In fact, the Athanasian paradox that one is three, and three but one, is so incomprehensible to the human mind, that no candid man can say he has any idea of it, and how can he believe what presents no idea? He who thinks he does, only deceives himself. He proves, also, that man, once surrendering his reason, has no remaining guard against absurdities the most monstrous, and like a ship without rudder, is the sport of every wind. With such persons, gullibility, which they call faith, takes the helm from the hand of reason, and the mind becomes a wreck.

I write with freedom, because, while I claim a right to believe in one God, if so my reason tells me, I yield freely to others that of believing in three. Both religions, I find, make honest men, and that is the only point society has any right to look to. Although this mutual freedom should produce mutual indulgence, yet I wish not to be brought in question before the public on this or any other subject, and I pray you to consider me as writing under that trust... . At the age of eighty, tranquillity is the greatest good of life, and the strongest of our desires that of dying in the good will of mankind. And with the assurance of good will to Unitarian and Trinitarian, to Whig and Tory, accept for yourself that of my entire respect.

ME XV 383-85 Dr. Benjamin Waterhouse 6-26-22

But much I fear, that when this great truth [Unitarianism] shall be re-established, its votaries will fall into the fatal error of fabricating formulas of creed and confessions of faith, the engines which so soon destroyed the religion of Jesus, and made of Christendom a mere Aceldama; that they will give up morals for mysteries, and Jesus for Plato. How much wiser are the Quakers, who, agreeing in the fundamental doctrines of the Gospel, schismatize about no mysteries, and, keeping within the pale of common sense, suffer no speculative differences of opinion, any more than that of feature, to impair the love of their brethren. Be this the wisdom of Unitarians, this the holy mantle which shall cover within its charitable circumference all who believe in one God, and who love their neighbor! [The Unitarians did not abolish their creed until about 1926].

The Separation of Church and State

ME XIV 232-34 Charles Clay, Esq. 1-29-15

Government, as well as religion, has furnished its schisms, its persecutions, and its devices for fattening idleness on the earnings of the people. It has its heirarchy of emperors, kings, princes, and nobles, as that has of popes, cardinals, archbishops, bishops, and priests. In short, cannibals are not to be found in the wilds of America only, but are revelling on the blood of every living people. Turning, then, from this loathsome combination of Church and State, and weeping over the follies of our fellow men who yield themselves the willing dupes and drudges of these mountebanks, I consider reformation and redress as desperate, and abandon them to the Quixotism of more enthusiastic minds.

ME XI 428-30 Rev. Samuel Miller 1-23-08

I consider the government of the United States interdicted by the Constitution from intermeddling with religious institutions, their doctrines, discipline, or exercises. This results not only from the provision that no law shall be made respecting the establishment or free exercise of religion, but from that also which reserves to the States the powers not delegated to the United States.

Certainly, no power to prescribe any religious exercise, or to assume authority in religious discipline, has been delegated to the General Government. It must then rest with the States, as far as it can be in any human authority. But it is only proposed that I should *recommend,* not prescribe, a day of fasting and prayer. That is, that I should *indirectly* assume to the United States an authority over religious exercises which the Constitution has directly precluded them from. It must be meant, too, that this recommendation is to carry some authority, and to be sanctioned by some penalty on those who disregard it; not indeed of fine and imprisonment, but of some degree of proscription, perhaps in public opinion. And does the change in the nature of the penalty make the recommendation less a *law* of conduct for those to whom it is directed? I do not believe it is for the interest of religion to invite the civil magistrate to direct its exercises, its discipline, or its doctrines; nor of the religious societies, that the General Government should be invested with the power of effecting any uniformity of time or matter among them.

Fasting and prayer are religious exercises; the enjoining them an act of discipline. Every religious society has a right to determine for itself the times for these exercises, and the objects proper for them, according to their own particular tenets; and this right can never be safer than in their own hands, where the Constitution has deposited it.

I am aware that the practice of my predecessors may be quoted. But I have ever believed, that the example of State executives led to the assumption of that authority by the General Government, without due examination, which would have discovered that what might be a right in a State government, was a violation of that right when assumed by another. Be this as it may, every one must act according to the dictates of his own reason, and mine tells me that civil powers alone have been given to the President of the United States, and no authority to direct the religious exercises of his constituents.

ME XVI 281-82 The Danbury Baptist Association 1-1-02

The affectionate sentiments of esteem and approbation which you are so good as to express towards me, on behalf of the Danbury Baptist Association, give me the highest satisfaction. My duties dictate a faithful and zealous pursuit of the interests of my constituents, and in proportion as they are persuaded of my fidelity to those duties, the discharge of them becomes more and more pleasing.

Believing with you that religion is a matter which lies solely between man and his God, that he owes account to none other for his faith or his worship, that the legislative powers of government reach actions only, and not opinions, I contemplate with sovereign reverence that act of the whole American people which declared that their legislature should "make no law respecting an establishment of religion, or prohibiting the free exercise thereof," thus building a wall of separation between Church and State. Adhering to this expression of the supreme will of the nation in behalf of the rights of conscience, I shall see with sincere satisfaction the progress of those sentiments which tend to restore to man all his natural rights, convinced he has no natural right in opposition to his social duties.

I reciprocate your kind prayers for the protection and blessing of the common Father and Creator of man, and tender you for yourselves and your religious association, assurances of my high respect and esteem.

22. Jesus and the Jefferson "Bible"

Commentary

A manuscript entitled The Life and Morals of Jesus of Nazareth *(sometimes referred to as* The Jefferson Bible), *was purchased by the National Museum in Washington in 1895. Originally, this consisted of 46 pages in English only, but it was later expanded to 82 pages, each one of which has four columns in Greek, Latin, French, and English; the text consists almost entirely of discourses attributed to Jesus; scarcely any of narration. Only 8 columns are from Mark and John — 70 verses from the former and 162 from the latter. Because the great bulk of these statements occur in Matthew and Luke, 40 columns are taken from the former and 32 from the latter. The entire manuscript is photographically reproduced in Volume XX of the* Writings of Thomas Jefferson, *published in 1905 by the Jefferson Memorial Association.*

Since it was Jefferson's intent to portray Jesus, not as a God-man or an atoning savior, but simply as a great moral teacher, Chapter 1 and 2 of Matthew and part of the third are omitted; and from Luke the first chapter as well as verses 8 to 40 of the second and 24 to 38 of the third, which describe the Annunciation, the virgin birth, the stories of the wise men and the shepherds, the flight to Egypt, the murder of the children by Herod, the presentation of the babe in the temple, and the geneologies of Joseph; also the many miracles, the expected parousia or second coming, and the post-crucifixion appearances of Jesus are omitted, as are the long Johannine theological dissertations and the bitter denunciations of the Scribes and Pharisees.

We include in this study Jefferson's statements concerning his Testament *as well as his "Syllabus of Jesus' Teachings Compared to Those of the Greek Philosophers"; his declarations which delineate Jesus as a great reformer of Jewish religion, practices, and morals; various passages which pay tribute to the elevation of his teachings; others also which seek a restitution and reconstruction thereof in order to rescue them from the perversions of dishonest and rapacious priesthoods; and, finally, his explanation of certain elements in the Gospels which may be genuine but with which he found himself in disagreement.*

It is indeed interesting to note that, even after returning to private life, and, in spite of his many explicit declarations to intimate friends, Jefferson cautioned them to respect his confidence in complete privacy, for, should his statements become known to the public, an avalanche of denunciations would be certain to ensue. He was often called the Anti-Christ foretold in Scripture. Although he would neither alter his convictions nor keep them entirely to himself, he denounced and refuted the dishonest accusations of atheism, etc., which his enemies levelled at him. It is also interesting to note that he distrusted the post office and therefore often sent his letters by private delivery.

We should be happy that the bigotry and outrages common in Jefferson's day have now to a large extent abated, a development due, at least in part, to his constant exposure and condemnation of them.

A study of Jefferson's writings reveals that in theology he was closest to what may be called Socinianism, a concept in which Jesus becomes a human being like all others, but endowed with great powers of persuasion and understanding and deeply devoted to basic reformation and morality. In this, he was very near to the viewpoint of the Deist, Thomas Paine, and the philosophic position of Joseph Priestley; it is doubtful that he would have been comfortable in the company of William Ellery Channing, the accepted American founder of Unitarianism, who adopted a credalized theology (a thing Jefferson abhorred), which approximated that of the Arians or the Semi-Arians of the early centuries who projected a species of Trinitarianism called the homoiousian — *in which Jesus appears, although still the Creative Word, as a power not identical with the Father-Creator, because he is subsequent, created, and inferior, but nevertheless of similar divine substance.*

As indicated in his "Bible," and in his written statements dealing with the subject, Jefferson rejected all supernaturalistic doctrines concerning Jesus as the fabrications invented by priesthoods to secure and enhance their power and wealth. Most of his references are general, rather than specific; he regarded Jesus as the great reformer of the Jewish system of religion and morals; there are only a few passages in which Jefferson spells out what he considered the fraudulent doctrines engrafted upon his original teachings. However, in one passage he declares that the story of Jesus' virgin birth will, in time, be equated with the generation of Minerva from the brain of Jove; and in another footnote he lists the specific orthodox doctrines which he rejected and abhorred.

The Preparation for the Gospel Testament

ME X 445-48 Doctor Joseph Priestley 1-29-04

I rejoice that you have undertaken the task of comparing the moral doctrines of Jesus with those of the ancient philosophers. You are so much in possession of the whole subject, that you will do it easier and better than any other person living. I think you cannot avoid giving, as preliminary to the comparison, a digest of his moral doctrines, extracted in his own words from the Evangelists, and leaving out everything relative to his personal history and character. It would be short and precious. With a view to do this for my own satisfaction, I had sent to Philadelphia to get two testaments (Greek) of the same edition, and two English, with a design to cut out the morsels of morality, and paste them on the leaves of a book, in the manner you describe as having been pursued in forming your Harmony.

ME XIII 387-92 John Adams 10-13-13

We must reduce our volume to the simple evangelists, select, even from them, the very words only of Jesus, paring off the amphibologisms into which they have been led, by forgetting often, or not understanding, what had fallen from him, by giving them our misconceptions as his dicta, and expressing unintelligibly for others what they had not understood themselves. There will be found remaining the most sublime and benevolent code of morals which has ever been offered to man. I have performed this operation for my own use, by cutting verse by verse out of the printed book and arranging the matter which is evidently his, and which is as easily distinguishable as diamonds in a dunghill. The result is an octavo of forty-six pages, of pure and unsophisticated doctrines, such as were professed and acted on by the unlettered apostles, the Apostolic Fathers, and the Christians of the first century.

ME XV 2-3 F. A. Van der Kemp 4-25-16

I made, for my own satisfaction, an extract from the Evangelists of His morals, selecting those only whose style and spirit proved them genuine, and His own... . I gave it the title "The Philosophy of Jesus Extracted from the Text of the Evangelists." To this... if a history of His life can be added, the world will see, after the fogs shall be dispelled, in which... He has been enveloped by jugglers to make money of Him, when the genuine character shall be exhibited which they have dressed up in the rags of an impostor, the world, I say, will at length see the immortal merit of this first of human sages.

ME XIV 385-87 Charles Thompson 1-9-16

I, too, have made a wee-little book... , which I call the Philosophy of Jesus; it is a paradigma of His doctrines, made by cutting the texts out of the book, and arranging them... in a certain order of time and subject. A more beautiful or precious morsel of ethics I have never seen; it is a document in proof that *I* am a *real Christian*, that is to say, a disciple of the doctrines of Jesus, very different from the Platonists, who call *me* infidel and *themselves* Christians and preachers of the gospel, while they draw all their characteristic dogmas from what its Author never said or saw.

They have compounded from the heathen mysteries a system beyond the comprehension of man, of which the Great Reformer of the vicious ethics and deism of the Jews, were He to return to earth, would not recognize one feature. If I had time, I would add to my little book the Greek, Latin, and French texts, in columns side by side. [This he did later, as we have noted.]

The Jefferson Syllabus

ME X 374-76 Dr. Joseph Priestley 4-9-03

In consequence of some conversations with Dr. Rush... I had promised some day to write him a letter giving him my view of the Christian system... . I should first take a general view of the moral doctrines of the most remarkable of the ancient philosophers..., say Pythagoras, Epicurus, Epictetus, Socrates, Cicero, Seneca, Antoninus... . I should then take a view of the deism and ethics of the Jews, and show in what a degraded state they were, and the necessity they presented of a reformation.

I should then proceed to a view of the life, character, and doctrines of Jesus, who, sensible of the incorrectness of their ideas of the Deity, and of morality, endeavored to bring them to the principles of a pure deism, and juster notions of the attributes of God, to reform their moral doctrines to the standard of reason, justice, and philanthropy, and to inculcate the belief of a future state. This view would purposely omit the question of his divinity, and even his inspiration. To do him justice, it would be necessary to remark the disadvantages his doctrines had to encounter, not having been committed to writing by himself, but by the most unlettered of men, by memory, long after they had heard them from him; when much was forgotten, much misunderstood, and presented in every paradoxical shape. Yet such are the fragments remaining as to show a master workman, and that his system or morality was the most benevolent and sublime probably that has ever been taught, and consequently more perfect than those of any of the ancient philosophers.

His character and doctrines have received still greater injury from those who pretend to be his special disciples, and who have disfigured and sophisticated his actions and precepts, from views of personal interest, so as to induce the unthinking part of mankind to throw off the whole system in disgust, and to pass sentence as an impostor on the most innocent, the most benevolent, the most elequent and sublime character that ever has been exhibited to man.

ME X 379-85 Doctor Benjamin Rush 4-21-03

In some of the delightful conversations with you in the evenings of 1798-99... , the Christian religion was sometimes our topic; and I then promised you, that one day or other, I would give you my views of it.

They are the result of a life of enquiry and reflection, and very different from that anti-Christian system imputed to me by those who know nothing of my opinions.

To the corruptions of Christianity I am, indeed, opposed; but not to the genuine precepts of Jesus himself. I am a Christian in the only sense in which he wished any one to be; sincerely attached to his doctrines, in preference to all others ascribing to himself every *human* excellence; and believing he never claimed any other... . The result was, to arrange in my mind a syllabus, or outline of such an estimate of the comparative merits of Christianity... . This I now send to you, as the only discharge of my promise I can probably ever execute.

And in confiding it to you, I know it will not be exposed to the malignant perversions of those who take every word from me a text for new misrepresentations and calumnies. I am moreover averse to the communication of my religious tenets to the public; because it would countenance the presumption of those who have endeavored to draw them before that tribunal, and to seduce public opinion to erect itself into that inquisition over the rights of conscience, which the laws have so justly proscribed. It behooves every man who values liberty of conscience for himself, to resist invasions of it in the case of others; or their case may, by change of circumstances, become his own. It behooves him, too, in his own case, to give no example of concession, betraying the common right of independent opinion, by answering questions of faith, which the laws have left between God and himself.

ME XV 1-2 F. A. Van der Kemp 4-25-16

The Syllabus, which is the subject of your letter, was addressed [confidentially] to a friend to whom I had promised a more detailed view... I have used this caution lest it should get out in connection with my name; and I was unwilling to draw on myself a swarm of insects, whose buzz is more disquieting than their bite. As an abstract thing, and without any intimation from what quarter derived, I can have no objection to its being committed to the consideration of the world. I believe it may even do good by producing discussion and finally a true view of the merits of this great reformer.

ME XV 243-48 William Short 4-13-20

...as you request, a copy of the syllabus is now enclosed. It was originally written to Dr. Rush... . At the request of another friend, I had given him a copy. He lent it to *his* friend, who copied it, and in a few months it appeared in the Theological Magazine of London. Happily, that repository is scarcely known in this country, and the syllabus, therefore, is still a secret and, in your hands, I am sure it will continue so.

ME XV 179-85 Doctor Benjamin Rush 4-21-03

Syllabus of an Estimate of the Merit of the Doctrines of Jesus, Compared with Those of Others

In a comparative view of the Ethics of the enlightened nations of antiquity, of the Jews and of Jesus, no notice should be taken of the corruptions of reason among the ancients, to wit, the idolatry and supperstition of the vulgar, nor of the corruptions of Christianity by the learned among its professors.

Let a just view be taken of the moral principles inculcated by the most esteemed of the sects of ancient philosophy, or of their individuals; particularly Pythagoras, Socrates, Epicurus, Cicero, Epictetus, Seneca, Antoninus.

I. Philosophers. 1. Their precepts related chiefly to ourselves, and the government of those passions which, unrestrained, would disturb our tranquillity of mind. In this branch of philosophy they were really great.

2. In developing our duties to others, they were short and defective. They embraced, indeed, the circles of kindred and friends, and inculcated patriotism, or the love of our country in the aggregate, as a primary obligation: towards our neighbors and countrymen they taught justice, but scarcely viewed them as within the circle of benevolence. Still less have they inculcated peace, charity and love to our fellow men, or embraced with benevolence the whole family of mankind.

II. Jews. 1. Their system was Deism; that is, the belief in one only God. But their ideas of him and of his attributes were degrading and injurious.

2. Their Ethics were not only imperfect, but often irreconcilable with the sound dictates of reason and morality, as they respect intercourse with those around us; and repulsive and anti-social, as respecting other nations. They needed reformation, therefore, in an eminent degree.

III. Jesus. In this state of things among the Jews, Jesus appeared. His parentage was obscure; his condition poor; his education, null; his natural endowments great; his life correct and innocent; he was meek, benevolent, patient, firm, disinterested, and of the sublimest eloquence.

The disadvantages under which his doctrines appear are remarkable.

1. Like Socrates and Epictetus, he wrote nothing himself.

2. But he had not, like them, a Xenophon or an Arrian to write for him. I name Plato, who only used the name of Socrates to cover the whimsies of his own brain. On the contrary, all the learned of his country, entrenched in its power and riches, were opposed to him, lest his labors should undermine their advantages; and the committing to writing his life and doctrines fell on unlettered and ignorant men; who wrote, too, from memory, and not till long after the transactions had passed.

3. According to the ordinary fate of those who attempt to enlighten and reform mankind, he fell an early victim to the jealousy and combination of the altar and the throne, at about thirty-three years of age, his

reason having not yet attained the *maximum* of its energy, nor the course of his preaching, which was but of three years at most, presented occasions for developing a complete system of morals.

4. Hence the doctrines which he really delivered were defective as a whole, and fragments only of what he did deliver have come to us mutilated, misstated, and often unintelligible.

5. They have been still more disfigured by the corruptions of schismatizing followers, who have found an interest in sophisticating and perverting the simple doctrines he taught, by engrafting on them the mysticisms of a Grecian sophist, frittering them into subtleties, and obscuring them with jargon, until they have caused good men to reject the whole in disgust, and to view Jesus himself as an impostor.

Notwithstanding these disadvantages, a system of morals is presented to us, which, if filled up in the style and spirit of the rich fragment he left us, would be the most perfect and sublime that has ever been taught by man.

The question of his being a member of the Godhead, or in direct communication with it, claimed for him by some of his followers, and denied by others, is foreign to the present view, which is merely an estimate of the intrinsic merits of his doctrines.

1. He corrected the Deism of the Jews, confirming them in their belief of one only God, and giving them juster notions of his attributes and government.

2. His moral doctrines, relating to kindred and friends, were more pure and perfect than those of the most correct of the philosophers, and greatly more so than those of the Jews; and they went far beyond both in inculcating universal philanthropy, not only to kindred and friends, to neighbors and countrymen, but to all mankind, gathering all into one family, under the bonds of love, charity, peace, common wants and common aids. A development of this head will evince the peculiar superiority of the system of Jesus over all others.

3. The precepts of philosophy, and of the Hebrew code, laid hold of actions only. He pushed his scrutinies into the heart of man; erected his tribunal in the region of his thoughts, and purified the waters at the fountain head.

4. He taught, emphatically, the doctrines of a future state, which was either doubted, or disbelieved, by the Jews; and wielded it with efficacy, as an important incentive, supplementary to the other motives to moral conduct.

Jesus As a Great Jewish Reformer

ME XV 425-30 John Adams 4-11-23

Calvin's character of this Supreme Being seems chiefly copied from that of the Jews. But the reformation of these blasphemous attributes, and substitution of those more worthy, pure, and sublime, seems to have been the chief object of Jesus in His discourses to the Jews... .

ME XIII 349-53 John Adams 8-22-13

It is with great pleasure I can inform you, that Priestley finished the comparative view of the doctrines of the philosophers of antiquity, and of Jesus... . But he has omitted the important branch, which, in your letter of August the 9th, you say you have never seen executed, a comparison of the morality of the Old Testament with that of the New. And yet, no two things were ever more unlike. I ought not to have asked him to give it. He dared not. He would have been eaten alive by his intolerant brethren, the Cannibal priests.

ME XIII 397-90 John Adams 10-13-13

To compare the morals of the Old, with those of the New Testament, would require an attentive study of the former, a search through all its books for its precepts, and through all its history for its practices, and the principles they prove. As commentaries, too, on these, the philosophy of the Hebrews must be inquired into, their Mishna, their Gemara, Cabbala, Jezirah, Sohar, Cosri, and their Talmud, must be examined and understood, in order to do them full justice. Brucker, it would seem, has gone deeply into these repositories of their ethics, and Enfield, his epitomizer, concludes in these words: "Ethics were so little understood among the Jews, that in their whole compilation called the Talmud, there is only one treatise on moral subjects. Their books of morals chiefly consisted in a minute enumeration of duties. From the law of Moses were deduced six hundred and thirteen precepts, which were divided into two classes, affirmative and negative, two hundred and forty-eight in the former, and three hundred and sixty-five in the latter. It may serve to give the reader some idea of the low state of moral philosophy among the Jews in the middle age, to add that of the two hundred and forty-eight affirmative precepts, only three were considered as obligatory upon women, and that in order to obtain salvation, it was judged sufficient to fulfil any one single law in the hour of death; the observance of the rest being deemed necessary, only to increase the felicity of the future life. What a wretched depravity of sentiment and manners must have prevailed, before such corrupt maxims could have obtained credit! It is impossible to collect from these writings a consistent series of moral doctrine."

It was the reformation of this "wretched depravity" of morals which Jesus undertook. In extracting the pure principles which he taught, we should have to strip off the artificial vestments in which they have been muffled by priests, who have travestied them into various forms, as instruments of riches and power to themselves.

The Sublime Gospel Morality

ME XV 219-224 William Short 10-31-19

But the greatest of all the reformers of the depraved religion of his own country was Jesus of Nazareth. Abstracting what is really His form the rubbish in which it is buried, easily distinguished by the lustre from the dross of His biographers, and as separable from that as the diamond from the dunghill, we have the outlines of a system of the most sublime morality which has ever fallen from the lips of man;... . The establishment of the innocent and genuine character of this benevolent Moralist, and the rescuing it from the imputation of imposture, which has resulted from artificial systems, invented by ultra-Christian sects, unauthorized by a single word ever uttered by Him, is a most desirable object, and one to which Priestley has successfully devoted his labors and learning. It would in time, it is to be hoped, effect a quiet euthanasia of the heresies of bigotry and fanaticism which have so long triumphed over human reason, and so generally and deeply afflicted mankind... .

ME XV 287-88 Rev. Jared Sparks 11-4-20

I adhere to the principles of the first age; and consider all subsequent innovations as corruptions of His religion, having no foundation in what came from Him. The metaphysical insanities of Athanasius, of Loyola, and of Calvin, are, to my understanding, mere relapses into polytheism, differing from paganism only by being more unintelligible. The religion of Jesus is founded in the Unity of God, and this principle chiefly, gave it triumph over the rabble of heathen gods, then acknowledged.

ME XV 202-04 Ezra Stiles 6-25-19

I am... of His theology, believing that we have neither words nor ideas adequate to that definition [of God]. And if we could all, after His example, leave the subject as undefinable, we should all be of one sect, doers of good, and eschewers of evil. No doctrines of His lead to schism. It is the speculations of crazy theologists which have made a Babel of religion, the most moral and sublime ever preached to man, and calculated to heal, and not to create differences. These religious animosities I impute to those who call themselves His ministers, and who engraft their casuistries on the stock of His simple precepts. I am sometimes more angry with them than is authorized by the blessed charities which He preaches.

Gospel Subversion and Restitution

ME XV 219-24 William Short 10-31-19

... rescuing it [the system established by Jesus] from the imputation of imposture, which has resulted from artificial systems,[a] invented by ultra-Christian sects, unauthorized by a single word ever uttered by Him, is a most desirable object, and one to which Priestley has successfully devoted his labors and learning.

ME XV 257-64 William Short 8-4-20

My aim was to justify the character of Jesus against the fictions of his pseudo-followers, which have exposed Him to the inference of being an impostor. For if we could believe that He really countenanced the follies, the falsehoods, and the charlatanisms which His biographers father upon Him, and admit the misconstructions, interpolations, and theorizations of the fathers of the early, and the fanatics of the latter ages, the conclusion would be irresistible by every sound mind, that He was an impostor... .[b]

I say, that this free exercise of reason [in rejecting what is contrary to experience] is all I ask for the vindication of the character of Jesus. We find in the writings of His biographers matter of two distinct descriptions. First, a groundwork of vulgar ignorance, of things impossible, of superstitions, fanaticisms, and fabrications. Intermixed with these, again, we find sublime ideas of the Supreme Being, aphorisms, and precepts of the purest morality and benevolence, sanctioned by a life of humility, innocence, and simplicity of manners, neglect of riches, absence of worldly ambition and honors, with an eloquence and persuasiveness which have not been surpassed. These could not be inventions of the grovelling authors who relate them. They are far beyond the powers of their feeble minds. They show that there was a character, the subject of their history, whose splendid conceptions were above all suspicion of being interpolations from their hands.

a. In the footnote to this letter, the following are listed as the impostures which have been engrafted upon the teachings of Jesus by priests and theologians:

"E.G., The Immaculate conception of Jesus, His deification, the creation of the world by Him, His miraculous powers, His resurrection and visible ascension, His corporeal presence in the Eucharist, the Trinity, original sin, atonement, regeneration, orders of hierarchy, etc., etc."

b. Here follows a long discussion, the intent of which is to reject the miracles attributed in the Gospels to Jesus and the fantastic stories told about him, such as his virgin birth, resurrection, and physical assumption.

ME XV 322-24 Timothy Pickering 2-27-21

No one sees with greater pleasure than myself the progress of reason in the advances towards rational Christianity. When we shall have... unlearned everything which has been taught since His [Jesus'] day, we shall then be truly and worthily His disciples; and my opinion is that if nothing had ever been added to what flowed purely from His lips, the whole world would at this day have been Christian... . The religion builders have so distorted and deformed the doctrines of Jesus, so muffled them in mysticisms, fancies, and falsehoods, have caricatured them into forms so monstrous and inconceivable, as to shock reasonable thinkers, to revolt them against the whole, and drive them rashly to pronounce its Founder an impostor. Had there never been a commentator, there never would have been an infidel... .

I do not wish to trouble the world with mine [my religious beliefs], nor to be troubled for them. These accounts are to be settled only with Him who made us; and to Him we leave it, with charity for all others, of whom, also, He is the only rightful and competent judge. I have little doubt that the whole of our country will soon be rallied to the unity of the Creator, and, I hope, to the pure doctrines of Jesus also.

In saying to you so much, and without reserve, on a subject on which I never permit myself to go before the public, I know that I am safe against the infidelities which have so often betrayed my letters to the strictures of those for whom they were not written, and to whom I never meant to commit my peace.

ME XV 383-385 Benjamin Waterhouse 6-26-22

The doctrines of Jesus are simple, and tend all to the happiness of man.

1. That there is one only God, and He all perfect.
2. That there is a future state of rewards and punishments.
3. That to love God with all thy heart and thy neighbor as thyself, is the sum of religion. These are the great points on which He endeavored to reform the religion of the Jews. But compare with these the demoralizing dogmas of Calvin.

1. That there are three Gods.
2. That good works, or the love of our neighbor, are nothing.
3. That faith is everything, and the more incomprehensible the proposition, the more merit in its faith.
4. That reason in religion is of unlawful use.
5. That God, from the beginning, elected certain individuals to be saved, and certain others to be damned; and that no crimes of the former can damn them; no virtues of the latter save.

Now, which of these is the true and charitable Christian? He who believes and acts on the simple doctrines of Jesus? Or the impious dogmatists, as Athanasius and Calvin? Verily I say these are the false shepherds foretold as to enter not by the door into the sheepfold, but to climb up some other way. They are mere usurpers of the Christian name, teaching a counter-religion made up of the *deliria* of crazy imaginations... . I rejoice that in this blessed country of free enquiry and belief, which has surrendered its creed and conscience to neither kings nor priests, the genuine doctrine of one only God is reviving, and I trust that there is not a *young man* now living in the United States who will not die an Unitarian.

ME XV 425-30 John Adams 4-11-23

The truth is, that the greatest enemies to the doctrines of Jesus are those, calling themselves the expositors of them, who have perverted them for the structure of a system of fancy absolutely incomprehensible, and without any foundation in His genuine words. And the day will come, when the mystical generation of Jesus, by the Supreme God as His Father, in the womb of a virgin, will be classed with the fable of the generation of Minerva in the brain of Jupiter. But we may hope that the dawn of reason, and freedom of thought in these United States, will do away with all the artificial scaffolding, and restore to us the primitive and genuine doctrines of the most venerated Reformer of human errors.

An Apology and Explanation

ME XV 243-44 William Short 4-13-20

But while this syllabus is meant to place the character of Jesus in its true and high light, as no impostor Himself, but a great Reformer of the Hebrew code of religion, it is not to be understood that I am with Him in all of His doctrines. I am a Materialist; he takes the side of Spiritualism; he preaches the efficacy of repentance towards forgiveness of sin; I require a counterpoise of good works to redeem it, etc., etc. It is the innocence of His character, the purity and sublimity of His moral precepts, the eloquence of His inculcations, the beauty of the apologues in which he conveys them, that I so much admire; sometimes, indeed, needing indulgence to eastern hyperbolism.

My eulogies, too, may be founded on a postulate which all may not be ready to grant. Among the sayings and discourses imputed to Him by His biographers, I find many passages of fine imagination, correct morality, and of the most lovely benevolence; and others, again, of so much ignorance, so much absurdity, so much untruth, charlatanism and imposture, as to pronounce it impossible that such contradictions should have proceeded from the same Being. I separate, therefore, the gold from the dross; restore to Him the former, and leave the latter to the stupidity of some, and roguery of others of His disciples. Of this band of dupes and impostors, Paul was the great Coryphaeus, the first corrupter of the doctrines of Jesus. These palpable interpolations and falsifications of His doctrines, led me to try to sift them apart. I found the work obvious and easy and that His part composed the most beautiful morsel of morality which has been given to us by man. The Syllabus is therefore of His doctrines, not *all* of *mine*. I read them as I do those of other ancient and modern moralists, with a mixture of approbation and dissent.

ME XV 275-64 William Short 8-4-20

There are, I acknowledge, passages not free from objection, which we may, with probability, ascribe to Jesus Himself; but claiming indulgence from the circumstances under which He acted. His object was the reformation of some articles in the religion of the Jews, as taught by Moses. That sect had presented for the object of their worship, a Being of terrific character, cruel, vindictive, capricious, and unjust. Jesus, taking for His type the best qualities of the human head and heart, wisdom, justice, goodness, and adding to them power, ascribed all of these, but in infinite perfection, to the Supreme Being, and formed Him really worthy of their adoration. Moses had either not believed in a future state of existence, or had not thought it essential to be explicitly taught to his people. Jesus inculcated that doctrine with emphasis and precision. Moses had bound the Jews to many idle ceremonies, mummeries, and observances, of no effect towards producing the social utilities which constitute the essence of virtue; Jesus exposed their futility and insignificance. The one instilled into his people the most anti-social spirit towards other nations; the other preached philanthropy and universal charity and benevolence.

The office of reformer of the superstitions of a nation, is ever dangerous. Jesus had to walk on the perilous confines of reason and religion; and a step to right or left might place Him within the grasp of the priests of the superstition, a bloodthirsty race, as cruel and remorseless as the Being whom they represented as the family God of Abraham, of Isaac and of Jacob, and the local God of Israel. They were constantly laying snares, too, to entangle Him in the web of the law. He was justifiable, therefore, in avoiding these by evasions, by sophisms, by misconstructions and misapplications of scraps of the prophets, and in defending Himself with these their own weapons, as sufficient, *ad homines*, at least.

That Jesus did not mean to impose Himself on mankind as the Son of God, physically speaking, I have been convinced by the writings of men more learned than myself in that lore. But that He might conscientiously believe Himself inspired from above, is very possible. The whole religion of the Jew, inculcated on him from His infancy, was founded in the belief of divine inspiration. The fumes of the most disordered imaginations were recorded in their religious code, as special communications of the Deity;

and as it could not but happen that, in the course of ages, events would now and then turn up to which some of these vague rhapsodies might be accommodated by the aid of allegories, figures, types, and other tricks upon words, they have not only preserved their credit with the Jews of all subsequent times, but are the foundation of much of the religions of those who have schismatised from them.

Elevated by the enthusiasm of a warm and pure heart, conscious of the high strains of an eloquence which had not been taught Him, he might readily mistake the coruscations of His own fine genius for inspirations of an higher order. This belief carried, therefore, no more personal imputation, than the belief of Socrates, that himself was under the care and admonition of a guardian Daemon. And how many of our wisest men still believe in the reality of these inspirations, while perfectly sane on all other subjects. Excusing, therefore, on these considerations, those passages in the Gospels which seem to bear marks of weakness in Jesus, ascribing to Him what alone is consistent with the great and pure character of which the same writings furnish proofs, and to their proper authors their own trivialities and imbecilities, I think myself authorized to conclude the purity and distinction of His character, in opposition to the impostures which these authors would fix upon Him... .

23. On His Public Service

Commentary

Although this chapter deals primarily with Jefferson's personal life, we consider it significant and enlightening; for it reflects the basics of his activity and desires. It depicts poignantly the endless conflict which dominated his emotions: the yearning, on the one hand, for the privacy of an individual philosopher and scientist confronted with a passion, or obsession, to establish a political and economic system which would serve the general welfare, together with his own conviction that, when called upon for service, he must forgo personal for public good.

From thousands of letters, we have culled excerpts which delineate this lifelong struggle. His repugnance for office, pomp, power, or rule was iterated again and again. When he resigned his position as Secretary of State in 1793 — following the use of military force to suppress the Pennsylvania Whiskey Rebellion — he declared that in this capacity he had exchanged everything he loved for everything he hated, without a single gratification in possession or prospect. On retiring to his farm, he found that his personal losses, because of deterioration in his absence, had been enormous. In addition, therefore, to personal misery, his service to the public had cost him dearly. In 1794, he declared with finality that never again could anything tempt him into public life. He stated, soon thereafter, while his name was in nomination for the presidency and vice-presidency, that he had no desire to govern; and that neither the power nor the splendor of high office had any attractions for him. Some years later, he declared that no honest man can feel pleasure in the exercise of power over his fellow-citizens. However, when James Monroe made plans to retire in 1804, Jefferson wrote him that when Nature endows men with the capacity for serving the human race, it becomes their duty and destination to do so. He had expressed similar sentiments in a letter to Washington in 1792.

Thus, again and again, Jefferson was determined to retire, but when his country called, he never refused; as a consequence, with few interruptions, this became his destiny from 1764 to 1824. In 1775, a year after penning the

Summary View *and a year before composing the Declaration of Independence, he wrote to John Randolph that he intended to withdraw from the public stage and spend the remainder of his life "in domestic ease and tranquillity, banishing every desire of ever hearing what passes in the world."*

Alas and alack! this was not to be: for it was not long before he became governor of Virginia and soon thereafter a member of Congress. In 1792, when preparing to resign his post in the Department of State, he declared that he looked forward to retirement like a waveworn mariner when in sight of land. Soon, we find him in ecstasy at his farm and in his study, which he thought would occupy him for the remainder of his life. However, the demands of the electorate shortly put an end to this idyllic condition, and he became vice-president under John Adams in 1796.

As his second term in the presidency approached its end in 1807-09, his decision became irrevocable — and was fortified by his conviction that the Federalists were finally defeated and the government set on a solid republican course. "Never did a prisoner," he exulted, "released from his chains, feel such relief as I shall on shaking off the shackles of power."

Intertwined with his other drives, we find also that Jefferson craved the approbation of his fellow-citizens, whom he served so sacrificially and magnificently; and never has there been a statesman whose service was more completely without personal interest. Even in 1788, he declared that he could not be accused of making money from public employment; it was his philosophy that those who worked in such capacities receive as compensation only their actual expenses. When he retired from more than five years in France, he reluctantly accepted his appointment as Secretary of State. He stated after twenty-five years of service, that he was much poorer than when he entered it; and in 1907, he wrote that he had the consolation of retiring "with hands as clean as they are empty." He was, in fact, heavily in debt.

Constantly, we find Jefferson yielding to the call for service which he never sought, because he felt that it was his patriotic duty or because it was necessary to save the republican form of government. When he came within one vote of being elected president in 1796, he accepted the role of vice-president as a duty, happy to escape the misery of the first magistracy. When, in 1800, his name was advanced along with that of Aaron Burr, and the electoral college was tied during 32 ballots, he refused to raise a finger or say one word in behalf of his candidacy or make the slightest concession which would have insured its immediate success.

However, again and again we find him rejoicing in the approbation of his fellow-citizens. This alone was what pleased him in the election of 1796; and in 1804, he declared that because of the torrents of Federalist abuse and calumny, he was motivated to seek another testimonial from the people. Finally, when he retired in 1809, he thanked God for the opportunity of retiring from the boisterous ocean of political passions without censure and carrying with him the most consoling proofs of public approbation.

Jefferson Magnificent Populist

When he returned to Monticello in 1809 — never again to visit Washington — he dreamed of enjoying a quiet life with his family, his books, his friends: but this was scarcely to be. When the great sage left the world, the world came to him in the form of a constant stream of visitors and an avalanche of mail. Although he complained constantly of his dislocated wrist he continued to pour out letters which fill several volumes and constitute one of the great American literary treasures. He wrote that sometimes he had to pen so many letters that he could not read a page from his beloved books for an entire week. At the close of one epistle which fills 23 pages in the Memorial Edition, he stated at the age of 82, that in spite of two crippled wrists, he was sometimes lured into composing letters of unmerciful length when unbosoming himself to friends. And his voluminous correspondence continued year after year to the very end; the last letter — in which he declined an invitation to attend the 50th celebration of the signing of the Declaration of Independence in Washington — was written ten days before the end.

The letters which discuss his health, his diet, and the process of aging, are, we think, extremely interesting; and we leave them to the pleasant perusal of the reader.

One of Jefferson's most poignant and moving declarations was that he addressed to the Virginia legislature, when, at the age of eighty, he was facing bankruptcy, the inability to pay his creditors, and the loss of his entire patrimony. In this, found among his Miscellaneous Papers, *he gives a resume of his three-score years of service to, and sacrifice for, his country and its republican ideals. The great depression beginning in 1819, brought on the closing of a great many banks, an extreme paucity of money, plummetting prices for goods and lands, and the bankruptcy of wealthy individuals on every hand. For all his services in the public good, Jefferson asked not one penny of remuneration; he would not, he declared, accept anything to be taken from any one else; he merely asked that the authorities make it possible for him to sell a considerable portion of his estate at reasonable prices, first, to satisfy his creditors, second, to leave him something to sustain him during his remaining days, and, third, to leave at least a little for his one living daughter and her family.*

As a result of this desperate appeal, help came from various sources which enabled him to pay most of his creditors, die in peace in a bed at Monticello — the Beautiful Mountain — and to leave a small patrimony to his beloved family. We understand that gifts totalling about $25,000 were bestowed upon him by friends and admirers.

Repugnance for Public Office

ME I 385-86 Anas Conversations with George Washington 8-6-93

I expressed to him my excessive repugnance to public life, the particular uneasiness of my situation in this place, where the laws of society oblige me always to move exactly in the circle which I know to bear me peculiar hatred; that is to say, the wealthy aristocrats, the merchants connected closely with England, the newly created paper fortunes; that thus surrounded, my words were caught, multiplied, misconstrued, and even fabricated and spread abroad to my injury; that he saw also, that there was such an opposition of views between myself and another part of the Administration, as to render it peculiarly unpleasing, and to destroy the necessary harmony.

ME IX 117-21 James Madison 6-9-93

The motion of my blood no longer keeps time with the tumult of the world. It leads me to seek for happiness in the lap and love of my family, in the society of my neighbors and my books, in the wholesome occupations of my farm and my affairs, in an interest or affection in every bud that opens, in every breath that blows around me, in an entire freedom of rest, of motion, of thought, and actions. What must be the principle of that calculation which should balance against those circumstances of my present existence [as Secretary of State], worn down with labors from morning to night, and day to day; knowing them as fruitless to others as they are vexatious to myself; committed singly in desperate and eternal contest against a host who are systematically undermining the public liberty and prosperity; even the rare hours of relaxation sacrificed to the society of persons in the same intentions, of whose hatred I am conscious even in those moments of conviviality when the heart wishes most to open itself to the expressions of friendship and confidence; cut off from my family and friends, my affairs abandoned to chaos and derangement; in short, giving everything I love in exchange for everything I hate, and all this without a single gratification in possession or prospect... .

ME IX 286-88 George Washington 5-14-94

I find on a more minute examination of my lands than the short visits heretofore made to them permitted, that the ten years' abandonment of them to the ravages of overseers, has brought on a degree of degradation far beyond what I had expected.

ME IX 290-92 To the Secretary of State 9-7-94

No circumstances, my dear Sir, will ever more tempt me to engage in anything public. I thought myself perfectly fixed in this determination when I left Philadelphia, but every day and hour since has added to its inflexibility.

ME IX 355-57 John Adams 12-28-96

I have no ambition to govern. It is a painful and thankless office.

ME IX 376-79 James Sullivan 2-9-97

Neither the splendor, nor the power, nor the difficulties, nor the fame, or the defamation, as may happen, attached to the first magistracy have any attractions for me.

ME XI 242-48 Dr. Casper Wistar 6-21-07

At any rate, it has permitted me, for a moment, to abstract myself from the dry and dreary waste of politics, into which I have been impressed by the times on which I happened, and to indulge in the rich fields of nature, where alone I should have served as a volunteer, if left to my natural inclinations and partialities.

ME XVIII 250-53 Martha Jefferson Randolph 11-23-07

I am tired of a life of contention and of being the personal object for the hatred of every man who hates the present state of things. I long to be among you, where I know nothing but love and delight, and where, instead of being chained to a writing table, I could be indulged as others are with the blessings of domestic society and pursuits of my own choice.

ME XIII 206-13 John Melish 1-13-13

An honest man can feel no pleasure in the exercise of power over his fellow citizens. And considering as the only offices of power those conferred by the people directly, that is to say, the executive and legislative functions of the General and State governments, the common refusal of these, and multiplied resignations, are proofs sufficient that power is not alluring to pure minds, and is not, with them, the primary principle of contest. This is my belief of it; it is that on which I have acted; and had it been a mere contest who should be permitted to administer the government according to its genuine republican principles, there has never been a moment of my life in which I should have relinquished for it the enjoyments of my family, my farm, my friends, and books.

The Deep Yearning for Retirement

ME IV 28-31 John Randolph 8-25-75

I hope the returning wisdom of Great Britain will, ere long, put an end to the unnatural contest. There may be people to whose tempers and dispositions contention is pleasing, and who, therefore, wish a continuance of confusion, but to me it is, of all states but one, the most horrid. My first wish is a restoration of our just rights; my second, a return to the happy period, when, consistently with duty, I may withdraw myself totally from the public stage, and pass the rest of my days in domestic ease and tranquillity, banishing every desire of ever hearing what passes in the world.

ME VIII 341-49 The President of the United States 5-23-92

The fear or suspicion that any selfish motive of [my dis-] continuance in office may enter into this solicitation on my part [to resign], obliges me to declare that no such motive exists... . It is a thing of mere indifference to the public whether I retain or relinquish my purpose of closing my term with the first periodical renovation of the government. I know my own measure too well to suppose that my services contribute anything to the public confidence, or the public utility... . I have, therefore, no motive to consult but my own inclination, which is bent irresistibly on the tranquil enjoyment of my family, my farm, and my books.

ME VIII 394-408 The President of the United States 9-9-92

When I came into this office, it was with a resolution to retire from it as soon as I could with decency. It pretty early appeared to me that the proper moment would be the first of those epochs at which the Constitution seems to have contemplated a periodical change or renewal of the public servants... . I look to that period with the longing of a wave-worn mariner, who has at length the land in view, and shall count the days and hours which still lie between me and it. In the meantime, my main object will be to wind up the business of my office, avoiding as much as possible all new enterprise.

ME IX 283-84 George Washington 4-25-94

I return to farming with an ardor which I scarcely knew in my youth, and which has got the better entirely of my love of study. Instead of writing ten or twelve letters a day, which I have been in the habit of doing as a thing of course, I put off answering my letters now, farmer-like, till a rainy day, and then find them sometimes postponed by other necessary occupations.

ME IX 301-04 James Madison 4-27-95

For as to myself, the subject had been thoroughly weighed and decided on, and my retirement from office had been meant from all office, high or low, without exception... . But the idea was forced upon me by continual insinuations in the public papers, while I was in office. As all these came from a hostile quarter, I knew that their object was to poison the public mind as to my motives, when they were not able to charge me with facts... .

I decided then on those general grounds which could alone be present to my mind at the time, that is to say, reputation, tranquillity, labor... . If these general considerations were sufficient to ground a firm resolution never to permit myself to think of the office, or to be thought of for it, the special ones which have supervened on my retirement, still more insuperably bar the door to it... .

The little spice of ambition which I had in my younger days has long since evaporated, and I set still less store by a posthumous than present fame. In stating to you the heads of reasons which have produced my determination [to retire from public life], I do not mean opening for future discussion, or that I may be reasoned out of it. The question is forever closed with me; my sole object is to avail myself of the first opening ever given me from a friendly quarter (and I could not with decency do it before), of preventing any division or loss of votes, which might be fatal to the republican interest. If that has any chance of prevailing, it must be by avoiding the loss of a single vote, and by concentrating all its strength on one object. Who this should be, is a question I can more freely discuss with anybody than yourself.

ME IX 311-13 Monsieur Odit 10-14-95

I am now a private man, free to express my feelings... as the expressions of a private man... . My books, my family, my friends, and my farm furnish more than enough to occupy me the remainder of my life, and of that tranquil occupation most analogous to my physical and moral constitution.

ME XI 181-83 Monsieur le Comte Diodati 3-29-07

At the end of the present term, of which two years are yet to come, I propose to retire from public life, and to close my days on my patrimony of Monticello, in the bosom of my family. I have hitherto enjoyed uniform health; but the weight of public business begins to be too heavy for me, and I long for the enjoyments of rural life, among my books, my farms, and my family. Having performed my *quadragena stipendia,* I am entitled to my discharge, and... I have, therefore, requested my fellow-citizens to think of a successor for me, to whom I shall deliver the public concerns with greater joy than I received them. I have the consolation too of having added nothing to my private fortune, during my public service, and of retiring with hands as clean as they are empty.

ME XI 411-12 Robert B. Livingston 1-3-08

It is now among my most fervent longings to be on my farm, which, with a garden and a fruitery, will constitute my principal occupation in retirement.

ME XI 443-45 James Monroe 2-18-08

My longings for retirement are so strong that I with difficulty encounter the daily drudgeries of my duty.

ME XII 258-60 Monsieur Dupont de Nemours 3-2-09

Within a few days, I retire to my family, my books, and farms; and, having gained the harbor myself, I shall look on my friends still buffeting the storms, with anxiety, indeed, but not with envy. Never did a prisoner, released from his chains, feel such relief as I shall on shaking off the shackles of power. Nature intended me for the tranquil pursuits of science, by rendering them my supreme delight. But the enormities of the times in which I have lived, have forced me to take a part in resisting them, and to commit myself on the boisterous ocean of political passions. I thank God for the opportunity of retiring from them without censure, and carrying with me the most consoling proofs of public approbation. I leave everything in the hands of men so able to take care of them, that if we are destined to meet misfortune, it will be because no human wisdom could avert them.

ME XIII 144-49 James Maury 4-25-12

I have withdrawn myself from all political intermeddlings, to indulge the evening of my life with what have been the passions of every portion of it, books, science, my farms, my family, and friends. To these every hour of the day is now devoted. I retain a good activity of mind, not quite as much of body, but uninterrupted health. Still the hand of age is upon me.

Duties and Rewards for Service

ME VII 31-35 John Jay 5-27-88

I think I am so far known to many of the present Congress, as that I may be cleared of all views of making money out of my public employment, or desiring anything beyond actual and decent expenses, proportioned to the station in which they have been pleased to place me, and to the respect they wish to see attached to it.

ME VIII 341-49 George Washington 5-23-92

I am perfectly aware of the oppression under which your present office lays your mind, and of the ardor with which you pant for domestic life. But there is sometimes an eminence of character on which society have such peculiar claims as to control the predilections of the individual for a particular walk of happiness, and restrain him to that alone arising from the present and future benedictions of mankind.

This seems to be your condition, and the law imposed on you by providence in forming your character, and fashioning the events on which it was to operate; and it is to motives like these, and not to personal anxieties of mine or others who have no right to call on you for sacrifices, that I appeal, and urge a revisal of it, on the ground of change in the aspect of things. Should an honest majority result from the new and enlarged representations; should those acquiesce whose principles or interest they may control, your wishes for retirement would be gratified with less danger... .

ME I 288-89 Anas Conversations with President Washington 1793

I told him that no man had ever had less desire of entering into public office than myself; that the circumstances of a perilous war, which brought everything into danger, and called for all the services which every citizen could render, had induced me to undertake the administration of the government of Virginia... .

ME IX 352-55 Edward Rutledge 12-27-96

I had retired after five and twenty years of constant occupation in public affairs, and total abandoment of my own. I retired much poorer than when I entered the public service, and desired nothing but rest and oblivion. My name, however, was again brought forward without concert or expectation on my part [in the present election], as a matter of fact... . On principles of public respect I should not have refused, but I protest before my God, that I shall, from the bottom of my heart, rejoice at escaping... . I shall highly value, indeed, the share which I may have had in the late vote, as an evidence of the share I hold in the esteem of my countrymen... . I have no ambition to govern men; no passion which would lead me to ride the storm... . This is certainly not the moment to covet the helm... .

There is [however] a debt of service due from every man to his country proportioned to the bounties which nature and fortune have measured to him... . There is no bankrupt law in heaven, by which you can put off with shillings in the pound; with rendering to a single State what you owed to the whole confederacy.

ME IX 360-65 Mr. Volney 1-8-97

I value the late vote highly; but it is only as an index of the place I hold in the esteem of my fellow-citizens. In this point of view, the difference between sixty-eight and seventy-one votes is little sensible, and still less that between the real vote, which was sixty-nine to seventy... [T. J. fell just one vote short of becoming president in 1796.]

ME IX 370-72 John Langdon 1-22-97

I had no right to a will on the subject [of refusing public office], much less to control that of the people of the United States in arranging us according to our capacities... . I wish for neither honors nor offices. I am happier at home than I can be elsewhere. Since, however, I am called out, an object of great anxiety to me is that those with whom I am to act, shutting their minds to the unfounded abuse of which I have been the object, will view me with the same candor with which I shall certainly act.

ME IX 380-86 Elbridge Gerry 5-13-97

When I retired from this place and the office of Secretary of State, it was in the firmest contemplation of never more returning here. There had indeed been suggestions in the public papers, that I was looking towards a succession in the President's chair, but feeling a consciousness of their falsehood, and observing that the suggestions came from hostile quarters, I considered them as intended merely to excite public odium against me. I never in my life exchanged a word with any person on the subject, till I found my name brought forward generally, in competition with that of Mr. Adams. Those with whom I then communicated, could say, if it were necessary, whether I met the call with desire, or even with a ready acquiescence, and whether from the moment of my first acquiescence, I did not devoutly pray that the very thing might happen, which has happened [i.e., his election to the vice-presidency]. The second office in the government is honorable and easy, the first is but splendid misery.

ME X 301-03 John Dickenson 12-19-01

The approbation of my ancient friends is, above all things, the most grateful to my heart. They know for what objects we relinquished the delights of domestic society, tranquillity and science, and committed ourselves to the ocean of revolution, to wear out the only life God has given us here in scenes the benefits of which will accrue only to those who follow us. Surely we had in view to obtain the theory and practice of good government; and how any, who seemed so ardent in this pursuit, could as shamelessly have apostasized, and suppose we meant only to put our government into other hands, not other forms, is indeed wonderful. The lesson we have had will probably be useful to the people at large, by showing to them how capable they are of being made the instruments of their own bondage. A little more prudence and moderation in those who had mounted themselves on their fears, and it would have been long and difficult to unhorse them. Their madness had done in three years what reason alone, acting against them, would not have effected in many;

and the more, as they might have gone on forming new entrenchments for themselves from year to year.

ME X 343-46 James Monroe 1-13-03

I am sensible after the measures you have taken for getting into a different line of business, that it will be a great sacrifice on your part, and presents from the season and other circumstances, serious difficulties. But some men are born for the public. Nature, by fitting them for the service of the human race on a broad scale, has stamped them with the evidences of her destination and their duty.

ME X 439-41 Governor George Clinton 12-31-03

The uniform tenor of a man's life furnishes better evidence of what he has said or done on any particular occasion than the word of an enemy... . Our business is to march straight forward to the object which has occupied us for eight and twenty years, without either turning to the right or the left. My opinion is that two or three years more will bring back to the fold of republicanism all our wandering brethren whom the cry of "wolf" scattered in 1798. Till that is done, let every man stand to his post, and hazard nothing by change. And when that is done, you and I may retire to the tranquillity which our years begin to call for, and review with satisfaction the efforts of the age we happened to be born in, crowned with complete success. In the hour of death, we shall have the consolation to see established in the land of our fathers the most wonderful work of wisdom and disinterested patriotism that has ever yet appeared on the globe.

ME XI 38-42 Philip Mazzei 7-18-04

I should have retired at the end of the first four years, but that the immense load of tory calumnies... have obliged me to appeal once more to my country for a justification. I have no fear but that I shall receive honorable testimony by their verdict on these calumnies.

ME XII 9-10 Richard M. Johnson 3-10-08

I cannot but be deeply sensible of the good opinion you are pleased to express of my conduct in the administration of our government. This approbation of my fellow-citizens is the richest reward I can receive. I am conscious of having always intended to do what was best for them; and never for a single moment, to have listened to any personal interest of my own... . I suppose, indeed, that in public life, a man whose political principles have any decided character, and who has energy enough to give them effect, must always expect to encounter political hostility from those of adverse principles.

ME XVI 97-100 Joseph C. Cabell 1-11-25

I have ever found in my progress through life, that, acting for the public, if we do always what is right, the approbation denied in the beginning, will surely follow us in the end. It is from posterity we are to expect remuneration for the sacrifices we are making for their service, of time, quiet, and good will. And I fear not the appeal. The multitude of fine young men whom we shall redeem from ignorance, who will feel they owe to us the elevation of mind, of character, and station they will be able to obtain from the result of our efforts, will insure their remembering us with gratitude. We will not, then, be "weary in well-doing."

Accident to Wrist

ME VI 11-15 Charles Thompson 12-17-86

A dislocation of my right wrist has for three months past, disabled me from writing except with my left hand, which was too slow and awkward to be employed often.

ME VI 63-73 James Madison 1-30-87

In a former letter, I mentioned to you the dislocation of my wrist. I can make not the least use of it, except for the single article of writing, though it is going on five months since the accident happened. I have great anxieties, lest I should never recover any considerable use of it.

ME XV 388-90 William T. Barry 8-2-22

Age, debility, an ancient dislocated, and now stiffened wrist, render writing so slow and painful, that I am obliged to decline everything possible requiring writing.

ME XV 430-32 General Samuel Smith 5-3-23

I am rendered a slow correspondent by the loss of the use, totally, of the one, and almost totally of the other, wrist, which renders writing scarcely and painfully practicable.

ME XV 439-52 William Johnson 6-12-23

The close of my second sheet warns me that it is time to relieve you from this letter of unmerciful length. Indeed, I wonder how I have accomplished it, with two crippled wrists, and one scarcely able to hold my pen, the other to hold my paper. But I am lured sometimes beyond the sense of pain, when unbosoming myself to friends who harmonize with me in principle.

Health, Diet, and the Process of Aging

ME VIII 42-45 James Monroe 6-20-90

An attack of periodical headache, which, though violent for a few days only, yet kept me long in a lingering state, has hitherto prevented me sooner acknowledging the receipt of your favor... .

ME X 360-65 Colonel Benjamin Hawkins 2-18-03

I retain myself very perfect health, having not had twenty hours of fever in forty-two years past. I have sometimes had a troublesome headache, and slight rheumatic pains; but now sixty years old nearly, I have had as little to complain of in point of health as most people.

ME XII 365-70 Gen. Thaddeus Kosciusko 2-26-10

My health is perfect; and my strength considerably reinforced by the activity of the course I pursue; perhaps it is as great as usually falls to the lot of near sixty-seven years of age... . A part of my occupation... is the direction of studies of such young men as ask it. They... have the use of my library and counsel, and make a part of my society... . I endeavor to keep their attention fixed on the objects of all science, the freedom and happiness of man.

ME XIII 123-25 John Adams 1-21-12

You and I have been wonderfully spared, and myself with remarkable health, and a considerable activity of body and mind... .

ME XVI 385-87 Charles Thompson 1-9-16

I retain good health, am rather feeble to walk much, but ride with ease, passing two or three hours a day on horseback, and every three or four months taking in a carriage journey of ninety miles to a distant possession, where I pass a good deal of my time. My eyes need the aid of glasses by night, and with small print in the day also; my hearing is not quite so sensible as it used to be; no tooth shaking yet, but shivering and shrinking in body from the cold we now experience... .

ME XV 186-88 Doctor Vine Utley 3-21-19

I have been blest with organs of digestion which accept and concoct, without ever murmuring, whatever the palate chooses to consign to them... .

ME XVI 112-15 Edward Livingston 3-25-25

When I had the pleasure of being a fellow-laborer with you in the public service, age had ripened, but not yet impaired whatever of mind I had at any time possessed. But five and twenty chilling winters have since rolled over my head, and whitened every hair of it.

ME XVI 119-21 Frances Wright 8-7-25

My own health is very low, not having been able to leave the house for three months, and suffering much at times. In this state of body and mind, your letter could not have found a more inefficient counsellor, one scarcely able to think or write. At the age of eighty-two, with one foot in the grave, and the other uplifted to follow it, I do not permit myself to take part in new enterprises, even for bettering the condition of man... which has been through life that of my greatest anxiety.

The Sage in Retirement

ME XIII 1-10 Doctor Benjamin Rush 1-16-11

...the few hours I can pass in my cabinet, are devoured by correspondences; not those with my intimate friends, with whom I delight to interchange sentiments, but with others, who, writing to me on concerns of their own in which I have had an agency, or from motives of mere respect and approbation, are entitled to be answered with respect and a return of good will. My hope is that this obstacle to the delights of retirement, will wear away with the oblivion which follows that, and that I may at length be indulged in those studious pursuits, from which nothing but revolutionary duties would ever have called me.

ME XIX 193-95 Abigail Adams 8-22-13

And yet so it is, that in no course of life have I been ever more closely pressed by business than at present. Much of this proceeds from my own affairs, much from the calls of others; leaving little time for indulgence in my greatest of all amusements, reading. Dr. Franklin used to say that when he was young and had time to read, he had no books; and now that he had become old and had books, he had no time... . Excepting for this [rheumatism] I have enjoyed general health; for I do not consider as a want of health the gradual decline and increasing debility which is the natural diathesis of age; this last, comes on me fast. I have not been able to walk much, though I still ride without fatigue and take long and frequent journeys to a distant possession.

ME XIV 41-45 Thomas Leiper 1-1-14

I receive letters from all quarters, some from known friends, some from those who write like friends, on various subjects. What am I to do? Am I to button myself up in Jesuitical reserve, rudely declining any answer, or answering in terms so unmeaning as only to prove my distrust? Must I withdraw myself from all interchange of sentiment with the world? I cannot do this. It is at war with my habits and temper. I cannot act as if all men were unfaithful because some are so; nor believe that all will betray me, because some do. I had rather be the victim of occasional infidelities than relinquish my general confidence in the honesty of man.

ME XIV 386-87 Charles Thompson 1-9-16

My greatest oppression is a correspondence afflictingly laborious, the extent of which I have been long endeavoring to curtail. This keeps me at the drudgery of the writing-table all the prime hours of the day, leaving for the gratification of my appetite for reading, only what I can steal from the hours of sleep. Could I reduce this epistolary corvee within the limits of my friends and affairs, and give the time redeemed from it to reading and reflection, to history, ethics, mathematics, my life would be as happy as the infirmities of age would admit... .

ME XV 202-04 Ezra Stiles 6-25-19

...the drudgery of letter-writing often denies [me] the leisure of reading a single page in a week.

A Summary of Jefferson's Services

ME I 256-59 Note G Appendix Cir. 1800

I have sometimes asked myself, whether my country is the better for my having lived at all? I do not know that it is. I have been the instrument of doing the following things; but they would have been done by others, some of them, perhaps, a little better... .

The Declaration of Independence.

I proposed the demolition of the church establishment, and the freedom of religion... . I prepared the act for religious freedom in 1777, as part of the revisal, which was not reported to the Assembly till 1779, and that particular law was not passed till 1785, and then by the efforts of Mr. Madison.

The act putting an end to entails.

The act prohibiting the importation of slaves.

The act concerning citizens, and establishing the natural right of man to expatriate himself, at will.

The act changing the course of descents, and giving the inheritance to all the children, etc., equally, I drew up as part of the revisal.

The act for apportioning crimes and punishments, part of the same work, I drew. When proposed to the legislature by Mr. Madison, in 1785, it failed by a single vote... . The public was ripe for this in 1796, when Mr. Taylor proposed it... .

In 1789 and 1790, I had a great number of olive plants, of the best kind, sent from Marseilles to Charleston, for South Carolina and Georgia. They were planted, and are flourishing; and, though not yet multiplied, they will be the germ of that cultivation in those States... .

The greatest service which can be rendered any country is, to add an useful plant to its culture; especially, a bread grain; next in value to bread is oil.

Whether the act for the more general diffusion of knowledge will ever be carried into complete effect, I know not... .

ME XVII 458-65 Miscellaneous Papers 1822-24

I came of age in 1764, and was soon put into the nomination of justice of the county in which I live, and at the first election following I became one of its representatives in the legislature.

I was then sent to the old Congress.

Then employed two years with Mr. Pendleton and Mr. Wythe, on the revisal and reduction to a single code of the whole body of the British statutes, the acts of our Assembly, and certain parts of the common law.

Then elected Governor.

Next to the Legislature, and to Congress again.

Sent to Europe as Minister Plenipotentiary.

Appointed Secretary of State to the new government.

Elected Vice-President, and

President. And lastly, a Visitor and Rector of the University. In these different offices, with scarcely any interval between them, I have been in the public service now sixty-one years, and during the far greater part of the time, in foreign countries or in other States. Every one knows how inevitably a Virginia estate goes to ruin, when the owner is so far distant as to be unable to pay attention to it himself; and the more especially, when the line of his employment is of a character to abstract and alienate his mind entirely from the knowledge necessary to good, and even to saving management.

If it were thought worthwhile to specify any particular services rendered, I would refer to the specification of them made by the legislature itself in their Farewell Address, on my retiring from the Presidency, February, 1809. There is one, however, not therein specified, the most important in its consequences, of any transaction in any portion of my life; to wit, the head I personally made against the federal principles and proceedings, during the administration of Mr. Adams. Their usurpations and violations of the Constitution at that period, and their majority in both Houses of Congress, were so great, so decided, and so daring, that after combating their aggressions, inch by inch, without being able in the least to check their career, the republican leaders thought it would be best for them to give up their useless efforts there, go home, get into their respective legislatures, embody whatever of resistance they could be formed into, and if ineffectual, to perish there in the last ditch.

All, therefore, retired, leaving Mr. Gallatin alone in the House of Representatives, and myself in the Senate, where I then presided as Vice-President. Remaining at our posts, and bidding defiance to the brow-beatings and insults by which they endeavored to drive us off also, we kept the mass of republicans in phalanx together, until the legislature could be brought up to the charge; and nothing on earth is more certain, than that if myself particularly, placed by my office of Vice-President at the head of the republicans throughout the Union, would have given up in despair, the cause would have been lost forever.

By holding on, we obtained time for the legislatures to come up with their weight; and those of Virginia and Kentucky particularly, but more especially the former, by their celebrated resolutions, saved the Constitution at its last gasp. No person who was not a witness of the scenes of that gloomy period, can form any idea of the afflicting persecutions and personal indignities we had to brook. They saved our country, however. The spirits of the people were so much subdued and reduced to despair by the XYZ imposture, and other stratagems and machinations, that they would have sunk into apathy and monarchy, as the only form of government which could maintain itself.

If legislative services are worth mentioning, and the stamp of liberality and equality, which was necessary to be imposed on our laws in the first crisis of our birth as a nation, was of any value, they will find that the leading and most important laws of that day were prepared by myself, and carried chiefly by my efforts: supported, indeed, by able and faithful coadjutors from the ranks of the House, very effective as seconds, but who would not have taken the field as leaders.

The prohibition of the further importation of slaves was the first of these measures in time... . [Then came the laws against Entails, Primogeniture, and the established Anglican State Church].

To these particular services, I think I might add the establishment of our University, as principally my work, acknowledging at the same time, as I do, the great assistance received from my able colleagues of the Visitation. But my residence in the vicinity threw, of course, on me the chief burden of the enterprise, as well of the buildings as of the general organization and care of the whole. The effect of this institution on the future fame, fortune, and prosperity of our country, can as yet be seen but at a distance. But an hundred well-educated youths, which it will turn out annually, and ere long, will fill all its offices with men of superior qualifications, and raise it from its humble state to an eminence among its associates which it has never yet known; no, not in its brightest days. That institution is now qualified to raise its youth to an order of science unequalled in any other State; and this superiority will be the greater from the free range of mind encouraged there, and the restraint imposed at other seminaries by the shackles of a domineering hierarchy, and a bigoted adhesion to ancient habits.

Those now on the theatre of affairs will enjoy the ineffable happiness of seeing themselves succeeded by some of a grade of science beyond their own ken. Our sister States will also be repairing to the same fountain of instruction, will bring hither their genius to be kindled at our fire, and will carry back the fraternal affections which, nourished by the same *alma mater,* will knit us to them by the indissoluble bonds of early personal friendships. The grand Old Dominion, the blessed mother of us all, will then raise her head with pride among the nations, will present to them that splendor of genius which she has ever possessed, but has too long suffered to rest uncultivated and unknown, and will become a centre of ralliance to the States whose youth she has instructed, and, as it were, adopted.

I claim some share in the merits of this great work of regeneration. My whole labors, now for many years, have been devoted to it, and I stand pledged to follow it up through the remnant of life remaining to me. And what remuneration do I ask? Money from the treasury? Not a cent. I ask nothing from the earnings or labors of my fellow citizens. I wish no man's comforts or labors to be abridged for the enlargement of mine. For the services rendered on all occasions, I have been always paid to my full satisfaction. I never wished a dollar more than what the laws had fixed...

[How many others have] devoted three-score years and one of their lives, uninterruptedly, to the service of their country? Have the times of those services been as trying as those which have embraced our Revolution, our transition from a colonial to a free structure of government? Have the stations of their trial been of equal importance? Has the share they have borne in holding their new government to its genuine principles, been equally marked? And has the cause of their distress... proceeded, not merely from themselves, but from errors of the public authorities, disordering the circulating medium, over which they had no control... ?

The single feature of a sixty-years' service, as no other instance of it has yet occurred in our country, so it probably never will again... .

My request is, only to be permitted to sell my own property freely to pay my own debts. To *sell* it, I say, and not to sacrifice it, not to have it gobbled up by speculators to make fortunes for themselves, leaving unpaid those who have trusted my good faith, and myself without resource in the last and most helpless siege of life...

ME XVI 181-82 Roger C. Weightman 6-24-26 (Jefferson's Last Letter)

Respected Sir, — The kind invitation I received from you, on the part of the citizens of the city of Washington, to be present with them at their celebration of the fiftieth anniversary of American Independence as one of the surviving signers of an instrument pregnant with our own, and the fate of the world, is most flattering to myself, and heightened by the honorable accompaniment proposed for the comfort of such a journey. It adds sensibly to the sufferings of sickness, to be deprived by it of personal participation in the rejoicings of that day. But acquiescence is a duty, under circumstances not placed among those we are permitted to control. I should, indeed, with peculiar delight have met and exchanged there congratulations personally with the small band, the remnant of that host of worthies, who joined with us on that day, in the bold and doubtful election we were to make for our country, between submission or the sword; and to have enjoyed with them the consolatory fact, that our fellow citizens, after half a century of experience and prosperity, continue to approve the choice we made. May it be to the world what I believe it will be, (to some parts sooner, to others later, but finally to all,) the signal of arousing men to burst the chains under which monkish ignorance and superstition had persuaded them to bind themselves, and to assume the blessings and security of self-government. That form which we have substituted, restores the free right to the unbounded exercise of reason and freedom of opinion. All eyes are opened, or opening, to the rights of man. The general spread of the light of science has already laid open to every view the palpable truth, that the mass of mankind has not been born with saddles on their backs, nor a favored few booted and spurred, ready to ride them legitimately, by the grace of God. These are grounds of hope for others. For ourselves, let the annual return of this day forever refresh our recollections of these rights, and an undiminished devotion to them.

I will ask permission here to express the pleasure with which I should have met my ancient neighbors of the city of Washington and its vicinities, with whom I passed so many years of a pleasing social intercourse; an intercourse which so much relieved the anxieties of the public cares, and left impressions so deeply engraved in my affections, as never to be forgotten. With my regret that ill health forbids me the gratification of an acceptance, be pleased to receive for yourself and those for whom you write, the assurance of my highest respect and friendly attachments.

INDEX